The BIBLICAL HEBREW VERB

Learning Biblical Hebrew

Beginning Biblical Hebrew

Intermediate Biblical Hebrew

The Biblical Hebrew Verb

"With a plethora of figures and examples, Cook introduces the reader to the subtleties of the ancient Hebrew verb and the varieties of its recent linguistic analysis. His presentation succeeds in summarizing and succinctly explaining many alternative descriptions of the verbal system. Both the seasoned expert in the Hebrew Bible and those with less experience will learn a great deal here. This volume will be a valuable tool in my own future research and teaching."

—**Eric D. Reymond**, Yale Divinity School

"Building on his earlier works on the verbal system, Cook's new publication offers a comprehensive linguistic analysis of all verb forms attested in the Hebrew Bible. The book brings together the latest scholarship on the topic and provides copious examples from prose and poetry. Highly recommended for serious students and scholars of Biblical Hebrew."

—**Hélène M. Dallaire**, Denver Seminary

"With a rich background in both academic research and teaching, Cook skillfully bridges the gap between basic learning and scholarly analysis. His work stands out for its clarity and practical application, making complex linguistic theories accessible. Cook's insights into the Biblical Hebrew verb system are invaluable, offering an essential resource for both students and scholars seeking a deeper understanding of the language."

—**Elitzur A. Bar-Asher Siegal**, Hebrew University of Jerusalem

"Students looking for direction in demystifying verbal syntax and semantics will find a valuable resource in this volume. Cook brings together his extensive insight as a scholar and his years of experience as a teacher to help readers better understand the Biblical Hebrew verb. He deftly provides clear explanations of complicated grammar and linguistic discussions with extensive examples. *The Biblical Hebrew Verb* will prove to be a go-to presentation for years to come."

—**H. H. Hardy II**, Beeson Divinity School, Samford University

"Cook offers an updated treatment of the Hebrew verbal system, including an accessible introduction to formal approaches to linguistic modeling and illustrating the light these can shed on ancient linguistic systems. For advanced students and specialists who want a deeper understanding of Hebrew verbal syntax and semantics, *The Biblical Hebrew Verb* will be a most welcome resource."

—**Andrew Burlingame**, Wheaton College

"Cook has written an introduction to the Biblical Hebrew verbal system intended for an intermediate level between textbooks and scholarly treatises. Without simplifying too much, several views of the verbal forms are presented, and the reader is guided to linguistically sound and reasonable explanations of the many obscure uses in the system. Cook also guides the reader to further scholarly literature and facilitates the transition to advanced-level studies."

—**Bo Isaksson**, Uppsala University

The BIBLICAL HEBREW VERB

A Linguistic INTRODUCTION

JOHN A. COOK

a division of Baker Publishing Group
Grand Rapids, Michigan

Published by Baker Academic
a division of Baker Publishing Group
Grand Rapids, Michigan
BakerAcademic.com

Printed in the United States of America

Library of Congress Cataloging-in-Publication Data
Names: Cook, John A. (Professor), author.
Title: The Biblical Hebrew verb : a linguistic introduction / John A. Cook.
Description: Grand Rapids, Michigan : Baker Academic, a division of Baker Publishing Group, [2024] | Series: Learning Biblical Hebrew | Includes bibliographical references and indexes.
Identifiers: LCCN 2023040040 | ISBN 9781540967220 (casebound) | ISBN 9781540961129 (paperback) | ISBN 9781493444168 (ebook) | ISBN 9781493444175 (pdf)
Subjects: LCSH: Hebrew language—Verb—Textbooks.
Classification: LCC PJ4645 .C66 2024 | DDC 492.45/6—dc23/eng/20230909
LC record available at https://lccn.loc.gov/2023040040

Unless otherwise indicated, all Scripture quotations are the author's translation.

Baker Publishing Group publications use paper produced from sustainable forestry practices and postconsumer waste whenever possible.

24 25 26 27 28 29 30 7 6 5 4 3 2 1

CONTENTS

ILLUSTRATIONS

Figures

Tables

ACKNOWLEDGMENTS

Many people have contributed to this book in innumerable ways. My thinking about its subject matter has been sharpened by my interaction with other scholars and/or their published works, most notably my frequent coauthor Robert Holmstedt. Asbury Theological Seminary afforded me a sabbatical during which the majority of this book was written, and two of my students, Hannah Hopkinson and Ashley Klein, assisted me along the way. Finally, I am thankful to my wife, Kathy, who is an inestimable partner in all my endeavors.

ABBREVIATIONS

General and Bibliographic

Andersen-Forbes	Andersen-Forbes Database, developed by Francis I. Andersen and A. Dean Forbes (accessed in Accordance Bible Software)
Arnold-Choi	Bill T. Arnold and John H. Choi. *A Guide to Biblical Hebrew Syntax*. 2nd ed. Cambridge: Cambridge University Press, 2018.
ASV	Authorized Standard Version
BDB	Francis Brown, S. R. Driver, and Charles A. Briggs. *A Hebrew and English Lexicon of the Old Testament*. Oxford: Clarendon, 1951.
BH	Biblical Hebrew
BHRG	Christo H. J. van der Merwe, J. A. Naudé, and Jan Kroeze. *A Biblical Hebrew Reference Grammar*. 2nd ed. London: Bloomsbury T&T Clark, 2017.
BHS	*Biblia Hebraica Stuttgartensia*. Edited by Karl Elliger and Wilhelm Rudolph. Stuttgart: Deutsche Bibelgesellschaft, 1983.
CBH	Classical Biblical Hebrew
cf.	*confer*, compare
cont.	continued
DCH	*Dictionary of Classical Hebrew*. Edited by David J. A. Clines. 9 vols. Sheffield: Sheffield Phoenix, 1993–2014.
ed(s).	editor(s), edited by, edition
e.g.	*exempli gratia*, for example
ESV	English Standard Version
ET	English translation
et al.	*et alii*, and others
etc.	*et cetera*, and so forth
ETCBC	The ETCBC (WIVU) Linguistic Database, developed by the Werkgroep Informatica at the Free University of Amsterdam, edited by Eep Talstra. German Bible Society and Netherlands Bible Society, 2004, 2014 (accessed in Accordance Bible Software).
ex(s).	example(s)

fig(s).	figure(s); figuratively
Fr.	French
GKC	*Gesenius' Hebrew Grammar*. Edited by Emil Kautzsch. Translated by Arther E. Cowley. 2nd ed. Oxford: Clarendon, 1910.
Groves-Wheeler	Groves-Wheeler Westminster Hebrew Morphology, v. 4.20 (accessed in Accordance Bible Software)
HALOT	*The Hebrew and Aramaic Lexicon of the Old Testament*. Ludwig Koehler, Walter Baumgartner, and Johann J. Stamm. Translated and edited under the supervision of Mervyn E. J. Richardson. 4 vols. Leiden: Brill, 1994–99.
IBHS	*An Introduction to Biblical Hebrew Syntax*. Bruce K. Waltke and M. O'Connor. Winona Lake, IN: Eisenbrauns, 1990.
Joüon	Paul Joüon. *A Grammar of Biblical Hebrew*. Translated and revised by Takamitsu Muraoka. 2nd ed. Rome: Pontifical Biblical Institute, 2006.
KAI	*Kanaanäische und aramäische Inschriften*. Herbert Donner and Wolfgang Röllig. 2nd ed. Wiesbaden: Harrassowitz, 1966–69.
ketiv	the reading preserved in the consonantal text (Aramaic for "what is written")
KJV	King James Version
LBH	Late Biblical Hebrew
lit.	literally
n., n	note
NASB	New American Standard Bible
NIV	New International Version
NJPS	*Tanakh: The Holy Scriptures; The New JPS Translation according to the Traditional Hebrew Text*
NRSV	New Revised Standard Version
OED	*Oxford English Dictionary*. 2nd ed. 20 vols. Oxford: Oxford University Press, 1989.
qere	the reading preserved in the Tiberian vocalization (Aramaic for "what is read")
rev.	revised (by)
RSV	Revised Standard Version
s.v(v).	*sub verbo* (*verbis*), under the word(s)
vs.	versus
v(v).	verse(s)

Grammatical and Linguistic

1	first person	ACT	active
2	second person	ADJ, adj.	adjective
3	third person	ADV, adv.	adverb

AdvP	adverb phrase
AG	agent
AINF	adverbial infinitive
AP	adjective phrase
AspP	aspect phrase
C	common (gender)
CAUSE	cause
CauseP	cause phrase
COMP	complementizer
CP	complementizer phrase
DIR	directive
DIR-VOL	directive-volitive
DYN	dynamic
E	event time
e	event/situation
e_1, e_2, etc.	$event_1$, $event_2$, etc. of foreground
EF	event frame
EXIST	existential particle (יֵשׁ)
F	feminine
FUT	future time/tense
HI	Hiphil
HO	Hophal
HT	Hithpael
IMPV	imperative
INF	infinitive
intr.	intransitive
IPFV	imperfective
IR-PFV	irrealis-perfective
JUSS	jussive
LOC, LOC	location
M	masculine
MID	middle
MP	mood/modality phrase
N, *n*	noun
NEG-EXIST	negative existential particle (אַיִן)
NI	Niphal
NP	noun phrase
P	plural
PASS	passive
PAST	past time/tense
PAT	patient
PERF	perfect aspect
PerfP	perfect phrase
PFV	perfective
PI	Piel
PN	past narrative
PP	prepositional phrase
PPTC	passive participle
PredP	predicate phrase
PRES	present time/tense
PRET	preterite
PRO	pronoun copula
PROG	progressive
PTC	participle
PU	Pual
Q	Qal
R	reference point/time
R_X	modal accessibility relationship (e.g., $R_{DEONTIC}$)
RF	reference frame
R-MID	reflexive/reciprocal middle
S	singular
S	speech time
STA	stative
subst.	substantive
S-V	subject-verb word order
TAM	tense-aspect-mood/modality
TP	tense phrase
tr.	transitive
v	verb
VoiceP	voice phrase
VOL	volitive
vP	verb-classified root
VP	verb phrase
V-S	verb-subject word order
W	actual world
W′	possible world
xP	any (x) phrase

Symbols

Symbol	Meaning
′	prime sign indicating an intermediate or sub-phrase in the tree diagram figures (e.g., Pred′)
″	denotes the uninflected Hebrew root (e.g., הי״ה)
,	is simultaneous with (e.g., R,E = R is simultaneous with E)
?	grammatically awkward or questionable
*	unattested or reconstructed
&	conjunction *and*
±	positive/negative value for features
<	precedence relationship or derived from
=	is equal to
≠	is not equal to
>	follows hierarchically
–	negative value for features
+	positive value for features
≈	approximately equivalent to
⊂	is included in (e.g., A ⊂ B = A is included in B)
⊃	includes (e.g., A ⊃ B = A includes B)
→	diachronically develops into/shifts to
Ø	null constituent
/	or
√	root
%	percent
§(§)	section(s)
×	times

Old Testament / Hebrew Bible

The list below is in English canonical order, but Scripture references in the text and notes are listed in Hebrew canonical order to match *BHS*. Versification also follows *BHS* whenever it differs from traditional English Bible chapter and verse divisions.

Gen.	Genesis	2 Chron.	2 Chronicles	Dan.	Daniel
Exod.	Exodus	Ezra	Ezra	Hosea	Hosea
Lev.	Leviticus	Neh.	Nehemiah	Joel	Joel
Num.	Numbers	Esther	Esther	Amos	Amos
Deut.	Deuteronomy	Job	Job	Obad.	Obadiah
Josh.	Joshua	Ps(s).	Psalm(s)	Jon.	Jonah
Judg.	Judges	Prov.	Proverbs	Mic.	Micah
Ruth	Ruth	Eccles.	Ecclesiastes	Nah.	Nahum
1 Sam.	1 Samuel	Song	Song of Songs	Hab.	Habakkuk
2 Sam.	2 Samuel	Isa.	Isaiah	Zeph.	Zephaniah
1 Kings	1 Kings	Jer.	Jeremiah	Hag.	Haggai
2 Kings	2 Kings	Lam.	Lamentations	Zech.	Zechariah
1 Chron.	1 Chronicles	Ezek.	Ezekiel	Mal.	Malachi

INTRODUCTION

The verb is a central component a student must master to become proficient in a language. Such mastery begins with learning how to recognize (or parse) the forms of the verb (i.e., morphology). As students progress, the syntax and semantics of the verb forms become increasingly important for interpreting texts. The importance of the verb in any clause is largely self-evident. It is the constituent on which almost everything else in the clause depends, and it forms a crucial connection to preceding and subsequent clauses in the discourse.

The importance of the verb in mastering a language is matched by its complexity in comparison with other components of grammar. These complexities fall into two basic areas: valency and tense-aspect-mood/modality (TAM). Valency refers to how many constituents verbs require to be grammatical. For example, the English verb *run* is grammatical with just a subject (e.g., *Joseph ran*), whereas the verb *hit* requires both a subject and an object (e.g., *Aaron hit Jim*). Tense-aspect-mood/modality concerns the array of temporal ideas encoded by verbs. These parameters (i.e., tense, aspect, mood/modality) are closely intertwined, making any attempt to analyze one of them independent of the others a somewhat artificial exercise. Together they determine the time in which an event occurs (tense), the temporal character of the event itself (aspect), and whether the event is an actual occurrence or a potential one (mood/modality). Valency in Biblical Hebrew (BH) is determined by the binyan, or stem, used to create a verb out of a root. For example, the root דב"ר plus the Piel binyan yields the verb דִּבֵּר ("he spoke"), here the 3MS perfective form. In BH, tense-aspect-mood/modality is associated with the verbal conjugations, which have been subjected to as many analyses as they have labels (*qatal*, perfect, perfective, suffix; *yiqtol*, imperfect, imperfective, prefix; etc.).

With this volume, I aim to fill a niche that lies between textbook treatments of the BH verb and scholarly treatises on the verb, of which both sorts of works I have written. The textbook treatments lack the space (and students at that stage lack the capacity) for the sort of analysis required by the multifaceted character of verbal systems. The scholarly treatises tend to lose students in the larger linguistic debates about the nature of the typological categories (and subcategories) of tense, aspect, and mood/modality of the BH verb. Thus, here I largely eschew the conundrums of linguistic theory and the history of BH verb theory, though the interested reader can consult my earlier monograph on this (Cook 2012c). Textbook treatments of the verb supply students with the range of meanings available for a form or construction, but they often leave unstated (or at least understated) the factors that must be taken into account to arrive at the most suitable interpretation of a verb in a given context. I think of this division between textbook and treatise as the difference between description and explanation. Students wishing to progress in their mastery of the language must move from simply describing the meaning of a given verb to understanding the various factors that explain how that meaning is composed. Developing this skill requires both a linguistic framework that accounts for meaning compositionally and some knowledge of the history of the language, which is the primary form that linguistic explanations take. I have provided numerous examples throughout the present text (with additional references in the footnotes) to enable readers to further explore instances of a given category and to test the categorizations I have proposed.

I recognize that the English translations I have provided are awkwardly literal at times, but this is done to make the syntax and semantics of the Hebrew text more apparent; I do not intend them as elegant translations. A constant danger of working with a corresponding gloss language and analytical metalanguage is that the approach may veer into an analysis of the gloss translation rather than the language sample in question. Let the awkwardness of the English gloss translations remind the reader that the Hebrew text is the focus of the analysis.

Chapter 1 introduces the reader to some fundamental linguistic ideas relevant to analysis of the BH verb. The remaining chapters treat the verb sequentially from lower to higher levels of the linguistic hierarchy—that is, from morphemes to larger syntactical structures. Chapter 2 examines the unique status of some verb types, the binyanim, valency and related syntactic phenomenon, and compound verbal expressions that constitute phasal aspect. In chapter 3, I turn to the conjugations and TAM of the BH verb. Finally, chapter 4 deals with the verb within the highest linguistic level, the text or discourse. The examination of several stretches of text explicates the mutual interaction among verbal forms to shape the discourse temporally.[1]

1. Readers interested in further analysis of this nature can consult the growing selection of handbooks on the Hebrew Bible by me and/or Robert Holmstedt, such as Holmstedt, Cook, and Marshall 2017; Cook 2019; and Cook and Holmstedt (forthcoming).

Chapter 1

LINGUISTIC BACKGROUND

1.1 Introduction

Economy of language results in speakers/writers employing a single linguistic construction for a variety of functions. Native speakers are adept at both using and interpreting these one-to-many relationships. Non-native speakers, by contrast, may struggle to make sense out of the manifold meanings or functions that are associated with a form or construction. This problem can be exacerbated in biblical studies, where the language has traditionally been treated in the context of philology and exegesis. Philology is concerned with deciphering ancient texts, and exegesis is similarly concerned with understanding specific biblical texts. The lists of meanings for a word in the lexica or for grammatical constructions in the traditional grammars derive from the meanings determined for the words/forms through philological and exegetical examination of specific texts. The problem is that lexica and grammars provide only sporadic guidance as to which meanings belong to which occurrences in the text. It is easy to fall into the trap of treating these resources like an open menu from which we can select to our liking which meaning to apply to a given text, which is to say we instinctually choose which meaning best fits the context.

A Latin-based grammar framework is the traditional way to bring some order to the sprawling meanings or functions that are associated with a grammatical expression, because it provides a taxonomy of categories (parts of speech) and grammatical functions with which to organize the data. Thus יְהוָה in the bound, or construct, phrase דְּבַר־יְהוָה ("the word of Yhwh") can be described as the "genitive" based on its affinity with the "of" relation expressed by the Latin genitive case (GKC §89). Unsurprisingly, Latinate categories are frequently ill-suited to the Semitic language BH, and rather than helping, they may obscure the categorization and function of a BH construction. In contrast to the focus of philology and exegesis on the unique and the taxonomic approach of traditional grammar, the linguistic approach adopted here is primarily concerned with explicating the internal or cognitive structure of grammar. As a theory-based approach (i.e., theory of human language), this method seeks to rationally organize the language phenomena in a way that allows us to explain the grammatical structures and make predictions about the grammaticality and meaning of BH constructions.

1.2 Linguistic Theory

Every scientific field has theories and technical terminology, which can be a challenge to understanding the field. As the scientific study of language, linguistics is heavily indebted to the fields of logic and mathematics because these provide a "metalanguage" with which to describe human language itself without confusing the language of analysis with the language being analyzed. In this section, I introduce some of the basic principles employed in this treatment of the BH verb. Throughout the book I minimize the technical terminology and modeling as much as possible without losing their benefit. At the end of the book is a linguistic glossary, which will be of great benefit to the reader throughout the book.

In this study, I combine insights from a number of linguistic theories, including the minimalist program and distributed morphology, formal semantics and discourse representation theory, and linguistic typology. Such a synthesis is not to be done lightly, because many linguistic theories have conflicting underlying assumptions about human language. However, the only potential conflict among these particular theories is between linguistic typology, which is strongly associated with functionalist approaches to language, and the other four, which are all formalist in character. Distributed morphology developed out of and operates within the minimalist program. Similarly, discourse representation theory developed out of formal semantics, and though it has some divergent assumptions about language, there have been efforts to reconcile them with formal semantics (Partee 2016: 16). Although simplistic, one could say that formalist theories (which analyze language at the "deep," or abstract level) and typology (which classifies and generalizes at the "surface" level) approach the data from opposite sides, which can make them mutually informing rather than conflicting (so Baker and McCloskey 2007: 295; see Holmstedt 2016: 36–37).

1.2.1 The Minimalist Program and Distributed Morphology

Several structural insights that inform this work and the Cook and Holmstedt grammar volumes (2013; 2020) derive from the minimalist program and are shared or extended by distributed morphology. All of these are motivated at least in part by the overriding principle of parsimony or linguistic economy.

The first structural insight has to do with *constituency structure*. Constituency refers to the way in which words are grouped into increasingly larger units to make up a phrase or clause. While language occurs linearly, some words are syntactically more closely related to others, creating a hierarchy. Analyzing syntax hierarchically provides a way to resolve syntactic ambiguities of the sort illustrated by the phrase *American history teacher* (see other examples in Kroeger 2005: 27). Does this refer to a teacher of American history (fig. 1.1a) or an American who teaches history (fig. 1.1b)? These different interpretations are associated with two different hierarchical analyses, in which the closer two constituents are combined "first" (i.e., "lower" on the tree diagram or more embedded in the bracketing). In fig. 1.1a, "American" and "history" are the closer constituents and are thus combined first. In fig. 1.1b, the closer constituents are "history" and "teacher."

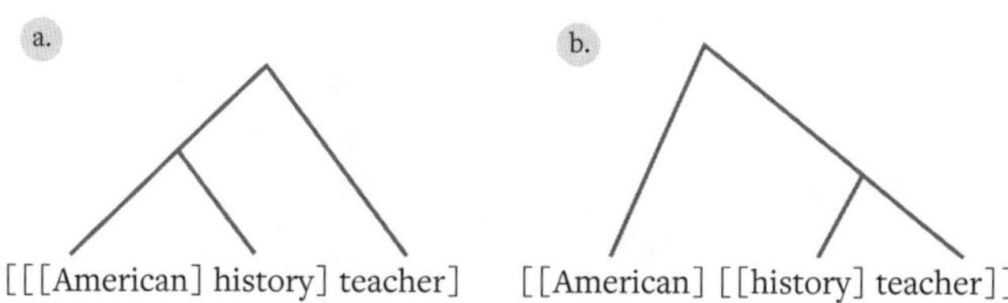

Figure 1.1. Hierarchical Phrase Structure

Distributed morphology extends this hierarchical structure downward into the domain of morphology. Hence slogans like "syntax all the way down" and "syntax within the word" are used to describe the theory of distributed morphology (Siddiqi 2009). The theory posits that word building (morphology) begins with an "underspecified" root, which is initially classified by word class (noun, verb, adjective, etc.). This word then combines with other words based on its classification and valency or syntactic role. Hence, the bottom of the distributed morphology tree looks like fig. 1.2, in which a root (√) is combined with a word class (*x* = classifier of any word class) to create a word of that class (xP = *x* phrase).

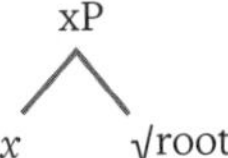

Figure 1.2. Bottom of Distributed Morphology Hierarchy

The hierarchical approach describes the clause construction as constituted by various values or functions that combine to create phrases, which are classified by the most important, or "head," word (hierarchically speaking) in the phrase. For example, *American history teacher* is a noun phrase (NP), because *teacher* is the "head" word modified by the other two words, regardless of which analysis from fig. 1.1 is adopted. Looking upward, the tree is divisible into a thematic domain and an inflectional domain, which are separated in fig. 1.3 by the curved line between them.

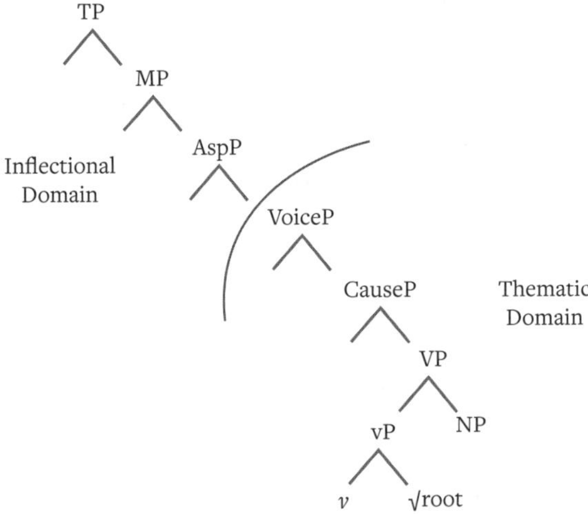

Figure 1.3. The Thematic and Inflectional Domains

The thematic domain is where valency (e.g., voice, transitivity, etc.) is determined, indicated by the voice phrase (VoiceP) and cause phrase (CauseP). Determinations by verb type (e.g., stative, dynamic, copular, etc.) and the system of binyanim in BH can be associated with the thematic domain. By contrast, the system of BH verbal conjugations is associated with the inflectional domain, where distinctions of tense, aspect, and mood/modality (TAM) are represented by the tense phrase (TP), aspect phrase (AspP), and mood/modality phrase (MP), respectively. There is also a "left-periphery" complementizer phrase (CP), which comes into play only in the discussion of the discourse הי"ה (see §4.2 and fig. 4.1). This hierarchy serves to make explicit the contribution of each constituent and parameter (e.g., voice, tense, etc.) to a clause.

The second insight from the minimalist program is *null constituents*. Null constituents contribute to the syntactic structure but are phonologically unexpressed. Like many other languages, BH allows clauses in which the subject or copular predicate is "unexpressed" (ex. 1). The lack of an overt subject is resolved by the recovery of an antecedent in the context that agrees with the verbal inflection (i.e., person, gender, and number). In ex. 1a the antecedent is the overt subject of the preceding clause, מִצְרַיִם ("Egyptians"). The null copula is interpreted as a "verbless" predication based on the juxtapositioning of the subject and predicate phrases (ex. 1b).

1a. Null Subject

וַיַּעֲבִדוּ מִצְרַיִם אֶת־בְּנֵי יִשְׂרָאֵל בְּפָרֶךְ׃ וַיְמָרְרוּ Ø אֶת־חַיֵּיהֶם

The Egyptians enslaved ‹hi.pn› the children of Israel ruthlessly, and (they) embittered ‹pi.pn› their lives. (Exod. 1:13–14)

1b. Null Copula

אָנֹכִי Ø אֱלֹהֵי אָבִיךָ

I (am) the God of your father. (Exod. 3:6)

In both cases, the interpretation of the clause depends on a subject or copula being *structurally* present, despite not being overtly expressed. This suggests the validity of a principle that has been a part of generative grammar since its earliest stage—namely, that a clause consists of a subject and a predicate (Chomsky 1957: 27). The absence of one of these two constituents (driven by the principle of parsimony) requires the positing of a null constituent. Otherwise, we would have to explain why the presence of a subject or verb seems to be "optional," since it is present in some clauses but not others.

Finally, a third principle that derives from the minimalist program is *constituent movement*. Here again, parsimony is the driving factor. By positing word-order movement in, for example, English interrogative clauses, the clauses in ex. 2, can be related to one another: the interrogative is derived from the declarative by "inversion of the subject and auxiliary" (Chomsky 1957: 90).

2a.

Abraham has become the father of many nations.

2b.

Has Abraham become the father of many nations?

1.2.2 Formal Semantics and Discourse Representation Theory

Semantics, the study of meaning, has a long history rooted in philosophy. Formal semantics traces its history back to philosophical logic studies of the 1970s, and notably the writings of Richard Montague (1974; see Partee 2016: 5–13; Portner and Partee 2002). A number of principles of semantics emerged from these studies and have become pervasive in semantic theory. The first and most fundamental of these is the compositionality principle, which treats the meaning of an expression as determined by the meaning of its parts and how they are combined (see Pagin and Westerståhl 2011). For example, the meaning of the sentence *Pam likes Broadway shows* is determined by the meaning of each of the constituents (*Pam, likes,* and *Broadway shows*) as they are syntactically combined (i.e., *Pam* is the subject, *likes* is the predicate, and *Broadway shows* is the object complement).

Any approach to meaning must first determine what *meaning* is. In answering this question, philosophers and linguists recognize two sorts of meaning, famously distinguished in Frege's (1892; ET 1948) essay (see Textor 2011; Abbott 2010, 2011) using the sentence in ex. 3a.

3a.

The morning star is the evening star.

3b.

The morning star is the morning star.

3c.

The evening star is the evening star.

Frege notes that the expressions *morning star* and *evening star* share the same reference or *extension*—the planet Venus; yet they have different senses or *intensions* (i.e., *morning star* describes the appearance of Venus at dawn whereas *evening star* describes it at dusk). This difference is evident from the tautological character of exs. 3b–c in contrast to the meaningfulness of ex. 3a. A referential or extensional approach to meaning is notably limited in being unable to account for meaning in modal expressions. For example, consider *George believes Mark Twain wrote* A Tale of Two Cities. Intensionally, if George really believes that Mark Twain was the author of *A Tale of Two Cities*, the sense of the statement is meaningful or true. However, extensionally it is false, because Charles Dickens is the actual author of *A Tale of Two Cities* (see Lyons 1977: chap. 7; Kroeger 2019: 225–26).

Three other principles of meaning from formal semantics are intertwined. Meaning is defined as truth conditional and model theoretic. These are related to each other in the correspondence theory of truth: that is, a statement is meaningful if it is true, and it is true if it corresponds to some state of affairs or model "world." Such an approach can adequately treat both extensional/referential and intensional/sense meanings by positing both the existing world and possible worlds. Consider again *George believes Mark Twain wrote* A Tale of Two Cities. Extensionally or referentially, a world in which Mark Twain authored such a book does not exist, and so it is false. However, in the model theoretic possible world of George's belief, Mark Twain did write the book, and so intensionally it is a true statement by virtue of that correspondence.

In the past few decades formal semantics has become concerned with the distinction between semantics and pragmatics. Pragmatics has to do with the context-dependency of meaning. Meaning can be dependent on the extralinguistic context, such as when I point to something and ask *What is that?* It can also be dependent on other sentences in the discourse or text. Dynamic semantic theories account for meaning as a product of "updating" from one sentence to the next in the discourse. One such theory, discourse representation theory, has focused on deictic and temporal references (see Kamp, Genabith, and Reyle 2011). For some deictic references to be meaningful, an anaphoric link is required between one clause and another. For example, in the sentence *George believes that Mark Twain wrote* A Tale of Two Cities, *but he is mistaken*, the pronoun *he* is uninterpretable (and so meaningless) unless the meaning of the second clause is analyzed in conjunction with the preceding one, which contains the antecedent. Successively reported events can be temporally related to one another in different ways, which similarly requires analyzing the meaning of a predicate based on the preceding one. For example, *Barbara arrived and Ron cooked dinner* suggests that the two events occur in succession: first Barbara arrived and *then* Ron cooked dinner. By contrast, *Ron was cooking dinner and Barbara arrived* is most naturally interpreted as Barbara arriving while Ron was cooking dinner. The temporality of the discourse is thus a matter of "updating" the temporal progression of events by incorporating one event into the preceding series of reported events.

1.2.3 Linguistic Typology

A fundamental question in the linguistic study of BH or any ancient language is *How do we know?* Linguists rely heavily on native speaker intuition to supply an answer to this question, using it to adjudicate whether something is grammatical and/or what an utterance means. In the case of an ancient language for which we lack native speakers, we must begin by assuming the grammaticality of the data unless some overwhelming weight of data indicates otherwise. The question of how we know an utterance means what we think it means has long plagued the BH verb debate. Linguistic typology offers a way forward.

Linguistic typology is the systematic study of cross-linguistic variation. Just as generative theory aims to determine universal principles and parameters (variations) in human language, typology seeks to identify the limits of variability in human language structures (see Daniel 2010). An ever-growing body of literature began in the 1980s on verbal systems in the world's languages. This literature provides a good profile of how verbal systems are configured and operate. It furnishes a sort of check on any theory of the BH verb. An analysis that shows no similarity to any of the rich array of other verbal systems is suspect because it lies beyond the known limits of variability in verbal systems. The subfields of diachronic typology and grammaticalization enrich the typological profiles of the world's verbal systems by examining them in their dynamic "change" over time, positing universal patterns not just of verbal system configuration but of their development (Croft 2003: chap. 8). Such data provide even more help in adjudicating analyses of the BH verb, since the BH data are diachronically diverse.

1.3 What Is Biblical Hebrew?

Recognizing that BH is diachronically diverse prompts the need to comment on what BH is. We rather casually regard BH as a language, but "language" can be understood in different ways. For example, Edward Ullendorff (1977: 16) famously rejected the notion that BH was a language, claiming that it was too incomplete to constitute "a system of communication." If we accept Ullendorff's restricted understanding of language, then we must concur that the Hebrew Bible contains only a fragment of the larger system of communication that is the ancient Hebrew language. Ullendorff's understanding of language is akin to our commonplace use of the term to refer to the Hebrew language, English language, Russian language, and so on, all of which also have strong political and/or sociological overtones. The early linguist Bloomfield (1926: 155) defines language as "the totality of utterances that can be made in a speech-community," which sidesteps any sociopolitical implications for the term. Chomsky (1986: 21–24) classifies definitions such as Bloomfield's (and, by extension, Ullendorff's) as "E[xternal]-language." He argues that the focus of linguistic study should be not on E-language but on "I[nternal]-language," which he defines as the static language system that holds in the mind of a speaker. Important to Chomsky's understanding is that linguistics studies the human language faculty and that each human mentally holds an internalized language structure or system.

This distinction clarifies both how the discipline of linguistics relates to the texts of the Hebrew Bible and whether a linguistic approach can say anything about the varieties of language found in those texts. Scholars have long recognized diachronic diversity in the texts of the Hebrew Bible, classifying them as examples of archaic, standard/classical, or late BH (e.g., Hurvitz 1972; 1982; 2000; Hurvitz et al. 2014; Polzin 1976). This scheme has justifiably been subject to reexamination in recent decades with suggestions that other sorts of variations also play a role in the diversity found in the Hebrew Bible, such as dialectal (i.e., regional) variation, differences of register (e.g., formal versus colloquial speech), and other variables (e.g., Rendsburg 1990a; 1990b; Young 1993; 1995; 1997).

More problematic (and disputed) is the claim that scribes have so muddled the texts of the Hebrew Bible that until the texts have been sorted out by text critics, linguists cannot succeed in making any sense out of the diversity found in them (e.g., Young 2005; Young, Rezetko, and Ehrensvärd 2008). There are two problems with this claim. First, it represents a confusion between text and language, which must be kept distinct. As Hale (2007: 22) explains, while textual artifacts may yield "features of the text" through philological examination, they require linguistic analysis in order to determine "features of the language of the text." Even if we admit that multiple scribal hands have contributed to the diversity found in the Hebrew Bible, linguistics focuses not on those language fragments themselves but on the "linguistic system" in the minds of those scribes responsible for those fragments (see Miller 2004; Holmstedt 2006). The texts are evidence of the scribes' "I-languages" or "idiolects," rather than constituting the direct focus of linguistic study. To the degree that idiolects are mutually comprehensible, we can speak of a common speech community or dialect, which is evidenced by most of those who contributed to the Hebrew Bible.

At times this book will use the standard categories of archaic, standard, or late BH with the understanding that we can discern differences in the idiolects of writers and scribes between philologically distinct texts. At other times, I make reference to diachronic developments that are common in verbal systems across times and languages to make sense out of the diverse uses of the BH verb. Often, however, we must content ourselves with more gross classifications of the Hebrew language, such as Biblical Hebrew versus Rabbinic Hebrew versus Modern Hebrew and so on. All this means that we must take the diversity in stride and aim to provide the majority data with the most coherent explanations possible. Edward Sapir (1921: 39) famously quipped that "all grammars leak." If this is true generally, then we must admit that grammars of ancient languages such as BH, which lacks native speakers and has a closed and fragmentary corpus, are particularly susceptible to leakage.

1.4 Terminology

The terms employed in discussions of the BH stems or binyanim are quite consistent. The vast majority of scholars employ simplified transliterated Hebrew terms, which are also used in this book: Qal, Niphal, Piel, Pual, Hithpael, Hiphil, and Hophal. By contrast, terminology for the BH conjugations varies widely and reflects a mixture of traditional terms, semantic labels, and attempts at semantically neutral terms. For convenience, table 1.1 lists in the left column some of the many labels that have been used, and in the right column are my corresponding semantically based terms. Throughout this book I employ terminology from the right column except when a transliterated form such as *qatal* or *yiqtol* helps to draw attention to the formal or morphological relationships among a BH conjugation and its Semitic cognate. I use the abbreviations both as a space-saving device and to avoid confusion between descriptive semantic terms and the identifying labels for the verbal conjugations.

Table 1.1. Labels for the Biblical Hebrew Conjugations

Finite Conjugations

Commonly Used Labels	Semantically Based Labels
perfect, suffix conjugation, past, *qatal*	perfective (PFV)
imperfect, prefix conjugation, future, *yiqtol*	imperfective (IPFV)
waw-consecutive/conversive imperfect, *wayyiqtol*	past narrative (PN)
waw-consecutive/conversive perfect, *wəqatal*	irrealis perfective (IR-PFV)

Directive-Volitive Conjugations[1]

<table>
<tr><th>Commonly Used Labels</th><th>Semantically Based Labels</th></tr>
<tr><td>imperative</td><td>imperative (IMPV)</td></tr>
<tr><td>jussive</td><td rowspan="2">jussive (JUSS)</td></tr>
<tr><td>cohortative</td></tr>
</table>

Nonfinite Conjugations

Commonly Used Labels	Semantically Based Labels
participle, verbal adjective	participle (PTC)
infinitive construct	infinitive (INF)
infinitive absolute	adverbial infinitive (AINF)

The conjugations are listed in three subgroups—the finite forms, the directive-volitive forms, and the nonfinite forms. Along with becoming familiar with the terminology in table 1.1, the reader will be immensely helped by referring to the glossary of linguistic terms at the end of the book. The various terms employed in the discussions are briefly defined in the glossary and often arranged by their logical relationships (e.g., the tense-aspect-mood/modality entry includes an array of tense, aspect, and mood/modality values as subentries).

1. The directive-volitive verb forms are also finite, but I have placed them in a separate table because they are a distinct subsystem of irrealis mood that warrants being singled out.

Chapter 2

THE THEMATIC DOMAIN

2.1 Introduction

The thematic domain is the lowest one in the minimalist program/distributed morphology hierarchic template. It includes the voice phrase (VoiceP), cause phrase (CauseP), and elements lower than them in the structure. It is at this level that roots are assigned a word class (e.g., verb, noun, adjective, adverb), and basic argument structure or valency can be modeled. I begin by examining the nonfinite forms (see table 1.1), which may be analyzed as having dual word classifications (§2.2). The following section (§2.3) introduces situation aspect in the Aristotelian tradition, which is important background for the subsequent sections. These include analyses of intransitive predications, including stative and copular varieties (§2.4), of transitive and ditransitive structures and the role of the binyanim (§2.5), and of phasal aspect (§2.6).

2.2 Root and Category: Dual-Category Forms

Distributed morphology is particularly suitable for analyzing Semitic languages and their (predominately triliteral) root system because distributed morphology posits that word building begins with "underspecified" roots (see §1.2.1). It is quite evident that roots in BH and the other Semitic languages are underspecified in precisely the ways distributed morphology suggests. For example, the root צד"ק does not belong to a particular word class, nor does it project any complements to satisfy valency until it is classified by means of a vowel pattern. For example, צֶדֶק and צְדָקָה (both "righteousness") are the result of nominal classification, צַדִּיק ("righteous") represents an adjectival classification, and צָדְקָה ("she is righteous") and הִצְדִּיקוּ ("they acquitted *x*") are each the product of a verbal classification. For most of this book, the focus is on roots that are classified verbal (*v*) and create a finite verb form (vP), but here I deal with the more complicated dual-classified nonfinite forms: INF, AINF, PTC, and STA.

2.2.1 The Infinitive: A Verbal Noun

Some grammars refer to the INF as a "verbal noun" (e.g., GKC §115a; Joüon §65a; *IBHS* §35.1a). Grasping its functions is intuitive for native English speakers, since Hebrew infinitives mirror to a good degree the ways in which the English infinitive functions. Using the distributed morphology framework, the INF may be modeled as shown in fig. 2.1: the root combines with the verb classification *v*, which introduces the ability for it to express predications (i.e., it is a verb); in turn, that verb is nominally classified by *n*, giving it nominal characteristics.

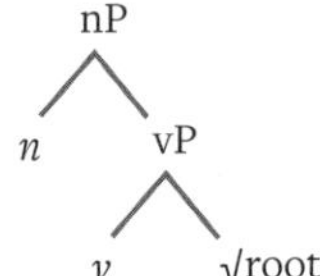

Figure 2.1. Infinitive (INF)

If one wanted to provide a more precise label, the INF might be called a "nominalized verb." This classification means that the INF exhibits features of both nouns and verbs, but it is also distinct from both. For example, like verbs distinctions of binyanim apply to the INF, but like nouns the form regularly appears as the complement of a preposition. It is noteworthy that the INF appears with both the possessive 1CS clitic pronoun (like nouns; see ex. 4a) and the objective 1CS clitic pronoun (like verbs; see ex. 4b). As a nonfinite form, it lacks inflection, in contrast to both nouns (gender-number) and verbs (person-gender-number).

4. Infinitive with Clitic Pronouns

4a

וַיֹּאמֶר לָבָן טוֹב תִּתִּי אֹתָהּ לָךְ מִתִּתִּי אֹתָהּ לְאִישׁ אַחֵר

Laban said ‹PN›, "Better (is) my giving ‹Q.INF› her to you than my giving ‹Q.INF› her to another man." (Gen. 29:19)[1]

4b

וָאֶקְרָאֶה לְךָ לְהוֹדִיעֵנִי מָה אֶעֱשֶׂה

I summoned ‹Q.PN› you to let me know ‹HI.INF› what I should do ‹Q.IPFV›. (1 Sam. 28:15)

The INF also employs the unique nonfinite negator בִּלְתִּי instead of לֹא or the directive-volitive negator אַל (see ex. 5).[2]

5. Infinitive with Preferred Negator בִּלְתִּי

וַאֲנַחְנוּ נִשְׁבַּעְנוּ בַיהוָה לְבִלְתִּי תֵּת־לָהֶם מִבְּנוֹתֵינוּ לְנָשִׁים

We have sworn ‹NI.PFV› by Yhwh to not give ‹Q.INF› to them any of our daughters for wives. (Judg. 21:7)

The dual classification gives the INF a unique syntactic distribution: it has a noun-like distribution with respect to hierarchically higher elements, and a verb-like distribution with respect to elements lower in the syntax hierarchy. As a noun, it can be the subject of a clause (ex. 6a), the complement of a preposition or verb (exs. 6b–c), and can appear in a bound phrase following a construct constituent (ex. 6d).

6. Infinitive in Relation to Its Governing Hierarchy

6a. Subject of Clause

שִׂמְחָה לַצַּדִּיק עֲשׂוֹת מִשְׁפָּט

Performing ‹Q.INF› justice (is) a joy for the righteous. (Prov. 21:15)[3]

1. 1 Kings 22:27; 2 Kings 5:18; Isa. 48:4; Jer. 7:18; 9:15; Ps. 40:14.

2. The adverb בִּלְתִּי negates the INF 86 times versus just 7 times with other verbal forms. The INF is preceded by the negator לֹא only once, and in that case the negated INF predication is the complement of a preposition: בְּלֹא רְאוֹת ("without seeing," Num. 35:23).

3. Gen. 2:18; 29:19; 30:15; Exod. 14:12; Num. 14:3; Judg. 9:2; 18:19; 1 Sam. 15:22; 16:4; 18:23; 23:20; 29:6; 1 Kings 16:31; Isa. 47:11; Jer. 2:19; 10:23; Ezek. 11:3; 18:3; Mal. 3:14; Pss. 40:6; 75:7;

6b. Complement of Preposition

וְרִבְקָה שֹׁמַעַת בְּדַבֵּר יִצְחָק אֶל־עֵשָׂו בְּנוֹ

Rebekah (was) listening ‹Q.PTC› while Isaac was speaking ‹PI.INF› to Esau, his son. (Gen. 27:5)[4]

6c. Clausal Complement of Verb

לֹא־יָדַעְתִּי דַּבֵּר כִּי־נַעַר אָנֹכִי

I do not know ‹Q.PFV› how to speak ‹PI.INF›, because I (am) just a boy. (Jer. 1:6)[5]

6d. Bound to a Construct Noun

בְּיוֹם בְּרֹא אֱלֹהִים אָדָם בִּדְמוּת אֱלֹהִים עָשָׂה אֹתוֹ

On the day God created ‹Q.INF› man, in the image of God he made ‹Q.PFV› him. (Gen. 5:1)[6]

The INF functions verbally with respect to syntactically lower elements in the hierarchy: it is accompanied by a subject, whether null or overtly expressed by a clitic pronoun (ex. 4a) or full NP (ex. 7a); it has valency that determines the number and type of VP complements expressed by a clitic pronoun (ex. 4b), NP (ex. 7b), or PP (ex. 7c).

7. Infinitive as Verb in Relation to Its Governed Hierarchy

7a. With Noun Phrase Subject

וְהוּא־יֹשֵׁב בַּנֶּגֶב בְּאֶרֶץ כְּנָעַן בְּבֹא בְּנֵי יִשְׂרָאֵל

He (was) dwelling ‹Q.PTC› in the Negev in the land of Canaan when the sons of Israel came ‹Q.INF›. (Num. 33:40)[7]

133:1; 147:1; Job 28:28; Prov. 10:23; 13:19; 16:12, 16, 19; 17:26; 18:5; 19:10; 21:3, 19; 25:2, 7, 24; 31:4; Esther 1:7; 1 Chron. 4:33; 7:5, 7, 9.

4. See exs. 8–9.

5. See exs. 10–14.

6. Lev. 7:36; Num. 8:17; Josh. 14:11; 1 Sam. 4:20; 1 Kings 2:42; 2 Kings 17:25; Jer. 11:4; Ezek. 31:15; Zeph. 3:8; Job 39:1; Neh. 13:15; 2 Chron. 6:39.

7. Gen. 4:15; Num. 26:10; Judg. 18:30; 2 Sam. 11:1; 1 Kings 22:36; 2 Kings 4:6; Ezek. 34:8; Joel 2:17; Amos 7:1; Jon. 2:8; Ps. 77:3; Job 10:4; Ruth 2:23; 1 Chron. 4:31; 2 Chron. 6:26.

7b. With Noun Phrase Complement

לֹא אוּכַל לָבוֹא בֵּית יְהוָה

I cannot ‹Q.IPFV› enter ‹Q.INF› the house of Yhwh. (Jer. 36:5)[8]

7c. With Prepositional Phrase Complement

וְלֹא אָבָה לִשְׁמֹעַ בְּקוֹלָהּ

He was unwilling ‹Q.PFV› to heed her voice ‹Q.INF›. (2 Sam. 13:14)[9]

The examples above demonstrate how the INF form relates syntactically to other elements of the clause. Semantically, the INF has four primary functions, broadly defined with respect to their correlation with certain syntagms (i.e., syntactic constituents).

First, the INF with the ל preposition is frequent as an adjunct clause expressing purpose, result, or elaboration of the governing predicate, which are closely related senses that are not always distinguishable in a given passage (see exs. 8a–c).

8. Infinitive with ל as Adjunct

8a. Purpose

וַיְהִי בַּיָּמִים הָהֵם וַיִּקְבְּצוּ פְלִשְׁתִּים אֶת־מַחֲנֵיהֶם לַצָּבָא
לְהִלָּחֵם בְּיִשְׂרָאֵל

[PAST] In those days the Philistines gathered ‹Q.PN› together their armies for war in order to fight ‹NI.INF› against Israel. (1 Sam. 28:1)[10]

8b. Result

וַיַּעֲשׂוּ דְּבָרִים רָעִים לְהַכְעִיס אֶת־יְהוָה

They did ‹Q.PN› wicked things so as to vex ‹HI.INF› Yhwh. (2 Kings 17:11)[11]

8. Gen. 6:7; Exod. 9:16; Lev. 26:44; Num. 3:7–8; Deut. 9:9; Josh. 22:29; Judg. 18:2, 14, 17; 1 Sam. 7:1; 2 Sam. 1:18; 1 Kings 12:15; Isa. 56:6; Jer. 7:31; Ezek. 22:27; Amos 8:11; Obad. 21; Zeph. 3:8.

9. Gen. 43:18; Exod. 17:10; Lev. 10:10; Num. 9:22; Deut. 8:6; Judg. 10:18; 2 Sam. 8:10; 1 Kings 9:4; Jer. 17:10; Ezek. 3:7; Hosea 5:4; Hag. 1:4; Zech. 2:6; Ps. 145:12; Job 1:6; Prov. 9:15; Esther 4:11, 13; Dan. 9:2, 13; Neh. 2:12; 1 Chron. 17:11.

10. Gen. 3:6; Exod. 5:10, 12, 21; Lev. 17:4; Num. 13:16–17; Deut. 2:15; Josh. 9:2; Judg. 20:25; 1 Sam. 7:1; 2 Sam. 16:21; 1 Kings 13:29; Isa. 40:20; Jer. 39:14; Ezek. 13:5; Hosea 6:3; Jon. 1:3; Zech. 14:16; Ps. 37:14; Job 2:1; Prov. 1:16; Ruth 2:8; Dan. 10:17, 20; 1 Chron. 21:15.

11. Lev. 20:3; Deut. 4:25; 2 Sam. 14:20; 1 Kings 2:27; Jer. 44:7; Ruth 2:10.

8c. Explanatory

הִנֵּה הָעָם חֹטְאִים לַיהוָה לֶאֱכֹל עַל־הַדָּם

Hey, the people (are) sinning ‹Q.PTC› against Yhwh by eating ‹Q.INF› with the blood. (1 Sam. 14:33)[12]

Second, the INF as complement of any one of several prepositions (most often ב or כ) serves as predicate of a temporal protasis clause (see exs. 9a–d). This syntagm with a ב or כ preposition frequently introduces a new scene or episode in narrative discourse, subordinate to a preceding or following PN clause and often preceded by the discourse ויהי, as illustrated in exs. 9a–b.

9. Infinitive in Temporal Protasis

9a

וַיְהִי בְּהַעֲלוֹת יְהוָה אֶת־אֵלִיָּהוּ בַּסְעָרָה הַשָּׁמָיִם וַיֵּלֶךְ אֵלִיָּהוּ וֶאֱלִישָׁע מִן־הַגִּלְגָּל

[PAST] When Yhwh took up ‹HI.INF› Elijah in a whirlwind (to) heaven, Elijah and Elisha traveled ‹Q.PN› from Gilgal. (2 Kings 2:1)

9b

וַיְהִי כִּשְׁמֹעַ הַמֶּלֶךְ אֵת דִּבְרֵי הַתּוֹרָה וַיִּקְרַע אֶת־בְּגָדָיו

[PAST] When the king heard ‹Q.INF› the words of the law, he tore ‹Q.PN› his garments. (2 Chron. 34:19)

9c

בְּזֵעַת אַפֶּיךָ תֹּאכַל לֶחֶם עַד שׁוּבְךָ אֶל־הָאֲדָמָה

By the sweat of your brow you shall eat ‹Q.IPFV› bread until you return ‹Q.INF› to the ground. (Gen. 3:19)[13]

9d

וַתָּקָם חַנָּה אַחֲרֵי אָכְלָה בְשִׁלֹה

Hannah arose ‹Q.PN› after eating ‹Q.INF› in Shiloh. (1 Sam. 1:9)[14]

12. Gen. 2:3; Exod. 31:16; 1 Sam. 12:17; 1 Kings 2:3; Jer. 16:12.

13. Gen. 43:25; Lev. 23:14; Num. 32:13; Deut. 7:20; Josh. 4:23; Judg. 6:18; 1 Kings 3:1; Jer. 1:3; Ezek. 24:13; 2 Chron. 18:10.

14. Gen. 5:4, 7, 10; Deut. 1:4; 12:30; 2 Sam. 1:10; 5:13; 1 Kings 13:31; 2 Kings 14:22; Jer. 36:27; Ezek. 46:12; 2 Chron. 25:14.

Third, the INF serves as complement, with or without prefixed ל, for three distinct groups of verbs. Group A consists of modal verbs and expressions, such as dynamic (exs. 10a–b), volitive (ex. 10c), and deontic modalities (ex. 10d).

10. Modal Verbs and Verb Phrases with Complementary Infinitive

10a

הִשִּׂיגוּנִי עֲוֺנֹתַי וְלֹא־יָכֹלְתִּי לִרְאוֹת

My iniquities have overtaken ‹HI.PFV› me and I am not able ‹Q.PFV› to see ‹Q.INF›. (Ps. 40:13)[15]

10b

וְאָנֹכִי נַעַר קָטֹן לֹא אֵדַע צֵאת וָבֹא

I (am) a small child; I do not know ‹Q.IPFV› how to go out ‹Q.INF› or come in ‹Q.INF›. (1 Kings 3:7)[16]

10c

וְלֹא־אָבָה יְהוָה לְהַשְׁחִית אֶת־יְהוּדָה

Yhwh was not willing ‹Q.PFV› to destroy ‹HI.INF› Judah. (2 Kings 8:19)[17]

10d

וְלֹא־נְתָנוֹ אֱלֹהִים לְהָרַע עִמָּדִי

But God did not allow ‹Q.PFV› him to cause harm ‹HI.INF› to me. (Gen. 31:7)[18]

15. Gen. 15:5; Exod. 33:20; Num. 14:16; Deut. 21:16; Josh. 24:19; Judg. 21:18; 1 Sam. 17:9, 33, 39; 2 Sam. 12:23; 1 Kings 13:4, 16; 2 Kings 16:5; Isa. 7:1; 59:14; Jer. 14:9; Ezek. 7:19; Hosea 5:13; Zeph. 1:18; Ps. 78:19–20; Prov. 30:21; Ruth 4:6; Song 8:7; Eccles. 7:13; Lam. 1:14; Ezra 2:59; Neh. 7:61; 1 Chron. 21:30; 2 Chron. 30:3.

16. Exod. 36:1; 1 Sam. 16:18; 1 Kings 5:20; Isa. 8:4; Jer. 15:15; Amos 3:10; Ps. 139:2; Eccles. 6:8; 2 Chron. 2:6–7, 13.

17. With אָבָה, Exod. 10:27; Lev. 26:21; Deut. 29:19; Josh. 24:10; 1 Sam. 15:9; 2 Sam. 14:29; 2 Kings 13:23; Isa. 28:12; Ezek. 3:7; Job 39:9; 1 Chron. 19:19; 2 Chron. 21:7. Negative with מָאֵן, Gen. 37:35; Exod. 16:28; Num. 20:21; 2 Sam. 2:23; 1 Kings 21:15; Jer. 8:5; Hosea 11:5; Zech. 7:11; Ps. 78:10; Job 6:7; Prov. 21:7; Neh. 9:17. With הוֹאִיל, Gen. 18:27, 31; 1 Chron. 17:27. With הִתְנַדֵּב, Neh. 11:2; 1 Chron. 29:5.

18. With נָתַן, Exod. 12:23; Num. 35:6; Judg. 3:28; 1 Sam. 24:7; 1 Kings 15:17; Hosea 5:4; Ps. 55:22; 2 Chron. 16:1. Once with נָטַשׁ ("leave"), Gen. 31:28, and once with מָשַׁל ("have the right"), Exod. 21:8.

Group B consists of phasal aspect verbs, which alter events so as to focus on their beginning or ending phases or to extend or repeat the event. These INF examples are discussed in the section on phasal aspect (§2.6).

In Group C, a handful of verbs that are neither modal nor phasal in character frequently take an INF complement simply because they are logically the sorts of events that feature an event complement. These include verbs that add an adverbial sense to the INF (ex. 11), verbs that take an event complement expressed by an INF (ex. 12), and verbs of speaking with complementary INF (ex. 13).

11. Adverbial Verbs with Complementary Infinitive

11a

לֹא תֹסִפוּן לִרְאוֹת פָּנָי

You will not again ‹HI.IPFV› see ‹Q.INF› my face. (Gen. 44:23)[19]

11b

מַה־זֶּה מִהַרְתָּ לִמְצֹא בְּנִי

What (is) this? You have been quick ‹PI.PFV› to find ‹Q.INF› (it). (Gen. 27:20)[20]

12. Other Verbs with Complementary Events Expressed by Infinitive

12a

אֲבַקֵּשׁ לְהַשְׁמִיד אֶת־כָּל־הַגּוֹיִם

I will seek ‹PI.IPFV› to destroy ‹HI.INF› all the nations. (Zech. 12:9)[21]

19. Usually with הוֹסִיף (HI): Gen. 8:21; 18:29; Exod. 8:25; 9:28, 34; Num. 22:15, 25; Deut. 3:26; 13:12; 28:68; 1 Sam. 3:6, 8, 21; 2 Sam. 14:10; 2 Kings 21:8; Isa. 7:10; 23:12; 29:14; Ezek. 36:12; Amos 5:2; 7:8, 13; Jon. 2:5; Nah. 2:1; Zeph. 3:11; Ps. 77:8; Job 27:1; 29:1; 2 Chron. 33:8. Ten times with יָסַף (Q): Gen. 8:12; 38:26; Lev. 26:18; Num. 32:15; Deut. 5:25; Judg. 8:28; 1 Sam. 7:13; 15:35; 27:4; 2 Sam. 2:28. Both verbs are sometimes accompanied in this construction by the adverb עוֹד ("again"; e.g., Gen. 8:12, 21). Note that this construction can also express *do x more* (e.g., Gen. 37:5, 8; 1 Sam. 18:29; 1 Kings 16:33; Hosea 13:2; 2 Chron. 28:22) or *continue to do x* (e.g., Exod. 5:7; see §2.6, below).

20. Gen. 18:7; Exod. 2:18; 12:33; 2 Sam. 15:14; Isa. 32:4; 59:7; Prov. 1:16; 6:18; Eccles. 5:1.

21. Gen. 43:30; Exod. 2:15; 4:24; Deut. 13:11; 1 Sam. 14:4; 19:10; 23:10; 2 Sam. 20:19; 21:2; 1 Kings 11:22, 40; Jer. 26:21; Zech. 6:7; 12:9; Pss. 27:4; 37:32; Eccles. 12:10; Esther 2:21; 3:6; 6:2.

12b

לֹא־יִבָּצֵר מֵהֶם כֹּל אֲשֶׁר יָזְמוּ לַעֲשׂוֹת׃

Anything that they plan ‹Q.IPFV› to do ‹INF› will not be too difficult ‹NI.IPFV› for them. (Gen. 11:6)[22]

12c

וּשְׁמוּאֵל יָרֵא מֵהַגִּיד אֶת־הַמַּרְאָה אֶל־עֵלִי׃

But Samuel was afraid ‹Q.PFV› of recounting ‹HI.INF› the vision to Eli. (1 Sam. 3:15)[23]

12d

וּבְתוֹרָתוֹ מֵאֲנוּ לָלֶכֶת

And in his teaching they refused ‹PI.PFV› to walk ‹Q.INF›. (Ps. 78:10)[24]

13. Verbs of Speaking with Complementary Infinitives

13a

וַיְצַוֵּהוּ לִבְנוֹת בַּיִת לַיהוָה אֱלֹהֵי יִשְׂרָאֵל

He commanded ‹PI.PN› him to build ‹Q.INF› a house for Yhwh the God of Israel. (1 Chron. 22:6)[25]

13b

וְיָבֹאוּ וְיִרְשׁוּ אֶת־הָאָרֶץ אֲשֶׁר־נִשְׁבַּעְתִּי לַאֲבֹתָם לָתֵת לָהֶם

. . . that they might go ‹Q.IPFV› and take possession ‹Q.IPFV› of the land that I swore ‹NI.PFV› to their fathers to give ‹Q.INF› to them. (Deut. 10:11)[26]

22. Deut. 19:19; Zech. 1:6; 8:14.

23. Gen. 19:30; 26:7; 46:3; Exod. 3:6; 20:20; 34:30; Num. 12:8; Deut. 5:29; 19:20; 25:18–19; 2 Sam. 1:14; 10:19; 12:18; Jer. 40:9; Pss. 46:3; 76:9–10; Job 32:6; Neh. 6:9; 1 Chron. 17:21; 2 Chron. 6:31; 32:18.

24. Gen. 37:35; Exod. 4:23; 7:14, 27; 9:2; 10:3–4; 16:28; 22:16; Num. 20:21; 22:13–14; Deut. 25:7; 1 Sam. 8:19; 2 Sam. 2:23; 13:9; 1 Kings 20:35; 21:15; Jer. 3:3; 5:3; 8:5; 9:5; 11:10; 13:10; 15:18; 25:28; 31:15; 38:21; 50:33; Hosea 11:5; Zech. 7:11; Ps. 77:3; Job 6:7; Prov. 21:7, 25; Esther 1:12; Neh. 9:17.

25. Exod. 35:1, 29; 36:5; Lev. 7:36; 8:5, 34; Num. 34:13, 29; 36:2; Deut. 18:20; 24:18, 22; 26:16; 2 Sam. 7:7; 17:14; 1 Kings 1:35; 17:4; Isa. 5:6; 10:6; Jer. 11:8; 13:6; 26:2, 8; Ps. 71:3; 1 Chron. 17:6.

26. Exod. 13:5; Num. 30:3; Deut. 1:35; 4:21; 7:13; Josh. 1:6; 21:43; Judg. 21:7; Isa. 54:9; Jer. 11:5; 32:22; Ps. 119:106; Neh. 5:12.

Fourth, the ל-INF sometimes serves as predicate complement of a null or overt copula, expressing a future (including future in the past) or a modal nuance (ex. 14).[27]

14. Copular Clauses with Complementary Infinitive

14a

שֹׁמֵר תְּבוּנָה לִמְצֹא־טוֹב

(One who) guards ‹Q.PTC› understanding (is) to find ‹Q.INF› goodness [i.e., One who guards understanding will find goodness]. (Prov. 19:8)

14b

מַה־לַּעֲשׂוֹת עוֹד לְכַרְמִי

What (is) to do ‹Q.INF› more for my vineyard [i.e., What could/should one do more for my vineyard]? (Isa. 5:4)

14c

וַיֹּאמֶר לְהַכּוֹת חָמֵשׁ אוֹ־שֵׁשׁ פְּעָמִים אָז הִכִּיתָ אֶת־
אֲרָם עַד־כַּלֵּה

He said ‹Q.PN›, "(Were you) to strike ‹HI.INF› five or six times, then you would have struck ‹HI.PFV› Aram until completion ‹PI.AINF› (it)." (2 Kings 13:19)

14d

מֶה לַעֲשׂוֹת לָךְ הֲיֵשׁ לְדַבֶּר־לָךְ אֶל־הַמֶּלֶךְ

What (is one) to do ‹Q.INF› for you? Shall ‹EXIST› (I) speak ‹PI.INF› for you to the king? (2 Kings 4:13)

14e

לָהֶם אֲזַבֵּחַ וְיַעְזְרוּנִי וְהֵם הָיוּ־לוֹ לְהַכְשִׁילוֹ וּלְכָל־יִשְׂרָאֵל

"To them I will sacrifice ‹PI.IPFV› and they will help ‹Q.IPFV› me." But they became ‹Q.PFV› for him to cause him to stumble ‹HI.INF› [i.e., a cause of his stumbling] and for all Israel. (2 Chron. 28:23)

For a few roots, the INF appears to have been reanalyzed into other word classes, notably nouns, since some noun patterns are morphologically identical

27. Gen. 15:12; Deut. 31:17; Josh. 2:5; Ezek. 30:16; Pss. 109:13; 119:173. See *IBHS* §36.2.3f–g.

with INF patterns. In these particular cases, the occurrence of *both* the INF and the noun, with notably divergent semantics, have led to differing classifications, such as דַּעַת and דֵּעָה (= Qal INF יד"ע), "knowledge," "knowing," "wisdom"; שֶׁבֶת (= Qal INF יש"ב), "sitting" (?); אַהֲבָה (= Qal INF אה"ב), "loving"; חֹם (= Qal INF חמ"ם), "warmth" (see *HALOT* s.vv.). Aside from the avalent/monovalent חֹם, the INF of these roots can be bivalent with patient complement or locative complement, which makes their thoroughgoing "nominal" use evident alongside the INF use. However, the lexica and morphological databases diverge in their analysis of these forms.

The most noteworthy reanalysis of an INF form, due to its frequency, is seen in the complementizer לֵאמֹר. The form functions only rarely as an INF (ex. 15a); in the vast majority of its almost 900 occurrences, it functions as an untranslatable reported direct speech complementizer (marked by [COMP]; ex. 15b). One clue to its shifted status is its vocalization, which is fixed and distinct from the expected INF vocalization לֶאֱמֹר (see Miller 2003: 161–212).

15. Infinitive and Complementizer לֵאמֹר

15a

וּבְצֵל יָדִי כִּסִּיתִיךָ לִנְטֹעַ שָׁמַיִם וְלִיסֹד אָרֶץ וְלֵאמֹר
לְצִיּוֹן עַמִּי־אָתָּה

And with the shade of my hand I covered ‹PI.PFV› you to plant[28] ‹Q.INF› (the) heavens, and to found ‹Q.INF› (the) earth, and to say ‹Q.INF› to Zion, "You (are) my people." (Isa. 51:16)[29]

15b

וַיֹּאמְרוּ לֵאמֹר הִנְנוּ עַצְמְךָ וּבְשָׂרְךָ אֲנָחְנוּ

They said ‹Q.PN› (saying) [COMP], "Hey, we are your bone and your flesh." (2 Sam. 5:1)

2.2.2 The Adverbial Infinitive: A Verbal Adverb

I have labeled this form, traditionally referred to as the infinitive absolute, the adverbial infinitive (following Cook and Holmstedt 2013; 2020) because, as others have recognized, it is "an *adverbial specifier* par excellence" (*BHRG* §20.2.1). In terms of a distributed morphology framework, the AINF can be modeled as an adverbialized verb (fig. 2.2). That is, the root is classified as

28. Many emend to לִנְטוֹת ("to stretch out"); see *BHS* and commentaries.
29. 2 Sam. 2:22; Mic. 3:11.

a verb (*v*), and then the resultant verb phrase (vP) is classified as an adverb (*adv*), which results in an adverb phrase (advP).[30]

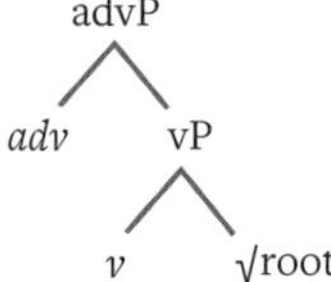

Figure 2.2. Adverbial Infinitive (AINF)

Like the INF, the AINF appears in different binyanim. But in contrast to the verbal *noun* INF, the *adverbial* AINF acts in accordance with an adverb: it is not only uninflected, but it also cannot be negated or modified (e.g., clitic pronouns); nor can it be the complement of a preposition.[31]

Over half of the AINFS occur paired with a following finite form of the same verb.[32] This configuration, which has been labeled the "tautological infinitive" (Kim 2009) or "paronomastic infinitive" (Callaham 2010), has been analyzed in a variety of ways.[33] Hatav (2017; 2021) has persuasively argued that the tautological AINF is a focus or topic marker of the event expressed by the finite verb.[34] The AINF marking contrastive focus, in which an event is chosen from a set of contextually established alternatives, is illustrated in ex. 16a: David rebuffs Ornan's offer of the land as a *gift* (v. 23) and insists on *buying* the land. Less often, the focus may be what linguists call "exhaustive"; that is, the focused event presents new information that does not necessar-

30. Hatav (2021: 125) proposes that this form is a "root phrase" that "names the eventuality of the verb in question." However, according to Arad (2005: 45, 161), the root phrase precedes (and so would not include) binyanim distinctions. The idea that the AINF represents a "reduced" verb, which simply preserves the lexeme without any other markings (i.e., a quintessential nonfinite verb), is attractive for explaining the frequent finite use of the "infinitive absolute" in Northwest Semitic (so Gai 1982), but the AINF in BH does not require such an analysis, because it rarely functions in this manner but instead is strongly adverbial in its usage.

31. The few exceptions prove the rule; see, e.g., 1 Sam. 1:9; 2 Kings 8:10 (*ketiv*); 2 Kings 13:17, 19 (see Joüon §123c).

32. The finite form occasionally precedes the AINF, and it may at times come from a different verb.

33. For example, Waltke and O'Connor (*IBHS* §35.2.1a) state that the AINF "may intensify" the event expressed by the finite verb; Callaham (2010) claims that it adds one of a variety of modal senses.

34. Although I follow Hatav's (2017; 2021) categories of meaning for the AINF, I do not agree with her classification of some of the examples she lists, and some of her footnoted examples seem to be muddled in the 2021 article: the reference in her n. 14 belongs in n. 15 with the other examples of the form used as a command; the last example in her n. 17 is not an adverbial use but a subject use that is featured as her ex. 18.

ily contrast with the alternatives. This is illustrated by ex. 16b, in which the construction marks out God's punishment of Eve, over and against other unspecified and not necessarily contrastive alternative punishments. Note the stress accent (marked by ′) naturally falls on the details of the punishment rather than the AINF and finite verb (see Hatav 2017: 221–22 for discussion of this example).

16. Tautological Adverbial Infinitive as Focus Marker[35]

16a

וַיֹּאמֶר הַמֶּלֶךְ דָּוִיד לְאָרְנָן לֹא כִּי־קָנֹה אֶקְנֶה בְּכֶסֶף מָלֵא

King David said ‹Q.PN› to Ornan, "No, but I will búy ‹Q.AINF+Q.IPFV› (it) for full price."
(1 Chron. 21:24; an acute accent indicates stress)

16b

אֶל־הָאִשָּׁה אָמַר הַרְבָּה אַרְבֶּה עִצְּבוֹנֵךְ וְהֵרֹנֵךְ

To the woman he said ‹Q.PFV›, "I will increase ‹HI.AINF+HI.IPFV› your páin and your chíldbearing."
(Gen. 3:16; an acute accent indicates stress)

The analysis of the tautological AINF as expressing modality (e.g., Callaham 2008–11; 2010; Cook and Holmstedt 2013: 77) can be accounted for by the frequency of its occurrence with the IPFV verb (about 80%) and the focus contrast the speaker may set up to express epistemic certainty or doubt with regard to the event. In ex. 17a, God assures Habakkuk of the certainty of the coming judgment, contrasted with its not coming, which could be wrongly inferred from its delay. In ex. 17b, the brothers respond with doubt to the interpretation of Joseph's dream, questioning the likelihood of it coming true.

17. Focus and Epistemic Modality with Tautological Adverbial Infinitive

17a

אִם־יִתְמַהְמָהּ חַכֵּה־לוֹ כִּי־בֹא יָבֹא

If it delays ‹HT.IPFV›, wait ‹PI.IMPV› for it, because it wíll come ‹Q.AINF +Q.IPFV›. (Hab. 2:3; an acute accent indicates stress)

35. Gen. 2:16; 31:30; 37:8, 10; 40:15; 44:5; Exod. 2:19; Num. 13:30; Deut. 13:10; 15:5, 8; 21:14; 22:1, 4; 24:13; 1 Sam. 8:9; 20:9; 26:25; 2 Sam. 17:16; 24:24; 1 Kings 22:28; 2 Kings 1:4; 8:10, 14; Isa. 36:15; Jer. 3:1; 14:19; 26:15; Amos 5:5; Job 13:5, 10; Esther 4:14.

17b

וַיֹּאמְרוּ לוֹ אֶחָיו הֲמָלֹךְ תִּמְלֹךְ עָלֵינוּ אִם־מָשׁוֹל תִּמְשֹׁל בָּנוּ

His brothers said ‹Q.PN› to him, "Will you réally reign ‹Q.AINF+Q.IPFV› over us or áctually rule ‹Q.AINF+Q.IPFV› us?" (Gen. 37:8; an acute accent indicates stress)

Hatav (2017: 223; 2021: 133) identifies just two examples of the tautological AINF marking *continuous* topic, illustrated in ex. 18a. The topic introduced by the embedded question in the preceding verse, "what Samuel said to you," is continued by the tautological construction. As a *temporal-setting* topic, the tautological AINF marks a nonspecific temporal setting for the event expressed by the finite verb, as illustrated in ex. 18b. The AINF marks off the parable as taking place in another, nonspecific (and nonreal) time.

18. Tautological Adverbial Infinitive as Topic Marker

18a

וַיֹּאמֶר דּוֹד שָׁאוּל הַגִּידָה־נָּא לִי מָה־אָמַר לָכֶם שְׁמוּאֵל׃ וַיֹּאמֶר שָׁאוּל אֶל־דּוֹדוֹ הַגֵּד הִגִּיד לָנוּ כִּי נִמְצְאוּ הָאֲתֹנוֹת

Saul's uncle said ‹Q.PN›, "Tell ‹HI.IMPV› me what Samuel said ‹Q.PFV› to you." Saul said ‹Q.PN› to his uncle, "What he told ‹HI.AINF+HI.PFV› us is that the donkeys were found ‹NI.PFV›." (1 Sam. 10:15–16)[36]

18b

הָלוֹךְ הָלְכוּ הָעֵצִים לִמְשֹׁחַ עֲלֵיהֶם מֶלֶךְ

Once the trees went ‹Q.AINF+Q.PFV› to anoint ‹Q.INF› over them a king. (Judg. 9:8)[37]

36. The English rendering follows Hatav (2021: 133). The other example Hatav identifies is 2 Sam. 5:19.

37. The other clear example Hatav (2017: 223–24) identifies is 2 Sam. 1:6, glossing the construction נִקְרֹא נִקְרֵיתִי as "The other day I happened to be . . ." Some of the other examples she lists (Hatav 2017: 224n20; cited in Hatav 2021: 134n13) are less convincing, though others that I have found as possibly expressing temporal setting include the following: Gen. 24:5; Num. 22:30; Deut. 17:15; Josh. 9:24; Judg. 16:11; 1 Sam. 2:30; 14:28, 43; 20:6, 28; 24:21; 26:25; 27:12; 2 Sam. 1:6; 19:43; 20:18; 1 Kings 20:39; 2 Kings 18:33; Jer. 3:1; Ezek. 28:9; Mic. 2:12. Based on Hatav's (2017: 224) discussion of the "problem" passage in Judg. 15:2, it seems that it and others of the examples I have listed here mark not a nonspecific temporal setting but a temporal

The focus and topic functions of the tautological AINF, though together comprising the majority of occurrences of the form, may be understood as pragmatic or grammaticalized extensions of its more basic adverbial character, i.e., a modifier of a verb or adverb (usually another AINF). A number of patterns of adverbial modification by the AINF can be identified (e.g., see Hatav 2021), but the distinctions among some of them are not always clear. First, an AINF (ex. 19a) or a conjoined pair of them (ex. 19b) may function as a simple adverbial modifier of a finite verb. Examples of single infinitive absolutes functioning adverbially are mostly limited to a handful of Hiphil forms, which semantically exhibit reanalysis as simple adverbs, while remaining formally identical with AINFs. In the case of הַרְבֵּה ("many"), it has become so bereft of verbal function that some lexica and databases classify it as an adverb and/or substantive rather than as an AINF.[38]

19. Adverbial Infinitive as Adverbial Modifier

19a

וְדָרְשׁוּ הַשֹּׁפְטִים הֵיטֵב

The judges should inquire ‹Q.IR-PFV› well ‹HI.AINF›. (Deut. 19:18)[39]

19b

קְבוּרַת חֲמוֹר יִקָּבֵר סָחוֹב וְהַשְׁלֵךְ מֵהָלְאָה לְשַׁעֲרֵי יְרוּשָׁלִָם

With a donkey's burial he will be buried ‹NI.IPFV›, dragged ‹Q.AINF› and cast ‹HI.AINF› beyond the gates of Jerusalem. (Jer. 22:19)[40]

In this first category belong a small number of cases in which a tautological infinitive *follows* rather than precedes the finite verb. Although Hatav (2017: 213) and Kim (2009: 85–89) both suggest that the order of the tautological infinitive and finite verb has little effect on the function of the construction,

---

setting *other* than the current one set by the dialogue: e.g., she translates אָמֹר אָמַרְתִּי in Judg. 15:2 as "But at that time I thought . . ."

38. For example, *HALOT* (s.v.) and Groves-Wheeler (cf. BDB, *DCH*, Andersen-Forbes, and ETCBC). The form הַרְבֵּה occurs 51 times (20 times modified by מְאֹד, "very"), either as an adverb (e.g., 2 Kings 10:8; 21:16; Neh. 2:2) or as an adjective (e.g., Deut. 3:5; 2 Sam. 8:8; 2 Chron. 14:2), including substantival uses (2 Sam. 1:4; Jon. 4:11). Note the ambiguity between adverb and substantival adjective in examples like Hag. 1:6: זְרַעְתֶּם הַרְבֵּה, "you have sown greatly [adv.]/plenty [subst.]."

39. Other examples with הֵיטֵב ("well") include Deut. 13:15; 17:4; 2 Kings 11:18. Examples with הַרְחֵק ("far off") include Gen. 21:16; Exod. 8:24; 33:7; Josh. 3:16.

40. Deut. 9:21; 27:8; 1 Sam. 3:12; 17:16; Isa. 3:16; Jer. 32:44.

it is telling that the adverbial functions occur predominantly when the AINF follows the predicate it modifies. In these cases the modifying AINF just happens to be a cognate of the finite verb, making the structure akin to that of cognate noun modifiers (see Boulet 2019: 200–204). These examples are quite rare (22 by my estimate; see the notes following ex. 21). Though a number of them are quite evidently adverbial modifiers (20a), others might arguably function as focus markers without fronting, as Hatav (2017: 213) has contended (ex. 20b).

20. Tautological Adverbial Infinitive Following Finite Verb Functioning Adverbially or as a Focus Marker

20a

שִׁמְעוּ שָׁמוֹעַ אֵלַי

Listen ‹Q.IMPV› carefully ‹Q.AINF› to me. (Isa. 55:2)[41]

20b

לָקֹב אֹיְבַי לְקַחְתִּיךָ וְהִנֵּה בֵּרַכְתָּ בָרֵךְ׃

To curse ‹Q.INF› my enemies I retrieved ‹Q.PFV› you, but hey, you blessed ‹PI.PFV› them blessingly ‹PI.AINF›. (Num. 23:11)[42]

Second, a pair of "stacked" AINFs may modify a finite verb, with one of them being a "copy" of the finite form (i.e., same root and binyan). By "stacked" I mean that rather than both modifying the finite verb (as in ex. 19b), one AINF modifies the other, which in turn modifies the main verb. The copied verb can occur either first or second. When it appears first, it acts as a "secondary predicate" (Hatav 2021: 130–31), which is then modified by the second AINF (ex. 21a). The copied verb in the second position occurs with only a couple of AINFs that have developed something like "light verb" (i.e., noncompositional or idiosyncratic) semantics, such as הָלוֹךְ (lit., "walking") → "continuously" (ex. 21b) and הַשְׁכֵּם (lit., "waking early") → "urgently." Note the distinction among the strict light verb construction, which consists of two conjoined finite verbs (see ex. 133 and discussion there, §3.4.2), this construction consisting of two AINFs, and the finite-INF construction employed to express continuation or repetition of an event (see §2.6 and the note attached to ex. 101).

41. Isa. 6:9; Jer. 22:10; 23:17; Job 13:17; 21:2; 37:2; Dan. 11:13.

42. Gen. 19:9; Num. 24:10; Josh. 7:7; 24:10; Judg. 5:23; 2 Sam. 3:24; 6:20; 2 Kings 5:11; Jer. 6:29; Ezek. 17:10; 25:12; Zech. 8:21; Job 6:25.

21. "Stacked" Adverbial Infinitives as Adverbial Modifiers

21a

וַאֲכַלְתֶּם אָכוֹל וְשָׂבוֹעַ

Then you will eat ‹Q.IR-PFV›, eating ‹Q.AINF› satiatingly ‹Q.AINF›. (Joel 2:26)[43]

21b

וַיִּסַּע אַבְרָם הָלוֹךְ וְנָסוֹעַ הַנֶּגְבָּה׃

Abram traveled ‹Q.PN›, continually ‹Q.AINF› traveling ‹Q.AINF› toward the Negev. (Gen. 12:9)[44]

Third, an AINF may serve as the predicate of a clause that is subordinate to a main clause, usually following it, and inheriting the TAM and agreement features of the lead verb in "serial-verb"–like fashion. Some examples are paratactic and clearly subordinate, modifying the main event in some way (ex. 22a). Others are hypotactic and connected with וְ ("and") or אוֹ ("or"). These examples of hypotactic coordination have been analyzed as consisting of an AINF "substitute" for a finite verb that adopts the TAM and agreement features of the clause to which it is joined (Rubinstein 1952; cf. Gai 1982). However, these are more likely cases of hypotactic subordination (see Holmstedt 2013a), given the adverbial modifier sense that can be seen in many of the examples, such as ex. 22b.[45] It is possible that while subordinate, the construction has a focusing element, as Hatav has suggested.[46] Example 22c, introduced by the focus word אַף, lends support to this view.

43. Gen. 8:7; Josh. 6:9, 13 (*qere*); Judg. 14:9; 1 Sam. 6:12; 2 Sam. 3:16; 15:30; 1 Kings 20:37; 2 Kings 2:10; Isa. 19:22; 59:13; Jer. 12:17.

44. Other examples with הָלוֹךְ ("continuously") are Gen. 8:3, 5; 26:13; Judg. 4:24; 1 Sam. 14:19; 2 Sam. 5:10; 1 Chron. 11:9. When the finite verb is a form of הל"ך, distinguishing this construction from the previous type in ex. 21a relies on discerning when the finite verb expresses literal or figurative motion: cf. 2 Sam. 3:16 (וַיֵּלֶךְ אִתָּהּ אִישָׁהּ הָלוֹךְ וּבָכֹה, "her husband walked with her, walking and weeping") versus 2 Sam. 5:10 (וַיֵּלֶךְ דָּוִד הָלוֹךְ וְגָדוֹל, "David proceeded, continually becoming greater"). Examples with הַשְׁכֵּם ("urgently," lit., "rising early") are Jer. 7:13; 11:7; 25:3–5; 26:5; 29:19; 32:33; 35:14–15; 44:4; 2 Chron. 36:15.

45. It might be possible to track a historical (and/or dialectal) development from a mostly hypotactic subordination to coordination and on to functioning as an independent "reduced" verb (see Gai 1982; note the increase of hypotactic examples in postexilic literature in n. 48), as exhibited in Eccles. 4:2, which includes an overt pronominal subject and seems awkward if interpreted as subordinate to anything: וְשַׁבֵּחַ אֲנִי אֶת־הַמֵּתִים . . . מִן־הַחַיִּים, "I praise the dead . . . more than the living." This is the only such example I have found, however.

46. Private communication cited in Screnock and Holmstedt 2015: 77 with respect to Esther 2:3.

22. Adverbial Infinitive in Subordinate Expressions

22a

אֶעֱבֹר בְּכָל־צֹאנְךָ הַיּוֹם הָסֵר מִשָּׁם כָּל־שֶׂה נָקֹד וְטָלוּא

Let me pass ‹Q.IPFV› through the whole of your flock today, removing ‹HI.AINF› from there every speckled and spotted ‹Q.PPTC› sheep. (Gen. 30:32)[47]

22b

וַיֹּאמֶר אֵלָיו רְאֵה הֶעֱבַרְתִּי מֵעָלֶיךָ עֲוֺנֶךָ וְהַלְבֵּשׁ אֹתְךָ מַחֲלָצוֹת

He said ‹Q.PN› to him, "Look ‹Q.IMPV›, I have removed ‹HI.PFV› from upon you your iniquity, clothing ‹HI.AINF› you in festal robes." (Zech. 3:4)[48]

22c

הוֹי מַשְׁקֵה רֵעֵהוּ מְסַפֵּחַ חֲמָתְךָ וְאַף שַׁכֵּר לְמַעַן הַבִּיט עַל־מְעוֹרֵיהֶם

Woe (to you who) offers ‹HI.PTC› his friend a drink, (who) pours out ‹PI.PTC› your wrath, even getting (him) drunk ‹PI.AINF› so as to gaze ‹HI.INF› upon their nakedness. (Hab. 2:15)

Another function of the AINF is as a substitute for a volitive form (ex. 23).

23. Adverbial Infinitive as Volitive Substitute

שָׁמוֹר אֶת־יוֹם הַשַּׁבָּת לְקַדְּשׁוֹ

Keep ‹Q.AINF› the sabbath day by sanctifying ‹PI.INF› it.

or (There should be) keeping ‹Q.AINF› of the sabbath day by sanctifying ‹PI.INF› it. (Deut. 5:12)[49]

47. Other possible examples include Exod. 30:36; 36:7; Lev. 2:6; Num. 6:23; Deut. 3:6; Josh. 6:3; 2 Sam. 8:2; Isa. 42:20; Jer. 31:2; Hosea 10:4; Mic. 6:13; Hab. 3:13; Zech. 14:12; Pss. 35:16; 65:11; Job 26:9; Prov. 25:4.

48. Other possible examples include Gen. 41:43; Exod. 8:11; Lev. 25:14; Num. 30:3; Deut. 14:21; Judg. 7:19; 1 Sam. 2:28; 1 Kings 9:25; Jer. 3:1; 19:13; 22:14; 37:21; Ezek. 23:47; Eccles. 8:9; Esther 2:3; 3:13; 6:9; 8:8; 9:1, 6, 12, 16–18; Dan. 9:5, 11; Neh. 7:3; 8:8; 9:8; 1 Chron. 5:20; 16:36; 2 Chron. 28:19.

49. Gen. 17:10; Exod. 12:48; 13:3; 20:8; Lev. 6:7; Num. 4:2, 22; 15:35; 25:17; Deut. 1:16; 15:2; 16:1; 24:9; 25:17; 27:1; 31:26; Josh. 1:13; 9:20; 1 Kings 22:30; 2 Kings 11:15; 19:29; Jer. 2:2; 3:12; 13:1; 17:19; 19:1; 32:14; 34:2; 35:2; 36:23; 39:16; Ezek. 21:24, 31; 23:46; 24:5, 10; Nah. 2:2; Zech. 6:10; 12:10; Prov. 17:12; Eccles. 9:11.

Hatav (2021: 136) explains this use on analogy with *-ing* expressions in English, such as *No feeding the monkeys!* She says that the construction performs "a directive with the absence of an interlocutor." In other words, it is overtly objective in its expression of deontic modality in contrast to the inherently subjective directive-volitive subsystem (see §3.8.2). The sense is difficult to capture in English, where the deontic *-ing* construction is usually prohibitive. In ex. 23 I have tried to reflect this understanding with the impersonal *there* construction.

In a handful of cases the AINF functions in a syntactic construction in which one would expect an INF instead (ex. 24). It is likely that either the spelling similarity with the INF or their categorical similarity (i.e., both infinitives) is to account for these examples, if not both.

24. Adverbial Infinitive Functioning like Infinitive

וַיֵּשֶׁב הָעָם לֶאֱכֹל וְשָׁתוֹ וַיָּקֻמוּ לְצַחֵק

The people sat ‹Q.PN› to eat ‹Q.INF› and drink ‹Q.AINF› and they rose ‹Q.PN› to play ‹Q.INF›. (Exod. 32:6)[50]

Finally, a handful of AINFs appear to express bare events in nominal syntactic positions such as subject or object (exs. 25a–b).

25. Adverbial Infinitive Functioning Nominally

25a

אָכֹל דְּבַשׁ הַרְבּוֹת לֹא־טוֹב

Eating ‹Q.AINF› honey greatly ‹HI.INF› (is) not good. (Prov. 25:27)[51]

25b

הֲגָנֹב רָצֹחַ וְנָאֹף וְהִשָּׁבֵעַ לַשֶּׁקֶר וְקַטֵּר לַבָּעַל וְהָלֹךְ אַחֲרֵי אֱלֹהִים אֲחֵרִים אֲשֶׁר לֹא־יְדַעְתֶּם׃

Is there to be stealing ‹AINF›, murdering ‹AINF›, and committing adultery ‹AINF›, and swearing falsely ‹AINF›, and burning incense ‹AINF› to Baal, and going ‹AINF› after other gods that you have not known ‹PFV›? (Jer. 7:9)

50. Other possible examples include Num. 23:20; 1 Sam. 1:9; 22:13; 25:26, 33; Isa. 42:24; Jer. 7:18; 44:17–18; Ezek. 36:3; Job 9:18; 13:3; Prov. 15:12.

51. Jer. 7:9; 9:24; Prov. 24:23; 28:21.

2.2.3 The Participle and the Stative: Verbal Adjectives

The PTC and STA (on the stative, see further §2.4.1) form a unique class of adjective: in contrast to typical adjectives that express properties or qualities, the PTC and STA adjectives encode event predicates (Cook 2008). In distributed morphology terms, they are both adjectivized verbs (fig. 2.3).

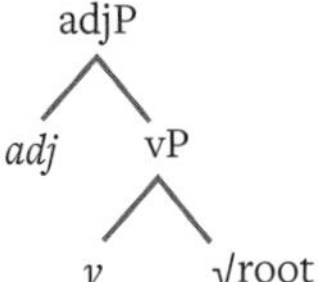

Figure 2.3. Participle/Stative (PTC/STA)

Like other adjectives, these verbal adjectives are declinable for gender and number, but unlike other adjectives, they express events and so are formed by binyanim. The eventive character is most evident by a comparison between verbal adjectives and substantive-based adjectives modifying a noun. The attributive adjective is phrasal, whereas the verbal adjective expresses a relative clause (ex. 26).[52]

26. Adjective versus Verbal Adjective in Attributive Position

הָעָם הַהֹלְכִים בַּחֹשֶׁךְ רָאוּ אוֹר גָּדוֹל

The people who (were) walking ‹Q.PTC› in darkness have seen a great ‹ADJ› light. (Isa. 9:1)

Although both the PTC and the STA are verbal adjectives, they are distinct. The STA exhibits a split encoding: sometimes it is inflected verbally (i.e., with person-gender-number affixes), and other times it is declined nominally, as the PTC is (i.e., with gender-number suffixes shared with nouns and other adjectives). Formal ambiguity (and so syntactic ambiguity) holds between the 3MS PFV and the MS adjective forms: if analyzed as a verbal form, it is a stand-alone predicate; if analyzed as an adjective, it requires copular support to form a predicate, as the PTC does (see below). Unlike the PTC, however, the STA appears only in the Qal binyan.

52. The semantic equivalence of an attributive adjective phrase and copular relative clause was already recognized by the Port-Royal grammarians of the seventeenth century (Lancelot and Arnauld 1975: 99, 181–88).

27. Stative Encoding: Verbal, Adjectival, and Ambiguous

27a

אֲנִי זָקַנְתִּי בָּאתִי בַּיָּמִים

I am old ‹Q.PFV›, advanced in days. (Josh. 23:2)

27b

וְאַבְרָהָם וְשָׂרָה זְקֵנִים בָּאִים בַּיָּמִים

Abraham and Sarah (were) old ‹STA›, advanced in days. (Gen. 18:11)

27c

וְאַבְרָהָם זָקֵן בָּא בַּיָּמִים

Abraham (was) old/was old ‹STA/Q.PFV›, advanced in days. (Gen. 24:1)

The status of the PTC has been debated. It has been described as having a "dual nature" (*Doppelnatur*), so that it is sometimes verbal and sometimes nominal (e.g., Kahan 1889; Sellin 1889). It has been described as an "intermediate" form, neither clearly nominal nor verbal (e.g., Gordon 1982). And it has been described as all of these: sometimes verbal, sometimes nominal, sometimes both, and sometimes "indeterminate" (Andersen and Forbes 2007). The solution is that the PTC and STA are both adjectival (Cook 2008). This is significant because typologically adjectives are not associated with any prototypical "encoding" strategy (Stassen 1997: 612), which explains why the STA is more like a verb in character (i.e., it can be inflected with person-gender-number affixes) while the PTC is more like a noun (i.e., it is restricted to sharing gender-number affixes with nouns and other adjectives).

That the PTC and STA can both have noun-like affixes and yet appear in binyan templates indicates that they both represent cases of "verb-switching" or, more specifically, a case in which verbal encoding has in part been taken over by a "nominal" strategy of predication (i.e., copula with predicate adjective). Stassen (1997: 242) notes that all such cases involve periphrastic expressions, which strongly suggests that all predicative PTCs and nominally encoded STAs (ex. 27b) are "supported" by a copula, whether overt or null/covert (ex. 28).[53]

53. The STA's split verb-adjective encoding, its restriction to the Qal binyan, and its general "nonproductiveness" in comparison to the PTC all suggest that the STA is an older verb-switching strategy that is falling out of use during the biblical period of the language. Based on the typological data presented by Stassen (1997), this is evidence of BH's drift away from aspect prominence toward tense prominence, inasmuch as verbal encoding of properties (i.e., the STA verbally encoded) is associated with aspect-prominent languages (see Cook 2008 for details).

28. Predicative Participle as Copular Complement

28a

וְהַנַּעַר הָיָה מְשָׁרֵת אֶת־יְהוָה אֶת־פְּנֵי עֵלִי הַכֹּהֵן

The lad was ‹Q.PFV› serving ‹PI.PTC› Yhwh before Eli the priest. (1 Sam. 2:11)

28b

וְהַנַּעַר שְׁמוּאֵל מְשָׁרֵת אֶת־יְהוָה לִפְנֵי עֵלִי

The lad Samuel (was) serving ‹PI.PTC› Yhwh before Eli. (1 Sam. 3:1)

The PTC is therefore not a "verbal form" (contra *BHRG* §20.3.1) but represents a sort of intrusion into the TAM system by a nominal strategy for predication (see Cook 2008). In the discussion below of the PTC's role in the TAM system, it will be evident that this intrusive role has resulted in a shift in TAM functions for the IPFV form in the system (§3.6–7).

2.3 Situation Aspect

Situation aspect in the Aristotelian tradition occurs widely in the linguistic literature in the form presented by Vendler 1957 (reprinted in Mani, Pustejovsky, and Gaizauskas 2005: 21–32; see also Pustejovsky 1991 [reprinted in Mani, Pustejovsky, and Gaizauskas 2005: 33–60]; and Filip 2011). Vendler classifies situations into four basic types, rooted in ideas from Aristotle: states, activities, accomplishments, and achievements. Rothstein (2004) has elegantly distinguished these four types with the properties of [±stages] and [±telic], as in table 2.1.

Table 2.1. Feature Chart for Situation Aspect (Adapted from Rothstein 2004: 12)

Situation aspect	[±Stages]	[±Telic]
State	–	–
Activity	+	–
Accomplishment	+	+
Achievement	–	+

These divisions are, however, only a starting point. First, states have been further subdivided into individual-level and stage-level types, based on the relative duration or permanency of the state. The distinction is motivated by, among other things, the fact that different copulas are associated with each type in some languages, such as Spanish *ser* and *estar* (see Wilson 2018: 88). While such data provide lexical evidence for the semantic distinction, that distinction seems not to be as firmly rooted in the verbal lexeme and argument structure as much as it is in real world knowledge. For example, we know that to *be asleep* is a stage-level (i.e., temporary) state in its literal sense, but can we say the same of its euphemistic use for death in *Lazarus is fallen asleep* (John 11:11)? The latter would seem to demand an individual-level (i.e., a permanent state) reading, as evidenced by Jesus's clarification a few verses later: *Lazarus is dead* (John 11:14).

Second, the delimitation of situation aspect is not always clear. For example, the term *stative* is traditionally associated with the lexical item, which I refer to as STA (e.g., זָקֵן, "he is old"; חָלָה, "he is sick"). However, *stativity* is associated with other constructions, such as generic expressions (ex. 29a), passives (ex. 29b), and anterior/perfect aspect (ex. 29c), in which a resultant state derives from a previous nonstative eventuality (see Rothmayr 2009: 35–36).

29. Varieties of Stative Expressions: Generic, Passive, Perfect

29a

לֵב אָדָם יְחַשֵּׁב דַּרְכּוֹ וַיהוָה יָכִין צַעֲדוֹ

A man's heart will plan ‹PI.IPFV› his path, but Yhwh will establish ‹HI.IPFV› his steps. (Prov. 16:9)

29b

וַתִּסָּגֵר מִרְיָם מִחוּץ לַמַּחֲנֶה

Miriam was shut ‹NI.PN› outside the camp. (Num. 12:15)

29c

וַיהוָה סָגַר רַחְמָהּ

Yhwh had closed ‹Q.PFV› her womb. (1 Sam. 1:5)

By contrast, STA lexemes are not limited to stative interpretations (as in ex. 30a) but are frequently interpreted dynamically, as an inchoative achievement (i.e., a transition from one state to another, as in ex. 30b; see §2.4.1).

30. Stative Expressing a State and an Inchoative Event

30a

וַיִּגְבַּהּ לִבּוֹ בְּדַרְכֵי יְהוָה

His mind was elevated ‹Q.PN› in the ways of Yhwh. (2 Chron. 17:6)

30b

וּכְחֶזְקָתוֹ גָּבַהּ לִבּוֹ

But when he became strong ‹Q.INF›[54] his mind became elevated ‹Q.PFV› [i.e., haughty]. (2 Chron. 26:16)

Unlike the contrast between *was* and *became* in the English glosses of exs. 30a–b, BH has no formal marking for this distinction. Rather, BH relies on contextual clues to distinguish stative and dynamic inchoative interpretations.

Third, situation aspect is affected by more than just the verbal categorization of a root; it is dependent on the arguments licensed by the verb. For example, the transitive verb עָשָׂה ("he did, worked, acted") is an activity when the object is unspecified (ex. 31a), an accomplishment when a single object complement is included (ex. 31b), and an activity if the object is pluralized (ex. 31c).

31. Effect of Argument Structure on Situation Aspect

31a

בַּעֲשֹׂתוֹ וְלֹא־אָחַז

When he acts ‹Q.INF›, I do not see. (Job 23:9)

31b

אֲשֶׁר עָשָׂה הַיְשׁוּעָה הַגְּדוֹלָה הַזֹּאת

. . . who has accomplished ‹Q.PFV› this great victory. (1 Sam. 14:45)

31c

כִּי־גָדוֹל אַתָּה וְעֹשֵׂה נִפְלָאוֹת

For you (are) great and work ‹Q.PTC› wonders. (Ps. 86:10)

54. The form is analyzed as a noun by some (e.g., *HALOT*, Groves-Wheeler) but clearly derives from an INF (see *DCH* s.v. חֶזְקָה) and functions as one here, and so may be parsed as one (so Andersen-Forbes).

Throughout my discussion, I will refer to these four basic types (i.e., states, activities, accomplishments, and achievements) as *situation aspects* with the caveat that verbal lexemes cannot always be assigned invariably to one of these types.

These situation aspects provide a foundation for building an event model by which to analyze the interaction of tense and aspect. Employing the ubiquitous space-time metaphor, measured in terms of intervals of time, the event model is composed of moments and (borrowing the phonological model of syllables) an onset, nucleus, and coda (fig. 2.4).

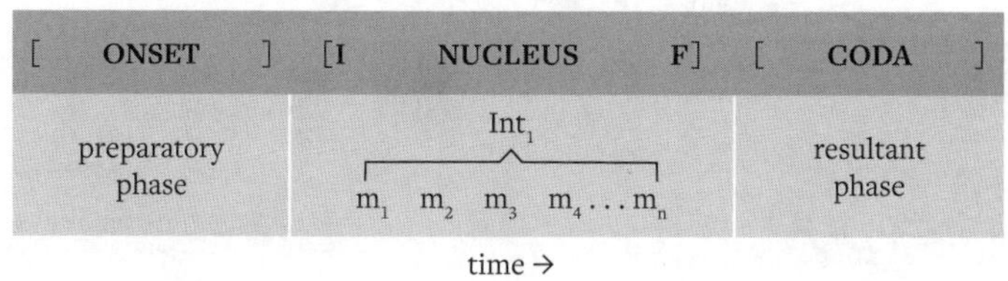

Key I = initial point | F = final point | Int = interval of time | m = moment of time

Figure 2.4. A Model of Events (Based on Cook 2012c: 58)

This model enables us to distinguish graphically among the four situation aspects listed above in terms of the nature of the nucleus intervals and the character of the "final" point of the nucleus. These are illustrated in fig. 2.5.

States (–stages, –telic) and activities (+stages, –telic) are distinguished by the feature of stages: if someone is *sick all day*, that state is consistent through all the intervals of time that make up that day (i.e., there are no "stages"). By contrast, if someone *goes walking* there is sense of progress or stages, whereby at each interval of time they are farther from their starting point and closer to their ending point of walking. Like activities, accomplishments (+stages, +telic) are distinguished from states in terms of stages, but accomplishments are also distinguished from activities in terms of telicity: nontelic situations "end," but telic ones have an inherent endpoint and so are "completed" or "finished." For example, whereas one ends *going for a walk*, one finishes *walking home*, because there is a specific point at which the event of *walking home* comes to a natural (rather than arbitrary) conclusion or endpoint.

This difference has been described in terms of the subinterval property, which belongs to states and activities but not to accomplishments or achievements. The property is illustrated by and explains what is known as the "imperfective paradox," which is stated in terms of entailments: the progressive/

a. States (e.g., חל"ה be sick)

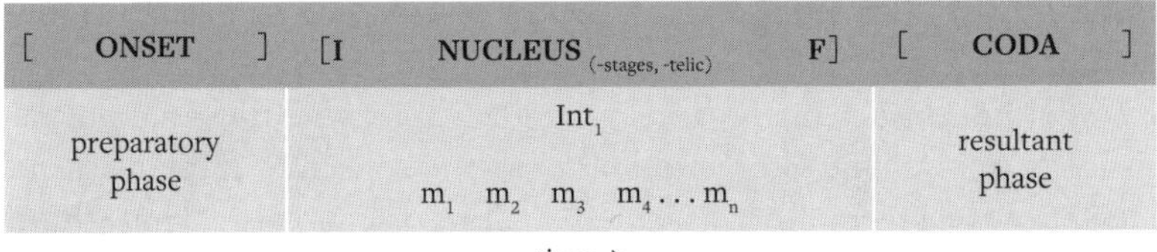

time →

b. Activities (e.g., הל"ך walk)

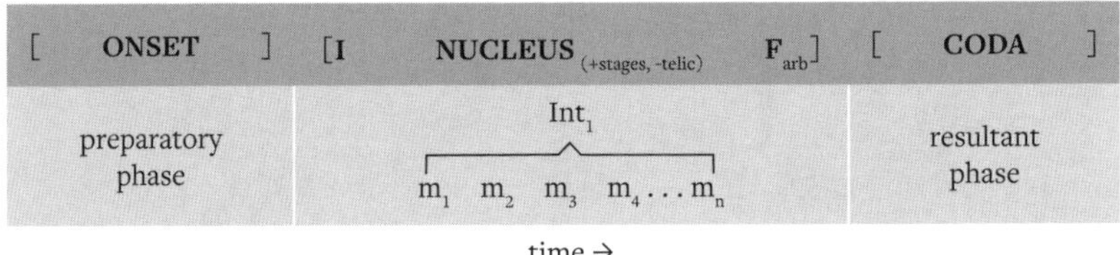

time →

c. Accomplishments (e.g., בנ"ה build [something])

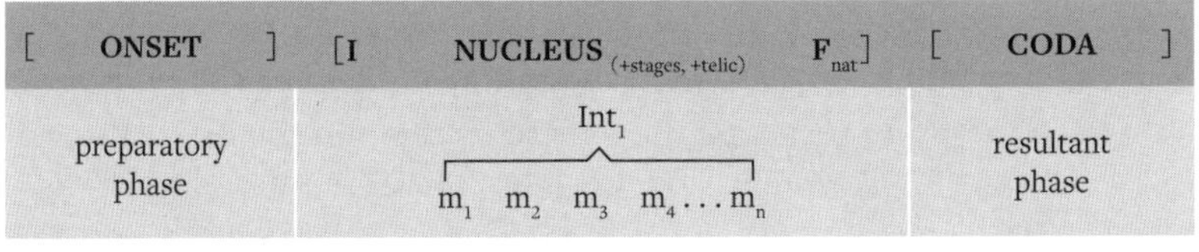

time →

d. Achievements (e.g., מות die)

[ONSET]		[CODA]
preparatory phase	[-stages, +telic]	resultant phase

time →

Key I = initial point | F_{arb} = arbitrary final point | F_{nat} = natural final point | Int = interval of time
m = moment of time

Figure 2.5. Event Models for Situation Types (Based on Cook 2012c: 63)

imperfective activity הוּא הֹלֵךְ "he (was) walking ‹Q.PTC›" (e.g., Gen. 18:16) entails the perfective הוּא הָלַךְ "he walked/has walked ‹Q.PFV›" (e.g., Exod. 17:5), because the arbitrary nature of the endpoint means the event is "effected" in a single interval of walking; by contrast, the progressive/imperfective accomplishment הוּא בֹּנֶה חַיִץ "he (was) building ‹Q.PTC› a wall" (Ezek. 13:10) does not entail the perfective הוּא בָּנָה חַיִץ "he built/has built ‹Q.PFV› a wall" (cf. Deut. 20:5), because there is a final point that has not been reached during the intermediate interval of *building a wall*. This distinction is important to the discussion of viewpoint aspects discussed in the following chapter.

Finally, achievements (–stages, +telic) are distinct from the previous three situation types by their entire lack of nucleus (and concomitant lack of stages). Rather than a nucleus with intervals, an achievement is constructed of an onset and coda juxtaposed to represent an instantaneous change of state (i.e., +telic). Thus, in contrast to states and activities, accomplishments and achievements are both +telic, but accomplishments are +stages, whereas achievements lack a nucleus and stages. This lack of a nucleus is evident from a comparison of the progressive construction of an accomplishment, like the above-cited example הוּא בֹּנֶה חַיִץ ("he [was] building ‹Q.PTC› a wall," Ezek. 13:10), and an achievement like אֲנַחְנוּ בָאִים בָּאָרֶץ ("we [are] entering ‹Q.PTC› into the land," Josh. 2:18). Whereas the former describes stages or progress toward completing the wall, the latter describes a preparatory phase leading up to the change of state, at which point the people will instantaneously transition from *entering* the land to *having entered* the land—the resultant state.

2.4 The Verb Phrase and Intransitive Predications

Moving up the distributed morphology tree, verb-classified intransitive predications consist of a verb-classified root (vP) combined with a thematic phrase of any category (xP, where x = any category) to create a verb phrase (VP; fig. 2.6).

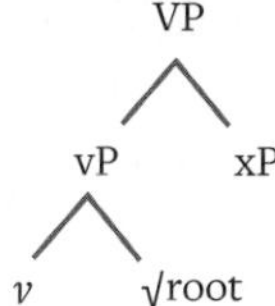

Figure 2.6. Intransitive Verb Phrase

The realization of this xP and its semantic relationship with the situation expressed by the verb allows us to distinguish an array of intransitive predications—notably, various stative predications, including copulars and existentials.

2.4.1 Stativity and the Stative in Biblical Hebrew

The term *stative* is multifaceted. First and foremost, in BH grammar it refers to a morphological distinction evident in the Qal binyan, the STA (§2.2.3). Semantically, however, it encompasses a variety of subtypes of stative constructions that lack both progress or stages [–stages] and an inherent endpoint [–telic] (§2.3). The significance of the semantic (versus morphological) class of stative extends beyond valency analysis to understanding how events unfold in relationship to each other in discourse (§4.3–4).

The morphological distinction between stative and dynamic in BH refers to two unique characteristics that distinguish between the two classes only in the Qal binyan. First, there is a variation of vocalization between the two classes of verbs, as delineated in table 2.2.

Table 2.2. Stative-Dynamic Morphological Distinction

	i-Class stative	*u*-Class stative	Dynamic
Suffix pattern (PFV)	כָּבֵד ("he is heavy")	קָטֹן ("he is small")	שָׁמַר ("he guarded")
Prefix pattern (IPFV, IMPV, INF)	יִכְבַּד ("he will be heavy")	יִקְטַן ("he will be small")	יִשְׁמֹר ("he will guard")

Note: The *i*-class and *u*-class labels refer to the historical form of the theme vowels, which are stress-lengthened to tsere and holem, respectively, in the 3MS PFV forms listed in the table.

Second, STAs feature an adjective form that in the masculine singular is morphologically identical with the 3MS PFV form, but STAs typically lack an active PTC form (e.g., *כֹּבֵד). Nevertheless, this distinction between STA and dynamic can be obscured by phonetic factors (e.g., the influence of guttural and weak consonants on the vowel pattern) and historical factors, such as the development of active PTC forms for some STAs (e.g., יֹודֵעַ, "is knowing"; אֹהֵב, "is loving") and the shift of some STAs into the dynamic category both in vowel pattern and meaning (e.g., קָרֵב, "is drawn near" → קָרַב, "drew/has drawn near"; see G. Driver 1936: 47–49). It is unsurprising, then, that alongside the label stative-dynamic to identify this distinction (e.g., Joüon §§41, 112; *IBHS* §22.2.1), other labels have been proposed, notably intransitive-transitive (e.g.,

GKC §43a) and middle-active voice (e.g., Tropper 1998: 182; Joosten 1998: 207). These differing identifications are understandable given the overlap of these categories seen among the STAs. For example, most STAs are intransitive, though not all are, including in BH (e.g., אָהֵב, "loves/loved"; שָׂנֵא, "hates/hated"); and many STAs, like the middle voice, encode the "undergoer" as subject (rather than as the "agent"), but, again, there are exceptions (cf. כָּבֵד, "is/was heavy" versus יָדַע, "knows/knew").

If we concede that any semantic label for this morphological distinction is only completely accurate as an etymological identification, the stative-dynamic label is the most coherent and comprehensive in accounting for the typological and historical-comparative evidence. Typologically, the STA in BH is recognized as aligning with stative predicates in other languages. For example, Stassen (1997: 496) describes the BH stative class in the following way:

> A restricted number of adjectival predicates (such as "old," "heavy," "hungry," "pure," "near," "small," "full," and "dead") is still associated with a productively used stative verb. As was the case in Akkadian, these verbs have a dynamic-ingressive interpretation when appearing in the imperfect, while the perfect expresses resultative-perfective meaning. But even these "adjectival verbs" allow for a stative, nominal-adjectival form. Since this nominal form is frequently identical to the third-person singular masculine of the perfect of the stative verb, there can be ambiguity in a number of cases between a stative (zero copula) reading and a verbal, resultative-perfective, reading of the item.

BH STAs also behave with the PN and PFV grams (i.e., grammatical constructions) in a pattern with statives in other languages as well (see Cook 2012c: 198–99). For example, STAs with the PN consistently express a *past*-time situation (ex. 32a), whereas with the PFV, STAs express by default a *present*-time situation (ex. 32b) and require contextual indicators to force a past-time interpretation (ex. 32c), and the interpretation may at times be ambiguous between past or present (ex. 32d).[55] Significantly, this pattern of interaction reinforces not only the stative identity of these forms but also the past-tense and perfective-aspect identity of these two conjugations, respectively.

55. The ambiguity arises because a stative cannot be "bounded" by the PFV, so Yhwh loving Israel in the past does not preclude his loving them still in the present time of speaking (see further §3.3.2 and §4.3). In Cook (2012c: 198–99), I note that the data from 49 STA roots show that while they consistently express past states or inchoative events in the PN, they express or may express (ambiguous) present states with the PFV more than half the time (54%), which rises to 78 percent if only reported speech is examined. See Cook 2012c: 198n33 for a list of the STAs examined.

32. Statives in Past Narrative and Perfective Conjugations[56]

32a

וַיֶּאֱהַב הַמֶּלֶךְ אֶת־אֶסְתֵּר מִכָּל־הַנָּשִׁים

The king loved ‹Q.PN› Esther more than all the women. (Esther 2:17)

32b

וְהָיָה כִּי־יֹאמַר אֵלֶיךָ לֹא אֵצֵא מֵעִמָּךְ כִּי אֲהֵבְךָ וְאֶת־בֵּיתֶךָ

[IRREALIS] If he says ‹Q.IPFV› to you, "I will not depart ‹Q.IPFV› from you," because he loves ‹Q.PFV› you and your house, . . ." (Deut. 15:16)

32c

וְתַחַת כִּי אָהַב אֶת־אֲבֹתֶיךָ וַיִּבְחַר בְּזַרְעוֹ אַחֲרָיו

And because he loved ‹Q.PFV› your fathers, he chose ‹Q.PN› his seed after him. (Deut. 4:37)

32d

וַיַּהֲפֹךְ יְהוָה אֱלֹהֶיךָ לְּךָ אֶת־הַקְּלָלָה לִבְרָכָה כִּי אֲהֵבְךָ
יְהוָה אֱלֹהֶיךָ׃

Yhwh your God turned ‹Q.PN› for you the curse into a blessing, because Yhwh your God loved (NRSV)/loves (NJPS) ‹Q.PFV› you. (Deut. 23:6)

Semantically, statives were described above as lacking both progress or stages [–stages] and an inherent endpoint [–telic] (§2.3). Within this classification, linguists recognize several subtypes of statives, which are historically

56. Compare the other 17 occurrences of PN אה"ב (Gen. 24:67; 25:28 [2×]; 29:18, 30; 34:3; Judg. 16:4; 1 Sam. 16:21; 18:1, 20; 2 Sam. 13:1; 1 Kings 3:3; Hosea 11:1; Mal. 1:2; Pss. 109:17; 119:167; 2 Chron. 11:21) versus 38 of 65 occurrences of PFV אה"ב (excluding 6 cases of the IRPFV) with a present stative sense (Gen. 22:2; 27:4, 9; 44:20; Exod. 21:5; Deut. 15:16; Judg. 14:16; 16:15; 1 Sam. 18:22; Isa. 43:4; Jer. 5:31; Hosea 12:8; Amos 4:5; Mal. 2:11; Pss. 11:7; 26:8; 47:5; 78:68; 116:1; 119:47, 48, 97, 113, 119, 127, 140, 159, 163; Prov. 8:36; Ruth 4:15; Song 1:3, 4, 7; 3:1, 2, 3, 4; Eccles. 9:9). Of the remaining 27 cases, 10 are ambiguous between a present and past stative reading (Deut. 23:6; Isa. 48:14; Jer. 2:25; 14:10; Ezek. 16:37; Hosea 4:18; 9:1; Pss. 52:5–6; 99:4) and 17 are more clearly past or perfect (Gen. 27:14; 37:3, 4; Deut. 4:37; 1 Sam. 1:5; 18:28; 20:17; 2 Sam. 12:24; 13:15; 1 Kings 11:1; Isa. 57:8; Jer. 8:2; 31:3; Mal. 1:2 [2×]; Ps. 45:8; Job 19:19).

or developmentally linked to perfective grams (see §3.5 below). The simple stative implies neither a previous dynamic event nor any agency (ex. 33a), and stative verbs are distinct from the other types in that the only dynamic interpretation available is an inchoative, the entrance into a state (ex. 33b).

33. Stative Expressing a State and an Inchoative Event

33a. Simple Stative

וּבַל־יֹאמַר שָׁכֵן חָלִיתִי

An inhabitant will not say ‹Q.IPFV›, "I am sick ‹Q.PFV›." (Isa. 33:24)[57]

33b. Inchoative Stative

בַּיָּמִים הָהֵם חָלָה חִזְקִיָּהוּ לָמוּת

In those days Hezekiah became sick ‹Q.PFV› to (the point of) dying ‹Q.INF›. (Isa. 38:1)[58]

By contrast, the resultative and perfect are stative constructions in which dynamic predicates can occur, because both constructions denote a prior (dynamic) event that is the cause of the current state. However, while the resultative construction leaves the agent of the prior event unexpressed and ambiguous, the perfect equates the subject of the state with the agent of the past event (see Detges 2000: 348–50).[59] The distinction can be captured by the different translations of the perfective verb in 1 Sam. 14:3: the earlier English versions employed a resultative (ex. 34a), which leaves ambiguous whether Jonathan was the agent of going away (e.g., he could have been taken away by someone); the modern versions, by contrast, employ the perfect construction (ex. 34b), which makes Jonathan's agentive role clear. It has been observed that the interpretation of the connection between the previous event and the current state can be more pragmatic than semantic; that is, the clause itself in 1 Sam. 14:3 tells us neither how nor why Jonathan went away but only that he is no longer present with the rest of the people. The how and why

57. Gen. 18:12–13; 19:31; 24:1; 27:1–2; 41:57; 47:20; Josh. 13:1; 23:1–2; 1 Sam. 2:22; 4:18; 8:1, 5; 12:2; 17:12; 2 Sam. 7:22; 19:33; 1 Kings 1:1, 15; 2 Kings 4:14; Isa. 3:16; 55:9; Jer. 44:10; Ezek. 11:8; 28:2; Hosea 10:2; Pss. 37:25; 92:6; 104:1; Prov. 23:22; Ruth 1:12; 1 Chron. 23:1.

58. Gen. 19:13; 26:13; Josh. 17:13; Judg. 1:28; 1 Kings 1:50; 2 Kings 3:26; Jer. 5:27; Ezek. 22:4; Ps. 76:9; Ezra 9:6; 1 Chron. 21:4; 2 Chron. 25:3; 28:20.

59. The perfect passive is an exception to this agent-subject equation since the passive allows for an overt expression of agent that need not be identical with the subject.

of the past act must be deduced (to the degree possible) from the broader pragmatic context.

34. Resultative Stative and Perfect (Stative)

וְהָעָם לֹא יָדַע כִּי הָלַךְ יוֹנָתָן

The people knew not ‹Q.PFV› that Jonathan was gone ‹Q.PFV›. (resultative stative; 1 Sam. 14:3 KJV, ASV)[60]

or The people did not know ‹Q.PFV› that Jonathan had gone ‹Q.PFV›. (perfect [stative]; 1 Sam. 14:3 RSV, NRSV, ESV; cf. NJPS)

The passive construction can also be considered a type of stative, as what is considered resultative in one language may be considered a passive expression in another (Bybee, Perkins, and Pagliuca 1994: 63). The distinction between the two depends on the transitivity of the event: unlike the resultative (ex. 34a), the passive construction is derived from a transitive active by means of promoting the object to the subject position, leaving the option of overtly expressing the agentive subject with an instrumental PP (ex. 35).

35. Passive Stative

וְהָאָרֶץ תֵּעָזֵב מֵהֶם

The land will be left ‹NI.IPFV› by them. (Lev. 26:43)

In BH, however, these stative subtypes are not uniformly constructed (e.g., with a copula or auxiliary). Rather, as seen above, simple statives may be associated with the morphological class of statives, while the resultative and perfect sense is associated with the perfective gram generally, and passive voice is associated with inter-binyan alternations, such as Qal-Niphal, Piel-Pual, and Hiphil-Hophal. Below we will return to both the binyanim alternations and the perfective conjugation (§2.5 and §3.5). Here I turn attention to copular and existential predicates, apart from the copular-supported PTC, which is treated in §3.6.

60. Cf. these versions in Num. 21:28; 1 Sam. 14:17; 2 Sam. 3:23; 1 Kings 1:25; 21:18; Isa. 15:8; 38:8; 45:23; 51:5; Jer. 4:7; 14:2; 23:19; Ezek. 7:10; 19:14; Mic. 2:13; Pss. 19:5; 88:17; Prov. 7:19; Ruth 1:13, 15; Song 6:2.

2.4.2 Copular and Existential Clauses[61]

Copular and existential clauses constitute some of the simplest types of intransitive predications. In BH, as in other languages, they are both semantically interrelated and employ some of the same grammatical constructions. Copular expressions in BH employ a form of הי״ה (ex. 36a), a phonological null or covert copula (36b), a pronoun as a substitute copula (ex. 36c), or the positive or negative "existential" יֵשׁ or אַיִן, respectively (exs. 36d–e).

36. Copular Constructions

36a

וּרְחַבְעָם הָיָה נַעַר

Rehoboam was ‹Q.PFV› a lad. (2 Chron. 13:7)

36b

עֲצַבֵּי הַגּוֹיִם Ø כֶּסֶף וְזָהָב

The idols of the nations (are) silver and gold. (Ps. 135:15)

36c

וְעַתָּה יְהוָה אַתָּה־הוּא הָאֱלֹהִים

And now, Yhwh, you are ‹PRO› God. (1 Chron. 17:26)

36d

גַּם אָנֹכִי כָּכֶם אֲדַבֵּרָה לוּ־יֵשׁ נַפְשְׁכֶם תַּחַת נַפְשִׁי

Also I like you could speak ‹PI.IPFV› if your life were ‹EXIST› in the place of my life. (Job 16:4)

36e

אֵינֶנּוּ גָדוֹל בַּבַּיִת הַזֶּה מִמֶּנִּי

He is not ‹NEG-EXIST› greater in this house than I. (Gen. 39:9)

Existential predications in BH are typically associated with יֵשׁ and אַיִן (exs. 37a–b), but forms of הי״ה are also employed (exs. 37c–d).

61. This section has greatly benefited from the treatment in Wilson 2018. On avalent discourse הי״ה, see §4.2.

37. Existential Constructions

37a

יִתֵּן בֶּעָפָר פִּיהוּ אוּלַי יֵשׁ תִּקְוָה

Let him put ‹Q.IPFV› his mouth in dust; perhaps there is ‹EXIST› hope. (Lam. 3:29)

37b

וַיִּתְהַלֵּךְ חֲנוֹךְ אֶת־הָאֱלֹהִים וְאֵינֶנּוּ כִּי־לָקַח אֹתוֹ אֱלֹהִים

Enoch walked ‹HT.PN› with God, and he was not ‹NEG-EXIST›, because God took ‹Q.PFV› him. (Gen. 5:24)

37c

וַיְהִי־אִישׁ מֵהַר־אֶפְרָיִם וּשְׁמוֹ מִיכָיְהוּ

There was ‹Q.PN› a man from the hill country of Ephraim, and his name (was) Micah. (Judg. 17:1)

37d

וְלֹא־הָיָה מַיִם לָעֵדָה

There was ‹Q.PFV› no water for the congregation. (Num. 20:2)

These data raise two questions. What is the difference between copular and existential predications? And are there any discernible patterns to the use of the various constructions?

The semantic and formal similarities between the copular and existential constructions are enough to create ambiguity in quite a few instances, specifically those with a locative adjunct. The clause in ex. 38 may mean that a famine occurred (copula) in the land or that a famine existed (existential), specifically in the land of Judah. In English, the difference can be made more explicit through the use of explicative *there* to mark the expression as existential.

38. Ambiguity between Copular and Existential Readings

וַיְהִי רָעָב בָּאָרֶץ

A famine was ‹Q.PN› in the land. (copula)

or There was ‹Q.PN› a famine in the land. (existential; Ruth 1:1)[62]

62. Gen. 12:10; 18:24; 26:1; 41:54; 47:6, 13; Exod. 7:21; 10:22; 16:13; 17:7; Num. 14:42; Deut. 1:42; 31:17; Josh. 5:1; Judg. 9:51; 18:1; 19:1; 21:25; 1 Sam. 5:11; 20:8; 28:20; 2 Sam. 14:32; 2 Kings 5:15; Isa. 43:12; Hab. 2:19; Zech. 9:11; Mal. 1:14; Ps. 144:14; Job 1:1; 2 Chron. 25:8.

Despite the ambiguity in certain instances, copula and existential clauses are semantically distinct, and distributed morphology provides a means to model that difference. A copular clause links a NP subject and a NP, AP, or PP predicate complement using a semantically minimal (or even null) verb, so that the predicate complement, rather than the verb, forms the major semantic content of the predicate (Mikkelsen 2011: 1805; Wilson 2018: 1). Within distributed morphology, copular expressions are analyzed as consisting of an embedded small clause within a thematic predicate phrase (PredP), as shown in fig. 2.7 (Myler 2018: 6–7).[63] In this model, the v_{BE} is the copular verb, the NP is the subject, and the NP/AP/PP is the predicate complement.[64]

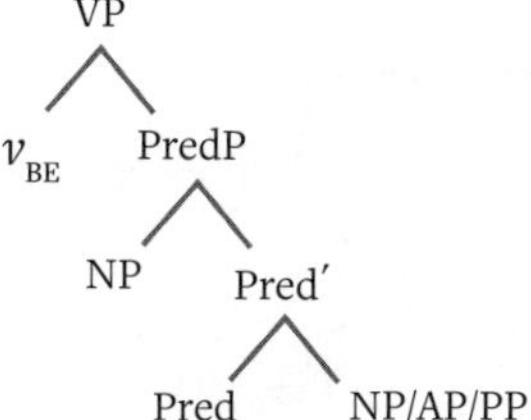

Figure 2.7. Copular Clause

By contrast, existential clauses express the presence or existence of someone or something (McNally 2011: 1830). This suggests that an existential has an inherent locative idea, which is capitalized on by distributed morphology in modeling existentials (fig. 2.8): the thematic PredP consists of a locative HERE, and the "sub-phrase" Pred′ features an existential predicate and the NP subject (Myler 2018: 18).

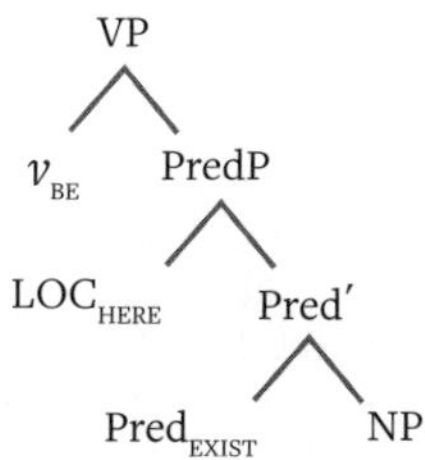

Figure 2.8. Existential Clause

63. A small clause is a predication without a full verb, such as *Michael smart* in *Joe thinks Michael smart*.

64. The prime sign with Pred′ marks it as an intermediate or sub-phrase of PredP; see van Gelderen 2013: 8–14.

Thus the ambiguity in the case of ex. 38 resides in its locative PP, which serves as the predicate complement in a copular analysis but an optional locative adjunct in an existential one.[65] Existential clauses consisting of just a subject and no predicate adjuncts have been called "one-place existentials" (see Wilson 2018: 94) and are illustrated in ex. 39. For many of the examples of one-place existential clauses with הי"ה (see exs. 39c–d and the references in the accompanying note), the predicate is more dynamic than a simple statement of existence, such as the English gloss "occurred" might convey.

39. One-Place Existential Clauses

39a

יִתֵּן בֶּעָפָר פִּיהוּ אוּלַי יֵשׁ תִּקְוָה

Let him put ‹Q.IPFV› his mouth in dust; perhaps there is ‹EXIST› hope. (Lam. 3:29)[66]

39b

וַיִּתְהַלֵּךְ חֲנוֹךְ אֶת־הָאֱלֹהִים וְאֵינֶנּוּ כִּי־לָקַח אֹתוֹ אֱלֹהִים

Enoch walked ‹HT.PN› with God, and he was not ‹NEG-EXIST›, because God took him. (Gen. 5:24)[67]

39c

וַיַּרְא פַּרְעֹה כִּי הָיְתָה הָרְוָחָה וְהַכְבֵּד אֶת־לִבּוֹ

Pharaoh saw that there was ‹Q.PFV› relief, and he hardened ‹HI.PFV› his heart. (Exod. 8:11)[68]

65. The optional character of a locative expression with a clause is why it is helpful to define existential clauses as expressing presence or existence and not locating something somewhere. Contrast Myler (2018: 17), who writes of the existential subject being "instantiated at a particular location." Wilson (2018: 2) instead helpfully refers to a "contextual domain," since the location need not be literal or overtly expressed in the clause.

66. 1 Kings 18:10; 2 Kings 9:15; Jer. 31:6; Job 11:18; 33:32; Prov. 19:18; 24:14; Eccles. 1:10; 2:21; 4:8; 5:12; 6:1; 8:14; 10:5; Esther 3:8.

67. Gen. 37:30; 41:49; 42:13, 32, 36; 44:31; Exod. 12:30; 21:11; 32:18; Num. 21:5; Deut. 4:39; 28:29; 1 Sam. 14:17; 20:2, 21; 1 Kings 5:18; 8:46; 10:21; 18:26, 29, 43; 2 Kings 4:31; Isa. 44:12; 48:22; Jer. 8:11; 31:15; 49:10; Ezek. 13:16; Hosea 3:4; 4:1; Pss. 10:4; 14:1; 37:10, 36; 53:2; 69:3; 74:9; 103:16; 144:14; Job 3:21; 8:22; 19:7; 23:8; 24:24; 27:19; Prov. 6:15; 23:5; 28:3; 29:1, 9; Eccles. 4:8; 1 Chron. 29:15; 2 Chron. 6:36.

68. For other one-place existential clauses with הי"ה in any conjugation, see Gen. 1:3, 5–6, 8, 13–14, 19, 23, 31; Exod. 9:24, 26; 21:22–23; Deut. 3:4; 18:22; Josh. 11:19; Amos 7:6; Hab. 1:3; Dan. 12:1; Neh. 8:17.

39d

הַקֹּלוֹת יֶחְדָּלוּן וְהַבָּרָד לֹא יִהְיֶה־עוֹד

The thunder will cease ‹Q.IPFV› and hail will be ‹Q.IPFV› no more. (Exod. 9:29)

Copular clauses have been subclassified into a number of different types, which is helpful for explaining the distribution of the copular constructions in BH. Stassen (1997) distinguishes between *identity* statements (illustrated in ex. 40) and *predicational* expressions (illustrated in ex. 41) using the concept of a "mental file" to explain the difference: whereas identity statements index the "mental file" of the subject (e.g., in ex. 40b the mental file of יְהוָה is identified with הָאֱלֹהִים), predicative expressions add information to the "mental file" associated with the subject (e.g., classification as a כָּלְבִּי, "Calebite"; property of being שִׁכֹּר עַד־מְאֹד, "very drunk"; and location of בָּאָרֶץ, "in the land" in exs. 41b–d, respectively).

40. Identity Statements[69]

40a. Presentational (Points Out a Thing by Its Identity)

אֵלֶּה הָיוּ עָרֵי הַמּוּעָדָה לְכֹל בְּנֵי יִשְׂרָאֵל

These were ‹Q.PFV› the designated cities for all the sons of Israel. (Josh. 20:9)[70]

40b. Equative (Identifies Things as Referentially Identical)

כִּי יְהוָה הָאֱלֹהִים

For Yhwh (is) God. (Josh. 22:34)[71]

40c. Specificational (Identifies Something by an Alternative Designation)

וְרֹאשׁ אֶפְרַיִם שֹׁמְרוֹן

The head of Ephraim (is) Samaria. (Isa. 7:9)[72]

69. The latter two are contextually distinguished; see Stassen (1997: 101–6) for more details.

70. For other examples with an overt copula, see Gen. 36:13–14; Lev. 14:2; 15:3; Deut. 18:3; 1 Sam. 8:11; Jer. 31:33; Ezek. 16:49; Zech. 14:12, 19; Ps. 119:56; Eccles. 2:10; 1 Chron. 2:33, 50; 3:1. Hundreds of examples occur with null copula, particularly in genealogical lists (e.g., 24 times in Gen. 36).

71. Gen. 18:27; 29:25; 35:10; 48:7; Exod. 6:8; 1 Kings 18:31; Dan. 10:4; Neh. 11:11; 1 Chron. 2:45; 3:9–14; 4:4, 25; 5:15; 7:12, 25; 16:14.

72. Gen. 46:8; Num. 2:3, 5, 7, 10, 12, 14, 18, 20, 22, 25, 27, 29; 3:24, 30, 32, 35; Ezek. 16:46.

Stassen (1997: 13) notes that the types of predications in ex. 41 align with the four major word classes: verb, noun, adjective, and adverb (i.e., adverbial PP).

41. Intransitive Predication

41a. Event (Verb)

לָכֵן שָׂמַח לִבִּי

Therefore my heart is glad ‹Q.PFV›. (Ps. 16:9)

41b. Class (NP)

וְהוּא כָלִבִּי

He (was) a Calebite. (*qere*; 1 Sam. 25:3)[73]

41c. Property (AP)

וְהוּא שִׁכֹּר עַד־מְאֹד

He (was) very drunk. (1 Sam. 25:36)[74]

41d. Location (PP)

קוֹל מִלְחָמָה בָּאָרֶץ

The sound of battle (is) in the land. (Jer. 50:22)[75]

When used as a copula, הי"ה (like any other copula) contributes minimal semantic content to its clause. However, it can be a full verb, expressing an event. In such cases it may express an inchoative event (i.e., an achievement [–stages, +telic]).[76] Based on Wilson (2018: 107), we can model the inchoative

73. For other examples, especially in genealogies, see Gen. 46:8–14; Num. 26:30–32; Ezek. 16:3, 45; 1 Chron. 1:32–42.

74. Gen. 2:12; 3:1; 13:13; 24:16; 29:17, 31; 37:24; Exod. 11:3; 19:16; 21:28; Num. 13:28; 24:21; Deut. 1:28; 32:5; Judg. 11:1; 13:2; 18:10; 1 Sam. 2:4; 3:1; 4:19; 25:2, 15; 2 Sam. 11:2; 14:9, 20; 15:3; 17:7, 14; 1 Kings 1:4; 2:38, 42; 11:28; 15:14; 2 Kings 2:19; 5:1; Isa. 54:13; Jer. 15:18; 20:17; Ezek. 7:7; 30:3; 32:25; Amos 8:3; Obad. 15; Zeph. 1:14; 3:5; Zech. 3:3; Pss. 19:8–10; 32:10; 33:1; 34:19; 48:2; 103:8; 111:2; 145:3; 147:5; Job 3:7; 6:12; 11:4; 26:6; 36:5, 26; Prov. 12:10, 15; 29:12; Song 1:3; 2:3; 4:3; 5:10; Eccles. 5:11; 11:7; Ezra 10:13; Neh. 5:9; 7:4; 1 Chron. 4:40; 2 Chron. 2:4; 15:17.

75. Gen. 8:11; 24:10; 43:21; Exod. 1:5; 17:9; 26:28; Num. 17:21; 24:7; Josh. 2:19; 7:21–22; Judg. 7:16; 9:51; 1 Sam. 17:40, 57; 18:10; 19:9; 22:6; 23:15; 28:20; 2 Sam. 2:16; 22:10; 1 Kings 2:37; 2 Kings 4:42; 6:25; Ezek. 9:2; 21:37; 22:25; 24:23; Hosea 9:6; Mic. 6:14; Hab. 2:20; Zeph. 3:15; Zech. 5:9; Mal. 2:6; 3:20; Pss. 11:4; 18:10; 37:31; 55:11; 66:17; 105:31; 118:15; Job 15:21; Prov. 3:16; 12:20; 19:21; Song 4:11; 8:3; Eccles. 2:14; Lam. 1:9; Neh. 7:72; 1 Chron. 17:1; 2 Chron. 23:5.

76. Although I adopt Wilson's (2018: 107) distributed morphology model for the eventive הי"ה, I depart from his strict constructionist approach to הי"ה. He argues that הי"ה is never a full verb but an auxiliary whose various meanings are dictated by allosemous heads in the

use of ה״יה as featuring a dynamic Pred ($Pred_{DYN}$; see fig. 2.9). Compare the stative/non-dynamic Pred in the copular model in fig. 2.7.

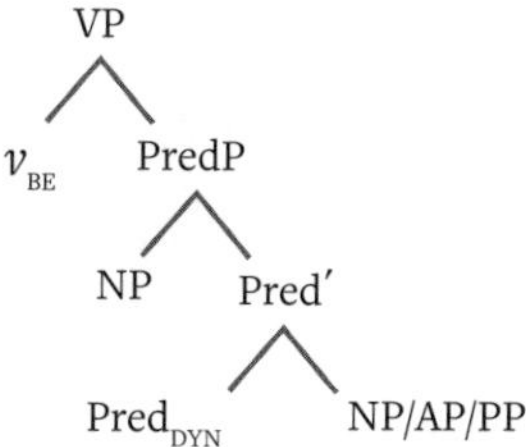

Figure 2.9. Inchoative ה״יה Clause

Wilson (2018: 107) draws attention to the Hebrew grammars that associate this inchoative sense especially with a ל PP predicate complement (ex. 42a). However, the inchoative sense is not restricted to that construction but is dependent on the discourse context and pragmatics. For example, a simple stative (identity) interpretation of ex. 42b, that "all the dust . . . was gnats," makes poor sense based on the discourse context and knowledge about dust and insects—that they are not one and the same thing.

42. Inchoative ה״יה

42a

וַיְהִי הָאָדָם לְנֶפֶשׁ חַיָּה

The man became ‹Q.PN› a living being. (Gen. 2:7)[77]

42b

כָּל־עֲפַר הָאָרֶץ הָיָה כִנִּים בְּכָל־אֶרֶץ מִצְרָיִם

All the dust of the land became ‹Q.PFV› gnats throughout all the land of Egypt. (Exod. 8:13)[78]

distributed morphology template. By contrast, I suggest that ה״יה is a full verb when eventive, while it is an auxiliary in its copular and existential functions. (The term *allosemy* appears in distributed morphology studies, where it refers to the ability of morphemes to have multiple semantic realizations; see, e.g., Wilson 2018: 5–6.)

77. Gen. 2:10, 24; 9:15; 17:16; 18:18; Exod. 34:12; Num. 11:20; 14:3; 26:10; Deut. 1:39; Josh. 7:5, 12; 14:9, 14; 24:32; Judg. 1:30, 33, 35; 2:3; 1 Sam. 14:15; 18:21; 25:37, 42–43; 2 Sam. 7:24; 11:27; 1 Kings 2:15; 9:7; 13:34; Isa. 1:14, 21–22, 31; 42:22; Jer. 3:1; 5:13; 6:10; 7:34; 42:18; 44:8; 49:2; Ezek. 16:8; 17:6, 8, 23; 22:19; 26:5; 36:4; 37:17; Hosea 5:9; Joel 4:19; Amos 5:5; Mic. 7:13; Zeph. 2:15; Pss. 69:11, 23; 94:22; 118:14, 21; Ruth 4:13; Lam. 1:1, 5; 1 Chron. 23:11.

78. Gen. 3:22; 19:26; 21:20; 34:15; 39:2; 48:19; Exod. 7:19; 9:10; 22:23; 23:29; Num. 17:5; Deut. 7:26; 15:7; Judg. 11:39; 1 Sam. 16:21; 28:16; 2 Kings 19:26; 24:1; Isa. 1:9, 18; 17:1; 37:27;

In addition to inchoative, הי״ה as a full verb expresses the idea of "happen, befall, come upon" (ex. 43a) and a specialized sense of "come to" when referring to the delivery of a word from Yhwh (ex. 43b). As in the case of the inchoative use, these uses can be classified as [–stages, +telic], referring to the achievement of an event "befalling" someone or the "arrival" of the divine word.[79]

43. Dynamic הי״ה

43a

זְכֹר יְהוָה מֶה־הָיָה לָנוּ

Remember ‹Q.IMPV›, Yhwh, what has happened ‹Q.PFV› to us. (Lam. 5:1)[80]

43b

וַיְהִי דְבַר־יְהוָה אֵלַי

The word of Yhwh came ‹Q.PN› to me. (Jer. 1:4)[81]

The choice of overt הי״ה copula or null copula is based on the present parameter (see Cook 2012c: 229; Stassen 1997: 314; and Wilson 2018). That is, the copula need not be overtly expressed unless it requires some TAM marking that departs from the default current time (i.e., time of the speaker or discourse time). Examples of הי״ה overtly signaling TAM include the same array of meanings found with other verbs: the PN copula expressing past tense (ex. 44a), the PFV copula expressing varieties of perfect (exs. 44b–c), the IPFV copula for past habitual (ex. 44d) and future (ex. 44e), and the JUSS and IMPV copulas for directive-volitive (exs. 44f–g).[82]

49:5; Jer. 7:11; 12:8; 18:21; 23:14; 27:17; Ezek. 12:20; 23:10; Mic. 3:12; 7:1; Zeph. 2:9; Zech. 10:7; Pss. 31:12–13; 69:9; 79:4; 89:42; 119:83; Job 19:15; Lam. 1:1, 6; 2:5; 3:14; 4:8.

79. It is possible to analyze these two events as identical, the divine communication being perceived as something that "happens to" or "befalls" a prophetic figure. However, the persistent use of a locative preposition in the latter construction suggests that the idiom has a directional sense to it.

80. Gen. 7:6, 10; Exod. 9:11; Num. 24:2; Judg. 19:30; 21:3; 1 Sam. 4:7; 19:9, 20, 23; 2 Kings 3:15; 7:20; 24:3; Jer. 5:30; 48:19; Joel 1:2; 1 Chron. 7:23; 27:24; 2 Chron. 15:1; 20:14; 24:18.

81. Gen. 15:1; 1 Sam. 15:10; 2 Sam. 7:4; 24:11; 1 Kings 6:11; 13:20; 16:1, 7; 17:2, 8; 18:1, 31; 19:9; 21:17, 28; 2 Kings 20:4; Jer. 1:13; 2:1; 13:3, 8; 16:1; 18:5; 24:4; Ezek. 6:1; 7:1; 11:14; 12:1, 8, 17, 21; Hag. 2:20; Zech. 1:7; 4:8; 6:9; 1 Chron. 17:3; 22:8.

82. This is just a sampling and not exhaustive of TAM functions, for which see §§3.4–8 on the individual conjugations.

44. Overt Copular for Tense-Aspect-Mood/Modality Marking

44a

וַיְהִי בְכוֹרוֹ אַמְנוֹן

His firstborn was ‹Q.PN› Amnon. (2 Sam. 3:2)

44b

אַנְשֵׁי מִקְנֶה הָיוּ עֲבָדֶיךָ מִנְּעוּרֵינוּ וְעַד־עַתָּה

Men of livestock your servants have been ‹Q.PFV› since our youth and until now. (Gen. 46:34)

44c

עַד־הַמָּקוֹם אֲשֶׁר־הָיָה שָׁם אָהֳלוֹ בַּתְּחִלָּה

. . . to the place that his tent had been ‹Q.PFV› at the beginning. (Gen. 13:3)

44d

חֹדֶשׁ יִהְיוּ בַלְּבָנוֹן שְׁנַיִם חֳדָשִׁים בְּבֵיתוֹ

A month they would be ‹Q.IPFV› in Lebanon, two months (they would be) at his house. (1 Kings 5:28)

44e

וְאַתָּה תִּהְיֶה כְּאַחַד הַנְּבָלִים בְּיִשְׂרָאֵל

And you will be ‹Q.IPFV› like one of the fools in Israel. (2 Sam. 13:13)

44f

וִיהִי כְנַעַן עֶבֶד לָמוֹ

Let Canaan be ‹Q.JUSS› a servant to him. (Gen. 9:27)

44g

הִתְהַלֵּךְ לְפָנַי וֶהְיֵה תָמִים

Walk before ‹HT.IMPV› me and be ‹Q.IMPV› blameless. (Gen. 17:1)

The use of a pronoun as a copula in BH is disputed. Tripartite verbless constructions, illustrated in ex. 45, have been analyzed either as left (initial) dislocation of the subject with a resumptive pronoun or as cases of the pronoun functioning as a copula (for recent analyses of the pronoun used as copula in BH, see Kummerow 2013; Holmstedt and Jones 2014).

45. Tripartite Verbless Clause: Left Dislocation or Pronominal Copula

וַיֹּאמְרוּ יְהוָה הוּא הָאֱלֹהִים

They said, "As for Yhwh, he (is) God."

or They said, "Yhwh is ‹PRO› God." (1 Kings 18:39)[83]

However, because the pronoun as a substitute copula does not always exhibit *person* agreement, examples like ex. 46a provide good evidence of a copular function; the pronoun as a substitute copula does show *number* agreement (ex. 46b).

46. Pronominal Copula[84]

46a

וְעַתָּה יְהוָה אַתָּה־הוּא הָאֱלֹהִים

And now, Yhwh, you are ‹PRO› God. (1 Chron. 17:26)

46b

אֵלֶּה הֵם מוֹעֲדָי

These are ‹PRO› my appointed festivals. (Lev. 23:2)

Because of the reduced agreement features and the inability of the pronoun to carry TAM marking, Wilson (2018: 147–53) argues that the label "pronominal copula" is misleading and that it should instead be understood as a case of the third-person pronoun functioning as a "substitute" for a copula (so also Cook and Holmstedt 2013: 34). The pronominal as a substitute copula in BH is limited to present-tense specificational and equative identity expressions.[85] However, it is optional, as illustrated by the minimal pair in ex. 47, leading Wilson (2018: 151) to conclude that the precise semantic nuance added by the pronoun "remains an open question."

83. Holmstedt and Jones (2014: 85–86) identify the following also as ambiguous between a left dislocation and pronominal copula analysis: Lev. 20:21; Deut. 4:35, 39; 7:9; Josh. 2:11; 1 Kings 8:60; Eccles. 1:9; 1:17; Dan. 8:21; 2 Chron. 33:13.

84. Other examples of pronominal copula Holmstedt and Jones (2014: 83–85) identify are Gen. 2:19; 15:2; 25:16; 27:38; 36:8; 42:6; Exod. 12.27; Lev. 14:13; 25:33; Num. 3:20, 21, 27, 33; Deut. 10:9, 17–18; 12:23; 18:2; Josh. 13:14, 33; 1 Sam. 4:8; 2 Sam. 7:28; 2 Kings 19:15; Isa. 9:14; 37:16; Jer. 14:22; 30:21; Zeph. 2:12; Pss. 24:10; 44:5; Lam. 1:18; Neh. 9:6, 7; 1 Chron. 1:31; 8:6; 22:1; 2 Chron. 20:6.

85. Naudé (2001: 110–11) associates the pronoun serving as copula with specification clauses, while Wilson (2018: 103n34, 153) states that it occurs only in equative clauses. As mentioned above (see the note to ex. 40), the distinction between these is contextual.

47. Optionality of Pronoun as Substitute Copula[86]

47a

אַתָּה־הוּא הָאֱלֹהִים לְבַדְּךָ

You are ‹PRO› God alone. (Isa. 37:16)

47b

כִּי אַתָּה ___ יְהוָה אֱלֹהָי

For you (are) Yhwh my God. (Jer. 31:18)

The particles יֵשׁ and אַיִן are often referred to as "existential" particles (e.g., *IBHS* §10.3.2b), and that seems likely to have been their historical origin (see Naudé and Miller-Naudé 2016; Naudé, Miller-Naudé, and Wilson 2021), but both particles developed copular functions alongside their existential ones through their reanalysis in ambiguous contexts like ex. 38, cited above (see Wilson 2018: 180). As particles (i.e., noninflecting forms), they cannot indicate TAM distinctions but are dependent on the discourse time for their temporal interpretation, as shown by the contrastive past and present interpretations in ex. 48a. They can appear interchangeably with the הי״ה construction, even in the same passage, as illustrated in ex. 48b.

48a. Contextual Temporal Interpretation of Existential Particle

וַיַּרְא יַעֲקֹב כִּי יֶשׁ־שֶׁבֶר בְּמִצְרָיִם וַיֹּאמֶר יַעֲקֹב לְבָנָיו לָמָּה
תִּתְרָאוּ׃ וַיֹּאמֶר הִנֵּה שָׁמַעְתִּי כִּי יֶשׁ־שֶׁבֶר בְּמִצְרָיִם

Jacob saw ‹Q.PN› that there was ‹EXIST› grain in Egypt, and he said ‹Q.PN› to his sons, "Why are you looking at each other ‹HT.IPFV›?" He said ‹Q.PN›, "Hey, I have heard ‹Q.PFV› that there is ‹EXIST› grain in Egypt." (Gen. 42:1–2)[87]

86. Examples are from Wilson 2018: 150.
87. Cited in Wilson 2018: 167.

48b. Interchangeability of Existential Particles and הי״ה

בַּעֲבוּר הָאֲדָמָה חַתָּה כִּי לֹא־הָיָה גֶשֶׁם בָּאָרֶץ . . . כִּי גַם־
אַיֶּלֶת בַּשָּׂדֶה יָלְדָה וְעָזוֹב כִּי לֹא־הָיָה דֶּשֶׁא׃ וּפְרָאִים עָמְדוּ
עַל־שְׁפָיִם שָׁאֲפוּ רוּחַ כַּתַּנִּים כָּלוּ עֵינֵיהֶם כִּי־אֵין עֵשֶׂב׃

. . . on account of the ground being shattered ‹Q.PFV›, because there has been ‹Q.PFV› no rain in the land. . . . Indeed, even the hind in the field has given birth ‹Q.PFV› abandoning ‹Q.AINF› [it], for there has been ‹Q.PFV› no grass. The wild asses have stood ‹Q.PFV› on the heights and panted ‹Q.PFV› for air like jackals. Their eyes have failed ‹Q.PFV› because there is no vegetation ‹NEG-EXIST›. (Jer. 14:4–6)[88]

A couple of syntactic features set apart יֵשׁ and אַיִן from הי״ה. First, they may take a clitic pronoun as the clausal subject. In the case of אַיִן, this syntagm appears in both existential (ex. 49a) and copula expressions (ex. 49b). Both יֵשׁ and אַיִן can have a clitic pronoun subject as a copula supporting a PTC (exs. 49c–d).

49. Existential Particles with Clitic Pronouns as Clausal Subject

49a

וְכֹל מִזְרַע יְאוֹר יִיבַשׁ נִדַּף וְאֵינֶנּוּ

All the sown land of the Nile will dry up ‹Q.IPFV›, have been driven away ‹NI.PFV›, and no longer exist ‹NEG-EXIST›. (Isa. 19:7)[89]

49b

וּמִן־הַבְּהֵמָה אֲשֶׁר אֵינֶנָּה טְהֹרָה

And from the animals that they are not ‹NEG-EXIST› clean . . . (Gen. 7:8)[90]

49c

וְעַתָּה אִם־יֶשְׁכֶם עֹשִׂים חֶסֶד וֶאֱמֶת אֶת־אֲדֹנִי הַגִּידוּ לִי

And now, if you are ‹EXIST› going to do ‹Q.PTC› steadfast love and faithfulness with my master, tell ‹HI.IMPV› me. (Gen. 24:49)[91]

88. Cited in Wilson 2018: 168.

89. Gen. 37:30; 42:13, 32, 36; 1 Kings 20:40; Isa. 17:14; Jer. 10:20; 31:15; 49:10; 50:20; Ezek. 26:21; Zech. 8:10; Pss. 37:10, 36; 39:14; 59:14; 103:16; 104:35; Job 3:21; 7:8, 21; 8:22; 23:8; 24:24; 27:19; Prov. 12:7; 23:5; Lam. 5:7.

90. Gen. 30:33; 31:2, 5; 39:9; 44:26, 30, 34; Lev. 13:21, 26, 34; Deut. 1:42; 29:14; 2 Sam. 3:22; 2 Kings 17:34; Ezek. 27:36; 28:19; 33:32; Ps. 73:5–6; Eccles. 1:7; 6:2; 8:13.

91. Only Gen. 24:42; 43:4; Deut. 13:4; 29:14; Judg. 6:36; Esther 3:8.

49d

וַיֹּאמְרוּ אֶל־הָעָם לֵאמֹר כֹּה אָמַר פַּרְעֹה אֵינֶנִּי נֹתֵן לָכֶם
תֶּבֶן

They said ‹Q.PN› to the people [COMP], "Thus has said ‹Q.PFV› Pharoah, 'I am not ‹NEG-EXIST› going to give ‹Q.PTC› straw to you.'" (Exod. 5:10)[92]

Second, יֵשׁ (and to a lesser degree אַיִן) more frequently than הי״ה hosts the interrogative הֲ (ex. 50).[93]

50. Existental יֵשׁ as Interrogative Host

הֲיֵשׁ־בִּלְשׁוֹנִי עַוְלָה

Is there ‹EXIST› iniquity on my tongue? (Job 6:30)[94]

The last structure included in this section is the copular-locative construction used to express possession. Stassen (2009: 48–69) observes that possessive constructions in the world's languages fall into those that feature a *have* verb and those that utilize a *be* verb. Of the *be*-verb type, he identifies three possessive constructions: the locative construction, the *with* construction, and the topic construction. Although Bar-Asher (2009) identifies all three of these *be*-verb types in BH, the locative construction, using a ל PP copular complement, is by far the dominant one (ex. 51a).[95] Clear examples of the *with* construction, using עִם or אֵת, are more difficult to identify (ex. 51b), because most such uses appear in the context of motion, leaving ambiguous whether possession or accompaniment is being expressed (e.g., Judg. 19:3,

92. Gen. 20:7; 30:33; 43:5; Exod. 3:2; 8:17; Lev. 11:4; Deut. 1:32; 4:12, 22; 21:18, 20; Judg. 3:25; 1 Sam. 11:7; 19:11; 2 Sam. 19:8; 1 Kings 21:5; 2 Kings 12:8; 17:26, 34; Isa. 1:15; Jer. 7:16–17; 11:14; 14:12; 32:33; 37:14; 38:4; 44:16; Ezek. 3:7; 20:39; Mal. 2:2, 9; Eccles. 4:17; 5:11; 8:7, 16; 9:2, 5, 16; 11:5–6; Esther 3:8; 5:13; Neh. 2:2; 13:24; 2 Chron. 18:7.

93. See Wilson (2018: 169–70), who also highlights the relative frequency of יֵשׁ versus הי״ה with אִם ("if"), אוּלַי ("perhaps"), לוּ ("if"), כִּי ("if"), כִּי־אִם ("except"), and פֶּן ("lest"). However, the contrast with הי״ה is slight in most cases (e.g., אוּלַי occurs twice with יֵשׁ and never with הי״ה).

94. Gen. 24:23; 43:7; 44:19; Exod. 17:7; Num. 13:20; Deut. 13:4; Judg. 4:20; 1 Sam. 9:11; 2 Kings 4:13; 10:15; Isa. 44:8; Jer. 14:22; 23:26; 37:17; Pss. 14:2; 53:3; Job 5:1; 25:3; 38:28. Less often with אַיִן: Judg. 14:3; 1 Kings 22:7; 2 Kings 3:11; Jer. 7:17; 49:7; 2 Chron. 18:6. Cf. with הי״ה: Deut. 4:32; 2 Kings 7:2, 19; Joel 1:2.

95. Bar-Asher (2009: 417) identifies a fourth type, the bound construction, which he classifies as a "subgroup" of the topic type: cf. this type in Ps. 115:7 יְדֵיהֶם with the locative example in v. 6 אָזְנַיִם לָהֶם. Bar-Asher appears to treat this type as predicative, labeling it a genitive predicate possessive construction with the caveat that "it may more simply be treated as a one-place existential: יְדֵיהֶם וְלֹא יְמִישׁוּן, 'their hands (exist), but they cannot feel.'" Given doubts about the clausal character of this type, I have not included it in the list of types.

10). The example Bar-Asher (2009: 369) provides of topic possession (1 Sam. 25:6) is uncertain (see Wilson 2018: 183–84), and in any case a possessive interpretation of the construction is a matter of pragmatics rather than semantics (Bar-Asher 2009: 378).

51. Possessive Copular Constructions

51a. Locative

הִנֵּה־נָא לִי שְׁתֵּי בָנוֹת

Hey now, I (have) two daughters. (Gen. 19:8)[96]

51b. With

מָה אִתָּנוּ

What do we (have) [lit., what (is) with us]? (1 Sam. 9:7)[97]

51c. Topic

וְאַתָּה שָׁלוֹם וּבֵיתְךָ שָׁלוֹם וְכֹל אֲשֶׁר־לְךָ שָׁלוֹם

May you (have) peace! May your house (have) peace! May all that belong to you (have) peace! (1 Sam. 25:6)[98]

Although null copula is most frequent in the locative possessive expression, other copula strategies can be employed (ex. 52).

52. Possessive Copular Constructions with Overt Copulas

52a

וַיְהִי לִפְנִנָּה יְלָדִים וּלְחַנָּה אֵין יְלָדִים

Peninnah had ‹Q.PN› children, but Hannah did not have ‹NEG-EXIST› children. (1 Sam. 1:2)[99]

96. Also Gen. 43:23; Judg. 17:5; Ruth 1:12 (with יֵשׁ).

97. Possibly also Judg. 19:3, 10; 1 Sam. 12:2; 25:25; 2 Sam. 15:27.

98. Translation from Tsumura 2007: 578.

99. Gen. 12:16; 30:42; Exod. 21:4, 34; Num. 35:3; 36:4; Deut. 22:29; Josh. 17:1; 24:32; Judg. 11:6; 17:12; 1 Sam. 17:9; 18:17; 2 Sam. 8:6; 1 Kings 4:11; 2 Kings 24:7; Isa. 55:13; Jer. 16:2; 35:9; 52:6; Ezek. 29:18; 34:23–24; 37:23; Hab. 2:7; Zech. 2:15; Pss. 31:3; 71:3; Song 8:11; 1 Chron. 11:21.

52b

כִּי יֵשׁ לָעֵץ תִּקְוָה

Indeed, a tree has ‹EXIST› hope. (Job 14:7)[100]

52c

וַתֹּאמֶר אֵין לְשִׁפְחָתְךָ כֹל בַּבַּיִת כִּי אִם־אָסוּךְ שָׁמֶן

She said ‹Q.PN›, "Your servant has nothing ‹NEG-EXIST› in the house except a jar of oil." (2 Kings 4:2)[101]

52d

כַּחַטָּאת הָאָשָׁם הוּא לַכֹּהֵן

Like the sin offering, the guilt offering belongs ‹PRO› to the priest. (Lev. 14:13)[102]

2.5 The Binyanim, Valency Alternations, and Non-overt Complements

Stems, themes, binyanim, and templates all refer to the patterns of vowels and (in some cases) affixes that apply to a root to create a verb. The seven standard binyanim are Qal, Niphal, Piel, Pual, Hithpael, Hiphil, and Hophal. The latter six are named after their 3MS PFV form of the paradigm verb פע"ל ("do, make"); the Qal is so called because it is the "light" (vs. "heavy") pattern (see *HALOT* s.v. קַל) in that it lacks binyan affixes and gemination or lengthening/doubling. Although the binyanim are most fundamentally requisite templates for creating verbs out of a root, they are also a means of encoding valency alternations among verbs built from the same root. This split function along with historical shifts (see below §2.5.1) has skewed the presumably originally "systematic" binyanim. Rather than attempt to reconstruct and analyze an original pristine system, we should recognize the lack of semantic regularity

100. Gen. 31:29; 33:9, 11; 39:4–5, 8; 44:19–20; Judg. 19:19; 1 Kings 17:12; Jer. 31:16–17; 41:8; Mic. 2:1; Job 25:3; 28:1; 38:28; Ruth 1:12; Eccles. 4:9; 1 Chron. 29:3; 2 Chron. 15:7.

101. Gen. 11:30; 47:4; Exod. 22:1–2; Num. 27:8–11; 35:27; Deut. 12:12; 25:5; Josh. 18:7; 22:25; Judg. 11:34; 18:7; 1 Sam. 14:6; 18:25; 2 Sam. 18:18; 21:4; 1 Kings 22:17; 2 Kings 4:14; 19:3; Isa. 1:30; 55:1; Jer. 8:17; 12:12; 50:32; Ezek. 38:11; 42:6; Hosea 8:7; 10:3; Joel 1:18; Amos 3:4–5; Nah. 3:3; Mal. 1:10; Pss. 3:3; 34:10; 73:4; Job 22:5; 32:12; Prov. 5:17; 30:27; Song 8:8; Eccles. 2:16; 8:15; Lam. 1:2, 7, 21; 4:4; Esther 2:7; Dan. 9:26; 11:45; Neh. 2:14; 5:5; 2 Chron. 12:3; 18:16.

102. Gen. 18:10; 19:8; Exod. 16:23; 19:5; Lev. 25:4; Deut. 4:43; 10:14; 29:28; Judg. 8:24; 10:4; 17:5; 1 Sam. 25:36; 2 Sam. 13:1; 1 Kings 7:30; Isa. 44:5; Jer. 8:9; Ezek. 1:4; Hosea 12:3; Amos 5:20; Jon. 2:10; Pss. 24:1; 25:14; 115:5–6; Prov. 16:11; 30:2; Eccles. 6:11; Dan. 9:8; 1 Chron. 25:22–26; 2 Chron. 9:18.

and instead focus on the sorts of valency alternation that are most frequently encoded by the binyanim.[103] This is what I undertake below in §2.5.2–3 after first providing some observations about the dual character of the binyanim (§2.5.1). The last subsection deals with valency alternation unrelated to the binyanim, between overt and non-overt object complements (§2.5.4).

2.5.1 The "System" of Binyanim[104]

The traditional assumption is that each of the binyanim has a more or less discrete syntactic-semantic value and that the relationships among the binyanim for a given root are systematic.[105] This assumption is reinforced by the ubiquity of charts like table 2.3 (e.g., Arnold-Choi appendix B; GKC §39f; Joüon §40; *IBHS* §21.2.2n; Weingreen 1959: 100). Such charts suggest that meaning relationships are predictable. For example, given the Qal of a root, the Hiphil of that same root can be expected to provide the corresponding causative verb.

Table 2.3. The System of Binyanim

	Active	Passive	Middle
Simple	Qal	Qal passive→	Niphal
Intensive/Factitive	Piel	Pual	Hithpael
Causative	Hiphil	Hophal	

This assumption is misleading because it is so often inaccurate.[106] The binyanim can be thought of as systematic only in an etymological sense; that

103. Previous studies are of limited value insofar as they almost uniformly presume that binyanim relationships and functions are systematic if only rightly understood. A common approach focuses on Piel as the key to understanding the system (so *IBHS* §21.2.2a), either concentrating on the relationship between the Qal and Piel (e.g., Goetze 1942; Beckman 2015; see also Ryder 1974; Kouwenberg 1997) or between the Piel and Hiphil (e.g., Jenni 1968). The middle-passive-reflexive binyanim have been analyzed at times individually (e.g., Klein 1992; van Wolde 2019, 2021; Jones 2020) but more often comparatively, seeking to tease out semantic distinctions among them (e.g., Bicknell 1984; Siebesma 1991; Boyd 1993; Benton 2009; Jenni 2012). In recent decades, attention has been given to the interaction of situation aspect with the binyanim (e.g., Creason 1995; Jenni 2000; Benton 2009; Gzella 2009).

104. This section draws heavily on Cook 2023.

105. I.e., "marked by thoroughness and regularity," *Merriam-Webster's Dictionary*, s.v. "systematic," def. 3b, https://www.merriam-webster.com/dictionary/systematic.

106. Blau (2010: 227) attempts to maintain the traditional view of semantic consistency while dismissing any practical benefit to such a view: "The meanings of the various verbal stems are quite fixed but not to the extent they are predictable."

is, we may assume that in its abstracted and reconstructed form, the binyanim applied to roots in a thorough and regular way (so Cook 2023). Etymology, however, is not a reliable guide to meaning in actual usage (Barr 1961: 107), and usage paints a picture that is different from the one implied by table 2.3. The binyanim are neither fully thorough nor fully regular. The Qal binyan dominates, accounting for almost 70% of the verbs in the Hebrew Bible, while the Hiphil accounts for just 13%, the Piel 9%, and the Niphal less than 6%. The remaining binyanim account for just 4% of the verbs, with the nonstandard binyanim accounting for less than 1% (see *IBHS* §21.2.3e). Almost half the roots that are used as verbs in BH appear in only one binyan, and another quarter of the roots appear in just two binyanim (fig. 2.10).

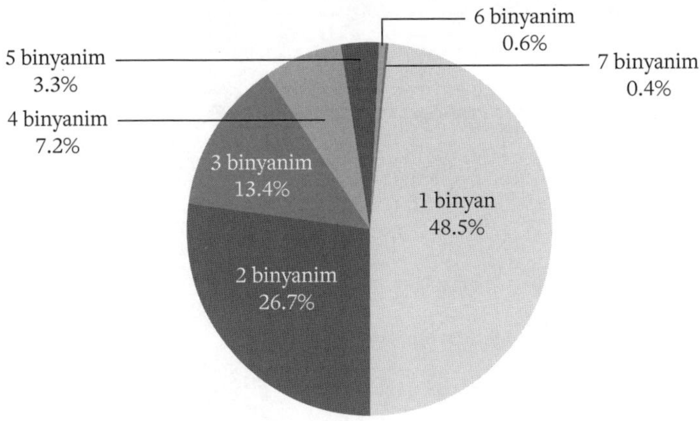

Figure 2.10. Percentage of Roots Occurring in 1–7 Binyanim

Only five roots (of more than 1600) occur in all seven standard binyanim (פק״ד, יד״ע, חל״ה, גל״ה, בק״ע).[107] Of these, only יד״ע and חל״ה show the expected regular meaning relationships among the binyanim (exs. 53a–b).

107. Two other roots included in the tally in fig. 2.10 occur in seven binyanim but not in all seven standard ones. That is, חי״ל occurs in Qal, Piel, Pual, Hithpael, Hiphil, Hophal, and Hithpelpel, and קל״ל occurs in Qal, Niphal, Piel, Pual, Hiphil, Pilpel, and Hithpalpel.

53a. Meaning Relations among Binyanim for ידʺע

Qal	יָדַע	knows/knew
Niphal	נוֹדַע	make oneself known, be known
Piel	יִדַּע	make something known
Pual	יֻדַּע	be made known
Hithpael	הִתְוַדַּע	make oneself known
Hiphil	הוֹדִיעַ	make someone know something
Hophal	הוֹדַע	be made known

53b. Meaning Relations among Binyanim for חלʺה

Qal	חָלָה	be(come) sick/weak
Niphal	נֶחֱלָה	show oneself/be sick/weak
Piel	חִלָּה	sicken/weaken someone
Pual	חֻלָּה	be made sick/weak
Hithpael	הִתְחַלָּה	pretend to be sick (< ? show oneself sick/weak)
Hiphil	הֶחֱלָה	make someone sick/weak
Hophal	הָחֳלָה	be wounded (< ? be made sick/weak)

That even just a couple of examples like ידʺע and חלʺה exist calls for some explanation as to why the system shows regular meaning relationships like these (exs. 53a–b) and yet also features many nonsystematic relations, such as those illustrated in exs. 54 and 55.[108]

108. The regularity of חלʺה across the binyanim is less clear than ידʺע: the semantic distinction between Qal and Niphal is not always evident (cf. 1 Sam. 30:13; Dan. 8:27); the Piel with this meaning appears just once (Deut. 29:21), whereas in its other fifteen occurrences it means to "appease"; and both the Hithpael and Hophal verbs also exhibit idiosyncratic meanings that can only be etymologically related to the basic sense of the root as exhibited in the other binyanim.

54. Binyan Homonyms

54a. Qal-Piel (≈ 9%)[109]

חָלָה "grow weak" and חִלָּה "appease"

פָּתַח "open" (tr.) and פִּתַּח "untie"

בִּין "understand" and בֹּנֵן "care for"

54b. Qal-Hiphil (≈ 3%)

סָגַר "shut" (tr.) and הִסְגִּיר "hand over"

דָּבַק "stick to something" and הִדְבִּיק "overtake"

פָּרַס "break bread" and הִפְרִיס "have a divided hoof"

54c. Piel-Hiphil (≈ 16%)

חִלֵּץ "despoil" and הֶחֱלִיץ "make strong"

חִלֵּל "profane" and הֵחֵל "begin"

כִּתֵּת "crush" and הִכְתִּית "scatter"

55. Binyan Synonyms

55a. Qal-Piel (≈ 53%)

בָּלַע and בִּלַּע "engulf"

בָּקַע and בִּקֵּעַ "split"

גָּלָה and גִּלָּה "uncover"

55b. Qal-Hiphil (≈ 19%)

זָנַח and הִזְנִיחַ "reject"

זָעַק and הִזְעִיק "cry"

יָרַשׁ and הוֹרִישׁ "take possession of"

55c. Piel-Hiphil (≈ 65%)

אִבַּד and הֶאֱבִיד "kill, destroy"

חִלֵּף and הֶחֱלִיף "change" (tr.)

עֹרֵר and הֵעִיר "stir up"

109. The statistics in this section refer to the percentage of the 1621 roots that occur in the binyanim indicated. They are all approximate (≈) because they are based on an analysis of glosses in the lexica rather than an exhaustive survey of the occurrences in context. Even allowing for fluctuations in the estimates, the impression given by the data remains valid.

As with most linguistic explanations (as opposed to descriptions), the explanation for the systematic/nonsystematic mixed character of the binyanim in BH is a historical one. Although the binyanim can be reconstructed as a pristine "system" in which roots appear in a full range of binyanim with regular and predictable meaning relationships among verbs of the same root, such an etymological portrait is insufficient as a guide to how the binyanim actually function in BH.[110] This is because historical shifts presumably or demonstrably have occurred to the "system" of binyanim.

One of these shifts has obscured the passive of the "simple" binyanim (table 2.3). The Qal passive has been assimilated to the Pual in the suffix pattern and to the Hophal in the prefix pattern, leaving only the participle form as a vestige of the Qal passive binyan (see Joüon §50c n. 4, §58). The lexica and databases vary in their parsing and/or identification of the nonparticiple forms as either Qal passive or a Pual or Hophal verb, because these lexical analyses rely on establishing a clear semantic relationship between the passive form and an existing or posited Qal active of the same root.[111]

In addition to the conflation of Qal passive with the Pual and Hophal patterns, the decline of the Qal passive correlates with the accretion of its functions in the Niphal.[112] This was originally the simple middle voice binyan, but with the decline of an overt simple passive binyan in BH, it has shifted to become a medio-passive (i.e., expressing either/both middle and passive; ex. 56).[113]

110. Jespersen (1921: 316), critically citing Max Müller's 1861 *Lectures on the Science of Language*, explains the attraction ("overestimation") of etymology in language description as "largely attributable to the 'conviction that there can be nothing in language that had not an intelligible purpose, that there is nothing that is now irregular that was not at first regular, nothing irrational that was not originally rational.'"

111. The timing and causes of the loss of the Qal passive are conjectural. Creason (1995: 290) suggests that the Qal passive was still productive during the biblical period, but that it fell out of use sometime between the fixing of the consonantal text and the emergence of the Masoretic tradition of vocalization; the Masoretes in ignorance assimilated the Qal passive forms with the Pual and Hophal. Gzella (2009: 311) by contrast states, "Even though the Gp [Qal passive] ceased to be a productive form during the history of Hebrew, a number of particularly frequent verbs kept their passive counterparts to a more than rudimentary extent." Fassberg (2001) contends that the Qal passive shift to Pual is a parallel development to a shift from Qal to Piel, which is part of a larger shift away from Qal to more easily identifiable binyanim, including Piel and Hiphil.

112. Whether the Niphal marginalized the Qal passive by coopting some of its functions, leading to its decline, or whether the independent decline of the Qal passive prompted the accretion of its functions to the Niphal is unanswerable (see Gzella 2009: 307, 312).

113. Alexiadou and Doron (2012: 5) define medio-passive as the ambiguous interpretation of a middle construction as either middle or passive in the absence of a designated passive construction, which fits well the situation in BH, in which the decline of Qal passive correlates with the shift of Niphal from middle voice to medio-passive.

56. Qal-Niphal Active–Medio-Passive Alternation (≈ 78%)

אָסַף "gather" (tr.) and נֶאֱסַף "gather (intr.)/be gathered"
טָמֵא "be unclean" and נִטְמָא "defile oneself"
אָמַר "say" and נֶאֱמַר "be said"

Another historical loss is of a causative middle (see table 2.3), which arguably would have originally been a part of the "system" based on the comparative evidence (see Boyd 2017: 87). This lack may explain why some Hiphil verbs exhibit both an active causative and a middle anticausative meaning (i.e., "internal" Hiphil; see *IBHS* §21.2.2n), as illustrated in ex. 57.

57. Active Causative and Middle Anticausative Hiphil of אר"ך ("Lengthen")

57a

וְהַאֲרַכְתֶּם יָמִים בָּאָרֶץ

and you might lengthen ‹HI.IR-PFV› days in the land (Deut. 5:33)

57b

לְמַעַן יַאֲרִיכֻן יָמֶיךָ

in order that your days might lengthen ‹HI.IPFV› (Deut. 5:16)

A third historical shift is the amalgamation of a group of *t*-infixed binyanim into the Hithpael, similar to the case of the conflation of Qal passive with the Pual and Hophal (so Creason 1995: 291). Comparative evidence is illuminating in this regard, in that we find BH Niphal verbs semantically equivalent to *t*-infixed binyan in other Northwest Semitic languages: for example, נִלְחַם, "fight" (BH), versus התלחם, "fight" (Moabite, *KAI* 181; see comments in Gzella 2009: 307–8). Whereas the function of the simple *t*-infixed binyan (Gt) has been absorbed by the Niphal in the case of לח"ם, in other cases a Hithpael expresses the middle or passive of a Qal verb of the same root (ex. 58).

58. Qal-Hithpael with No Attested Piel Active-Middle/Passive Alternation (≈ 51%)

רָאָה "look" and הִתְרָאָה "look at one another"
רָעַע "smash" and הִתְרֹעַע "be smashed/smash one another"
שָׁלַל "plunder" and אֶשְׁתּוֹלֵל "be plundered"[114]

Instead of providing caveats to the misleading impression that the binyanim are systematic,[115] we should affirm that the binyanim are only *partially* systematic in that they encode valency alternations among the verbs of *certain roots*.

Among these alternations, the most regular is the active-passive alternation found in the Piel-Pual and Hiphil-Hophal verb pairs (ex. 59).

59. "Internal" Active-Passive Alternations

59a. Piel-Pual (≈ 86%)

שִׁלַּח "send away" and שֻׁלַּח "be sent away"
שִׁלֵּם "recompense" and שֻׁלַּם "be recompensed"
הִלֵּל "praise" and הֻלַּל "be praised"

59b. Hiphil-Hophal (≈ 91%)

הִגִּיד "inform" and הֻגַּד "be informed"
הִכָּה "strike" and הֻכָּה "be struck"
הִשְׁלִיךְ "throw" and הֻשְׁלַךְ "be thrown"

Although the data is incomplete (almost half of all Pual verbs lack a corresponding Piel, and more than a quarter of Hophal verbs do not exhibit a Hiphil of the same root) and skewed by the conflation of the Qal passive with these passive binyanim, the high incidence of active-passive alternations associated with these binyanim pairs strongly suggests that these passives are not independent binyanim at all but "internal" passive patterns built off of their active counterparts. That is, they are exceptions to the rule that binyanim are templates that create verbs from *roots*; instead, these passives are derived from their active counterparts.[116] In addition to the Qal-Niphal

114. The Hithpael verb אֶשְׁתּוֹלֵל exhibits metathesis of the ת and שׁ, and the א prefix instead of the expected ה is attributed to Aramaic influence (so *HALOT* s.v.).

115. See, e.g., Seow (1995: 175): "It is not always possible to fit a piel verb into one of these categories. Sometimes there is no obvious reason why a certain verb occurs in piel."

116. This is supported by Semitic studies that treat Pual, Hophal, and the Qal passive (and their cognates) as "internal" passive constructions (i.e., constructed from the active counterparts

active–medio-passive alternation (ex. 56), the Piel and Hithpael also frequently encode an active-middle or (less often) active-passive alternation (ex. 60).

60. Piel-Hithpael Active-Middle/Passive Alternation (≈ 42%)

גִּלַּח "shave" (tr.) and הִתְגַּלַּח "shave oneself"
טִהַר "cleanse" and הִטַּהֵר "clean oneself"
עִוֵּת "bend" (tr.) and הִתְעַוֵּת "be stooped over"

Alongside the above valency-reducing alternations, valency-increasing causative alternations are common between Qal and Piel and between Qal and Hiphil verbs of the same root (ex. 61).[117]

61. Causative Alternations

61a. Qal-Piel (≈ 32%)

אָמַץ "be strong" and אִמֵּץ "strengthen"
טָהַר "be clean" and טִהַר "cleanse"
לָמַד "learn" and לִמֵּד "teach"

61b. Qal-Hiphil (≈ 47%)

מָלַךְ "be king" and הִמְלִיךְ "install as king"
אָכַל "eat" and הֶאֱכִיל "feed someone"
בָּא "come" and הֵבִיא "bring"

There are also regular valency alternations evident among some triads of binyanim, which combine the active-middle and active-causative alternations illustrated in the above pairs (ex. 62).

62a. Qal-Niphal-Hiphil Active/Stative–Medio-Passive–Causative Alternation (≈ 41%)

רָאָה "see" and נִרְאָה "appear/present oneself" and הֶרְאָה "show"
שָׁמַע "hear" and נִשְׁמַע "be heard" and הִשְׁמִיעַ "cause to hear"

---

by means of vowel gradation; e.g., Lipiński 2001: 408; Gzella 2009: 297) and by Arad's (2005: 108) claims about Pual and Hophal in Modern Hebrew.

117. For these data, I focused on whether the Piel or Hiphil represents a valency-increasing counterpart of the Qal verb, without distinguishing between stative and dynamic Qal or between subclasses of causative (e.g., active causative vs. factitive).

62b. Qal-Niphal-Piel Active/Stative–Medio-Passive–Causative Alternation (≈ 23%)

רָפָה "grow slack" and נִרְפָּה "be slack" and רִפָּה "make slack"
יָרֵא "fear" and נוֹרָא "be afraid" and יֵרָא "make afraid"

Once we move to examining roots in four binyanim, we quickly reach the single digits of roots with regular valency alternations. The largest collection of roots that occur across four binyanim are the nineteen that occur in Qal, Niphal, Piel, and Hiphil.[118] In many of these cases the Qal and Piel verbs or the Piel and Hiphil verbs exhibit either homonymous or synonymous meanings.

Notably missing from this discussion are possible systematic meaning relationships among binyanim that do not manifest syntactically. For example, the Piel has been interpreted as a pluractional counterpart to Qal, such as with שב״ר as glossed in *HALOT*: Qal שָׁבַר ("smash, shatter") versus Piel שִׁבֵּר ("smash into fragments"; e.g., Ps. 29:5). The lack of syntactic alternation between such verbs throws one back onto exegesis of specific passages to discern meaning relationships.[119] Complicating this task, the lexica's root-based entries give the expectation of regular meaning relationships of some sort among the binyanim of a root. *HALOT* in particular also relies heavily on Jenni's (1968) study of Qal-Piel and Piel-Hiphil relations in its entries, despite Jenni's study being criticized for lack of clear theory and scholarly rigor.[120]

118. חל״ץ, חת״ם, חת״ת, יר״ש, כב״ש, כז״ב, נח״ת, נש״ה, עב״ר I, עו״ה, צמ״ת, צע״ק, קר״ב, קש״ה, רצ״ה II, שׂב״ע, שׁא״ל, שׁו״ה I, שׁמ״ע.

119. Having argued for a pluractional analysis of the Piel (vs. Qal), Garr (2021: 259) rightly observes that "sometimes . . . it is difficult to isolate a single factor that drives the pluractional Piel." In such cases, "the pluractional Piel may be governed by one factor or a conspiracy of factors."

120. Jenni appears to have adopted a *semantic* rather than *syntactic* approach to transitivity, in line with GKC §43a–b and an oft-cited subsequent study of transitivity by Hopper and Thompson (1980). This approach, which treats transitivity as a semantic cline rather than a syntactic distinction, appears to have prompted Hillers's (1969: 212) negative comment in his review that "no consistent or acceptable definition of transitive or intransitive is offered, in spite of the fact that much of the structure of Jenni's argument is based on a distinction between these two categories, and that the terms occur on almost every page. If this reviewer grasps the concept as Jenni intended, transitive and intransitive are for him not syntactic categories at all, in spite of the book's subtitle: He speaks, not so much of a verb being used intransitively in a given sentence, or of intransitive verbs, as of 'intransitiven Grundbedeutung,' intransitive *meaning*." Subsequently, Jenni (2000; reprinted 2005: 77–106) turned to Vendlerian situation aspect as a key to analyzing the binyanim (see §2.3 above). This approach has been followed by others, such as Boyd (2017: 125), who, however, continues in the vein of the default approach, positing a neat system of binyanim relationships as "an essential starting point" before cautioning that conclusions about the meanings of the various binyanim "should be tempered by actual usage, which not infrequently veers from the straight and narrow."

2.5.2 Voice and the Binyanim

The most long-standing descriptions of the binyanim are grounded in voice distinctions (i.e., active, passive, middle/reflexive; e.g., GKC §§39f, 51c, 54e; Joüon §40a; Gzella 2009). The distinction between active and passive voice is straightforward: linguists describe the passive as "derived" from the more basic active construction by "promoting" the patient complement of the verb to the subject position and "demoting" the agent of the active construction from the subject to an optional oblique PP expression.[121] The contrast is expressed by a number of binyanim pairs with differing degrees of frequency, illustrated by exs. 63–68.

63. Active:Passive Qal and Qal Passive[122]

63a

וַיִּקַּח אַבְרָם אֶת־שָׂרַי אִשְׁתּוֹ

Abram took ‹Q.PN› Sarai his wife. (Gen. 12:5)

63b

וַתֻּקַּח הָאִשָּׁה בֵּית פַּרְעֹה

The woman was taken ‹QALP.PN› (into) the house of Pharaoh. (Gen. 12:15)

64. Active:Passive Piel and Pual[123]

64a

הַלְלוּ אֶת־שֵׁם יְהוָה

Praise ‹PI.IMPV› the name of Yhwh. (Ps. 113:1)

64b

מְהֻלָּל שֵׁם יְהוָה

The name of Yhwh (is) praised/praiseworthy ‹PU.PTC›. (Ps. 113:3)

121. This fundamental understanding of the passive as "derived" from the active supports the contention that Pual and Hophal are not independent binyanim but are "internal passives" derived from their active counterparts, Piel and Hiphil, respectively (see the note following ex. 59b).

122. Gen. 41:50; Exod. 21:20–21; Num. 35:33; 2 Kings 5:1 and 17; Isa. 1:19–20; 27:7; Jer. 49:11, 25; Ezek. 15:3.

123. Num. 36:2; Judg. 16:17 and 19; 2 Sam. 7:29; Isa. 50:1; Ps. 78:38 and Prov. 16:6; Prov. 13:13 and 21; Esther 2:15 and 23; Ezra 3:6 and 10.

65. Active:Passive Hiphil and Hophal[124]

65a

וַיַּשְׁלִיכֵהוּ אַרְצָה

He cast ‹HI.PN› him to the ground. (Dan. 8:7)

65b

וְהֻשְׁלַךְ מְכוֹן מִקְדָּשׁוֹ

The place of his sanctuary was overthrown ‹HO.PFV› (Dan. 8:11)

66. Active:Passive Qal and Niphal[125]

66a

וְתֹכֶן לְבֵנִים תִּתֵּנוּ

The (same) quantity of bricks you must give ‹Q.IPFV›. (Exod. 5:18)

66b

וְתֶבֶן לֹא־יִנָּתֵן לָכֶם

Straw will not be given ‹NI.IPFV› to you. (Exod. 5:18)

67. Active:Passive Piel and Hithpael[126]

67a

וַיָּקֻמוּ כָל־בָּנָיו וְכָל־בְּנֹתָיו לְנַחֲמוֹ

All his sons and daughters rose up ‹Q.PN› to comfort ‹PI.INF› him. (Gen. 37:35)

67b

וַיְמָאֵן לְהִתְנַחֵם

He refused ‹PI.PN› to be comforted ‹HT.INF›. (Gen. 37:35)

124. Gen. 31:20 and 22; 43:12; 2 Kings 12:5; 14:6; Jer. 38:22–23; Hosea 14:6 and 9:16; Nah. 2:4, 6; Esther 2:6.

125. Gen. 18:30; 20:9; 32:29; 34:7; 35:10; Exod. 14:16 and 21; 25:31; Josh. 7:17; Judg. 20:32 and 35; 1 Sam. 10:2; 2 Sam. 22:45; 2 Kings 18:10; Isa. 49:55; 62:12; Jer. 31:4; Ezek. 30:22; Pss. 24:7; 109:14, 16; 2 Chron. 28:5.

126. Gen. 22:3 and Josh. 9:13; Isa. 5:24 and 52:5; Eccles. 7:13 and 12:3.

68. Active:Passive Qal and Hithpael

68a

שְׁלָחַנִי אֶל־הַגּוֹיִם הַשֹּׁלְלִים אֶתְכֶם

He sent me ‹Q.PFV› to the nations that (were) plundering ‹Q.PTC› you. (Zech. 2:12)

68b

אֶשְׁתּוֹלְלוּ אַבִּירֵי לֵב

The brave of heart were plundered ‹HT.IPFV›. (Ps. 76:6)[127]

In contrast to the active/passive voice distinction, middle voice presents a number of challenges. First, linguists are divided on whether and how middle voice constructions are derivationally related to active and passive voice (see Doron 2003). Second, a variety of predicates have been classified as middle voice, as illustrated in ex. 69 (based on Alexiadou and Doron 2012: 4).

69. Varieties of Middle Voice

69a. Reflexive

וַיִּטַּהֲרוּ הַכֹּהֲנִים וְהַלְוִיִּם

The priests and the Levites cleansed themselves ‹HT.PN›. (Neh. 12:30)[128]

69b. Reciprocal

עָשִׁיר וָרָשׁ נִפְגָּשׁוּ

Rich and poor met each other ‹NI.PFV›. (Prov. 22:2)[129]

69c. Medio-Passive

וְנִרְאֲתָה הַקֶּשֶׁת בֶּעָנָן

The bow will appear/be seen ‹NI.IR-PFV› in the cloud. (Gen. 9:14)[130]

127. The verb אֶשְׁתּוֹלְלוּ exhibits metathesis of the ת and שׁ, and the א prefix instead of the expected ה is attributed to Aramaic influence (so *HALOT* s.v.).

128. Other verbs that are or can be reflexive include טמ״א (NI, HT), "make oneself unclean"; לב״ש (Q), "clothe oneself"; רח״ץ (Q, HT), "wash oneself"; קד״ש (HT), "consecrate oneself"; נד״ב (HT), "willingly offer oneself"; ענ״ג (HT), "delight/pamper oneself"; חפ״שׂ (HT), "disguise oneself"; חז״ק (HT), "strengthen oneself."

129. Other verbs that are or can be reciprocal include יע״ץ (HT), "take counsel together"; יע״ד (NI), "meet together"; רא״ה (HT), "look at one other"; נק״שׁ (Q), "kiss each other"; חב״ר II (Q, HT), "join/make an alliance together"; אס״ף (NI, HT), "gather together."

130. Other verbs that can be medio-passive (i.e., either middle or passive) include יד״ע (NI), "make oneself known/be known"; קב״ץ (NI), "gather together/be gathered"; ית״ר (NI), "remain/be left"; נח״ם (NI), "console oneself/be sorry"; גל״ה (NI), "appear/be revealed"; סת״ר (NI), "hide/be hidden."

69d. Dispositional Middle

וַיֵּרָאוּ רָאשֵׁי הַבַּדִּים מִן־הָאָרוֹן עַל־פְּנֵי הַדְּבִיר וְלֹא יֵרָאוּ הַחוּצָה

The ends [lit., heads] of the poles were visible ‹NI.PN› from the ark before the holy place; they could not be seen ‹NI.IPFV› from outside. (2 Chron. 5:9)[131]

69e. Anticausative

וְנָמַסּוּ הֶהָרִים תַּחְתָּיו וְהָעֲמָקִים יִתְבַּקָּעוּ כַּדּוֹנַג מִפְּנֵי הָאֵשׁ

The mountains will melt ‹NI.IR-PFV› under him and the valleys will split ‹HT.IPFV› like wax before the fire. (Mic. 1:4)[132]

Third, these semantically classified middles are not uniformly associated with middle morphology (in BH or cross-linguistically). Rather, some are expressed by active constructions (e.g., anticausative Hiphil of אר״ך, ex. 57b; English anticausative, *the shadows lengthened*), others by middles (e.g., BH Hithpael), and still others by medio-passive forms (i.e., morphology that encodes middle and passive expressions, such as the Greek middle-passive inflection; e.g., BH Niphal). Unsurprisingly, the lack of uniformity or sharing of morphological encoding results in uncertainty when distinguishing among different voice constructions.

Of the variety of middles given in ex. 69, the reflexive and reciprocal are the most straightforward, as it is rather transparent that the "roles Agent and Patient are conflated in a single participant" in these structures (van Wolde 2021: 455). In particular, this conflation is effected by "argument identification," in which the agent and patient are co-indexical (see Alexiadou and Doron 2012: 25). That is, this argument identification manifests as a single constituent as the subject of the event, fulfilling both a patient and agent role.[133]

131. Gen. 8:5; Exod. 13:7; Num. 12:7; Deut. 7:9; 1 Kings 6:18; Prov. 25:13, 26; 27:6; Eccles. 4:12; Song 2:12.

132. Other verbs that are or can be anticausative include אר״ך (Q, HI), "lengthen"; פק״ח (NI), "open"; שב״ר (NI), "break"; סג״ר (NI), "shut"; סת״ר (NI), "hide"; ית״ר (NI), "remain."

133. BH lacks reflexive pronouns (cf. Greek and Latin), and although it can express the same sense by the ל preposition with pronominal complement, such constructions do not typically appear with reflexive or reciprocal verbs but instead, with active verb constructions, denote in whose interest something is done: וַיִּבְחַר־לוֹ לוֹט אֵת כָּל־כִּכַּר הַיַּרְדֵּן, "Lot chose for himself the whole Jordan Valley" (Gen. 13:11). Other lexical expressions can be employed to create reciprocal events of active verbs: וַיִּשְׁאֲלוּ אִישׁ־לְרֵעֵהוּ לְשָׁלוֹם, "They asked, each his companion, (about his) welfare" (Exod. 18:7).

That there is a conflation of agent and patient (i.e., both roles are associated with the verb even if co-indexical) correctly suggests that middle reflexive and reciprocal verbs have active voice counterparts consisting in non–co-indexical agent and patient, as illustrated by the contrastive pairs in exs. 70–71.

70. Reflexive Middle and Active טה״ר

70a

וַיִּטַּהֲרוּ הַכֹּהֲנִים וְהַלְוִיִּם

The priests and the Levites cleansed themselves ‹HT.PN›. (Neh. 12:30, repeated from ex. 69a)

70b

וַיְטַהֵר אֶת־יְהוּדָה וְאֶת־יְרוּשָׁלִָם

He cleansed ‹PI.PN› Judah and Jerusalem. (2 Chron. 34:5)

71. Reciprocal Middle and Active פג״ש

71a

עָשִׁיר וָרָשׁ נִפְגָּשׁוּ

Rich and poor met each other ‹NI.PFV›. (Prov. 22:2, repeated from 69b)

71b

וַיֵּלֶךְ וַיִּפְגְּשֵׁהוּ בְּהַר הָאֱלֹהִים

He went ‹Q.PN› and he met ‹Q.PN› him at the mountain of God. (Exod. 4:27)

While reflexives can have a singular (Job 9:30) or plural (ex. 70a) agent/patient, reciprocals require plural ones (ex. 71a).

The other three middle voice varieties (exs. 69c–e) are unified in their lack of an agent, either overt or implied. The only argument is the patient, which undergoes the action expressed by the verb. This contrasts with the passive voice, which introduces an agent, whether overt or implicit. Alexiadou and Doron (2012) contend that this feature of [±agency] is fundamental to distinguishing the middle and passive voices. They posit (using a distributed morphology framework) two distinct voice heads, of which only the passive introduces its own "external" (to the VP) argument in the oblique case, the *by*-NP agent of the passive action (fig. 2.11a). The middle voice allows for only an "internal" argument, the patient of the action (fig. 2.11b). In the case of the reflexive and reciprocal middles, those specific middle heads introduce an external agent that "combines" with the thematic (VP-internal) NP in the process of "argument identification," denoted by the connecting line and subscript *i*'s with the two NPs in fig. 2.11c (Alexiadou and Doron 2012: 25).

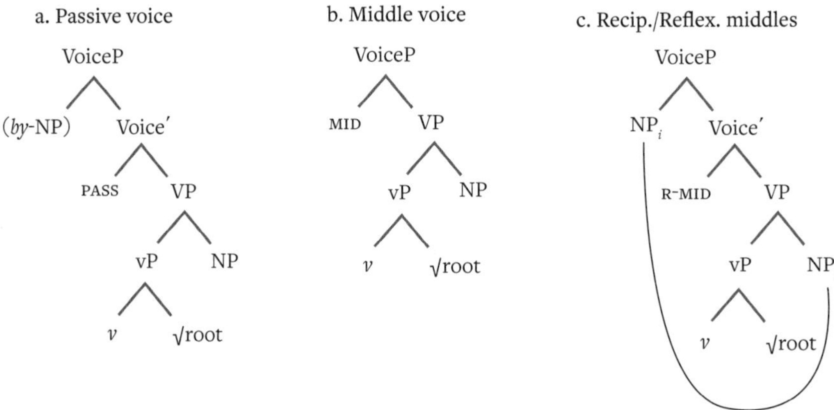

Figure 2.11. Passive and Middle Voice

This distinction is fine in the abstract, but it leaves some practical difficulties with respect to distinguishing middle and passive in BH. First, BH rarely expresses an agent overtly with passive constructions (Joüon §132ca), as in ex. 72.

72. Passive with Agent Prepositional Phrase

שֹׁפֵךְ דַּם הָאָדָם בָּאָדָם דָּמוֹ יִשָּׁפֵךְ

(Whoever) sheds ‹Q.PTC› the blood of a man, by a man his blood will be shed ‹NI.IPFV›. (Gen. 9:6)[134]

Second, as Joüon (§132ca) notes, the distinction between agency and instrument (ex. 73a) or cause (ex. 73b) is quite slight, and the latter two can occur with middle as well as passive, whereas agency is limited to the passive.[135]

134. The agent is typically expressed by a ב or ל PP (e.g., Gen. 31:15; Exod. 12:16; 29:33; Num. 36:2; Deut. 33:29; Judg. 17:2; 1 Sam. 23:21; 25:7; 2 Sam. 2:5; Isa. 45:17; Ps. 115:15; Prov. 25:15; Ruth 2:20; 3:10), but other prepositions are also used (e.g., מפני Exod. 8:20; מן 2 Sam. 7:29; Ps. 37:23; מעם Isa. 29:6), as is the bound structure (e.g., Deut. 33:13; Isa. 54:13; Ps. 37:22).

135. Van Wolde (2021) argues that the agent must be overt in passive constructions, thus allowing her to argue that the Niphal is not passive but middle. However, the grammars recognize

73a. Reflexive Middle with Instrumental Prepositional Phrase

וְלֹא תִטַּמְּאוּ בָּהֶם

Do not make yourselves unclean ‹HT.IPFV› through them. (Lev. 18:30)

73b. Anticausative Middle with Causative Prepositional Phrase

וְגַם־נָמֹגוּ כָּל־יֹשְׁבֵי הָאָרֶץ מִפָּנֵינוּ

Also all the inhabitants of ‹Q.PTC› the land have melted ‹NI.PFV› because of us. (Josh. 2:24)

And third, especially in the case of Niphal, which has assumed the functions of the Qal passive, many times a middle or passive reading of a middle verb is equally possible (ex. 69c). Alexiadou and Doron (2012: 5) explain that the medio-passive is dependent on the system lacking a morphologically distinct passive construction. As such, a medio-passive classification applies well to many Niphal verbs, whereas it applies to far fewer Hithpaels because of the availability of the Pual passive.

This potential for ambiguity between passive and varieties of middle applies also to dispositional (ex. 69d) and anticausative middles (ex. 69e): in both cases, absent of context, a passive interpretation is equally possible. Dispositional middles are stative generic expressions derived from transitive activity or accomplishment verbs (Kit 2014), such as English *This bread cuts easily* and the BH example (ex. 69d): in the context of describing the temple construction, the description of the visibility of the poles of the ark conveys the static character of the temple configuration (i.e., "visible") rather than a specific event ("were seen"). The distinction between dispositional middle and passive is therefore dependent on the character of the event in its discourse-pragmatic context.

Anticausatives (ex. 69e) are a subtype of unaccusatives, though the terms are often used interchangeably. Unaccusatives can be classified into two subtypes: the anticausative, which lacks an agent but for which we might envision one (ex. 74a),[136] and autocausatives, which are more or less spontaneous or "agentless" (ex. 74b). The latter are not so easily confused with passives, because the idea of an agent is ill-suited to the root's meaning.[137]

---

that passives can be "incomplete" (e.g., *IBHS* §23.2.2f). That is, an *overt* agent is *licit* but not required with passives. Van Wolde's (2021: 444–45) treatment of Gen. 9:6 (ex. 72) is as tortured a non-agentive reading of the passage as Joüon's (§132e), which she rightly criticizes.

136. Notice that the English anticausative gloss *opened* in ex. 74a does not allow for the agent PP *by God*, whereas the passive gloss *was opened* does.

137. My use of autocausative differs from that of Geniušienė 1987, in which autocausative and decausative are subcategories of reflexive. Her decausative (vs. autocausative)

74a. Anticausative Middle/Passive Interpretation

וַאֲרֻבֹּת הַשָּׁמַיִם נִפְתָּחוּ׃

The windows of the heavens opened/were opened ‹NI.PFV› (by God). (Gen. 7:11)

74b. Autocausative Middle

יָבֵשׁ חָצִיר נָבֵל צִיץ כִּי רוּחַ יְהוָה נָשְׁבָה בּוֹ

The grass has dried up ‹Q.PFV› and the flower has withered ‹Q.PN› because/when the spirit of Yhwh has blown ‹Q.PFV› on it. (Isa. 40:7)

What should be noted at this point is that the correspondence between voice and binyanim is limited. To the extent we can align them, it is an abstraction or an etymological reconstruction. Nevertheless, as generalizations about the binyanim's role in encoding voice alternations, we can state the following: Qal, Piel, and Hiphil are all active voice binyanim, although the Qal's STA forms can be confused with the passive voice (see ex. 29 above); when a root appears in both Qal and Niphal, the Niphal functions as a medio-passive of active Qal; similarly, the Hithpael functions as the middle voice to active Piel; Pual, Hophal, and Qal passive are consistently passive voice alternations of their active counterparts (i.e., Piel, Hiphil, and Qal active, respectively).

2.5.3 Transitivity, Causation, and Ditransitive Clauses

A similar partial regularity can be found with valency-increasing alternations between binyanim. To appreciate how causation applies to different roots, it is important to recognize two major types of intransitive expressions: unaccusatives and unergatives. Anticausative and autocausative (illustrated in exs. 74a–b) are subtypes of unaccusatives, all of which feature the patient of the event as subject (ex. 75a). By contrast, unergatives are intransitives in which the agent is encoded as subject (ex. 75b). As such, "with respect to the active-passive dimension, unergatives are more active-like and unaccusatives are more passive-like" (Lyngfelt and Solstad 2006: 3).

---

semantically parallels ex. 74b, and her autocausative:anticausative contrast greatly overlaps the unergative:unaccusative distinction; on which see §2.5.3 and exs. 75a–b there.

75. Unaccusative and Unergative

75a

וַתִּכְלֶינָה שֶׁבַע שְׁנֵי הַשָּׂבָע

The seven years of plenty ended ‹Q.PN›. (Gen. 41:53)[138]

75b

וַיַּעַל מֹשֶׁה וְאַהֲרֹן נָדָב וַאֲבִיהוּא וְשִׁבְעִים מִזִּקְנֵי יִשְׂרָאֵל׃

Moses and Aaron, Nadab and Abihu, and seventy of the elders of Israel went up ‹Q.PN›. (Exod. 24:9)[139]

Certain verbs from either category of intransitive may exhibit alternation with a transitive counterpart, as illustrated in ex. 76 (cf. ex. 75). In both cases, the subject of the intransitive is "demoted" to the object complement, but its role (patient or agent) is maintained with respect to the event proper versus the causing event.[140]

76. Causative Alternations of Unaccusative and Unergative

76a

וּתְכַל תְּלוּנֹּתָם מֵעָלַי

. . . so you might end ‹PI.IPFV› their grumblings against me. (Num. 17:25)

76b

וַיָּבֹאוּ אַנְשֵׁי קִרְיַת יְעָרִים וַיַּעֲלוּ אֶת־אֲרוֹן יְהוָה

The men of Kiriath-jearim came up ‹Q.PN› and brought up ‹HI.PN› [lit., caused to go up] the ark of Yhwh. (1 Sam. 7:1)

This suggests that these predicates are "bieventive," consisting of a causative event and the underlying root-expressed event. Thus, the alternation

138. Other unaccusative roots include מו"ת (Q), "die"; אב"ד (Q), "perish"; יב"ש (Q), "dry up"; נפ"ל (Q), "fall"; שב"ר (Q), "break"; מו"ג (NI), "melt"; פת"ח (Q, NI), "open"; מל"ט (NI), "escape." There is some overlap in terms of classifying unaccusatives, statives, and passives, evident in part from the medio-passive character of Niphal anticausatives listed here and Perlmutter's (1978: 162) classification of English expressions with *be* and an adjective (e.g., *be heavy*; cf. BH כָּבֵד) as unaccusatives.

139. Other unergative roots include הל"ך (Q), "walk"; רו"ץ (Q), "run"; שכ"ם (HI), "rise early"; סו"ר (Q), "turn aside"; בו"א (Q), "come"; נו"ס (Q), "flee."

140. This is not to suggest that the causatives are derived from the noncausative counterparts or vice versa; linguists do not agree on the derivational relationship of these alternations.

involved between exs. 75 and 76 can be modeled in distributed morphology terms as a difference of a single event versus two events—a causing event and the event that is caused, as illustrated in fig. 2.12.[141]

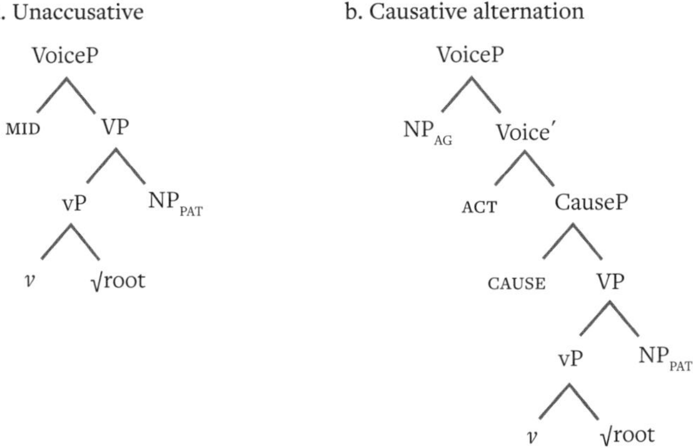

Figure 2.12. Unaccusative and Causative Alternation

Note that the unaccusative (anticausative) is modeled as middle voice here, in contrast to the causative, which has an active voice phrase that introduces an external argument—the "causer" agent (AG). We can extend this contrast further by including the passive-causative (ex. 77), modeled in distributed morphology terms in fig. 2.13. In contrast to the middle anticausative, which does not introduce an external argument, and unlike the active causative, which introduces an external cause as subject, the passive causative introduces a *by*-NP external argument which may or may not be realized overtly, as shown by the parentheses in the diagram.

77. Passive Derivation of Causative Unaccusative

וַיְכֻלּוּ הַשָּׁמַיִם וְהָאָרֶץ וְכָל־צְבָאָם (בֵּאלֹהִים)

The heavens and the earth and all their host were completed ‹PU.PN› (by God) [lit., were caused to be completed]. (Gen. 2:1)

141. Linguists analyze causatives in a number of ways; the distributed morphology-based approach followed here is presented in Pylkkänen (2008: chap. 3).

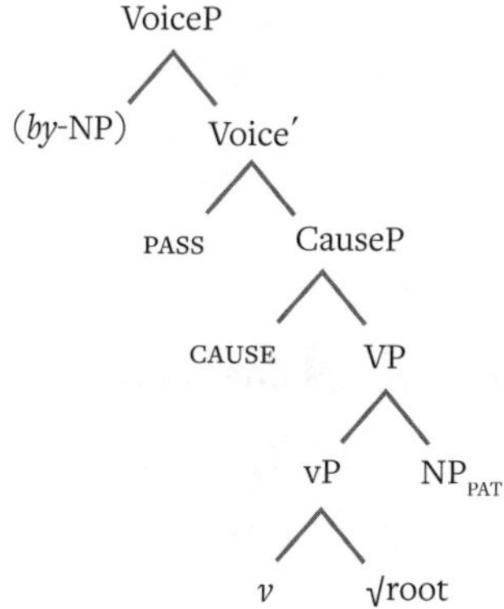

Figure 2.13. Passive Causative

In the case of unergatives, the single agentive argument moves up the tree to the external position introduced by the active voice phrase. The line in fig. 2.14a, which models ex. 75b, indicates the constituent movement, and the co-indexical *t* signifies its "trace" in its original position. By contrast, in the causative of an unergative (ex. 76b), the external argument (the subject) is the "causer" agent, and the internal argument remains in place, just as with the causative of an unaccusative (fig. 2.12b), except that the internal argument is interpreted as the agent (AG) of the subevent rather than its patient (PAT) (fig. 2.14b).

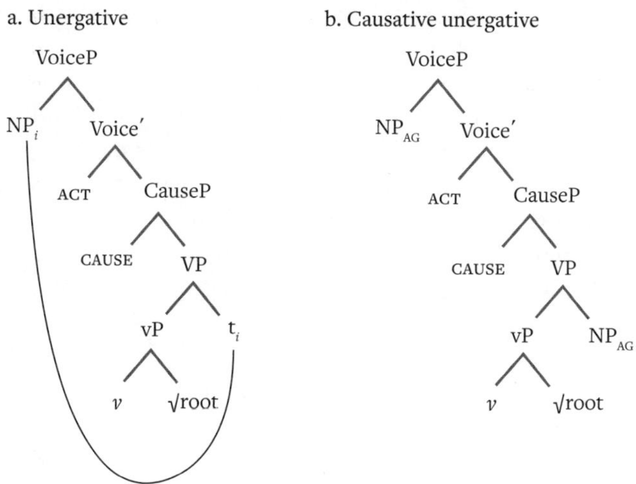

Figure 2.14. Unergative and Causative Unergative

As with the causative of unaccusatives, passives can also be derived from causatives of unergatives, as illustrated by ex. 78 and modeled in fig. 2.15. As with the causative of an ergative, the internal agent NP remains, but the passive voice leaves the external *by*-NP, the agent of the caused event, optional rather than required.

78. Passive Derivation of Causative Unergative

וְאֵת הַפָּר הַשֵּׁנִי הֹעֲלָה עַל־הַמִּזְבֵּחַ הַבָּנוּי (בְּגִדְעוֹן)

And the second bull was made to go up ‹HO.PFV› upon the altar that (was) built ‹Q.PPTC› (by Gideon). (Judg. 6:28)

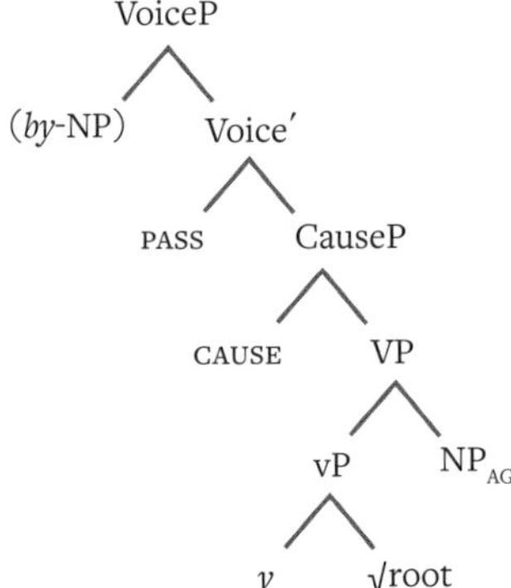

Figure 2.15. Passive-Causative Ergative

The CauseP can be used to model trivalent or ditransitive verbs (ex. 79). In these cases, the "internal" argument actually consists of a NP-PP small clause consisting in the patient and location complements of the verb. The active voice introduces the external argument as the agentive "cause" subject. This analysis understands the expression to entail an agent who *causes* something to *be* somewhere (fig. 2.16).[142]

142. Compare copular and existential clauses modeled above in figs. 2.7 and 2.8 (§2.4.2): whereas the small clauses in those cases appear within a predicate phrase (PredP) under the VP, in trivalent/ditransitive clauses the small clause is immediately in the VP.

79. Trivalent/Ditransitive

וַיָּשֶׂם אֶת־מִזְבַּח הַזָּהָב בְּאֹהֶל מוֹעֵד לִפְנֵי הַפָּרֹכֶת

He placed ‹Q.PN› the golden altar in the tent of meeting before the curtain. (Exod. 40:26)[143]

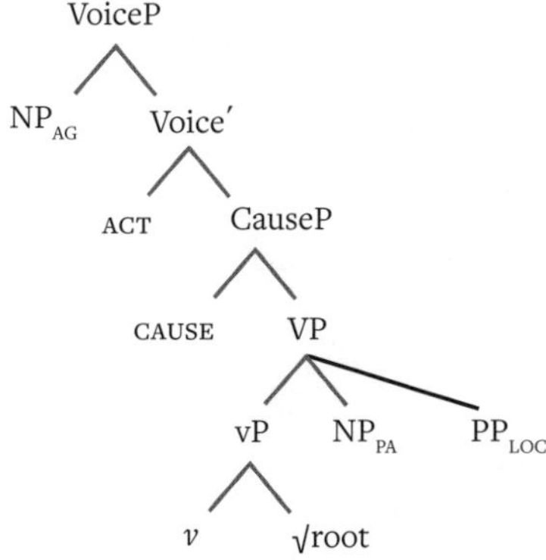

Figure 2.16. Trivalent/Ditransitive Clause

Again, the partial regularity justifies some degree of generalization, but such generalizations are limited to cases where the binyanim show valency alternations for a root and where no skewing from historical shifts has disturbed the "regularity" of the reconstructed "system." Otherwise, many verbs retain idiosyncratic meanings related to but not predictable from the root or binyan in isolation. What we can affirm is that Piel and Hiphil are active binyanim that often function as valency-increasing counterparts of Qal verbs of the same root. The Piel can show a valency increase with respect to both Qal STA (and unaccusative) and dynamic verbs, which the standard grammars often distinguish in terms of "factitive" (i.e., make *x* be *y*, expressible with a predicate adjective; ex. 80) versus "resultative" (i.e., make *x* be *y*-ed, expressible by a past participle; ex. 81; see *IBHS* §24.3a; Joüon §52d; Arnold-Choi §3.1.3).

143. Gen. 1:17; 2:8; 6:16; 18:8; Deut. 28:56; 30:15; Josh. 10:18; Judg. 1:15; 2 Sam. 17:25; 2 Kings 4:43; Pss. 40:3; 78:5; 2 Chron. 19:5; 23:19.

80. Qal Stative/Unaccusative and Piel Factitive[144]

80a

יָרֵאתִי אֶת־הָעָם

I was afraid ‹Q.PFV› of the people. (1 Sam. 15:24)

80b

יֵרְאֻנִי הָעָם

The people made me (be) afraid ‹PI.PFV›. (2 Sam. 14:15)

81. Qal Dynamic and Piel Resultative[145]

81a

הִנְנִי קֹבֵץ אֶתְכֶם אֶל־תּוֹךְ יְרוּשָׁלִָם

Hey, I (am) going to gather you together ‹Q.PTC› into the midst of Jerusalem. (Ezek. 22:19)

81b

וַאֲנִי אֲקַבֵּץ אֶת־שְׁאֵרִית צֹאנִי מִכֹּל הָאֲרָצוֹת

I myself will make (to be) gathered together ‹PI.IPFV› the remnant of my flock from all the lands. (Jer. 23:3)

This Qal-Piel causative alternation is contrasted with the active causative sense of the Hiphil with respect to the Qal. The Hiphil manifests in causative (often inchoative) for STAs and unaccusatives (i.e., make *x* be[come] *y*; ex. 82) and causative active for dynamic and unergatives (i.e., make *x* to do *y*; ex. 83; see *IBHS* §27.1d; Joüon §54d; Arnold-Choi §3.1.6).

144. Others include טמ״א, "be unclean" (Q), "make unclean" (PI); טה״ר, "be clean" (Q), "purify" (lit., "make clean"; PI); אמ״ץ, "be strong" (Q), "make strong" (PI); יש״ר, "be straight" (Q), "make straight" (PI); דמ״ה, "be like" (Q), "make like" (PI).

145. Others include רפ״א, "heal" (Q), "make healed" (PI); קש״ר, "bind" (Q), "make bound" (PI); למ״ד, "learn" (Q), "teach" (lit., "make learned"; PI); חל״ץ, "withdraw" (Q), "make withdrawn" (PI); נק״ם, "avenge" (Q), "make avenged" (PI).

82. Qal Stative/Unaccusative and Hiphil Inchoative[146]

82a

וַיִּמְלֹךְ רְחַבְעָם בְּנוֹ תַּחְתָּיו

Rehoboam his son became king ‹Q.PN› in his place. (1 Kings 11:43)

82b

וַיַּמְלִיכוּ אֹתוֹ עַל־כָּל־יִשְׂרָאֵל

They made him (become) king ‹HI.PN› over all Israel. (1 Kings 12:20)

83. Qal Dynamic/Unergative and Hiphil Causative[147]

83a

בָּאתִי לְגַנִּי אֲחֹתִי כַלָּה

I came ‹Q.PFV› to my garden, my sister, bride. (Song 5:1)

83b

הֱבִיאַנִי אֶל־בֵּית הַיָּיִן

He brought ‹HI.PFV› me [lit., made me to go] to the house of banqueting [lit., the wine]. (Song 2:4)

However, neither this neat distinction between Piel and Hiphil nor the regularity of the Qal-Piel/Hiphil causative alternation holds in a good number of cases. For both STA Qal verbs (ex. 84) and dynamic ones (ex. 85), the Piel and Hiphil are frequently synonymous.

84. Piel and Hiphil Synonyms of Qal Stative קד"ש ("Be Holy")[148]

84a

קַדֶּשׁ־לִי כָל־בְּכוֹר פֶּטֶר כָּל־רֶחֶם בִּבְנֵי יִשְׂרָאֵל

Consecrate ‹PI.IMPV› to me every firstborn, firstborn of every womb among the children of Israel. (Exod. 13:2)

146. Others include בו"ש I, "be ashamed" (Q), "make become ashamed" (HI); גב"ה, "be high" (Q), "make become high" (HI); שפ"ל, "be low" (Q), "make become low" (HI); תמ"ם, "be complete" (Q), "make become complete" (HI); שק"ט, "be peaceful" (Q), "make become peaceful" (HI).

147. Others include יצ"א, "go out" (Q), "make go out" (HI); על"ה, "go up" (Q), "make go up" (HI); רא"ה, "see" (Q), "show" (lit., "make see"; HI); אכ"ל, "eat" (Q), "feed" (lit., "make eat"; HI); זכ"ר, "remember" (Q), "make remember" (HI).

148. Others include יד"ע, "know" (Q), "make know" (PI, HI); כע"ס, "be vexed" (Q), "vex (someone)" (PI, HI); רח"ק, "be far" (Q), "remove" (lit., "make far away"; PI, HI); יב"ש, "be dry" (Q), "make dry" (PI, HI); שכ"ר, "be drunk" (Q), "make drunk" (PI, HI).

84b

הִקְדַּשְׁתִּי לִי כָל־בְּכוֹר בְּיִשְׂרָאֵל מֵאָדָם עַד־בְּהֵמָה

I consecrated ‹HI.PFV› to me every firstborn in Israel from human to animal. (Num. 3:13)

85. Piel and Hiphil Synonyms of Qal Dynamic שו"ב ("Return")[149]

85a

וְשֹׁבַבְתִּי אֶת־יִשְׂרָאֵל אֶל־נָוֵהוּ

I will return ‹POLEL.IR-PFV› Israel to its habitation. (Jer. 50:19)

85b

וַהֲשִׁבֹתִים אִישׁ לְנַחֲלָתוֹ וְאִישׁ לְאַרְצוֹ

I will return ‹HI.IR-PFV› them, each to his inheritance and each to his land. (Jer. 12:15)

Synonyms also exist between Qal and Piel/Hiphil verbs of the same root (exs. 86–87).

86. Qal and Piel Synonyms[150]

86a

הֵמָּה יִשְׂאוּ קוֹלָם יָרֹנּוּ

They are lifting up their voice ‹Q.IPFV›, they are shouting ‹Q.IPFV›. (Isa. 24:14)

86b

נָשְׂאוּ קוֹל יַחְדָּו יְרַנֵּנוּ

They have lifted up ‹Q.PFV› their voice, together they are shouting ‹PI.IPFV›. (Isa. 52:8)

149. Others include קו"ם, "stand up" (intr. Q), "erect" (PI, HI); פש"ט, "strip" (intr. Q), "strip" (tr. PI, HI); רפ"ה, "loosen" (intr. Q), "loosen" (tr. PI, HI); שכ"ן, "settle" (intr. Q), "settle" (tr. PI, HI); פנ"ה, "turn" (intr. Q), "turn (away)" (tr. PI, HI).

150. Others include אר"ר, "curse" (Q, PI); גל"ה, "uncover" (Q, PI); חש"ב, "think, plan" (Q, PI); נא"ף, "commit adultery" (Q, PI); נה"ג, "lead" (Q, PI).

87. Qal and Hiphil Synonyms[151]

87a

וּמְרִיתֶם אֶת־פִּי יְהוָה

You will rebel ‹Q.IR-PFV› against the command of Yhwh. (1 Sam. 12:15)

87b

וַתַּמְרוּ אֶת־פִּי יְהוָה אֱלֹהֵיכֶם

You rebelled ‹HI.PN› against the command of Yhwh your God. (Deut. 1:26)

There are a few cases in which a single verb shows the sort of causative alternation associated with Qal-Piel/Hiphil pairs (exs. 88–90).

88. Anticausative-Causative Alternating Qal[152]

88a

יִזְּלוּ־מָיִם

Water flows ‹Q.IPFV›. (Ps. 147:18)

88b

וְעַפְעַפֵּינוּ יִזְּלוּ־מָיִם

Our eye(lids) will pour ‹Q.IPFV› water. (Jer. 9:17)

89. Anticausative-Causative Alternating Piel[153]

89a

וְאַל־תְּאַשֵּׁר בְּדֶרֶךְ רָעִים

Do not proceed ‹PI.JUSS› into the path of evil people. (Prov. 4:14)

89b

וְאַשֵּׁר בַּדֶּרֶךְ לִבֶּךָ

Lead ‹PI.IMPV› your mind in the path. (Prov. 23:19)

151. Others include יס״ף, "do again" (Q, HI); צל״ח, "succeed" (Q, HI); נט״ף, "drip" (tr. Q, HI); סכ״ך, "shut off" (Q, HI); נח״ה I, "lead" (Q, HI).

152. Also נט״ף (Q), "drip" (intr./tr.); בק״ע (Q), "split open" (intr./tr.).

153. Also בק״ע (PI), "split open" (intr./tr.).

90. Anticausative-Causative Alternating Hiphil[154]

90a

לְמַעַן יַאֲרִיכֻן יָמֶיךָ

. . . in order that your days <u>might lengthen</u> ‹HI.IPFV›. Deut. 5:16; cf. יַאַרְכוּ הַיָּמִים, "the days <u>are lengthening</u> ‹Q.IPFV›," Ezek. 12:22)

90b

וְהַאֲרַכְתֶּם יָמִים בָּאָרֶץ

You <u>might lengthen</u> ‹HI.IR-PFV› days in the land. (Deut. 5:33)

All this suggests that a verb-by-verb approach must be taken to mastering both vocabulary and valency of Hebrew verbs, relying only cautiously on generalizations about the regularity of valency alternations among binyanim. There are other factors that may disambiguate seemingly synonymous verbs, such as the pluralizing/frequentive Piel (e.g., *IBHS* §24.5; Joüon §52d; Arnold-Choi §3.1.3c). However, such contrasts can be more difficult to demonstrate, as exs. 91a–b illustrate, than transitivity-affecting changes of voice and causation.[155]

91. Qal and Pluralizing/Frequentive Piel

91a

קוֹל יְהוָה שֹׁבֵר אֲרָזִים וַיְשַׁבֵּר יְהוָה אֶת־אַרְזֵי הַלְּבָנוֹן׃

The voice of Yhwh <u>breaks</u> ‹Q.PTC› the cedars; Yhwh <u>broke/shattered</u> ‹PI.PN› the cedars of Lebanon. (Ps. 29:5)[156]

91b

וָאֲשַׁלְּחֵהוּ בִּשְׁרִירוּת לִבָּם יֵלְכוּ בְּמוֹעֲצוֹתֵיהֶם׃ לוּ עַמִּי
שֹׁמֵעַ לִי יִשְׂרָאֵל בִּדְרָכַי יְהַלֵּכוּ׃

I dismissed ‹PI.PN› them in the stubbornness of their heart, (that) they might <u>walk</u> ‹Q.IPFV› in their own councils. Oh that my people (were) listening ‹Q.PTC› to me, [oh that] in my ways Israel <u>might walk</u> ‹PI.IPFV›. (Ps. 81:13–14)

154. Also בי״ן (HI), "understand," "cause someone to understand."

155. Dialectal, register, and diachronic distinctions, which have not been studied much, also might explain the distribution and/or overlapping meaning among some verbs.

156. Others of this classification include דל״ג, "leap" (Q), "leap around" (PI); צע״ק, "cry out" (Q), "cry incessantly" (PI); צח״ק, "laugh" (Q), "mock" (PI); לק״ק, "lap" (Q), "lap incessantly" (PI); שא״ל, "ask" (Q), "beg" (PI).

2.5.4 *Valency and "Missing" Objects*[157]

Up until now, the concern in this section has been steered by valency alternations that alter the syntax. Thus the sentences in ex. 92 could be thought of as contrasting in transitivity, since the verbs in ex. 92a have direct objects and those in ex. 92b do not.

92. Transitive-Intransitive Variation with אכ״ל and שת״ה

92a

לֹא־אָכַל לֶחֶם וְלֹא־שָׁתָה מַיִם

He did not eat ‹Q.PFV› bread and did not drink ‹Q.PFV› water. (1 Sam. 30:12)

92b

וַיֶּחֱזוּ אֶת־הָאֱלֹהִים וַיֹּאכְלוּ וַיִּשְׁתּוּ

They saw ‹Q.PN› God and they ate ‹Q.PN› and they drank ‹Q.PN›. (Exod. 24:11)

However, a valency approach combines syntax with semantics and pragmatics to account for our instinctual sense that אכ״ל (Q), like its English counterpart *eat*, is more basically a transitive verb than an intransitive. To put it in valency terms, אכ״ל (Q) seems best classified as a bivalent verb involving an agent subject and patient object, whether it appears as syntactically transitive or intransitive. Our lexical semantic knowledge about what eating entails leads us to infer that the agent subject must have eaten *something edible*, and our pragmatic sense leads us to determine as precisely as possible the implicit edible item from the context. This pragmatic sense has been described as the I-principle, the information principle (ex. 93).

93. I-Principle (from Levinsohn 2000: 114)

Speaker's maxim: The maxim of Minimization. "Say as little as necessary"; that is, produce the minimal linguistic information sufficient to achieve your communicational ends. . . .

Recipient's corollary: The Enrichment Rule. Amplify the informational content of the speaker's utterance, by finding the most specific interpretation. . . . Specifically:

. . . Assume that stereotypical relations obtain between referents or events. . . .

157. This section is based on Cook 2020.

> . . . Avoid interpretations that multiply entities referred to (assume referential parsimony); specifically, prefer coreferential readings of reduced NPs (pronouns or zeros).

This principle helps elucidate four different types of "missing" objects, as illustrated by ex. 94.

94. Types of "Missing" Objects in Biblical Hebrew

94a. Anaphoric Null

וַעֲשֵׂה־לִי מַטְעַמִּים כַּאֲשֶׁר אָהַבְתִּי וְהָבִיאָה לִּי וְאֹכֵלָה

Prepare ‹Q.IMPV› for me some tasty food$_i$ just as I love ‹Q.PFV›, and bring ‹HI.IMPV› (it$_i$) to me that I may eat ‹Q.IPFV› (it$_i$). (Gen. 27:4)[158]

94b. Deictic Implicit

וַיֹּאמֶר לוֹ קוּם אֱכוֹל׃ וַיַּבֵּט וְהִנֵּה מְרַאֲשֹׁתָיו עֻגַת
רְצָפִים וְצַפַּחַת מָיִם

And he said ‹Q.PN› to him, "Get up ‹Q.IMPV›, eat ‹Q.IMPV›." And he looked ‹HI.PN› and, hey, at his head (was) a hot-stones baked cake and a jar of water. (1 Kings 19:5–6)

94c. Contextual Implicit

וַיִּישַׂם לְפָנָיו לֶאֱכֹל וַיֹּאמֶר לֹא אֹכַל עַד אִם־דִּבַּרְתִּי דְּבָרָי

And he set ‹Q.PN› (something) before him to eat ‹Q.INF›, but he said ‹Q.PN›, "I will not eat ‹Q.IPFV› (that or anything else) until I have spoken ‹PI.PFV› my words." (Gen. 24:33)[159]

94d. Generic Implicit

וַיֹּאכְלוּ וַיִּשְׁתּוּ הוּא וְהָאֲנָשִׁים אֲשֶׁר־עִמּוֹ

He and the men who were with him ate ‹Q.PN› and drank ‹Q.PN›. (Gen. 24:54)[160]

158. Gen. 22:6; 25:34; 28:11; Exod. 17:12; 24:6; Lev. 8:26; Deut. 26:2; Josh. 7:11; Judg. 9:48–49; 1 Sam. 7:12; 9:24; 24:18; 2 Sam. 12:31; 1 Kings 18:33; Zech. 6:11; Song 5:1.

159. Reading the Qal active וַיָּשֶׂם instead of the Qal passive *ketiv* (וַיִּישָׂם) or Hophal *qere* (וַיּוּשַׂם; see GKC §73f; Joüon §81e). The text may evidence some confusion about who is the active topic at this point in the narrative, whether "the man" or "Laban." In any case, the textual uncertainty does not affect the point made here.

160. 1 Kings 18:41; Prov. 23:7.

Several factors distinguish these types. First, anaphoric nulls (ex. 94a) are a type of pronoun drop, akin to null subjects: the reader seeks the nearest linguistically acceptable antecedent to supply the content of the phonologically null constituent. In contrast, the implicit types are not simply phonologically null but are syntactically absent. Here the extralinguistic context comes into greater play: deictic implicit objects (ex. 94b) are items pointed out in the discourse context; contextually implicit items (ex. 94c) lack a linguistic antecedent, but the context leads one to deduce with a degree of specificity the semantic content of the missing object; finally, with generic implicit objects (ex. 94d), absent any contextual clues, the reader is left to deduce a more-or-less stereotypical or generic object. The majority of "missing" objects in BH are generic implicit or anaphoric null.

2.6 Lexical Expression of Phasal Aspect

Phasal aspect creates an activity "subevent" out of the situation expressed by the main verb. Varieties of phasal aspect are distinguished by their contrastive focal points on different stages of the situation types modeled in fig. 2.5 (see §2.3 above) and the underlying aspectual character of the event to which they apply.[161]

95. Phasal Aspect Focal Points

95a. Focus on Onset

Inchoative: Beginning of [+state] situation (e.g., *Tage became sick*).

Inceptive: Beginning of a [−state] situation (e.g., *Colin began writing*).

95b. Focus on Coda

Cessative: End of a [−telic] situation (e.g., *Colin stopped writing*).

Completive: End of a [+telic] situation (e.g., *Colin finished writing his report*).

95c. Alteration of Middle Phase(s)

Iterative: Repetition of a semelfactive situation (e.g., *Jared knocked for five minutes*).[162]

161. Based on Cook 2012c: 25. For other taxonomies, see Binnick 1991: 202–7.

162. The status of semelfactive is disputed. While some linguists classify it as a fifth situation aspect (see §2.3), Rothstein (2004: 29) observes that semelfactives always have a corresponding

Habitual: Regular repetition of a situation (e.g., *Evan [always] walks to school*).

Continuative: Continuation of a situation without a pause (e.g., *Jared continued studying*).

Resumptive: Resumption of a situation after a pause (e.g., *Colin resumed studying his lesson*).

Almost all the phasal aspects in the English examples in ex. 95 are lexically expressed, whether by an aspectual verb and *-ing* form (e.g., *continued knocking*) or by means of an adverbial modifier (e.g., *for five minutes*). Note, however, that a lexical expression is not always required. For example, the adverb *always* is optional in the above habitual example. This is because the simple present in English often expresses habituality by itself in light of the preference for the progressive present to describe actual present events (cf. *Evan is walking to school [right now]*). Similarly, combining a semelfactive with a progressive construction would yield an iterative expression simply lacking a specific number of iterations, in contrast to the iterative example above: *Jared was knocking*.

The case of phasal aspect in BH is similar. Phasal aspect may be expressed lexically, such as by an aspectual verb plus a finite or infinitive verb or by means of an adverb phrase.[163] At the same time, other constructions may express certain phasal aspects without the need of aspectual verbs or adverbs. Notably, as illustrated in ex. 96a, STA predicates freely alternate between a stative and inchoative interpretation, depending on the context. Parallel with English grammar, a semelfactive combined with progressive aspect (predicate PTC) may express iteration (ex. 96b). The use of IR-PFV or IPFV to express habituality is frequent (ex. 96c).

96. Pragmatically Interpreted "Phasal" Aspects

96a

אַחֲרֵי בְלֹתִי הָיְתָה־לִּי עֶדְנָה וַאדֹנִי זָקֵן

After I have become worn out ‹Q.INF›, this pleasure will have become mine ‹Q.PFV›, and my husband (is)/has become old ‹STA/Q.PFV›? (Gen. 18:12)

activity (e.g., semelfactive *knock* versus activity *are knocking*), suggesting that the semelfactive is derivative, consisting of "activities used in [a] minimal way."

163. These dual-verb constructions include both light verb constructions, which involve two finite verbs (see Snider 2021), and verbs that take a complementary infinitive. Both groups consist of a limited number of verbs, and Snider (2021: 176) mentions that some linguists group them together as two varieties of light verb construction.

96b

אָדָם בְּלִיַּעַל אִישׁ אָוֶן הוֹלֵךְ עִקְּשׁוּת פֶּה׃ קֹרֵץ בְּעֵינָו מֹלֵל בְּרַגְלָו מֹרֶה בְּאֶצְבְּעֹתָיו׃

A worthless man, a wicked man goes about ‹Q.PTC› with a perverse mouth, winking ‹Q.PTC› with his eyes, shuffling ‹Q.PTC› with his feet, pointing ‹Q.PTC› with his fingers. (Prov. 6:12–13)

96c

וְגַם אָנֹכִי מָנַעְתִּי מִכֶּם אֶת־הַגֶּשֶׁם בְּעוֹד שְׁלֹשָׁה חֳדָשִׁים לַקָּצִיר וְהִמְטַרְתִּי עַל־עִיר אֶחָת וְעַל־עִיר אַחַת לֹא אַמְטִיר חֶלְקָה אַחַת תִּמָּטֵר וְחֶלְקָה אֲשֶׁר־לֹא־תַמְטִיר עָלֶיהָ תִּיבָשׁ

I even withheld ‹Q.PFV› from you the rain with yet three months till the harvest: I would cause it to rain ‹HI.IR-PFV› upon one city, and upon another city I would not cause it to rain ‹HI.IPFV›; one field would be rained upon ‹NI.IPFV›, and a field that it would not rain ‹HI.IPFV›[164] upon it would dry up ‹Q.IPFV›. (Amos 4:7)

This section is focused particularly on the lexical strategies employed to express phasal aspect in BH. Both inchoative and inceptive aspects can be expressed by the aspectual verb חל״ל (HI, "begin") with a complementary infinitive. Whether the construction is inchoative or inceptive depends on the situation aspect of the infinitive, as illustrated in ex. 97. The rarity of inchoative examples is due to the contextually available inchoative interpretation of STA verbs mentioned above (ex. 96a).

97. Onset-Focused Phasal Aspects[165]

97a. Inchoative

הוּא הֵחֵל לִהְיוֹת גִּבּוֹר בָּאָרֶץ

He began ‹HI.PFV› to be ‹Q.INF› a mighty one in the land. (1 Chron. 1:10 = Gen. 10:8)

164. The Hiphil תַמְטִיר is problematic here, conjoined with the passive Niphal and contrasting with the earlier causative Hiphils. The only possible understanding of the form is as a 3FS impersonal avalent "(rain) rained" with the relative head "a field" (וְחֶלְקָה) resumed by the PP עָלֶיהָ. See the similarly avalent תַּשְׁלֵג "(snow) snowed" (Ps 68:15).

165. Inchoative with חל״ל (HI) appears only in Gen. 9:20; 10:8; and 1 Chron. 1:10. For other inceptive examples with חל״ל (HI), see Gen. 4:26; 6:1; 11:6; 41:54; Num. 25:1; Deut. 2:31; 3:24; 16:9; Judg. 10:18; 13:5, 25; 16:19, 22; 20:31, 39–40; 1 Sam. 3:2; 14:35; 22:15; 2 Kings 10:32; 15:37; Jer. 25:29; Jon. 3:4; Esther 6:13; 9:23; Ezra 3:6; Neh. 4:1; 1 Chron. 27:24; 2 Chron. 3:1–2; 31:7, 10; 34:3.

97b. Inceptive

וַיָּחֶל יוֹנָה לָבוֹא בָעִיר מַהֲלַךְ יוֹם אֶחָד

Jonah began ‹HI.PN› to go ‹Q.INF› through the city, a day's journey. (Jon. 3:4)

As with onset-focused phasal aspect, there are two types of coda-focused phasal aspect, which apply to two different situation types: completive aspect appears with situations that have an inherent goal (i.e., +telic) while cessative aspect applies to situations lacking one (i.e., –telic). In addition, distinct aspectual verbs are used with each: שב"ת (Q) and חד"ל (Q), "cease, stop," are used with cessative constructions (exs. 98a–b), while כל"ה (PI), "complete, finish," is used with completive ones (ex. 98c).

98. Coda-Focused Phasal Aspects[166]

98a

וַתֵּרֶא כִּי־מִתְאַמֶּצֶת הִיא לָלֶכֶת אִתָּהּ וַתֶּחְדַּל לְדַבֵּר אֵלֶיהָ

She saw ‹Q.PN› that she (was) set ‹HT.PTC› on going ‹Q.INF› with her, and she ceased ‹Q.PN› speaking ‹PI.INF› to her. (Ruth 1:18)

98b

אִם־יָמֻשׁוּ הַחֻקִּים הָאֵלֶּה מִלְּפָנַי נְאֻם־יְהוָה גַּם זֶרַע
יִשְׂרָאֵל יִשְׁבְּתוּ מִהְיוֹת גּוֹי לְפָנַי כָּל־הַיָּמִים

If these ordinances will depart ‹Q.IPFV› from before me—declaration of Yhwh—also the seed of Israel will cease ‹Q.IPFV› from being ‹Q.INF› a nation before me forever. (Jer. 31:36)

98c

וַיְהִי בְּיוֹם כַּלּוֹת מֹשֶׁה לְהָקִים אֶת־הַמִּשְׁכָּן וַיִּמְשַׁח אֹתוֹ

[PAST] On the day Moses finished ‹PI.PFV› erecting ‹HI.INF› the tent, he anointed ‹Q.PN› it. (Num. 7:1)

166. For other examples with חד"ל (Q), see Gen. 11:8; 18:11; 41:49; Exod. 23:5; Num. 9:13; Deut. 23:23; 1 Sam. 12:23; 23:13; 1 Kings 15:21; Isa. 1:16; Jer. 44:18; 51:30; Ps. 36:4; 2 Chron. 16:5. For examples with שב"ת (Q), see Ezek. 34:10; Hosea 7:4 (with PTC and INF). For other examples with כל"ה (PI), see Gen. 17:22; 18:33; 24:15, 19, 22, 45; 27:30; 43:2; 49:33; Exod. 5:14; 31:18; 34:33; Lev. 16:20; 19:9; 23:22; 26:44; Num. 7:1; 16:31; Deut. 7:22; 20:9; 26:12; 31:24; 32:45; Josh. 8:24; 19:49, 51; Judg. 3:18; 15:17; 1 Sam. 10:13; 13:10; 18:1; 24:17; 2 Sam. 6:18; 13:36, 39; 1 Kings 1:41; 3:1; 7:40; 8:54; 9:1; 2 Kings 10:25; Isa. 10:18; Jer. 5:3; 26:8; 43:1; 51:63; Ezek. 43:23; Amos 7:2; Ruth 3:3; Dan. 9:24; 12:7; 1 Chron. 16:2; 2 Chron. 4:11; 29:29.

Nucleus-focused phasal aspects rely on adverbial modifiers to a greater degree than onset and coda types. The iteration of a semelfactive is not always easily identifiable (cf. Exod. 29:21 and Lev. 4:6) except in cases where it is enforced by an adverbial phrase, as in ex. 99a. Likewise, adverbial phrases clearly identify IR-PFVs and IPFVs as expressing habituality (exs. 99b–c).

99. Nucleus-Focused Iterative and Habitual Phasal Aspects[167]

99a

וַיְזוֹרֵר הַנַּעַר עַד־שֶׁבַע פְּעָמִים וַיִּפְקַח הַנַּעַר אֶת־עֵינָיו

The child sneezed ‹POEL.PN› seven times, and then the child opened ‹Q.PN› his eyes. (2 Kings 4:35)

99b

וְעָלָה הָאִישׁ הַהוּא מֵעִירוֹ מִיָּמִים יָמִימָה לְהִשְׁתַּחֲוֹת
וְלִזְבֹּחַ לַיהוָה צְבָאוֹת בְּשִׁלֹה

That man would go up ‹Q.IR-PFV› from his city periodically to worship ‹HISHTAPHEL.INF› and to sacrifice ‹Q.INF› to Yhwh of Hosts at Shiloh. (1 Sam. 1:3)

99c

וַתְּהִי־חֹק בְּיִשְׂרָאֵל: מִיָּמִים יָמִימָה תֵּלַכְנָה בְּנוֹת
יִשְׂרָאֵל לְתַנּוֹת לְבַת־יִפְתָּח הַגִּלְעָדִי אַרְבַּעַת יָמִים
בַּשָּׁנָה

It became ‹Q.PN› a custom in Israel that periodically the daughters of Israel would go ‹Q.IPFV› to lament ‹PI.INF› the daughter of Jephthah the Gileadite four days during the year. (Judg. 11:39–40)

Identifying continuative and resumptive phasal aspect in BH is challenging because alternate interpretations of the aspectual verbs are possible in some cases. For example, רב״ה (HI) may express continuation in some cases (ex. 100a), but in others it means to increase doing something (ex. 100b).

167. For other examples with מִיָּמִים יָמִימָה, see Exod. 13:10; Judg. 11:40; 21:19; 1 Sam. 2:19. For examples with הַיָּמִים, see 1 Sam. 1:21; Neh. 10:32.

100. Nucleus-Focused Continuative Phasal Aspect with רב״ה (HI)

100a

הִרְבְּתָה לְהִתְפַּלֵּל לִפְנֵי יְהוָה

She continued ‹HI.PFV› to pray ‹HT.INF› before Yhwh. (1 Sam. 1:12)

100b

הִרְבָּה לַעֲשׂוֹת הָרַע בְּעֵינֵי יְהוָה

He increased ‹HI.PFV› doing ‹Q.INF› (i.e., did much) evil in the eyes of Yhwh. (2 Kings 21:6)

Similarly, continuative interpretation may be more appropriate for יס״ף (HI) in exs. 101a–b than the more common light verb meaning to "do again" in ex. 11a (see §2.2.1 above).[168]

101. Nucleus-Focused Continuative Phasal Aspect with יס״ף (HI)[169]

101a

לֹא תֹאספוּן לָתֵת תֶּבֶן לָעָם לִלְבֹּן הַלְּבֵנִים כִּתְמוֹל שִׁלְשֹׁם

You should not continue ‹HI.IPFV› giving ‹Q.INF› [*or* give ‹Q.INF› again ‹HI.IPFV›] straw to the people to make ‹Q.INF› the bricks, as previously. (Exod. 5:7)

101b

וְאִם־עַד־אֵלֶּה לֹא תִשְׁמְעוּ לִי וְיָסַפְתִּי לְיַסְּרָה אֶתְכֶם שֶׁבַע עַל־חַטֹּאתֵיכֶם

If still at these things you will not heed ‹Q.IPFV› me, I will continue ‹Q.IR-PFV› punishing ‹PI.INF› [*or* punish you ‹PI.INF› again ‹Q.IR-PFV›] seven times for your sins. (Lev. 26:18)

Resumptive phasal aspect is heavily dependent on the interpretation of the whole passage, since, in the case of פנ״ה (Q) "turn," it relies on recognizing the possibility that פנ״ה (Q) has an aspectual sense of "resume" (ex. 102a) rather than its literal meaning of "to change direction" (ex. 102b).

168. The expression of *to do x again* is not classified here as a phasal aspect, because it does not create an activity subevent of the original event but simply adverbially modifies it (Cook 2012c: 193n23).

169. For other examples with יס״ף (HI), see Exod. 9:28; Deut. 5:25; Josh. 7:12; Judg. 2:21; 10:13; Isa. 1:13; 51:22; Hosea 9:15; Ps. 78:17; Lam. 4:15.

102. Nucleus-Focused Resumptive Phasal Aspect with פנ"ה (Q)

102a

וַיִּפְנוּ וַיֵּלֵכוּ וַיָּשִׂימוּ אֶת־הַטַּף וְאֶת־הַמִּקְנֶה וְאֶת־
הַכְּבוּדָּה לִפְנֵיהֶם

They resumed their journey ‹Q.PN+Q.PN› and placed ‹Q.PN› the little ones, the livestock, and the goods in front of them. (Judg. 18:21 NRSV; cf. ESV: "turned and departed").

102b

וַנֵּפֶן וַנִּסַּע הַמִּדְבָּרָה דֶּרֶךְ יַם־סוּף

We turned ‹Q.PN› and departed ‹Q.PN› toward the wilderness toward the Red Sea. (Deut. 2:1)

This chapter has treated the first major component of the Hebrew verb, the thematic structure of events. While the binyanim are a major component in determining these structures and their valency alternations, it should be clear from the discussion above that valency is in some sense inherent to certain event types. The next chapter turns to the inflectional domain, in which language allows the speaker/writer to portray the temporal unfolding and location of events from different viewpoints. These two areas intersect and interact in significant ways because, as the above discussion of situation aspect alluded to (see §2.3), inflectional viewpoints interact with the thematic structure of events in some predictable and constrained ways. Therefore, the above material, though distinct, is crucial background to the discussion of the inflectional domain in the next chapter.

Chapter 3

THE INFLECTIONAL DOMAIN

3.1 Introduction

The inflectional domain in the minimalist program/distributed morphology template contains those parameters that are most typically associated with the inflection of verbal forms, the triad frequently referred to as TAM: tense, aspect, and mood. Corresponding to these three and constituting the inflectional domain are the tense phrase (TP), the mood/modality phrase (MP), and the aspect phrase (AspP), under which appear (separated by the curved line) the thematic domain's phrases (see fig. 3.1).[1]

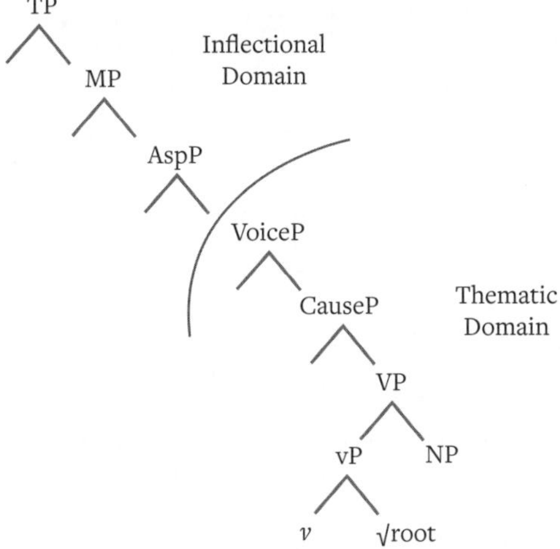

Figure 3.1. The Inflectional Domain

1. The order given here follows the typical order given in minimalist program/distributed morphology studies, though there is some uncertainty concerning the hierarchical order of the MP with respect to the TP and AspP (Gelderen 2013).

This chapter examines the various TAM values that these phrases can express to compositionally determine the semantics of the verbal construction and their respective clauses. The chapter begins with a brief overview of tense, aspect, and mood, illustrated with Hebrew examples (§3.2). Following that section is a condensed overview of the BH verbal system *as a system* (§3.3), which forms the backdrop to a discussion of each of the major verbal forms, their range of meanings, and their overlap and/or contrasts with other verbal constructions (§§3.4–8).

3.2 Tense-Aspect-Mood/Modality (TAM)

This brief introduction to each of the areas in the TAM triad does not follow the order of the distributed morphology template but instead reflects both the increasing complexity of each category and the historical development of linguistic focus on these parameters. In this section, I am not making any claims regarding the identification of particular BH verbal conjugations or constructions with any specific tense, aspect, or mood. Rather, the examples are meant to illustrate the various parameters, using BH examples along with English glosses that reflect the same or similar analysis.

3.2.1 Tense

Tense refers to the linguistic means of locating events in time. Tense distinctions have long been correlated with our intuitive sense of three times: past, present, and future. Linguists have formalized these and other tenses by ordering relationships between the time of the event (E) and the time of speech or speaking (S) using symbols to denote before (<) and simultaneous or overlapping (,), as illustrated in ex. 103.

103. Absolute Tenses

103a. Past: E<S

וַיֹּאמַר רָאִיתִי אֶת־בֶּן־יִשַׁי בָּא נֹבֶה אֶל־אֲחִימֶלֶךְ׃
בֶּן־אֲחִטוּב

He said ‹Q.PN›, "I saw ‹Q.PFV› the son of Jesse coming ‹Q.PTC› to Nob, to Ahimelech son of Ahitub." (1 Sam. 22:9)[2]

2. Gen. 20:10–11; 27:35; Num. 22:14; Judg. 6:8; 1 Sam. 3:5; 10:14, 16; 14:43; 19:17; 2 Sam. 1:4; 11:23; 12:7; 2 Kings 6:6; Ezek. 17:12; Jon. 2:3; Job 1:21; 2 Chron. 18:16.

103b. Present: E,S

כִּי יֹאמְרוּ נָסִים לְפָנֵינוּ

Because they will say ‹Q.IPFV›, "They (are) fleeing ‹Q.PTC› before us." (Josh. 8:6)[3]

103c. Future: S<E

וַיֹּאמֶר אֲלֵהֶם אַחְאָב עָבַד אֶת־הַבַּעַל מְעָט יֵהוּא יַעַבְדֶנּוּ הַרְבֵּה

He said ‹Q.PN› to them, "Ahab served ‹Q.PFV› the Baal little; Jehu will serve ‹Q.IPFV› him much." (2 Kings 10:18)[4]

Few if any languages feature just three tenses that fully align with these three temporal relationships. Rather, languages typically possess a broader array of tenses beyond these absolute ones, which can express more complicated temporal relationships. The complexity of such tenses has been identified with their ability to relate events not simply to the speech time but to other temporal reference points established by other events in the discourse. To describe these "relative" tenses, linguists employ a reference time R alongside E and S (ex. 104).

104. Relative Tenses

104a. Past in Past: E<R<S

וַיְהִי בָרָד וְאֵשׁ מִתְלַקַּחַת בְּתוֹךְ הַבָּרָד כָּבֵד מְאֹד אֲשֶׁר לֹא־הָיָה כָמֹהוּ בְּכָל־אֶרֶץ מִצְרַיִם מֵאָז הָיְתָה לְגוֹי׃

Hail was ‹Q.PN›—fire (was) flashing ‹HT.PTC› in the midst of the hail—very heavy, that had not happened ‹Q.PFV› like it in all the land of Egypt since it had become ‹Q.PFV› a nation. (Exod. 9:24)

3. Gen. 41:9; Judg. 3:24; 11:9; 19:18; 20:32; 1 Sam. 17:45; 19:14; 2 Sam. 10:3; 16:3; 18:27; 20:17; Isa. 47:10; Jer. 4:16; Ezek. 36:13; Zech. 5:2; Neh. 2:17.

4. Gen. 22:8; 27:41; Exod. 8:17; Num. 22:4; 26:45; 1 Sam. 3:14; 8:11; 9:17; 11:9; 13:12; 23:12; 28:23; Jer. 23:17; Zech. 8:20.

104b. Future in Past: R<E<S

וַנַּגֶּד־לוֹ עַל־פִּי הַדְּבָרִים הָאֵלֶּה הֲיָדוֹעַ נֵדַע כִּי יֹאמַר הוֹרִידוּ אֶת־אֲחִיכֶם

We replied ‹HI.PN› to him in accordance with these words. Could we really ‹Q.AINF› know ‹Q.IPFV› that he would say ‹Q.IPFV›, "Bring ‹HI.IMPV› your brother down"? (Gen. 43:7)

104c. Past in the Present: E<R,S

וַיֹּאמֶר יְהוָה לְנֹחַ בֹּא־אַתָּה וְכָל־בֵּיתְךָ אֶל־הַתֵּבָה כִּי־אֹתְךָ רָאִיתִי צַדִּיק לְפָנַי בַּדּוֹר הַזֶּה׃

Yhwh said ‹Q.PN› to Noah, "Enter ‹Q.IMPV›, you and all your household, into the ark, because I have seen ‹Q.PFV› you (are) righteous before me in this generation." (Gen. 7:1)

104d. Past in the Future: S<E<R

וִיהִי כְּשָׁמְעֲךָ אֶת־קוֹל הַצְּעָדָה בְּרָאשֵׁי הַבְּכָאִים אָז תֵּצֵא בַמִּלְחָמָה כִּי־יָצָא הָאֱלֹהִים לְפָנֶיךָ לְהַכּוֹת אֶת־מַחֲנֵה פְלִשְׁתִּים׃

When you hear ‹Q.INF› the sound of the march in the tops of the *baka* trees, then you should go forth ‹Q.IPFV› into battle, because God will have gone forth ‹Q.PFV› before you to strike ‹HI.INF› the camp of the Philistines. (1 Chron. 14:15)

In each of these cases, the event E is located not directly relative to S but relative to another temporal point established by another event in the context. For example, the past-in-the-past interpretation of the second and third ה״י verbs in ex. 104a recognizes that they speak of events that precede the narrative time denoted by וַיְהִי at the beginning of the verse. Similarly, the future in the past in ex. 104b must be interpreted in this way because the act of saying (יֹאמַר) logically follows the brothers' inability to know, set in the context of the PN. The case of the past in the present is slightly different, as it relies for its interpretation on a recognition that the event that it describes has some lasting relevance for the speech time, hence R is identified as concurrent with S. In ex. 104c, Yhwh's assessment (רָאִיתִי) of Noah's righteousness is not something disconnected from the present, since his assessment is that Noah *is* righteous, expressed with a null copula clause. Finally, with respect to ex. 104d, the time of Yhwh's going forth (יָצָא) logically occurs before the future/directive אָז תֵּצֵא, as it is the prompt for the signal to go forth into battle. It is worth noting that the temporal ordering of the events takes precedence over the specific verbal inflection in the interpretation of these passages, given that in the English renderings less precise verbal constructions could be employed in all but ex. 104b: simple past "happened" and "became" in ex. 104a; simple present "see" in ex. 104c, and present perfect "has gone forth" in ex. 104d (see §3.2.2.).

While this model of tense relationships using S, E, and R has been very influential in linguistics since it was first introduced by Reichenbach (1947), it is not without its shortcomings (see Cook 2012c: 4–18). Some criticisms have led to important insights. For instance, one early criticism contended, over and against Reichenbach's principle of the "permanence of the reference point" (Reichenbach 1947: 293), that instead the reference point is transitory in discourse, beginning initially at the speech time and being "transferred" to each successive event so as to create a reference point for the following event in the discourse (see Cook 2012c: 9–10). The rise of aspectual studies in linguistics has led linguists to regard all but the future in the past of the "tense" relations in ex. 104 as composed of the combination of tense and aspect rather than simply tense relations. The result of these responses to Reichenbach was the development of a theory of tense and viewpoint aspect based on the reference point, which is discussed in the next section.

3.2.2 Viewpoint Aspect

Comrie's (1976: 3) definition of aspect has been frequently taken to apply to a specific sort—*viewpoint aspect:* "Aspects are different ways of viewing the internal temporal constituency of a situation." This is important because the definition appropriately suggests that a speaker can *choose* to view (i.e., portray or express) a situation with one or another viewpoint aspect. This is quite different from situation aspect (§2.3), which is more lexically embedded in a verb, even though its determination depends on the entire VP structure.

The two viewpoint aspects most discussed in the linguistic literature are the contrasting *perfective* and *imperfective* aspects. Many different descriptive words have been applied to distinguish these two, such as "complete" versus "in progress." A more helpful approach is the metaphor of camera lenses, whose differences in focal length capture the contrastive features between these two viewpoints. Perfective aspect views a situation in the manner of a wide-angle camera lens: it has an expanded scope that includes the entire situation, including the onset and coda (fig. 2.4, §2.3). This wide scope, however, sacrifices a "close up" or detailed view of the individual intervals of the situation. By contrast, imperfective aspect views a situation as a telephoto lens does: it portrays greater "detail" of the intervals of the situation, but in so doing it fails to take the entire situation into its scope, presenting only some intervals of the situation (see Cook 2012c: 26–28, 65–67, and fig. 1.15 there).

Linguists have long observed that the effect of these contrastive perspectives or "views" on situations is manifest in how juxtaposed situations relate to one another temporally: two juxtaposed perfective events will be interpreted as happening in succession, especially in narrative discourse, where the default is to recount events in the order in which they occur (ex. 105a). By contrast, if one of the situations is presented with the imperfective aspect, the perfective event is understood as "intersecting" intervals of the imperfective verb (ex. 105b).[5]

105. Successive and Overlapping Situations with Perfective and Imperfective Aspect

105a

וְאַרְפַּכְשַׁד יָלַד אֶת־שָׁלַח וְשֶׁלַח יָלַד אֶת־עֵבֶר

Arpachshad fathered ‹Q.PFV› Shelah; and Shelah fathered ‹Q.PFV› Eber. (1 Chron. 1:18 = Gen. 10:24)[6]

105b

לָמָּה תַעֲמֹד בַּחוּץ וְאָנֹכִי פִּנִּיתִי הַבַּיִת וּמָקוֹם לַגְּמַלִּים

Why are you standing ‹Q.IPFV› outside? I prepared ‹PI.PFV› the house and a place for the camels? (Gen. 24:31)[7]

Note that the two events of fathering in ex. 105a are, obviously, distinct and successive: first Arpachshad fathered Shelah, and only afterward did Shelah father Eber. By contrast, the perfective event of preparing the house (פִּנִּיתִי) is

5. Some early studies of linguistic aspect associated these effects with perfective and imperfective aspects while others suggested that situation aspect was the determining factor. Linguists subsequently came to recognize that *(un)boundedness* is the crucial factor, which is determined not solely by viewpoint or situation aspect but by their combination as well as adverbial modification and contextual factors (see Cook 2004; 2012c: 41–42, 275–82). On (un)boundedness and the default temporal interpretation of the perfective and imperfective conjugations, see §3.3.1; on its role in structuring discourse, see §4.3.

6. Though not frequent due to the predominance of the PN, other examples are Gen. 29:34; 30:8; Deut. 5:27 (nonpast volitionals); Eccles. 2:5 (on the structure of the autobiographical "report," see Cook 2013: 320); 2 Chron. 7:12.

7. In past-tense discourse, this sort of overlap is much more frequently expressed using the PN and participle. A couple of other examples with the perfect and imperfect are found in Jer. 6:4 and Ps. 32:4.

assumed to have occurred simultaneously with some intervals of the servant standing outside (תַּעֲמֹד). This ability to overlap or intersect intervals of the imperfective viewpoint is what the notion of "detailed view" in the camera lens analogy is intended to capture.

In keeping with the situation model in fig. 2.5 (see §2.3 above) and the metaphor of camera lenses, linguists have employed symbols from set theory to model viewpoint aspect: the "reference frame" (RF) of perfective aspect is a superset of (⊃), or "includes," the temporal intervals of the "event frame" (EF) of the situation (ex. 106a); the reverse is the case for imperfective aspect—the RF is a subset of (⊂), or is "included" in, the temporal intervals of the EF (ex. 106b). This is to say, *all* of the intervals of the event (EF) "he did" (עָשָׂה) in ex. 106a are included in the scope of the perfective viewpoint (RF), conveying a sense of "completion" of the event. By contrast, only *some* of the intervals of the EF "are you weeping" (תִבְכִּי) are included in the imperfective RF, resulting in an "incomplete" or "in-progress" presentation of the activity.

106. Basic Model of Perfective and Imperfective Aspects

106a. RF⊃EF

כְּכֹל אֲשֶׁר צִוָּה אֹתוֹ אֱלֹהִים כֵּן עָשָׂה

According to everything that God commanded ‹PI.PFV› him, thus he did ‹Q.PFV›. (Gen. 6:22)

106b. RF⊂EF

וַיֹּאמֶר לָהּ אֶלְקָנָה אִישָׁהּ חַנָּה לָמֶה תִבְכִּי

Elkanah her husband said ‹Q.PN› to her, "Hannah, why are you weeping ‹Q.IPFV›?" (1 Sam. 1:8)

This model has been further refined by linguists to account for other aspects, notably perfect, or anterior, which was analyzed in terms of tense above (§3.2.1). Perfect aspect as opposed to perfective implies a continued state of affairs arising from the event. The distinction is illustrated by the contrastive pair in ex. 107: whereas the perfective aspect leaves ambiguous whether the ancestors are still in Egypt, the perfect viewpoint implies that Ahab is still in Naboth's vineyard, as the preceding clause underscores. Linguists have suggested that a useful way to model this distinction is to contrast more precisely where the RF and EF intersect: perfective and imperfective viewpoints intersect the nucleus of the event whereas the perfect intersects the coda (see fig. 2.5 in §2.3 above). Thus, the above analyses of perfective and imperfective can be revised to $\text{RF}\supset\text{EF}_{\text{NUCL}}$ and $\text{RF}\subset\text{EF}_{\text{NUCL}}$, respectively. By contrast, the perfect in ex. 107b will be expressed as $\text{RF}\supset\text{EF}_{\text{CODA}}$.

107. Perfective and Perfect Aspects

107a. Perfective: $\text{RF}\supset\text{EF}_{\text{NUCL}}$

בְּשִׁבְעִים נֶפֶשׁ יָרְדוּ אֲבֹתֶיךָ מִצְרָיְמָה וְעַתָּה שָׂמְךָ
יְהוָה אֱלֹהֶיךָ כְּכוֹכְבֵי הַשָּׁמַיִם לָרֹב׃

With seventy people your ancestors went down ‹Q.PFV› to Egypt, but now Yhwh your God has made ‹Q.PFV› you as the stars of heaven with respect to numerousness. (Deut. 10:22)

107b. Perfect: $\text{RF}\supset\text{EF}_{\text{CODA}}$

קוּם רֵד לִקְרַאת אַחְאָב מֶלֶךְ־יִשְׂרָאֵל אֲשֶׁר בְּשֹׁמְרוֹן
הִנֵּה בְּכֶרֶם נָבוֹת אֲשֶׁר־יָרַד שָׁם לְרִשְׁתּוֹ׃

Get up ‹Q.IMPV›, go down ‹Q.IMPV› to meet ‹Q.INF› Ahab king of Israel, who (is) in Samaria. Look, (he is) in the vineyard of Naboth, where he has gone down ‹Q.PFV› to take possession ‹Q.INF› of it. (1 Kings 21:18)

It is noteworthy that the contrast in ex. 107 is explicit in English but not so in BH (or in many other languages, such as French and German). That is, the PFV gram (i.e., grammatical construction) can freely express either perfective past (= English simple past) or perfect (= English perfect) as dictated by context. This suggests that rather than a temporal distinction between the two, the perfective and perfect aspects differ with respect to their focus (i.e., the nucleus of the event versus the coda), and as such in many (but not all) cases they appear in free variation. For example, ex. 107a might be glossed with an English perfect—though specifically the past perfect "had gone down"—as dictated by the discourse context, which is Moses's address to the people some forty years after they had left Egypt. Similarly, the PFV in ex. 107b might be glossed as a simple past "went down," since there is no risk of misunderstanding where Ahab is at the discourse time, since this is conveyed by the previous stative expression. The difference between the two options is whether the focus is on what Ahab did ("went down") or on the resultant state ("has gone down"), which must be interpreted pragmatically: and so he is now there. The preceding stative clause is thereby not redundant but makes clear what that resultant state is—hence the optionality of the perfect versus perfective-past interpretation.

That the perfect has past, present, and future varieties is why it could be treated adequately by the reference-point theory; it has characteristics of relative tense, whereby it places an event anterior to a past, present, or future discourse time (§3.2.1). However, the difference in focus or viewpoint between the perfective and perfect modeled in ex. 107 suggests the alternative analysis of the perfect as viewpoint aspect rather than as a tense gram. Accordingly, exs. 104a, c–d should be reanalyzed as a combination of tense and aspect by reanalyzing the reference-point theory's R-S relationship as tense and its E-R relationship as viewpoint aspect; hence, the reference-point model's E and R are identified with the aspectual model's EF and RF, respectively. The result, illustrated in exs. 108a–c along with exs. 104a, c–d, is that these tensed varieties of the perfect are modeled by a combination of (&) the perfect aspect ($\text{RF}\supset\text{EF}_{\text{CODA}}$) and absolute tense relations (i.e., RF<S; RF,S; S<RF) shown above in ex. 103.

108. Perfect Aspect and Tense

108a. ~~Past in the Past: E<R<S~~ Revised to Past Perfect: $\text{RF}\supset\text{EF}_{\text{CODA}}$ & RF<S

וַיְהִי בָרָד וְאֵשׁ מִתְלַקַּחַת בְּתוֹךְ הַבָּרָד כָּבֵד מְאֹד
אֲשֶׁר לֹא־הָיָה כָמֹהוּ בְּכָל־אֶרֶץ מִצְרַיִם מֵאָז הָיְתָה
לְגוֹי׃

Hail was ‹Q.PN›—fire (was) flashing ‹HT.PTC› in the midst of the hail—very heavy, that had not happened ‹Q.PFV› like it in all the land of Egypt since it had become ‹Q.PFV› a nation. (Exod. 9:24)

108b. ~~Past in the Present: E<R,S~~ Revised to Present Perfect: $\text{RF}\supset\text{EF}_{\text{CODA}}$ & RF,S

וַיֹּאמֶר יְהוָה לְנֹחַ בֹּא־אַתָּה וְכָל־בֵּיתְךָ אֶל־הַתֵּבָה כִּי־
אֹתְךָ רָאִיתִי צַדִּיק לְפָנַי בַּדּוֹר הַזֶּה׃

Yhwh said to Noah, "Enter ‹Q.IMPV›, you and all your household, into the ark, because I have seen ‹Q.PFV› you (are) righteous before me in this generation." (Gen. 7:1)

108c. ~~Past in the Future: S<E<R~~ Revised to Future Perfect: $\text{RF}\supset\text{EF}_{\text{CODA}}$ & S<RF

וִיהִי כְּשָׁמְעֲךָ אֶת־קוֹל הַצְּעָדָה בְּרָאשֵׁי הַבְּכָאִים אָז
תֵּצֵא בַמִּלְחָמָה כִּי־יָצָא הָאֱלֹהִים לְפָנֶיךָ לְהַכּוֹת אֶת־
מַחֲנֵה פְלִשְׁתִּים׃

When you hear ‹Q.INF› the sound of the march in the tops of the *baka* trees, then you should go forth ‹Q.IPFV› into battle, because

God will have gone forth ‹Q.PFV› before you to strike ‹HI.INF› the camp of the Philistines. (1 Chron. 14:15)

In addition to exhibiting tense distinctions, the perfect is unique in also being combinable with another viewpoint aspect, the progressive. In these cases, illustrated in ex. 109, the perfect aspect is indicated by the coda focus of the EF (i.e., EF_{CODA}), as above, and the progressive viewpoint is denoted by the subset relationship of the RF to the EF (i.e., RF⊂EF), the reverse of the perfect in ex. 108. As mentioned above in the discussion of the perfect in ex. 104, the perfect aspect is somewhat malleable in English, so that either of the examples in ex. 109 could be rendered with a simple progressive, such as "who were standing" and "you are seeking." These examples are given simply to illustrate the analysis of perfect progressive forms. I have not found any suitable examples of future perfect progressive in BH (i.e., "will have been doing *x*"), which is unsurprising given the rarity of the future perfect more generally. It would be analyzed as $RF \subset EF_{CODA}$ & S<RF.

109. Perfect Progressive

109a. Past Perfect Progressive: $RF \subset EF_{CODA}$ & RF<S

וַיִּוָּעַץ הַמֶּלֶךְ רְחַבְעָם אֶת־הַזְּקֵנִים אֲשֶׁר־הָיוּ עֹמְדִים אֶת־פְּנֵי שְׁלֹמֹה אָבִיו בִּהְיֹתוֹ חַי

King Rehoboam took counsel ‹NI.PN› with the elders who had been standing ‹Q.PFV+Q.PTC› before Solomon his father when he had been ‹Q.INF› alive. (1 Kings 12:6)

109b. Present Perfect Progressive: $RF \subset EF_{CODA}$ & RF,S

לֹא כֵן לְכוּ־נָא הַגְּבָרִים וְעִבְדוּ אֶת־יְהוָה כִּי אֹתָהּ אַתֶּם מְבַקְשִׁים

Not so! Let the men go ‹Q.IMPV› now and worship ‹Q.IR-PFV› Yhwh, because that you (have been) seeking ‹PI.PTC›. (Exod. 10:11)[8]

Two other viewpoint aspects are relevant particularly to the BH participle: continuous and prospective, which are both context-specific interpretations of the PTC. Continuous aspect represents a generalizing of a progressive gram. The generalized sense is especially evident in the aspect's combination with

8. A participle with null copula is relatively rare for expressing present perfect progressive. Usually it has an overt PFV form of הי״ה supporting the participle, as in Deut. 9:24.

stative predicates to express a generic or habitual sense, because, by contrast, progressives prototypically cannot be employed in these ways (Bybee, Perkins, and Pagliuca 1994: 139–41).[9] Stative predicates and generic and habitual expressions are all stative in character, putting them at odds with "progressive" grams, which are most felicitously combined with predicates that have stages (see §2.3), such as activities (e.g., *I am running late* versus **?I am being sick*; *Birds fly* versus *?Birds are flying*). However, progressives in some languages can be used in these ways, conveying a temporary character to the static events: *John is being clever* implies a temporary activity and not a simple stative situation (example from Bertinetto, Ebert, and de Groot 2000: 537). We can observe the same temporary sense with a habitual like *Bill is drinking coffee every day (this week)*. This habitual should strike a native English reader as poorly constructed, unless the temporal qualifier *this week* is added, creating a temporary activity of the habitual. Simple generic expressions do not appear to yet be available in the English progressive: *?Birds are flying* (cf. *Birds fly*). This nascent spread of the English progressive beyond the confines of prototypical progressive grams has suggested to scholars that it is developing into a continuous gram (Mair 2012: 817).[10]

Prospective aspect is conceptually the reverse of the perfect: the perfect implies a current situation that is the result of a past event; the prospective implies a future event that will emerge from the current situation, particularly in combination with achievement situations (Comrie 1976: 64). A frequent encoding of prospective aspect in English is the *going to* construction, as in *I am going to go now*. This construction views a future event as already underway and without any volitional idea, such as is implied by the *will* construction (e.g., *I will go now*). But this prospective aspect is not simply an alternative to future tense, because as with the perfect, the prospective can be combined with the three absolute tenses: *was going to*, *is going to*, and *will be going to*. While I have not located any clear examples of past or future prospective aspect in the Hebrew Bible, the present prospective is frequently expressed

9. Krifka et al. (1995: 16–18), followed by others (e.g., A. Cohen 2020: 127), distinguish generic and habitual based on the predication: habitual expressions have an "episodic" counterpart that generics lack. For example, the habitual *whales swim by nature* has an episodic counterpart (e.g., *whales are swimming in the bay, whales swam up to the boat*) that the generic *whales are mammals* lacks. By contrast, Langacker (1997: 195) distinguishes generic and habitual based on the subject NP: generics feature generic "kind-referring" NPs, whereas habituals have specific NPs. While in the above habitual and generic expressions *whales* is a kind-referring NP, in the episodic statements *whales* refers to specific whales.

10. Bertinetto, Ebert, and de Groot (2000: 538–39) appear to argue instead for a development continuous → progressive → imperfective in European languages (assuming their "durative" corresponds to continuous as used here). See further §3.6.1 below.

by the predicate PTC, distinguished from a simple progressive aspect by contextual clues, as illustrated in ex. 110. In this case, God has not yet begun the seven years of plenty, so his *doing* is technically in the future from Joseph's speech time; yet the dream underscores that the future is already determined by God, and so in a sense already underway in God's superintendence of the events. As suggested by its converse relationship to the PFV and in light of its *-ing* form (English) and PTC strategies, prospective aspect can be formulated in terms of the RF being a subset of the EF's *onset* phase, $RF \subset EF_{ONSET}$, which can then be combined with the absolute tense formulas.

110. Prospective Aspect: $RF \subset EF_{ONSET}$ & S,RF

וַיֹּאמֶר יוֹסֵף אֶל־פַּרְעֹה חֲלוֹם פַּרְעֹה אֶחָד הוּא אֵת אֲשֶׁר
הָאֱלֹהִים עֹשֶׂה הִגִּיד לְפַרְעֹה׃

Joseph said ‹Q.PN› to Pharaoh, "Regarding the dream of Pharaoh, it (is) one: that which God is going to do ‹Q.PTC› he has told ‹HI.PFV› to Pharaoh." (Gen. 41:25)

This intersection of the prospective with the onset of the EF closely associates it with the structure of achievement events: achievements lack a nucleus and consist of only a transition from an onset state to a coda state (see fig. 2.5d in §2.3 above). This lack of a nucleus means that progressive and imperfective viewpoint aspects (like prospective aspect) focus on the onset of the achievement ($RF \subset EF_{ONSET}$) while the broader scope of the perfective includes the entire event frame of the onset and coda in its scope ($RF \supset EF_{ONSET\text{-}CODA}$; ex. 111).

111. Imperfective and Perfective Aspects with Achievement Situations

111a. Imperfective and Achievement: $RF \subset EF_{ONSET}$ (cf. ex. 110)

נִסְתְּרָה דַרְכִּי מֵיְהוָה וּמֵאֱלֹהַי מִשְׁפָּטִי יַעֲבוֹר

My way has become hidden ‹NI.PFV› from Yhwh, and from my God my vindication is passing away ‹Q.IPFV›. (Isa. 40:27)

111b. Perfective and Achievement: $RF \supset EF_{ONSET\text{-}CODA}$

וְאֵהוּד נִמְלַט עַד הִתְמַהְמְהָם

Ehud escaped ‹NI.PFV› while they delayed ‹HITHPALPAL.INF›. (Judg. 3:26)

Up until now in this section, I have been illustrating the range of relevant viewpoint aspects using BH examples with English glosses. However, in anticipation of the fuller discussion of the matter in §3.3 below, a word must be said about the relationships between the perfect and PN and between the imperfect and progressive. The reader may have noticed that the imperfective and progressive aspects are both analyzed as RF⊂EF. Similarly, the perfective and past narrative may both be modeled as RF⊃EF. The passage in ex. 112 illustrates the semantic overlap between each of these pairs by their similar English glosses: simple past for both the PFV and PN, and progressive for both the IPFV and predicative PTC.

112. Semantic Overlap between PFV and PN and between IPFV and Predicative PTC

וַיִּמְצָאֵהוּ אִישׁ וְהִנֵּה תֹעֶה בַּשָּׂדֶה וַיִּשְׁאָלֵהוּ הָאִישׁ לֵאמֹר
מַה־תְּבַקֵּשׁ׃ וַיֹּאמֶר אֶת־אַחַי אָנֹכִי מְבַקֵּשׁ הַגִּידָה־נָּא לִי
אֵיפֹה הֵם רֹעִים׃ וַיֹּאמֶר הָאִישׁ נָסְעוּ מִזֶּה כִּי שָׁמַעְתִּי
אֹמְרִים נֵלְכָה דֹּתָיְנָה וַיֵּלֶךְ יוֹסֵף אַחַר אֶחָיו וַיִּמְצָאֵם בְּדֹתָן

A man found ‹Q.PN› him and, hey, he (was) wandering ‹Q.PTC› in the field. The man asked ‹Q.PN› him [COMP], "For what are you searching ‹PI.IPFV›?" He said ‹Q.PN›, "For my brothers I (am) searching ‹PI.PTC›. Please tell ‹HI.IMPV› me where they (are) shepherding ‹Q.PTC›." The man said ‹Q.PN›, "They moved on ‹Q.PFV› from this place, for I heard ‹Q.PFV› them saying ‹Q.PTC›, 'Let us go ‹Q.JUSS› to Dothan.'" Joseph went ‹Q.PN› after his brothers and found ‹Q.PN› them in Dothan. (Gen. 37:15–17)

Linguists have observed that lacking a specific perfective or imperfective form, the simple past and progressive forms in English contrast in a similar manner to these viewpoint aspects, based on cross-linguistic comparisons (Binnick 1991: 372). Herein lies a clue to understanding how these forms that often seem synonymous might nevertheless be distinct: while most (all?) languages have the ability to present the aspectual contrast exhibited in ex. 112, they might employ constructions different from inflected perfective and imperfective forms to do so, and they might even express the same or similar viewpoints with multiple forms. In §3.3 the relationship between the forms in each of these pairs will be fleshed out and the diachronic dimension that explains their relationship will be explored.

3.2.3 Mood and Modality

Modality is the ability of language to classify situations with respect to "reality" or "actuality"; *mood* refers to the grammatical constructions employed to express various modalities.[11] This association with reality makes mood and modality in one sense a binary phenomenon: real or actual events are situations that have either already occurred or hold at the present time; nonreal events are every sort of hypothetical, potential, or counterfactual situation—alternate realities. The division between *realis* and *irrealis* events, as I will refer to them here, has been portrayed as a branching timeline, as shown in fig. 3.2 (see Hatav 1997: 119; Portner 2009: 233).

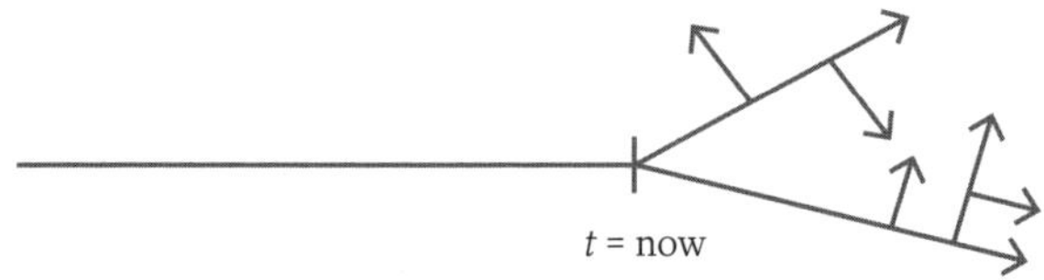

Figure 3.2. Branching Timeline

This portrayal casts the relationship of mood and modality as intertwined with tense: events occurring at or before the time (*t*) denoted by the vertical line, "now," are realis, whereas everything after that moment is irrealis. This explains why English, like some other languages, utilizes an irrealis mood auxiliary (*will*) to express "future tense."[12]

At the same time, irrealis is more rich and complex a category than a binary realis-irrealis portrayal of mood and modality suggests. As demonstrated in the discussion of tense (§3.2.1), the speech time is merely the default position of the reference time. Hence branching timelines or alternate realities are not restricted to future moments; there can be alternate (irrealis) situations in the past that were never realized (i.e., counterfactual conditions and statements). Generic and habitual ideas can also be expressed by irrealis forms, because such expressions do not refer to events occurring on the timeline at a particular time but describe the characteristic (generic) or regular (habitual) occurrence of a situation. Finally, qualifications of possibility and necessity of situations also classify an event as irrealis, since to the speaker the event may be more or

11. The approach adopted here owes much to Portner's work (2009; 2018). The far-ranging phenomena and backgrounds to the field have meant that, relative to tense and aspect, uncertainties remain in the semantic analysis of mood and modality in language.

12. "Future tense" is in quotes because linguists are not agreed on whether English has a future tense gram or whether *will* statements are always accompanied by an irrealis volitional sense, harking back to the auxiliary's volitional origin.

less possible or necessary and so not fully realized. This complexity is reflected in grammar, where the traditional labels *indicative* and *subjunctive* have been correlated with the realis-irrealis opposition (Palmer 2001: 5), while at the same time subjunctive constitutes only one of several traditional grammar "moods" that fit within the category of irrealis (e.g., imperative, optative, etc.).

Taxonomies of mood and modality vary widely (see Cook 2012c: 47–52). For the purposes of the present volume, the taxonomy in table 3.1 is appropriate. Note the major division between absolute and relative modalities. Whereas absolute or independent modalities relate possible situations directly to real or actual—speaker's "now"—relative or dependent modalities express a situation as contingent on another one (cf. absolute and relative tense in §3.2.1 above). The dependency in conditional clauses is mutual: the protasis is syntactically dependent on the apodosis, which is semantically (mood) dependent on the protasis.

Table 3.1. Taxonomy of Modalities (Based on Cook 2012c: 71)

Absolute Modalities	
Declarative (Neutral Epistemic)	general expression of speaker knowledge
Epistemic	qualification of speaker knowledge
Deontic	general expression of obligation
Directive-Volitive	imposition/expression of speaker will
Dynamic	expression of ability/genericity

Relative Modalities	
Conditional (protasis-apodosis)	contingent on postulated condition
Final (purpose)	contingent aim of postulated or real event
Result (consecution)	contingent outcome of postulated or real event

Linguists use the language of "possible worlds" and "accessibility" relationships to model modalities, which is a helpful way to regard the relationship between irrealis events and the "actual" timeline: irrealis modality expresses an "accessibility" relationship (R_X) of some modal sort (e.g., knowledge-based $R_{EPISTEMIC}$ or will/obligation-based $R_{DEONTIC}$, etc.) between the actual "world" (w) and a "possible world" (w'). For example, the event of arriving in *Arrive by 8 a.m.!* can be modeled as the logic formula $R_{DEONTIC}ww'$, in which the speaker's situation *w* ("now") is related to an alternative situation of arriving at 8 a.m. *w′* via a deontic relation specifying that the two situations are related via the speaker's imposition of his/her will—hence the use of the imperative.

Epistemic modality is knowledge based, as illustrated by the examples in ex. 113. Declarative (or indicative) expressions are the epitome of realis modality and can be thought of as epistemically neutral, lacking any qualification as to the certainty or dubiousness of the situation (ex. 113a). Over and against the realis declarative statement stands irrealis epistemic qualifications that cast the events in the realm of either more or less certain to be realized (exs. 113b–c).

113. Epistemic Modality

113a

בַּדֶּרֶךְ אֲשֶׁר־בָּא בָּהּ יָשׁוּב

By the way that he came ‹Q.PFV› he will return ‹Q.IPFV› (Isa. 37:34)

113b

אוּלַי יִמָּצְאוּן שָׁם אַרְבָּעִים

Perhaps forty will be found ‹Q.IPFV› there. (Gen. 18:29)[13]

113c

וַיֹּאמַר אָכֵן נוֹדַע הַדָּבָר

He said, "The incident must have become known ‹NI.PFV›." (Exod. 2:14)[14]

Alongside the knowledge-based epistemic modality stands the other major category of modality, the will-based deontic. In contrast to the epistemic's focus on a knowledge about a state of affairs, deontic modality expresses a speaker's will with respect to some action or event.[15] Directive-volitive, listed in table 3.1, is technically a subcategory of deontic (just as declarative is properly a subcategory of epistemic). The distinguishing feature of directive-volitive, at least in BH, is that it is limited to expressions of the *speaker's* will as opposed to expressing a general obligation or wish of someone else's (exs. 114a–b). By contrast, other deontic expressions may or may not identify the source of

13. Gen. 16:2; 18:28–32; Num. 23:3; Josh. 9:7; 1 Sam. 9:6; 14:6.

14. Examples with אָכֵן include Gen. 28:16; 1 Sam. 15:32; Isa. 40:7. Examples with אַךְ include Gen. 29:14; 1 Kings 22:32; Hosea 12:9.

15. Epistemic and deontic are frequently distinguished in the literature as "propositional" versus "event" modality (e.g., Palmer 1986: 7).

obligation or leave it ambiguous, much as English impersonal constructions like *Visitors are not to enter restricted areas* (ex. 114c).

114. Deontic Modality

114a

הַטֵּה יְהוָה אָזְנְךָ וּשֲׁמָע פְּקַח יְהוָה עֵינֶיךָ וּרְאֵה

Incline ‹HI.IMPV›, O Yhwh, your ear and listen ‹Q.IMPV›; open ‹Q.IMPV›, O Yhwh, your eyes and see ‹Q.IMPV›. (2 Kings 19:16)

114b

וַיֹּאמֶר יוֹאָב אֶל־הַמֶּלֶךְ וְיוֹסֵף יְהוָה אֱלֹהֶיךָ אֶל־הָעָם
כָּהֵם וְכָהֵם מֵאָה פְעָמִים

Joab said ‹Q.PN› to the king, "May Yhwh your God add ‹HI.JUSS› to the people, however many as they are, a hundred times." (2 Sam. 24:3)

114c

כִּי־נְבָלָה עָשָׂה בְיִשְׂרָאֵל לִשְׁכַּב אֶת־בַּת־יַעֲקֹב וְכֵן
לֹא יֵעָשֶׂה

Because a disgraceful thing he has done ‹Q.PFV› in Israel by lying ‹Q.INF› with the daughter of Jacob; and this must not be done ‹NI.IPFV›. (Gen. 34:7)

Dynamic modality entails expressions of ability and willingness (Palmer 2001: 76–79).[16] Neither of these describes actual occurrences of events. Instead, they refer to events that someone is capable of (ex. 115a) or willing to do (ex. 115b). Ambiguity between the two dynamic modal interpretations is evident in ex. 115b: Are the fathers and elders *capable* or both capable and *willing* to relate the past? Moreover, distinguishing willingness from futurity is even more difficult: In ex. 115c, is God predicting what *will* happen or describing Pharaoh's *willingness* (with reluctance) to dismiss Israel?

16. Portner (2009: 5) also includes in this category generics and habituals, which "can be seen as representing covert modality." While linguists have posited a generic operator common to both generics and habituals (see Krifka et al. 1995: 20–23; Langacker 1997: 194; A. Cohen 2020: 128), there is a lack of agreement on whether this operator is modal (cf. Boneh and Doron 2008; 2010; and A. Cohen 2018). I follow A. Cohen's (2018) argument that generics and habituals are intensional but not modal (contra Cook 2012c: 194), and therefore I have excluded them from the dynamic category. See the summary of his argument in §3.7.2.

115. Dynamic Modality

115a

מִי יוּכַל לְתַקֵּן אֵת אֲשֶׁר עִוְּתוֹ

Who is able to straighten ‹Q.IPFV+PI.INF› that which he has twisted ‹PI.PFV›? (Eccles. 7:13)

115b

זְכֹר יְמוֹת עוֹלָם בִּינוּ שְׁנוֹת דּוֹר־וָדוֹר שְׁאַל אָבִיךָ וְיַגֵּדְךָ
זְקֵנֶיךָ וְיֹאמְרוּ לָךְ׃

Remember ‹Q.IMPV› the days of old; consider ‹Q.IMPV› the years of generations. Ask ‹Q.IMPV› your father and he will recount ‹HI.IPFV› (them) to you; (ask) your elders and they will tell ‹Q.IPFV› (them) to you. (Deut. 32:7)

115c

וְשָׁלַחְתִּי אֶת־יָדִי וְהִכֵּיתִי אֶת־מִצְרַיִם בְּכֹל נִפְלְאֹתַי
אֲשֶׁר אֶעֱשֶׂה בְּקִרְבּוֹ וְאַחֲרֵי־כֵן יְשַׁלַּח אֶתְכֶם׃

I will stretch out ‹Q.IR-PFV› my hand and strike ‹HI.IR-PFV› Egypt with all of my wonders that I will do ‹Q.IPFV› in their midst, and after this he will dismiss ‹PI.IPFV› you. (Exod. 3:20)

Relative modalities consist of conditional, result, and purpose clauses. Conditional clauses, as broadly described in linguistics, include subtypes such as temporal and concessive (e.g., *if/when . . . then*; *although*; ex. 116). By virtue of their construction rather than choice of verb, the protasis and the apodosis clauses express irrealis mood—the protasis based on its conditionality (*if*) and the apodosis based on its contingent relationship (*then*) with the protasis. This is the case despite other additional modal nuances that may accompany the apodosis, such as deontic especially found in conditional law code apodoses (ex. 116a), or epistemic modality as illustrated in the protasis of ex. 116c. Note, however, that some (notably temporal) protasis-apodosis constructions are realis mood when both parts of the construction refer to actual events (ex. 116d). In this case, the temporal protasis event (חָזַק) simply provides the realis setting for the past apodosis event (וַיָּשֶׂם).

116. Conditional Modality

116a

וְאִם־מִזְבַּח אֲבָנִים תַּעֲשֶׂה־לִּי לֹא־תִבְנֶה אֶתְהֶן גָּזִית

If an altar of stones you make ‹Q.IPFV› for me, you must not build ‹Q.IPFV› it of hewn stones. (Exod. 20:25)

116b

וּבְפָרִשְׂכֶם כַּפֵּיכֶם אַעְלִים עֵינַי מִכֶּם

When you spread ‹PI.INF› your palms, I will hide ‹HI.IPFV› my eyes from you. (Isa. 1:15)

116c

כִּי־יִפֹּל לֹא־יוּטָל כִּי־יְהוָה סוֹמֵךְ יָדוֹ

Although he may fall ‹Q.IPFV›, he will not be hurled down ‹HO.IPFV›, because Yhwh (is) supporting ‹Q.PTC› his hand. (Ps. 37:24)[17]

116d

וַיְהִי כִּי־חָזַק יִשְׂרָאֵל וַיָּשֶׂם אֶת־הַכְּנַעֲנִי לָמַס

[IRREALIS] When Israel became strong ‹Q.PFV›, they put ‹Q.PN› the Canaanites to forced labor. (Judg. 1:28)

Result (or consecutive) and purpose (or final) modal clauses are grouped together here because in BH, as in some other languages, they may both be expressed by the same constructions (e.g., לְמַעַן, "so that"; *HALOT* s.v. מַעַן; Latin *ut* with the subjunctive) and may be difficult to differentiate in specific cases (ex. 117a; Joüon §168a). The major distinguishing feature is that of control: in purpose clauses the agent of the event in the main clause has some degree of control or agency with regard to the purpose clause event (i.e., it entails the agent's "intent"), whereas such control is absent in result clauses. Purpose and result clauses may be expressed by various predicates and with or without a subordinating word (see Joüon §§168–69), and they may be attached to a realis (exs. 117a–b) or irrealis (ex. 117c) main event.

17. Num. 22:18; Isa. 1:15, 18; 54:10; Ezek. 11:16; Ps. 23:4.

117. Purpose/Result Modal Clauses[18]

117a

הִנֵּה נָגַע זֶה עַל־שְׂפָתֶיךָ וְסָר עֲוֺנֶךָ

Hey, this has touched ‹Q.PFV› your lips so that (?for the purpose/with the result) your iniquity has been removed ‹Q.IR-PFV›. (Isa. 6:7)

117b

רַק אֵין־יִרְאַת אֱלֹהִים בַּמָּקוֹם הַזֶּה וַהֲרָגוּנִי עַל־
דְּבַר אִשְׁתִּי

Fear of God is certainly not ‹NEG-EXIST› in this place so that they will kill ‹Q.IR-PFV› me on account of my wife. (Gen. 20:11)

117c

רַק לֹא־יַרְבֶּה־לּוֹ סוּסִים וְלֹא־יָשִׁיב אֶת־הָעָם מִצְרַיְמָה
לְמַעַן הַרְבּוֹת סוּס

Only he must not increase ‹HI.IPFV› horses for himself and he must not return ‹HI.IPFV› the people to Egypt in order to increase ‹HI.INF› horse(s). (Deut. 17:16)

As with conditional clauses, so with purpose and result clauses: the construction itself classifies the expression as irrealis mood, even when the verb form itself may not be marked by an irrealis gram (e.g., INF in exs. 116b and 117c).

3.3 Biblical Hebrew TAM System: An Overview

One of the lasting insights of structuralist linguistics, going back to the "father" of modern linguistics, Ferdinand de Saussure, is that grammars may be described in terms of a set of oppositions whose definitions or meanings are dependent on those oppositions. Saussure (1959: 88–89) famously employed the analogy of a chess board to illustrate the structuralist character of grammar as well as to distinguish synchrony and diachrony. As he describes it, the state of the chess board at any given moment corresponds to a language's

18. Subordinate to a realis clause, see also 1 Kings 5:31; 6:6; 2 Kings 10:19; Zech. 13:4; 2 Chron. 25:20. Subordinate to an irrealis clause, see also Exod. 33:13; Josh. 3:4; Judg. 2:22; Ruth 4:5.

synchronic *state*, in which the meaning or function of each piece is dictated by its oppositional relationship to other pieces on the board. By contrast, the movement of any given piece in a player's turn corresponds to the isolated diachronic *shifts* that alter the language state. To adapt this analogy specifically to verbal systems, we can say that the configuration of the board at any given time—the number and placement of pieces—dictates the "strategies" that can be employed to express the endless variety of tensed, aspectual, and modal nuances of human language. Meanwhile, as each piece is moved, the configuration changes the potential strategies for which each piece can be employed.

Despite the inherent weakness of this adaption—namely, my conflation of chess moves as both strategies for constructing utterances and diachronic changes—it is helpful in underscoring several facets of a verbal system. First, the analogy should caution against the tendency to pigeonhole verbal conjugations with a single, narrowly defined meaning or function. This tendency has been the cause of the much-caricatured debates over whether the BH verbal system is "tense" or "aspect." Regardless of how the conjugations are defined in terms of TAM, which is mostly a necessary step to comparing the forms with like forms in other languages, the system is sufficient to express an endless array of TAM distinctions. That each form may be employed in an array of functions consistent with its basic meaning—just as chess pieces can be employed in a variety of strategies—is the result of economy of language, because developing an unwieldy set of grammatical constructions to correspond one-to-one with functions is unrealistic.

Second, though the chess pieces on the board are distinct from one another both in their defined role and their potential role given the current configuration, multiple pieces may be employed in the same way. For example, a bishop must be employed diagonally in a strategy, but so may the queen. At times it may be impossible to adjudicate the merits of employing one piece over another piece for a given strategy in the game. Likewise, verbal systems often feature overlapping functions among forms, and especially in the absence of native speakers (as is the case for BH), it may be difficult or impossible to entirely discern the semantic difference between the two constructions. Such a situation can be illustrated by the varied strategies for expressing a future anticipated event in English: *I am traveling next week*; *I will be traveling next week*; *I'm going to go traveling next week*; and so on. Even native English speakers are hard-pressed to tease out the nuanced differences among these strategies.

Third, I return to Saussure's analogy that movement of a chess piece equates to a diachronic change to the synchronic state of the board. Verbal systems, like all language, change through time. These changes may be viewed similarly as movements of individual pieces or verbal constructions that alter the configuration of the board. It can be tempting to assign "strategies" to such changes—as with chess moves—especially when some pressure from an opposing form or "piece" can be posited. However, changes to a language's grammar state are never "intentional" (e.g., no one decided to implement the Great Vowel Shift in English), and historical linguists observe that "there is hardly any bottom to causes" (Anttila 1989: 180), meaning that an ultimate or "first" cause for any chain of language change is beyond our reach. Language states can be "described," just as one would describe a chess board's configuration, but once the notion of strategy is excluded, the only "explanation" for the language state (or chess board's configuration) is a reconstruction of the historical changes from one language state to another, or one chessboard configuration to another (see Moravcsik 2007; Haspelmath 2004).

With these general principles in mind, the rest of this section provides the "big picture" of the BH verbal system as a prelude to discussing the details of the semantics of each of the inflectional forms. The first segment (§3.3.1) describes the system, and the second (§3.3.2) explains the system in terms of its diachronic development. The remainder of the chapter provides a more detailed analysis of the individual components of the system. Throughout, it must be borne in mind that applying labels to forms is not a substitute for analysis but rather a necessary step to drawing on valuable typological comparative data to elucidate the specific behavior (meanings or functions) of a construction. The detailed analyses in §§3.4–8 recognize that regardless of how comparable a form might be typologically, each system must be described "in its own terms" (see Matthews 2001: 119), as a set of unique oppositions among forms at varying places along universal trajectories of development.

3.3.1 Biblical Hebrew TAM *System Described*

The core of the BH verbal system consists of a viewpoint opposition between the perfective (PFV) and imperfective (IPFV) forms (ex. 118).

118. Opposition of Perfective (PFV) and Imperfective (IPFV) Grams

כִּי אַתָּה עָשִׂיתָ בַסָּתֶר וַאֲנִי אֶעֱשֶׂה אֶת־הַדָּבָר הַזֶּה נֶגֶד
כָּל־יִשְׂרָאֵל וְנֶגֶד הַשָּׁמֶשׁ׃

Although you did ‹Q.PFV› (it) in secret, I will do ‹Q.IPFV› this thing before all Israel and before the sun. (2 Sam. 12:12)[19]

19. Other verses in which the same verb appears contrastively in both conjugations include Gen. 18:5; 21:23; 26:29; 28:4; 35:12; Exod. 6:12; Lev. 4:20; 15:28; 26:35; Num. 18:12; 23:8, 26;

Unsurprisingly, these two forms occur more than any others in the biblical text, and together they compose over half of the occurrences of verbal forms in BH (more than 37,000 times).[20] This analysis also comports with typological studies, which have found the perfective versus imperfective aspectual opposition to be the most fundamental distinction in about every other human language in their databases (Bybee and Dahl 1989).[21] Both the PFV and IPFV can express either realis mood or irrealis mood, the difference marked by S-V word order for realis mood and V-S word order for irrealis mood (cf. exs. 118 and 119).

119. Irrealis Perfective (IR-PFV) and Imperfective (IPFV) Grams

119a

וּשְׁמַרְתֶּם אַתֶּם אֶת־חֻקֹּתַי וְאֶת־מִשְׁפָּטַי וְלֹא תַעֲשׂוּ מִכֹּל הַתּוֹעֵבֹת הָאֵלֶּה

You must ‹Q.IR-PFV› keep my statutes and my judgments and you must not do ‹Q.IPFV› any of these abominations. (Lev. 18:26)

119b

וְהָיָה כְּצֵאת מֹשֶׁה אֶל־הָאֹהֶל יָקוּמוּ כָּל־הָעָם וְנִצְּבוּ אִישׁ פֶּתַח אָהֳלוֹ

[IRREALIS] Whenever Moses went out ‹Q.INF› to the tent, the people would stand up ‹Q.IPFV› and each man would stand ‹Q.IR-PFV› (at) the entrance of his tent. (Exod. 33:8)

Deut. 2:5, 9, 19; 3:21; 6:16; 12:31; 28:63; Josh. 1:5, 17; 7:25; 24:15; Judg. 11:24; 14:16; 1 Sam. 6:6; 17:37; 2 Sam. 2:6; 10:2; 16:19; 1 Kings 3:14; 9:4; 12:11, 14; 20:34; 2 Kings 18:35; 19:4; 23:27; Isa. 33:1; 36:18; Jer. 2:32, 36; 3:7; 22:21; 31:28; Ezek. 5:9; 8:15; 18:14, 24; 20:36; 44:2; Hosea 4:6; 12:9; Hab. 2:8; Zech. 7:13; Prov. 24:29; Eccles. 1:9; 1 Chron. 14:15; 19:2; 2 Chron. 7:17; 24:5; 32:14, 17.

20. Even with computer databases, the statistics for the forms are difficult to pin down with complete accuracy. McFall's (1982: 186–87) tally has been cited widely (e.g., *IBHS* §29.1c; *BHRG* §19.1.1), but only his count of the PN closely aligns with the major databases (as searched in Accordance Bible Software version 14): 14,972 (McFall), 14,974 (ETCBC), 14,932 (Andersen-Forbes), and 15,036 (Groves-Wheeler). Only the Andersen-Forbes database distinguishes with grammatical tagging between *qatal* and the *wəqatal* or consecutive perfect and between the *yiqtol* and prefixed preterite (see §3.4.1 below). This accounts in part for their low tally of *yiqtol* forms (just 12,117 versus McFall's 14,299 and 16,000+ for both the ETCBC and Groves-Wheeler databases. Even Andersen-Forbes's tally of *qatal* minus *wəqatal* forms is higher than the average tally of the PN.

21. Crucially, this starting point is distinct from that adopted by Joosten (2012), who follows the work of Kuryłowicz (1973), who argued that relative tense is a more fundamental distinction of verbal systems than viewpoint aspect. For details on the divergent starting points, see Cook 2006; 2012c: 135–43; 2014.

This irrealis V-S word order applies likewise to the irrealis subsystem of directive-volitive modalities, consisting of the IMPV and JUSS forms (Shulman 1996; ex. 120). However, only the third-person JUSS regularly appears with an overt subject (ex. 120a).[22]

120. Directive-Volitive Irrealis Subsystem (IMPV and JUSS)

120a

יָרֶב בּוֹ הַבַּעַל כִּי נָתַץ אֶת־מִזְבְּחוֹ

Let Baal contend ‹Q.JUSS› with him, because he destroyed ‹Q.PFV› his altar. (Judg. 6:32)[23]

120b

וַיֹּאמֶר יְהוָה אֶל־שְׁמוּאֵל אַל־תַּבֵּט אֶל־מַרְאֵהוּ

Yhwh said ‹Q.PN› to Samuel, "Do not look ‹HI.JUSS› at his appearance." (1 Sam. 16:7)

120c

הִשְׁתַּחֲווּ לַיהוָה בְּהַדְרַת־קֹדֶשׁ חִילוּ מִפָּנָיו כָּל־הָאָרֶץ׃

Bow down ‹HISHTAPHEL.IMPV› to Yhwh in splendor of holiness; tremble ‹Q.IMPV› before him all the earth. (Ps. 96:9)

120d

וַיֹּאמֶר שְׁמוּאֵל אֶל־הָעָם לְכוּ וְנֵלְכָה הַגִּלְגָּל

Samuel said ‹Q.PN› to the people, "Come ‹Q.IMPV›, let us go ‹Q.JUSS› (to) Gilgal." (1 Sam. 11:14)

The PN and the predicatively employed PTC have significant semantic overlap with the PFV and IPFV, respectively. As will be explained in the next section, there

22. For a rare example of an overt subject with the IMPV, see ex. 119a.

23. A search of the Hebrew syntax database in Accordance shows that V-S order with morphologically distinctive JUSS forms occurs 4 times as often as S-V order. Examples with V-S order include Gen. 1:3; 19:20; Exod. 32:22; Lev. 9:6; Num. 24:7; Deut. 15:3; 33:6; Josh. 7:3; Judg. 6:32; 1 Sam. 10:24; 18:17, 21; 2 Sam. 16:16; 18:22–23; 19:38; 22:47; 1 Kings 1:25, 34, 39; 13:33; 20:32; 2 Kings 11:12; Isa. 47:3; 55:3; Jer. 38:20; 50:26, 29; Ezek. 9:5; Hosea 4:4; 14:7; Mic. 1:2; 4:11; 5:8; Pss. 14:7; 27:14; 31:25; 35:6; 53:7; 74:21; 96:11; 97:1; 104:20, 31; 109:13; 119:175; 122:7; Job 3:4, 7; 6:9, 29; 17:2; 21:2; 27:7; 34:29; Prov. 7:25; Dan. 5:10; Neh. 1:6; 1 Chron. 12:18; 16:31; 2 Chron. 23:11; 24:22. Examples of S-V order include Gen. 1:22; 37:27; 44:33; 45:20; Exod. 16:19; Deut. 1:11; 2 Sam. 14:17; 2 Kings 23:18; Jer. 20:14; Ezek. 45:10; Hosea 4:4; Ps. 109:14; Job 3:4, 7; 40:19; Prov. 3:8. For pragmatic explanations of the latter sort of S-V orders, see the next section (§3.3.2).

are good historical explanations for these overlaps. The PN, as the name implies, expresses past tense, predominantly within narrative discourse (ex. 121).

121. Past Narrative (PN) Gram

וַיָּבֹאוּ הַמְצֹרָעִים הָאֵלֶּה עַד־קְצֵה הַמַּחֲנֶה וַיָּבֹאוּ אֶל־אֹהֶל אֶחָד וַיֹּאכְלוּ וַיִּשְׁתּוּ וַיִּשְׂאוּ מִשָּׁם כֶּסֶף וְזָהָב וּבְגָדִים וַיֵּלְכוּ וַיַּטְמִנוּ וַיָּשֻׁבוּ וַיָּבֹאוּ אֶל־אֹהֶל אַחֵר וַיִּשְׂאוּ מִשָּׁם וַיֵּלְכוּ וַיַּטְמִנוּ׃

These lepers came ‹Q.PN› to the edge of the camp and they entered ‹Q.PN› into one of the tents and they ate ‹Q.PN› and they drank ‹Q.PN›, and they carried off ‹Q.PN› from there silver and gold and garments and they went ‹Q.PN› and hid ‹HI.PN› (them). Then they came back ‹Q.PN› and entered ‹Q.PN› another tent and they carried off ‹Q.PN› (more silver and gold and garments) from there and they went ‹Q.PN› and hid ‹HI.PN› (them). (2 Kings 7:8)[24]

As explained above (§2.2.3), the PTC is a dual-classified adjective and verb, and it features in the verbal system when employed predicatively (i.e., as the complement of a null or overt copula) to express progressive aspect (ex. 122).

122. Predicative Participle (PTC)

וַיַּחֲלֹם וְהִנֵּה סֻלָּם מֻצָּב אַרְצָה וְרֹאשׁוֹ מַגִּיעַ הַשָּׁמָיְמָה וְהִנֵּה מַלְאֲכֵי אֱלֹהִים עֹלִים וְיֹרְדִים בּוֹ׃

He dreamt ‹Q.PN› and, hey, a ladder (was) stood [lit., being made to stand] ‹PU.PTC› on the ground and its top (was) reaching ‹HI.PTC› to the heavens. And hey, messengers of God (were) ascending ‹Q.PTC› and descending ‹Q.PTC› on it. (Gen. 28:12)[25]

Although the PN exhibits V-S word order, its semantic similarity with realis PFV and predominance in realis-mood narrative discourse indicates that it is a realis mood verb. Its pervasive V-S word order is due to triggered inversion from the basic S-V order because of the distinctive proclitic -·וַ (see §3.3.2 below).

The INF and AINF forms lie at the margins of the TAM system, intersecting with it in only a few ways. These include, notably, the expression of obligation

24. For other verses with a preponderance of PN forms, see the note accompanying ex. 130.

25. Other verses with a preponderance of PTCs include Exod. 18:14; Deut. 21:20; Josh. 6:9, 13; 2 Sam. 15:23, 30; 1 Kings 3:23; 13:25; Jer. 6:28; Lam. 1:4, 16; Neh. 4:11; 2 Chron. 18:9; 23:13; 30:10.

with the INF as the complement of a copula or employment with aspectual verbs (§2.2.1), and the occasional substitute use of an AINF for an irrealis-mood form or its focal use to express various modal nuances (§2.2.2).

Fundamental to understanding this system is recognizing that, cross-linguistically, perfective and imperfective grams are closely associated semantically with past and nonpast tense, respectively. Typological studies have demonstrated that these aspectual grams may be employed to express tensed distinctions as well. In particular, studies by Smith (2006; 2008) have demonstrated a predictable pattern in which bounded events are interpreted by default as located in past time, whereas unbounded events are interpreted by default as located in present or nonpast time. Earlier linguistic studies associated the effects of boundedness invariably with viewpoint aspect (or telic situation types), such as the successive-overlapping contrastive interpretations illustrated above (see ex. 105 in §3.2.2). Subsequent studies have recognized that while perfective and imperfective aspect regularly effect boundedness and unboundedness, respectively, other factors such as situation aspect and adverbial modification also influence the interpretation of the event (see the note preceding ex. 105). This explains why, although events expressed by the BH PFV conjugation are *often* interpreted as occurring in the past, a major exception is its combination with STA predicates, in which case it defaults to a present-time interpretation (ex. 123): perfective aspect cannot create a bounded expression of a stative situation (see Smith 1999).

123. Perfective (PFV) Gram with Stative (STA) Predicate

מַה־גָּדְלוּ מַעֲשֶׂיךָ יְהוָה מְאֹד עָמְקוּ מַחְשְׁבֹתֶיךָ׃

How great ‹Q.PFV› are your works, Yhwh; (how) very deep ‹Q.PFV› are your thoughts. (Ps. 92:6)[26]

Tense distinctions expressed by the aspectual grams are most easily visible in the context of direct speech, where the reference time invariably corresponds to the speaker's deictic center, resulting in mostly absolute tense expressions. This context also makes evident the general confinement of the IPFV to non-past *future* due to the preference of the predicative PTC to describe *present*-time events (ex. 124). The case is somewhat analogous to the preference of the English progressive to describe real present events, resulting in a generic

26. For other examples of present stative expressed with the PFV conjugation, see the note accompanying ex. 33a above. See also that section (§2.4.1) for further discussion of the STA and its contrastive interaction with PFV and PN conjugations.

interpretation becoming attached to the simple present (cf. *I am teaching [right now]* versus *I teach [every day]*; see Bertinetto, Ebert, and de Groot 2000).

124. Tense Distinctions among TAM Grams in Direct Speech

וַיֹּאמֶר הַמֶּלֶךְ וְאַיֵּה בֶּן־אֲדֹנֶיךָ וַיֹּאמֶר צִיבָא אֶל־הַמֶּלֶךְ הִנֵּה יוֹשֵׁב בִּירוּשָׁלַםִ כִּי אָמַר הַיּוֹם יָשִׁיבוּ לִי בֵּית יִשְׂרָאֵל אֵת מַמְלְכוּת אָבִי׃

The king said ‹Q.PN›, "Where (is) the son of your master?" Ziba said ‹Q.PN› to the king, "Hey, (he is) remaining ‹Q.PTC› in Jerusalem, because he said ‹Q.PFV›, 'Today the house of Israel will return ‹HI.IPFV› to me the kingdom of my father.'" (2 Sam. 16:3)[27]

The system as described here can be modeled using a Venn diagram to visually show the areas of functional overlap among the various forms, excluding as relatively marginal the infinitive forms (fig. 3.3).

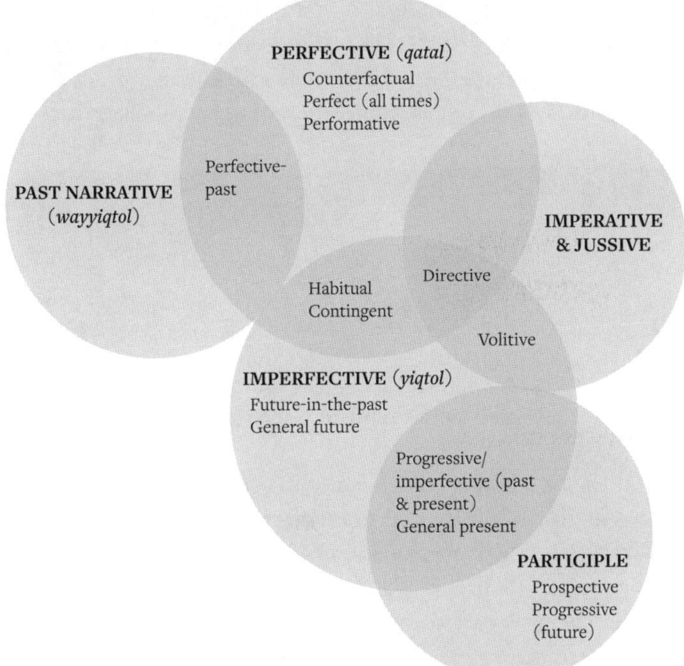

Figure 3.3. Semantic Mapping of the Biblical Hebrew Verbal System (Based on Cook 2012c: 270; Cook and Holmstedt 2013: 123)

27. Other illustrative examples are 1 Sam. 9:27; 16:1; 1 Kings 5:19; 2 Kings 1:6.

3.3.2 *Biblical Hebrew* TAM *System Explained*

As mentioned above (§3.3), some linguists point to diachronic reconstruction as the only sort of "explanation" that can be offered alongside a description of language states. For a "language" such as BH, which attests to multiple language states, a diachronic perspective of the verbal system is especially helpful, because not only does it explain how the "state" of the BH verbal system came to be what it is, but it explains why the profile differs slightly from one part of the canon to another—namely, diachronic changes are gradually but constantly shifting the system from one state to another, just as each chess move alters the state of the chess board.

Diachronic typology and grammaticalization studies have provided a wealth of insights into the "life cycle" of grammatical constructions. One such relevant insight is that languages are constantly developing new constructions that may overlap in meaning/function with previously developed ones. A historical case in point is the periphrastic → synthetic future verbal constructions in the Romance languages, illustrated in fig. 3.4 ("we will sing"). The pre-Latin periphrastic gram (i.e., constructed with an auxiliary verb) developed into a "fused" synthetic form in Latin (*cantabimus*), alongside of which a new periphrastic form developed (*cantare habemus*), which is the origin of the French periphrastic gram, which may at some point also become synthetic.

PRE-LATIN	LATIN	FRENCH
*?		
**kanta* b^h *umos* ⟶	*cantabimus*	
	cantare habemus ⟶	*chanterons allons chanter* ⟶ ?

Figure 3.4. Development of Latinate Futures (Based on Hopper and Traugott 2003: 9)

Not only does the emergence of a new construction itself alter the language state, the "competition" created between newer and older forms can also alter the state by recasting the functional distribution of the older form to "make room" in the system for the newer form. A case in point is the previously mentioned displacement of the older English simple present by the newer progressive construction to express "real" present events, as with *I drink coffee (every morning)* versus *I am drinking coffee (now)*.[28]

28. Compare the ambiguity of the present tense in German, French, and others: *Ich trinke Kaffee* can refer to a habitual event (*Ich trinke jeden Tag Kaffee*, "I drink coffee every day") or

Even without any competing forms, some words or constructions can expand to develop new, divergent uses. For example, the early English verb *wolde*, undoubtedly due to its volitional meaning of "want," developed a second function as an auxiliary verb, which has come into present-day English as *would* (fig. 3.5).

EARLY OLD ENGLISH	OLD-MIDDLE ENGLISH	PRESENT DAY ENGLISH
wolde "wanted" ⟶	*wolde* "wanted" *wolde* (auxiliary) ⟶	*would* (auxiliary)

Figure 3.5. Grammaticalization of English *Wolde/Would* (Based on Hopper and Traugott 2003: 48)

A more recent example is the development of *going to* into an auxiliary, which is sometimes reduced in form to *gonna*. That this is a distinct usage is evident from the fact that it can co-occur with the originating lexical construction: *He is going to/gonna be going home today* (see Hopper and Traugott 2003: 1–3).

The effect of both these historical trends in language—the development of new constructions and of new meanings or functions for existing ones—creates a "layered" effect in the grammar system, whereby constructions may overlap in some or many of their meanings or functions. Based on historical and typological data, this appears to be the best explanation for the overlap we find between the BH PFV and PN, on the one hand, and the IPFV and predicative PTC, on the other. Grammaticalization studies have documented a number of developmental "paths" along which verbal grams regularly travel in their life cycle. Multiple constructions developing along the same path can therefore overlap and/or compete, creating a layered grammar as well as reconfiguring the grammar system through redistributing the meanings/functions of one or another of the forms under pressure of competition.

Two such paths explain the overlap and competition between the BH verbal forms. The first is a well-documented path of development from a resultative

something I am doing right now (*Ich trinke jetzt Kaffee*, "I am drinking coffee now"). Although *be* plus the present participle construction goes back to Old English, it develops into an aspectual gram only in Middle English, and its role in the TAM system remains unsettled, showing a degree of promiscuousness with the simple present up until the early twentieth century. For example, compare "What <u>do</u> you <u>read</u>, my lord?" (Shakespeare, *Hamlet* 2.2.1294–95) and "What <u>are</u> you <u>reading</u>?" (Shakespeare, *Troilus and Cressida* 3.3.1968); and "She is always <u>seeing</u> Apparitions, and <u>hearing</u> Death-Watches" (Addison, *The Spectator*, no. 7) versus expected present-day English habitual "she always <u>sees</u> . . ." (exs. from Rissanen 1999: 216–22).

meaning to a perfective and/or past-tense one (ex. 125). Bybee, Perkins, and Pagliuca (1994: 105) posit that perfect (or anterior) grams may develop into either perfective or simple past-tense grams, but they also leave open the possibility that a past-tense form may represent a further development from a perfect → perfective shift (Bybee, Perkins, and Pagliuca 1994: 92).

125. Resultative to Perfective/Past Grammaticalization Path

Resultative → Perfect → Perfective → Past

The ancient Hebrew data appear to be an illustration of this two-stage development of perfective and past tense: in the biblical period the Hebrew PFV verb developed from a resultative to a perfective, while retaining its earlier perfect function. In the post-BH period, the form developed further into a past-tense form, as evidenced by its functions in Rabbinic Hebrew texts. Not coincidentally, the PN, which had already fully developed into a past-tense form in the biblical period, fell into disuse in the post-BH period and was replaced by the newly transitioned past-tense form from the old perfective gram. This relative age difference explains the distribution of these forms: the PN has become restricted to a literary construction whereas the perfective verb is used to express simple past in nonliterary contexts. In regard to both this distribution and the preservation of the PFV's earlier perfect sense, these forms relate analogously to the German *Präteritum* and *Perfekt* or the French *passé simple* and the *passé composé* (see further below).

The other established path relevant to the BH TAM system is the development from progressive to imperfective by way of continuous (ex. 126).

126. Progressive to Imperfective/Present Grammaticalization Path

Progressive → Continuous → Imperfective/Present

Although semantically there are challenges to distinguishing among these aspects, they differ in their distribution and/or construction. The progressive is confined to dynamic events, while a continuous gram may be used with statives. Whereas progressives are typically constructed periphrastically (i.e., with an auxiliary), imperfectives are synthetic forms (e.g., fig. 3.4)—a difference exhibited between the BH copular-supported PTC and IPFV (see Bybee, Perkins, and Pagliuca 1994: 141). Analogous with the development of the English progressive and simple present, in BH the newer (at least to the TAM system) periphrastic copula-PTC construction has largely displaced the IPFV to describe ongoing events in the present; and the PTC has begun to apply to stative predicates. In the face of this competition (and undoubtedly aided by its partial homonymy with the irrealis JUSS form), the IPFV has expanded its irrealis functions in a way seen with other "old" imperfective forms (Haspelmath 1998). As a result, the realis IPFV is distinguished from the irrealis IPFV and homonymous JUSS grams by a long-observed word-order distinction of S-V and V-S, respectively (see Cook 2012c: 132–33 and sources cited there).

The case of IR-PFV is analogous to that of *wolde*/*would* above (fig. 3.5): the PFV (realis) form appears to have developed an irrealis meaning apart from any specific competing form. More specifically, the development is likely to be a case of context-induced reinterpretation (Heine, Ulrike, and Hünnemeyer 1991: 71–72) in conditional structures. This seems a plausible context for such reinterpretation in light of the fact that a number of Semitic-language cognates of the BH PFV verb express a nonpast and/or irrealis TAM in conditional structures (see ex. 154 below). The conditional structure's semantics, consisting of a posited *if*/*when* as the condition for the realization of the *then* clause, imposes an irrealis semantic interpretation of the verbal forms that appear in the structure, and the two clauses regularly exhibit V-S order for irrealis mood clauses.[29] Once this contextual reinterpretation was well-enough established, the V-S–ordered PFV (i.e., IR-PFV) could be used in other contexts to express modalities regularly associated with conditional protasis and apodosis, such as result/purpose, habitual, and deontic.[30]

Word order is integral to understanding the verbal system, although word-order phenomena extend beyond just verbal semantics. As with the debate about the verbal system, debates over whether BH is best described as a V-S or S-V language are long-standing (cf. GKC §142a; Joüon 2006: §155k [since the 1923 French edition]). I find the typological classification of BH as a S-V language to be explanatorily superior to the alternative V-S classification (see Holmstedt 2009; 2011). This basic S-V order contrasts with inverted V-S order that is "triggered" by features that are syntactic (i.e., clause-initial function words like interrogatives, negatives, and relative and subordinating words), semantic (i.e., irrealis mood), or syntactic/pragmatic (i.e., fronting of constituents for topic or focus), as illustrated in ex. 127. In ex. 127a the basic S-V order of the first clause contrasts with the אֲשֶׁר-triggered V-S order in the relative clause. In ex. 127b the two הָיוּ verbs contrast semantically and thus exhibit contrastive word orders, the first a V-S ordered IR-PFV and the

29. This suggests that the conditional structure might have contributed to the development of irrealis meanings for IPFV also (so Cook 2012c: 234–35), but morphological overlap with the JUSS and functional pressure from the predicative PTC might have been sufficient causes for the shift of IPFV to irrealis as the more dominant realm of meaning for the form.

30. As stated above in the note in the introduction of ex. 115, I do not treat habitual as modal in BH; however, irrealis or modal forms can express habituality, and linguists have observed a semantic relationship between habitual and conditional expressions (Langacker 1997).

second a S-V realis mood PFV. In ex. 127c the fronted object, what Aaron did with the "breast" and "right thigh," is contrasted with the "fatty pieces" in the preceding verse and triggers V-S order after the fronted constituent.

127. Verses Illustrating Basic S-V Order and V-S Triggered Inversion

127a. Syntactic Triggering by Function Word

וְהַנָּחָשׁ הָיָה עָרוּם מִכֹּל חַיַּת הַשָּׂדֶה אֲשֶׁר עָשָׂה
יְהוָה אֱלֹהִים

The serpent was ‹Q.PFV› (S-V) craftier than all the animals of the field that Yhwh God created ‹Q.PFV› (V-S). (Gen. 3:1)[31]

127b. Semantic Triggering by Irrealis Mood

וְהָיוּ יָמָיו מֵאָה וְעֶשְׂרִים שָׁנָה׃ הַנְּפִלִים הָיוּ בָאָרֶץ
בַּיָּמִים הָהֵם

His days shall be ‹Q.IR-PFV› (V-S) one hundred twenty years. The Nephilim were ‹Q.PFV› (S-V) in the land in those days. (Gen. 6:3–4)[32]

127c. Pragmatic Triggering by Fronted Constituent

וַיַּקְטֵר הַחֲלָבִים הַמִּזְבֵּחָה׃ וְאֵת הֶחָזוֹת וְאֵת שׁוֹק
הַיָּמִין הֵנִיף אַהֲרֹן תְּנוּפָה לִפְנֵי יְהוָה

He burned ‹HI.PN› the fatty pieces on the altar, but the breasts and the right thigh Aaron waved ‹HI.PFV› (O-V-S) (as) a wave offering before Yhwh. (Lev. 9:20–21)[33]

31. Gen. 1:21; 5:24; 6:3; 8:9; 18:14; Exod. 4:19; 7:22; 14:20; 32:22; 40:35; Lev. 9:5; 14:36; 18:28; Num. 5:12; 27:4; 32:9; 36:7; Deut. 1:45; 12:21; 16:15; 29:3, 19; Josh. 11:22; 13:33; 18:7; Judg. 1:28; 8:20; 11:24; 1 Sam. 4:20, 22; 13:14, 22; 27:6; 2 Sam. 2:7; 10:14; 17:19; 1 Kings 3:21; 9:8; 12:15; 15:4; 2 Kings 7:17; 11:1; 14:11; Isa. 5:25; 40:2; 52:6; Jer. 2:32; 7:29; 9:8; 12:4; 15:18; 18:14; 23:12; Ezek. 5:11; 22:14; 46:7; 47:9; Hosea 4:4; Joel 1:16; 2:26; Amos 2:13; 7:10; Mic. 2:6; 3:12; Hab. 1:1; Zeph. 1:11–12; 2:7; Zech. 11:2; Pss. 2:1; 13:3; 16:9; 22:17; 40:13; 45:3; 66:14; 105:14; 139:15; Job 7:7; 31:14; 36:24; Prov. 6:28; 10:3; 11:4; 22:28; 25:1; Ruth 3:6; Eccles. 1:8; 5:17; Lam. 1:9, 16; 4:12; Esther 2:10, 20; 3:12; Dan. 1:20; 12:10; Ezra 6:22; 7:6; 1 Chron. 5:6; 6:34; 13:13; 17:25; 2 Chron. 5:14; 8:11; 24:5; 25:20.

32. Gen. 1:3, 9; 27:29; 41:34; Exod. 9:19; Lev. 9:6; 13:20, 25; 14:40; Num. 10:4; 21:27; Deut. 17:12; 20:2; 22:15; 32:2; 33:6; Judg. 9:7; 16:17; 19:6; 1 Sam. 10:24; 13:3; 2 Sam. 19:38; 22:47; 1 Kings 8:26; 14:12; Isa. 42:11; 45:8; 47:3; 55:3; Ezek. 4:17; Hosea 7:1; 10:11; Joel 2:16; 4:9; Jon. 3:8–9; Pss. 5:12; 14:7; 24:7; 31:25; 55:20; 69:35; 97:1; 104:22; 107:2; Job 6:9; 13:13; Prov. 4:4; Neh. 1:6; 2 Chron. 24:11, 22.

33. Gen. 4:3, 8; 10:5; Exod. 32:30; Lev. 19:34; Num. 36:2; Deut. 1:5; 2:36; 5:22; 7:20; 18:22; Josh. 6:25; 10:42; 11:12–13; 21:44; Judg. 14:14; 1 Sam. 2:15; 28:19; 2 Sam. 8:8; 1 Kings 14:12; 16:34; 2 Kings 17:6; 23:24; 25:11, 13; Isa. 55:13; Jer. 2:15; 39:8–9; 41:3; 52:15, 17; Ezek. 31:12;

The obligatory V-S order with the PN conjugation can be classified among those cases exhibiting a syntactic inversion triggered by a function word, the function word being "underspecified" but marked by the lengthening/doubling in the distinctive waw prefix (see §3.4.2).

A confluence of factors may contribute to the triggered V-S word order, such as the amalgamation of function words (e.g., עַל־מָה, "for what"; הֲלֹא, "is not?"; כִּי לֹא, "for not"; ex. 128a), the collocation of a function word with an irrealis verb (e.g., אִם, "if"; לְמַעַן, "so that"; אוּלַי, "perhaps"; אַל, "not" with directive-volitive verbs; ex. 128b), or the combination of any of the above with a pragmatically fronted constituent (ex. 128a).[34]

128. Compound Factors in Word-Order Inversion

128a

כִּי לֹא־יֵצֵא מֵעָפָר אָוֶן וּמֵאֲדָמָה לֹא־יִצְמַח עָמָל׃

For disaster does not come out ‹Q.IPFV› of the dust, and from the ground trouble does not sprout ‹Q.IPFV›. (Job 5:6)[35]

128b

אוּלַי יִשְׁמְעוּ בֵּית יְהוּדָה אֵת כָּל־הָרָעָה אֲשֶׁר אָנֹכִי
חֹשֵׁב לַעֲשׂוֹת לָהֶם לְמַעַן יָשׁוּבוּ אִישׁ מִדַּרְכּוֹ הָרָעָה

Perhaps the house of Judah will hear ‹Q.IPFV› all the evil that I (am) planning ‹Q.PTC› to do ‹Q.INF› to them so that each might return ‹Q.IPFV› from his evil way. (Jer. 36:3)[36]

The pragmatic fronting of the constituents can hamper recognition of word-order shifts effected by a syntactic or semantic element. For example, the V-S–triggered order of the JUSS clause in ex. 129a is altered by the focus fronting of the subject NP הַנַּעַר. Both the PN (ex. 129b) and the IR-PFV (ex. 129c) may occasionally be preceded by fronted constituents, which are cases of "extreme topic fronting" in which the --ְוּ conjunction serves as a "left-edge marker" (i.e., initial marker) of the phrase, separating the fronted element

37:9; Hosea 10:5; Joel 2:3; Hab. 3:16; Pss. 17:2; 21:2; 33:8; 44:2; 102:6; Job 18:16; 23:11; Prov. 14:13; 26:20; Ezra 9:8; Neh. 3:8, 13; 2 Chron. 4:16; 21:8; 32:9.

34. An important point to bear in mind, and one that often confuses beginning students being introduced to the manifold elements that can trigger inversion, is that the inversion is unidirectional. That is, multiple triggering factors will never trigger the clause to *revert back* to S-V order.

35. Deut. 27:5; 1 Sam. 21:10; 25:34; 2 Sam. 5:6; Isa. 5:25; Prov. 7:11.

36. Gen. 18:28–32; Judg. 21:21; 2 Sam. 14:15; Job 3:4; Prov. 7:25.

from the predicate and aiding the processing of the syntax (Holmstedt 2014: 141–49).[37]

129. Pragmatic Effects on Word Order

129a

וְעַתָּה יֵשֶׁב־נָא עַבְדְּךָ תַּחַת הַנַּעַר עֶבֶד לַאדֹנִי וְהַנַּעַר יַעַל עִם־אֶחָיו׃

Now, please let your servant remain ‹Q.JUSS› in place of the lad (as) a servant to my master, but let the lad go up ‹Q.JUSS› with his brothers. (Gen. 44:33)[38]

129b

בַּיּוֹם הַשְּׁלִישִׁי וַיִּשָּׂא אַבְרָהָם אֶת־עֵינָיו

On the third day Abraham lifted up ‹Q.PN› his eyes. (Gen. 22:4)[39]

129c

אֲשֶׁר יִמָּצֵא אִתּוֹ מֵעֲבָדֶיךָ וָמֵת

(Whoever it) is found with him from your servants should die ‹Q.IR-PFV›. (Gen. 44:9)[40]

It has been plausibly suggested that Hebrew originally exhibited V-S order, as other ancient Semitic languages, but that it developed into a basic S-V order through the repeated topicalization (or topic fronting) of the subject (so Holmstedt 2013b). The V-S order in subordinate clauses may reflect the relative conservative character of subordinate clauses (see Holmstedt 2013b: 21), and

37. Joosten (2012: 292) claims that "in biblical Hebrew the conjunction ו is always clause initial"—speaking of its role with verbs, not on words and phrases—and that "WEQATAL occurs in principle at the head of its clause." This view forces him to analyze cases like exs. 129b–c as instances of "extrapositioning" (i.e., left dislocation or *casus pendens*, in which the element appears *outside* the left/initial clause edge). Such a view—taken also by the first edition of *BHRG* (§46.1)—departs from the normal linguistic definition of left dislocation, which requires *resumption* of the dislocated element within the clause to distinguish it from fronting. In the second edition of *BHRG* (§48.1), Holmstedt's (2014) view, followed here, is presented alongside the analysis from their first edition.

38. Gen. 1:22; Deut. 1:11; 1 Sam. 26:19; 2 Kings 23:18; Hosea 4:4; Job 3:4.

39. 2 Sam. 16:13; Job 10:8; 1 Chron. 20:4; 2 Chron. 34:6–7.

40. Gen. 47:24; Exod. 16:5; 17:4; 30:33; Num. 9:21; 10:10; 23:3; 34:3; Judg. 16:2; Isa. 10:25; 29:17; Jer. 51:33, 58; Ezek. 34:20; 48:1, 28; Hosea 1:4–5; Joel 4:1–2; Zeph. 1:8; Zech. 8:23; Ps. 25:11.

this conservative character within specifically legal conditional clauses may therefore have contributed to the realis-irrealis mood word-order variation.

3.4 The Past-Narrative Conjugation

I begin the discussion of individual conjugations with the PN because it is the most straightforward of the forms. As the label suggests, the conjugation is a past-tense gram whose employment is largely limited to narrative discourse. Analogous with the French *passé simple* and German *Präteritum*, which are simple past-tense forms largely restricted to written (versus spoken) or formal discourse, the PN dominates BH narrative, except in reported speech, where the PFV is typically employed for past tense unless a narrative is embedded within the speech. Evidence of the PN's literary character is the absence of the form and its cognates in the Northwest Semitic epigraphic materials, except for a few royal inscriptions, which are lengthier and more "literary" in character (see details in Cook 2012c: 119n46).[41]

3.4.1 Diachronic Development of the Past Narrative

The most significant shift in understanding the BH verb in the twentieth century came from the deciphering of Akkadian in the nineteenth century. Akkadian exhibits, among other things, a prefixed past-tense conjugation. This led Bauer (1910) to hypothesize that BH exhibits reflexes of two distinct prefixed conjugations, a "short" **yaqtul* form and a "long" **yaqtulu* form. When, prior to the biblical period, ancient Hebrew deleted final short vowels, these two forms became partially homonymous. Scholars are now largely agreed that the JUSS and PN in BH represent reflexes (i.e., developments) of the **yaqtul* form and that the IPFV is a reflex of the **yaqtulu* form.[42]

A development that remains shrouded in some mystery is the distinct conjunction prefixed to the PN form (i.e., -·וַ). Ewald (1879: 19) notably suggested that the lengthening or doubling of the prefix represents an assimilated אָז

41. The form appears in a couple of Hebrew epistolary epigraphs (Lachish 4, Meṣad Ḥashavyahu), which suggests that relative length and narrative discourse are more relevant to the form's appearance than royal sponsorship.

42. The JUSS and PN both exhibit apocopation, or shortened forms, in 3MS, 3FS, and 2MS that make them more often homonymous than either are with the IPFV (i.e., JUSS יַ֫עַל, "let him go up," and PN וַיַּ֫עַל, "he went up"; versus IPFV יַעֲלֶה, "he is going/will go up"), suggesting that they derive from the same or homonymous short **yaqtul* form(s) (see Huehnergard 1988). The wide divergence in meaning between the PN and JUSS were presumably enough to avoid confusion between the two forms.

("then"), inasmuch as the PN regularly coincides with temporal succession and a number of times אָז appears with a prefixed verb that appears to demand a past-tense interpretation (e.g., Exod. 15:1; 1 Kings 8:1).[43] The approach I follow here is agnostic about the lexical or morphological origin of the lengthened prefix, recognizing it only as an "underspecified" function word (DeCaen 1995: 128) that is semantically bleached (i.e., has had its meaning diluted or lost) but triggers inversion, accounting for the consistent V-S word order with the form (see Holmstedt 2009: 125; Holmstedt forthcoming; Cook 2012c: 258–59).

The distinctive form of the waw conjunction with lengthened prefix consonant appears consistently enough to suggest that they are in the process of or already have been reanalyzed as part of the PN inflection. The occurrence of prefixed verb forms exhibiting what appear to be past-tense semantics but without this distinctive conjunction—as in the case of אָז—have exercised scholars and commentators, some of whom suggest that on occasion the past **yaqtul* has been employed in BH as an "archaic" past alongside and distinct from its past *narrative* form and function (e.g., Held 1962; Rainey 1986). It stands to reason that such forms occasionally occur in BH, and they appear in poetic texts, where the preservation of an archaic form is more expected than in prose narrative. That said, the ad hoc character of such identifications is insurmountable. That is, only when no other possible explanation for the semantics of the prefixed form can be found can the proposal of a "prefixed preterite" be compelling. Such identifications therefore remain scattered and tentative.[44]

43. The appearance of אָז with a prefixed verb expressing past tense is problematic because if the prefixed form in such constructions is a reflex of the short **yaqtul* (so *IBHS* §3.1.1d), it should exhibit an apocopated form where possible, but it does not. Only one example out of ten in which the verb could be apocopated is it (cf. 1 Kings 8:1 with Exod. 15:1; Num. 21:17; Deut. 4:41; Josh. 8:30; 1 Kings 11:7; 12:18; 15:16; 16:5; 2 Chron. 5:2), and in that one case the parallel text in 2 Chron. 5:2 shows a plene spelling, suggesting that it might have been read as a reflex of **yaqtulu* (cf. יַקְהֵל in 1 Kings 8:1 with יַקְהִיל in 2 Chron. 5:2). The most likely explanation is that these are indeed reflexes of short **yaqtul*, which have been replaced with the non-apocopated reflex of long **yaqtulu* in the process of transmission (so Bloch 2010). Prefixed verbs with טֶרֶם, which some also analyze as reflecting short **yaqtul* (e.g., *IBHS* §3.1.1d), are better analyzed as examples of future-in-the-past IPFVs (see ex. 206b below and discussion in Cook 2012c: 260–63).

44. Exod. 15:5–6, 12, 14; Deut. 32:8, 10, 11, 13; Judg. 5:26; 2 Sam. 22:14 (cf. Ps. 18:14), 16 (cf. Ps. 18:16); Isa. 43:28; Pss. 3:5; 18:7, 12 (cf. 2 Sam. 22:12), 17–18, 38–40; 24:2; 44:3; 47:5; 68:10, 12; 78:45, 47, 49–50; 80:9; 106:19; 107:29; Job 3:3; 15:7.

3.4.2 Semantics and Discourse Pragmatics of the Past Narrative in Prose

The native context for the BH PN form is past-narrative discourse, where it often appears in a string of PN forms expressing the temporally successive foreground events in the narrative (ex. 130).

130. PN in Temporally Successive Narrative Foreground

וַיֵּצֵא גְבוּל־בְּנֵי־דָן מֵהֶם וַיַּעֲלוּ בְנֵי־דָן וַיִּלָּחֲמוּ עִם־לֶשֶׁם
וַיִּלְכְּדוּ אוֹתָהּ וַיַּכּוּ אוֹתָהּ לְפִי־חֶרֶב וַיִּרְשׁוּ אוֹתָהּ וַיֵּשְׁבוּ
בָהּ וַיִּקְרְאוּ לְלֶשֶׁם דָּן כְּשֵׁם דָּן אֲבִיהֶם׃

The territory of the sons of Dan departed ‹Q.PN› from them. And the sons of Dan went up ‹Q.PN› and they fought ‹NI.PN› against Leshem and they captured ‹Q.PN› it and they struck ‹HI.PN› it with the edge of the sword and they took possession ‹Q.PN› of it and they dwelt ‹Q.PN› in it; and they named ‹Q.PN› Leshem Dan, after the name of Dan their father. (Josh. 19:47)[45]

Thus both semantic and discourse-pragmatic features define the form. Semantically, the form is past tense. Employing the distributed morphology template introduced at the beginning of this chapter provides a way to model the differences in meaning/function for the verbal conjugations by means of various combinations of values expressed at different branches of the template. In contrast to the previous chapter's focus on the voice phrase, (§§2.4–5), in this chapter I will ignore for simplicity's sake the details of the voice phrase where irrelevant to the interpretation of the inflectional nodes, the tense phrase (TP), the mood/modality phrase (MP), and the aspect phrase (AspP; see fig. 3.1 in §3.1 above). The PN can be analyzed as a past-tense, realis mood, perfective aspect expression (fig. 3.6).

The PN represents the furthest development along the grammaticalization path of resultative → perfect → perfective → past (ex. 125 in §3.3.2 above), suggesting that just as the perfective PFV gram retains its earlier perfect sense, so the PN retains perfective aspect semantics. There are no convincing examples in which the PN expresses past imperfective or imperfective in any other temporal sphere.

45. Other verses with a preponderance of PNs include Josh. 6:20; Judg. 4:21; 9:27; 14:19; 1 Sam. 17:51; 2 Sam. 2:23; 12:20; 17:23; 1 Kings 19:21; 2 Kings 1:13; 7:8; 10:15; Ezek. 16:8; Ruth 3:7; 1 Chron. 19:17; 20:1; 2 Chron. 28:15; 29:22.

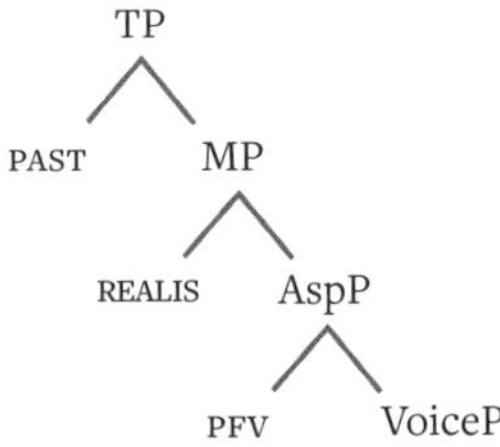

Figure 3.6. Past Tense (Realis Mood)

The discourse-pragmatic feature of the PN is that it relates the foreground events in the narrative. It appears to be a universal of narrative discourse that clauses can be divided into the categories of more salient foreground and less salient background. This instinct for prioritizing some information is illustrated by our annoyance when someone tells a story but keeps getting "off track" from the most salient points of the unfolding situation. Linguists have recognized that certain semantic features tend to correlate with foreground events, notably dynamic (versus stative) situation types (see §2.3), perfective aspect (which creates a bounded event of a dynamic situation), and realis mood (see Cook 2012c: 288). The first two of these features are most important, because dynamic situations with perfective aspect conjugations create bounded events, which effects temporal succession from one event to another (see Cook 2012c: 276–82). Temporal succession is defined by the irreversibility property, which states that given two events or clauses A and B, the order AB ≠ BA (Lakoff 1971: 126–31). To illustrate, consider the passage in ex. 131a and its made-up alternative in ex. 131b.

131. Temporal Succession and the Irreversibility Principle

131a. Original Text

וַיַּשְׁכֵּם אַבְרָהָם בַּבֹּקֶר וַיַּחֲבֹשׁ אֶת־חֲמֹרוֹ

Abraham rose early ‹HI.PN› in the morning and he saddled ‹Q.PN› his donkey. (Gen. 22:3)

131b. Rearranged Text

וַיַּחֲבֹשׁ אֶת־חֲמֹרוֹ וַיַּשְׁכֵּם אַבְרָהָם בַּבֹּקֶר

He saddled ‹Q.PN› his donkey and Abraham rose early ‹HI.PN› in the morning. (*Gen. 22:3)

As I have argued at some length drawing on Gestalt principles of perception,[46] temporal succession and foreground are highly correlative but distinct (Cook 2004, summarized in Cook 2012c: 275–98), and although the BH PN form is highly correlative with both, only foregrounding is a function of the form. It would be odd if the BH PN form overtly marked temporal succession, inasmuch as temporal succession is a general property of narrative discourse, its *ordo naturalis* as it has been termed (see Brown and Yule 1983: 125). It would be like prefacing every foregrounded event with *and then* (cf. S. Driver 1998: 71–72).

As such, the correlation of the PN with temporal succession should be explained not as part of its semantic meaning, as the traditional "consecutive" theory implies, but rather as a secondary effect of its perfective aspect and its use for narrative foreground where dynamic events predominate. This leaves unproblematic the various examples of nontemporally successive PNs. One common sort is the double speech frame (ex. 132), in which the two conjoined verbs refer to a single act of speaking. They may consist of two generic verbs of speaking (ex. 132a), or one may add a degree of specificity to the nature of the speech: e.g., עָנָה, "answer" (ex. 132b); קָרָא, "call" (Exod. 32:5); בֵּרֵךְ, "bless" (Gen. 27:27); צָעַק, "cry out" (2 Kings 6:5); זָעַק, "cry out" (Ezek. 9:8); מֵאֵן, "refuse" (1 Sam. 28:23); הִתְפַּלֵּל, "pray" (1 Sam. 2:1); צִוָּה, "command" (Gen. 28:1); נָדַר, "vow" (1 Sam. 1:11); and שָׁאַל, "ask" (Gen. 32:30).[47]

132. PN in Double Speech Frame

132a

וַיְדַבֵּר אֱלֹהִים אֶל־מֹשֶׁה וַיֹּאמֶר אֵלָיו

God spoke ‹PI.PN› to Moses and said ‹Q.PN› to him . . . (Exod. 6:2)[48]

46. Gestalt principles describe how we perceive the visual world. Reinhart (1984) applied by analogy some of these principles to narrative foreground-background. For example, visually we perceive things as consisting of a "figure" against the backdrop of a "ground," analogous to the foreground-background distinction. The principles of "closure" and "continuation," which help determine what part of the visual field is interpreted as the figure versus ground, explain why bounded (closure), temporally successive (continuation) events highly correlate with foreground (figure).

47. For a discussion of double speech frames, see Miller 2003: 147–57. Although these constructions have been analyzed as a sort of verbal hendiadys (Cook 2004: 259; 2012c: 291) in which both words are understood to refer to a single event rather than two different events, some or perhaps all of these constructions can alternatively be analyzed as two verbs of differing valency: an intransitive manner-of-speaking verb (sometimes with a recipient specified) followed by a transitive verb of speaking with the reported speech as complement (sometimes accompanied by a recipient). In this latter analysis, the two verbs do not violate the temporal succession rule of narrative (AB ≠ BA; e.g., "answer/speak and say" is not equivalent to "say and answer/speak").

48. Gen. 42:7; 2 Kings 5:13; 18:28; Ezek. 3:24; Dan. 9:22; 10:16.

132b

וָאַעַן וָאֹמַר אֶל־הַמַּלְאָךְ הַדֹּבֵר בִּי לֵאמֹר מָה־אֵלֶּה אֲדֹנִי

I answered ‹Q.PN› and said ‹Q.PN› to the messenger who (was) speaking ‹Q.PTC› with me [COMP], "What (are) these, my lord?" (Zech. 4:4)[49]

A second nontemporally successive pattern is light verb constructions, in which one of the conjoined verbs adds a noncompositional meaning to the other, often with respect to its aspectual character (see Snider 2021: 178). Snider (2021) limits his classification of light verb constructions to those featuring only finite verbs, excluding the sorts of constructions discussed above with the infinitive (§2.2.1) and classified as phasal aspect (§2.6), which some linguists would also include under this rubric. He identifies a relatively short list of eligible light verbs in BH (Snider 2021: 175), which includes the following, some of which also appear above (see §§2.2.1; 2.6) with complementary infinitives (listed with their noncompositional meaning): **שׁוּב**, "do again" (ex. 133); **הוֹסִיף**, "do again, more" (Job 36:1; Esther 8:3); **הוֹאִיל**, "do willingly" (Deut 1:5, with PFV; no examples occur with PN); **מִהַר**, "do quickly" (Exod. 34:8); **הִשְׁכִּים**, "rush to do" (Josh. 8:14); **הִרְבָּה**, "do a lot, continue to do" (no PN examples); **קוּם**, "begin to do, do immediately" (Judg. 8:21).

133. PN in Light Verb Constructions

וַיָּשָׁב וַיִּשְׁלַח אֵלָיו שַׂר־חֲמִשִּׁים אַחֵר וַחֲמִשָּׁיו

He sent again ‹Q.PN+Q.PN› to him another captain of fifty and his fifty. (2 Kings 1:11)[50]

Finally, in contrast to ex. 131, conjoined events such as eating and drinking show no interpretive change if reordered (ex. 134).

134. PN in Nontemporally Successive Contexts

וְיַעֲקֹב נָתַן לְעֵשָׂו לֶחֶם וּנְזִיד עֲדָשִׁים וַיֹּאכַל וַיֵּשְׁתְּ
וַיָּקָם וַיֵּלַךְ

49. For other examples with **עָנָה**, see Gen. 18:27; 40:18; Exod. 4:1; Num. 22:18; Deut. 1:41; 1 Sam. 1:15, 17; 2 Sam. 20:20; 1 Kings 1:43; 2 Kings 1:10–12; Isa. 21:9; Jer. 11:5; Joel 2:19; Amos 7:14; Hag. 2:14; Zech. 3:4; 4:6, 11–12; 6:4; Job 3:2; 35:1; Ruth 2:11; Esther 5:7; 1 Chron. 12:18; 2 Chron. 29:31.

50. Josh. 22:9; Judg. 19:7; 1 Sam. 1:19; 25:12; 27:9; 1 Kings 13:33; 19:6; 2 Kings 1:13; 19:9; 21:3; Zech. 5:1; 6:1; Ps. 78:41; 2 Chron. 19:4; 33:3.

Jacob gave ‹Q.PFV› Esau bread and lentil stew and he ate ‹Q.PN› and he drank ‹Q.PN› and he got up ‹Q.PN› and left ‹Q.PN›. (Gen. 25:34)[51]

While not temporally successive, the events are foregrounded by the PN verbs: the role of acceptance and consumption of the lentil stew as the basis for Esau's forfeiture of his birthright points to the salient foregrounded status of not only eating and drinking but the entire string of PNs.

Once the traditional attachment of temporal succession to the PN form is broken, it becomes understandable that on occasion isolated PN forms appear without any temporally successive relation to the juxtaposed events, as illustrated in ex. 135. This recognition makes the multiplication of special categories like "summarizing" or "explanatory" for isolated PN forms unnecessary (e.g., see comments in *IBHS* §33.2a; and Joüon §118i–j). The motivation for the grams's use is not to mark temporal succession but to indicate foregrounding.

135. Isolated PN

וַתֹּאמֶר אֲבָל אִשָּׁה־אַלְמָנָה אָנִי וַיָּמָת אִישִׁי׃ וּלְשִׁפְחָתְךָ שְׁנֵי בָנִים

She said ‹Q.PN›, "Alas, I (am) a widow; my husband died ‹Q.PN›. Your maidservant (has) two sons." (2 Sam. 14:5–6)[52]

This pattern can be interpretively significant, as in the passage in ex. 136, in which Laban and Jacob negotiate Jacob's wages. The foreground of events proceeds from Laban's reported speech in verse 15 (וַיֹּאמֶר) to the statement that Jacob loved Rachel in verse 18 (וַיֶּאֱהַב). The intervening material provides background information about Leah and Rachel, the latter of whom Jacob chooses as his wages. It makes poor sense to interpret the PN וַיֶּאֱהַב as indicating any sort of temporal succession with any of the preceding material, which would require an inchoative dynamic interpretation: "he began to love." Jacob presumably did not come to love Rachel in the course of his exchange with Laban, but instead had sometime previously come to love her and named her as his wages.[53] The choice of PN is intended to convey not temporal succession

51. Gen. 45:15; 1 Sam. 18:11.

52. Isa. 39:1; Hab. 1:14; 3:19; Pss. 8:6; 50:6; 52:9; Job 1:2; Prov. 20:26; Eccles. 4:1, 6.

53. While the idea of "love" here might be construed as all but synonymous with "choose" (e.g., Mal. 1:2) and so preserve strict temporal succession, interpreted literally, the background information about the two sisters suggests something of an attraction between Jacob and Rachel, which would undoubtedly have begun prior to the exchange.

but the saliency of Jacob's love of Rachel that had begun at some unspecified prior time. The stativity of the root allows such an interpretation, because the perfective aspect of the PN does not create a bounded event of a stative (see §2.4.1 and the note accompanying ex. 33b; and §4.3), leaving implicit that Jacob's love of Rachel extends some undetermined amount of time on either side of the deictic center established by the speech time.[54]

136. Nontemporally Successive Isolated PN

וַיֹּאמֶר לָבָן לְיַעֲקֹב הֲכִי־אָחִי אַתָּה וַעֲבַדְתַּנִי חִנָּם הַגִּידָה
לִּי מַה־מַּשְׂכֻּרְתֶּךָ׃ וּלְלָבָן שְׁתֵּי בָנוֹת שֵׁם הַגְּדֹלָה לֵאָה וְשֵׁם
הַקְּטַנָּה רָחֵל׃ וְעֵינֵי לֵאָה רַכּוֹת וְרָחֵל הָיְתָה יְפַת־תֹּאַר
וִיפַת מַרְאֶה׃ וַיֶּאֱהַב יַעֲקֹב אֶת־רָחֵל וַיֹּאמֶר אֶעֱבָדְךָ שֶׁבַע
שָׁנִים בְּרָחֵל בִּתְּךָ הַקְּטַנָּה׃

Laban said ‹Q.PN› to Jacob, "(Is) it because you are my kin that you serve ‹Q.IR-PFV› me for nothing? Tell me ‹HI.IMPV› what your wages (should be)." Now Laban (had) two daughters. The name of the older (was) Leah, and the name of the younger (was) Rachel. And the eyes of Leah (were) soft/weak, but Rachel was ‹Q.PFV› lovely and beautiful in appearance. Jacob loved ‹Q.PN› Rachel, and he said ‹Q.PN›, "I will serve ‹Q.IPFV› you seven years for Rachel your youngest daughter." (Gen. 29:15–18)

While the PN always expresses foreground, the expression of foreground is not limited to the PN. Many times the PFV form is employed to express foreground, as in the case of נָתַן in ex. 134. A noteworthy pattern juxtaposes a PN clause with a PFV clause to express two thematically coupled events, as illustrated in ex. 137.

137. PN and PFV for Thematically Related Events

וַיִּפֹּל עַל־צַוְּארֵי בִנְיָמִן־אָחִיו וַיֵּבְךְּ וּבִנְיָמִן בָּכָה עַל־צַוָּארָיו

He fell ‹Q.PN› on the neck of Benjamin his brother and he wept ‹Q.PN›. And Benjamin wept ‹Q.PFV› on his neck. (Gen. 45:14)[55]

54. Stativity accounts for other cases of overlapping (i.e., nontemporally successive) events expressed by the PN: e.g., two passive PNs in Gen. 6:11; PFV and PN in Ps. 45:7.

55. Gen. 1:5, 10, 27; 4:2–4; 8:18–19; 14:10, 16; 37:11; Exod. 9:33; 17:10; Num. 24:25; Josh. 10:13; Judg. 1:25; 3:19–20; 1 Sam. 14:41; 15:34; 1 Chron. 10:6; 2 Chron. 23:21.

Some scholars have claimed that the PN is not restricted to expressing foreground material but is found also in background or "off-line" material, notably following a PFV verb with a past perfect sense that interrupts the foreground narrative to provide background (e.g., Joosten 2012: 175).[56] Such data suggesting a past perfect meaning for the PN would challenge both the traditional (though incorrect) notion that the PN expresses temporal succession and the argument made here that the form expresses foregrounded events. First, if part of the semantics of the form were temporal succession, "it would thus be grammatically very irregular if a wayyiqtol had the value of a pluperfect [= past perfect]" (Joüon §118d n. 8). Unsurprisingly, Waltke and O'Connor admit that the claim that the PN may express past perfect "has been controversial" (*IBHS* §33.2.3a). Second, given that the *ordo naturalis* in narrative is temporal succession, a past perfect passage (even containing PNs) epitomizes background material, as illustrated in ex. 138, where verse 18 recounts actions taken by Absalom prior to his death, which was reported earlier in the passage.

138. PN in Past Perfect Passage

וַיִּתְקַע יוֹאָב בַּשֹּׁפָר וַיָּשָׁב הָעָם מִרְדֹף אַחֲרֵי יִשְׂרָאֵל כִּי־
חָשַׂךְ יוֹאָב אֶת־הָעָם׃ וַיִּקְחוּ אֶת־אַבְשָׁלוֹם וַיַּשְׁלִיכוּ אֹתוֹ
בַיַּעַר אֶל־הַפַּחַת הַגָּדוֹל וַיַּצִּבוּ עָלָיו גַּל־אֲבָנִים גָּדוֹל מְאֹד
וְכָל־יִשְׂרָאֵל נָסוּ אִישׁ לְאֹהָלָו׃ וְאַבְשָׁלֹם לָקַח וַיַּצֶּב־לוֹ
בְחַיָּו אֶת־מַצֶּבֶת אֲשֶׁר בְּעֵמֶק־הַמֶּלֶךְ כִּי אָמַר אֵין־לִי בֵן
בַּעֲבוּר הַזְכִּיר שְׁמִי וַיִּקְרָא לַמַּצֶּבֶת עַל־שְׁמוֹ וַיִּקָּרֵא לָהּ יַד
אַבְשָׁלֹם עַד הַיּוֹם הַזֶּה׃

Joab blew ‹Q.PN› on the horn and the people turned back ‹Q.PN› from pursuing after Israel, for Joab restrained ‹Q.PFV› the people. They took ‹Q.PN› Absalom and threw ‹HI.PN› him in the forest into a large pit and they set ‹HI.PN› over him a very large heap of stones; and all Israel fled ‹Q.PFV›, each man, to his tents. Now Absalom had taken ‹Q.PFV› and set up ‹HI.PN› for himself while alive [lit., in life] the pillar that (is) in the valley of the king, for he said ‹Q.PFV›, "I have no ‹NEG-EXIST› son in order to keep ‹HI.INF› my name in remembrance." And he named ‹Q.PN› the

56. GKC §111q ambiguously states, "An imperfect consecutive [= PN] occurs in dependence on a perfect which has the sense of a pluperfect." *BHRG* (§21.2) notes that "in discourse, a *wayyiqtōl* may also have a past or present perfect value," but provides no examples.

pillar by his name, and it is called ‹NI.PN› Absalom's monument until this day. (2 Sam. 18:16–18)[57]

To address these two issues in reverse order, the idea that PNs in contexts such as this express background information misses the fact that the foreground-background division is a relative one, so that narrative can contain successive layers of it: "The background itself can divide into (subsidiary) foreground and background" (Reinhart 1984: 785; see Cook 2012c: 287). Thus, the three shaded PNs in ex. 138 express the foreground of the subsidiary "flashback" storyline embedded in the background. This storyline is introduced by the leading past perfect PFV and interrupted by the background subordinate causal clause (כִּי אָמַר, "for he said") with reported speech.

As for the claim that PNs can have a past perfect sense, given their more generalized semantics (past tense compared with perfect aspect), they merely continue the temporally progressive storyline in such contexts, following the lead past perfect PFV without any misunderstanding. What is important to note is that the PN cannot *introduce* a subsidiary foreground sequence. Rather, the temporal scope of the past perfect PFV determines the temporal placement of the entire sequence without having to reassert the past perfect semantics. This makes sense since continuing with a past perfect would potentially lead to confusion about the order of events. That is, one could potentially express nesting past perfect events in which one represents an event prior to another past perfect event that is itself prior to an event established in the past narrative deixis. Such a case exists in the causal clause in ex. 138 (i.e., כִּי אָמַר), which can be glossed with a past perfect, conveying that the event preceded Absalom's taking and setting up the pillar: "Absalom had taken ‹PFV› and set up . . . for he had said ‹PFV›." Such explicitness is unnecessary, evidenced by the simple past rendering of the verb in all the major English translations. This is an important point: in English, where the perfect and simple tenses are distinct, the perfect is very frequently optional, and a simple tense could be employed equally well. For example, the PFV verbs in verses 16–17 in ex.

57. Gen. 39:13–14; Josh. 13:8–33; 1 Sam. 28:3; 30:1–3; 2 Sam. 5:18; 1 Kings 13:12 (but perhaps read as HI; see *BHS*); 2 Kings 7:6–20; 13:13–20; Isa. 39:1; see other examples in Baker (1973: 23–53). Some of the examples of the PN purportedly expressing past perfect aspect offered by Baker (1973) have been misconstrued: in most cases the PN events are actually temporally successive (e.g., Gen. 2:19; 29:12; Exod. 2:10; 14:8; 1 Sam. 7:13; 9:26; 2 Sam. 12:26–29; 13:28; 2 Kings 6:29); in other cases, a past perfect reading of a PN has been forced as a means of harmonizing redactional difficulties (e.g., Gen. 35:7, 15; Exod. 4:19 [see S. Driver 1913: 23; Propp 1999: 215]; Judg. 20:31–47; 2 Sam. 4:3, 7; 1 Kings 7:13); finally, in several of Baker's examples, the initial clause is not intended to be temporally successive with the following PNs, but introduces the discourse topic with a PFV form (e.g., Gen. 31:19; Exod. 19:1–2; Num. 1:47–49; Judg. 11:1).

138 could both be glossed as past perfect—“because Joab had restrained ‹PFV› the people” and “Israel had fled ‹PFV›”—since logically Joab’s restraint preceded the people’s return and Israel’s flight had preceded the burial of Absalom. But this is unnecessary to an accurate interpretation of the order of the events in the passage; a past perfect rendering is just more explicit and focuses the attention on the resultant state rather than the event proper. As such, no case can be made for a semantic past perfect meaning of the PN gram; it expresses simple past tense and foreground, even within the context of subsidiary foregrounds introduced by a past perfect PFV form.

The above passage (ex. 138) illustrates that the PN can function to foreground events in a subsidiary narrative. Such cases are particularly common in subordinate clauses, as illustrated in ex. 139. The PN וַיְסַתְּמוּם constitutes a foregrounded event within the subsidiary narrative introduced by אֲשֶׁר. The main foreground line of events resumes with וַיִּקְרָא, which itself is modified with another past perfect relative clause, though the PFV form in this case is isolated and does not continue with a PN form to establish any subsidiary narrative.

139. PN in Subsidiary Narrative in Subordinate Clause

וַיָּשָׁב יִצְחָק וַיַּחְפֹּר אֶת־בְּאֵרֹת הַמַּיִם אֲשֶׁר חָפְרוּ בִּימֵי
אַבְרָהָם אָבִיו וַיְסַתְּמוּם פְּלִשְׁתִּים אַחֲרֵי מוֹת אַבְרָהָם
וַיִּקְרָא לָהֶן שֵׁמוֹת כַּשֵּׁמֹת אֲשֶׁר־קָרָא לָהֶן אָבִיו׃

Isaac dug ‹Q.PN› again ‹Q.PN› the wells of water that they had dug ‹Q.PFV› in the days of Abraham his father, and the Philistines stopped them up ‹PI.PN› after the death of Abraham. And he named ‹Q.PN› them after the names that his father had called ‹Q.PFV› them. (Gen. 26:18)[58]

Multiple storylines, each with foreground-background distinctions, are the result of the limitation of narrative’s inherent linear character, in which events cannot be simultaneously recounted. Verb choice and syntax, along with other signals, can be used to alert the reader to the temporal relationship among these different storylines, as illustrated in ex. 140.

58. Gen. 28:6–8; 31:19, 34; Num. 14:36; 1 Sam. 30:21; 2 Sam. 2:23; 8:10.

140. PN in Multiple Storylines

וַיְהִי יָמִים רַבִּים וּדְבַר־יְהוָה הָיָה אֶל־אֵלִיָּהוּ בַּשָּׁנָה
הַשְּׁלִישִׁית לֵאמֹר לֵךְ הֵרָאֵה אֶל־אַחְאָב וְאֶתְּנָה מָטָר עַל־
פְּנֵי הָאֲדָמָה׃ וַיֵּלֶךְ אֵלִיָּהוּ לְהֵרָאוֹת אֶל־אַחְאָב וְהָרָעָב
חָזָק בְּשֹׁמְרוֹן׃ וַיִּקְרָא אַחְאָב אֶל־עֹבַדְיָהוּ אֲשֶׁר עַל־הַבָּיִת
וְעֹבַדְיָהוּ הָיָה יָרֵא אֶת־יְהוָה מְאֹד׃ וַיְהִי בְּהַכְרִית אִיזֶבֶל
אֵת נְבִיאֵי יְהוָה וַיִּקַּח עֹבַדְיָהוּ מֵאָה נְבִאִים וַיַּחְבִּיאֵם
חֲמִשִּׁים אִישׁ בַּמְּעָרָה וְכִלְכְּלָם לֶחֶם וָמָיִם׃ וַיֹּאמֶר אַחְאָב
אֶל־עֹבַדְיָהוּ לֵךְ בָּאָרֶץ אֶל־כָּל־מַעְיְנֵי הַמַּיִם וְאֶל כָּל־
הַנְּחָלִים אוּלַי נִמְצָא חָצִיר וּנְחַיֶּה סוּס וָפֶרֶד וְלוֹא נַכְרִית
מֵהַבְּהֵמָה׃ וַיְחַלְּקוּ לָהֶם אֶת־הָאָרֶץ לַעֲבָר־בָּהּ אַחְאָב הָלַךְ
בְּדֶרֶךְ אֶחָד לְבַדּוֹ וְעֹבַדְיָהוּ הָלַךְ בְּדֶרֶךְ־אֶחָד לְבַדּוֹ׃ וַיְהִי
עֹבַדְיָהוּ בַּדֶּרֶךְ וְהִנֵּה אֵלִיָּהוּ לִקְרָאתוֹ וַיַּכִּרֵהוּ וַיִּפֹּל עַל־פָּנָיו
וַיֹּאמֶר הַאַתָּה זֶה אֲדֹנִי אֵלִיָּהוּ׃

Storyline 1: Many days passed ‹Q.PN› and the word of Yhwh came ‹Q.PFV› to Elijah, in the third year (of the drought) [COMP], "Go ‹Q.IMPV› present yourself ‹NI.IMPV› to Ahab and I will give ‹Q.IPFV› rain on face of the land." And Elijah went ‹Q.PN› to present himself ‹NI.INF› to Ahab.

Storyline 2: Now the famine (was) severe in Samaria. And Ahab summoned ‹Q.PN› Obadiah, who (was) in charge of the palace.

Background storyline: Now Obadiah greatly feared ‹Q.PFV› Yhwh, and [PAST] when Jezebel was killing ‹HI.INF› the prophets of Yhwh, Obadiah took ‹Q.PN› a hundred prophets and hid ‹HI.PN› them fifty men in (each) cave, and he would sustain ‹PILPEL.IR-PFV› them with bread and water.

Storyline 2 (cont.): And Ahab said ‹Q.PN› to Obadiah, "Go ‹Q.IMPV› through the land to all the springs of water and to all the wadis; perhaps we will find ‹Q.IPFV› grass and keep the horses and mules alive ‹PI.IPFV›, and we will not have to destroy ‹HI.IPFV› some of the animals." They divided ‹PI.PN› for themselves the land to pass ‹Q.INF› through it. Ahab went ‹Q.PFV› in one direction on his own and Obadiah went ‹Q.PFV› in another direction on his own.

Convergence of storylines 1 and 2: Obadiah was ‹Q.PN› on the way and, hey, Elijah met ‹Q.INF› him. He recognized ‹HI.PN› him and fell ‹Q.PN› on his face and said ‹Q.PN›, “Are ‹PRO› you, my lord, Elijah?” (1 Kings 18:1–7)[59]

This passage reports two concurrent storylines that eventually converge in the discourse: Elijah goes to appear before Ahab (vv. 1–2), and Ahab and his servant Obadiah go out to look for pastureland (vv. 3, 5–6), at which point Elijah and Obadiah meet (v. 7). The relationship of the two storylines could justify inserting a “meanwhile” before the first foregrounded clause of the second storyline, at the head of verse 3. After this single foregrounded event, the second storyline is interrupted by a brief subsidiary narrative that describes Obadiah’s pious character in terms of his meritorious past actions for God’s prophets (v. 4), which is set off from the storyline by the topic-fronting of Obadiah and the shift to a PFV verb.

Another way of navigating multiple storylines is employing repetition to link portions of the same storyline together after an interruption (ex. 141).

141. Resumptive Repetition of PN

וַתַּעֲלֶה הַמִּלְחָמָה בַּיּוֹם הַהוּא וְהַמֶּלֶךְ הָיָה מָעֳמָד
בַּמֶּרְכָּבָה נֹכַח אֲרָם **וַיָּמָת** בָּעֶרֶב וַיִּצֶק דַּם־הַמַּכָּה אֶל־
חֵיק הָרָכֶב׃ וַיַּעֲבֹר הָרִנָּה בַּמַּחֲנֶה כְּבֹא הַשֶּׁמֶשׁ לֵאמֹר
אִישׁ אֶל־עִירוֹ וְאִישׁ אֶל־אַרְצוֹ׃ **וַיָּמָת** הַמֶּלֶךְ וַיָּבוֹא
שֹׁמְרוֹן וַיִּקְבְּרוּ אֶת־הַמֶּלֶךְ בְּשֹׁמְרוֹן׃

And the battle increased ‹Q.PN› that day, and the king was ‹Q.PFV› propped up ‹HO.PTC› in the chariot opposite Aram, and he died ‹Q.PN› in the evening, and the blood of the wound poured ‹Q.PN› into the bottom of the chariot. And the cry passed ‹Q.PN› through the camp when the sun went ‹Q.INF› (down) [COMP], “Each man to his city and each man to his country!” And (so) the king died ‹Q.PN› and he came ‹Q.PN› to Samaria, and they buried ‹Q.PN› the king in Samaria. (1 Kings 22:35–37)[60]

After recounting the injury and death of the king in his chariot, the narrator turns to recounting the rest of the battle before returning to the king and the aftermath of his death. The repetition of **וַיָּמָת** serves to alert the reader to the picking up of the storyline of the king’s death.

59. See also Gen. 19:28–29; 42:20; Num. 1:47–48; Deut. 5:22–27; Josh. 2:4; Judg. 1:7; 1 Sam. 19:11–14; 2 Sam. 4:4; 1 Kings 11:15–22; 2 Kings 14:1–16; see other examples in Talmon 1978: 17–26.

60. Lev. 6:6–11; 1 Sam. 14:1–6; 31:4–6; 2 Sam. 13:29–34; see discussion in Buth (1994: 142–43).

Claims that the PN has past perfect semantics are, wittingly or not, indebted to the lingering effects of eighteenth- and early nineteenth-century waw-relative and waw-inductive theories (see Cook 2012c: 85–86), inasmuch as the semantics of the PNs in such constructions are interpreted in line with the preceding form's TAM (e.g., Joüon §118o).[61] If we uncouple the semantics of the PN from various preceding forms, we find that not only the claims about a past perfect sense but also claims about non-past-tense, non-perfective-aspect semantics appear flimsy. Compare the glossing of the examples in ex. 142 found in grammars and other treatments of the BH verbal system with my consistently simple past glossing. In almost every case, a past-tense (with perfective aspect) interpretation is acceptable and preferred over adopting the semantics of the leading verb or a contextually based interpretation.

142. Consistency of Semantics of PN

142a

כֹּה אָמַר עַבְדְּךָ יַעֲקֹב עִם־לָבָן גַּרְתִּי וָאֵחַר עַד־עָתָּה

Thus said ‹Q.PFV› your servant Jacob, "With Laban I have sojourned ‹Q.PFV› and I tarried ‹Q.PN› until now." (Gen. 32:5)[62]

Cf. "I have been staying with Laban and have remained until now." (*IBHS* §33.3.1a ex. 3)

142b

וַיְהִי כִּי־זָקֵן יִצְחָק וַתִּכְהֶיןָ עֵינָיו מֵרְאֹת

[PAST] When Isaac (was)/had become old ‹STA/Q.PFV› and his eyes dimmed ‹Q.PN› from seeing ‹Q.INF› . . . (Gen. 27:1)[63]

Cf. "When Isaac was old and his eyes were dim so that he could not see . . ." (Joosten 2012: 178)

61. Waltke and O'Connor (*IBHS* §33.3a) make a point of rejecting the thoroughgoing inductive theory of Davidson (1901), averring that the PN always retains a perfective sense, though its temporal reference can be dependent on the preceding verb.

62. Gen. 31:34; 39:1–3; Exod. 4:23; Num. 22:11; 31:49–50; Josh. 4:9; 1 Kings 19:10; Isa. 30:12; Jer. 8:6; Ps. 119:90.

63. Isa. 2:6–7; 3:16; 40:24; 50:7; Nah. 3:16; Pss. 16:9; 41:13; Job 7:9; Prov. 11:2, 8; 12:13; 20:26; 22:12; 25:4; 30:25; Job 4:5; 6:21; 14:10. For a discussion of TAM in generic expressions, like some of these are, see below §3.5.2 on the PFV in such expressions.

142c

אָהַבְתָּ צֶּדֶק וַתִּשְׂנָא רֶשַׁע עַל־כֵּן מְשָׁחֲךָ אֱלֹהִים אֱלֹהֶיךָ
שֶׁמֶן שָׂשׂוֹן מֵחֲבֵרֶיךָ

You (have) loved ‹Q.PFV› righteousness and you hated ‹Q.PN› wickedness. Therefore, God your God has anointed ‹Q.PFV› you with oil of gladness above your companions. (Ps. 45:8)

Cf. "You love justice and you hate iniquity." (Joüon §118p)

142d

עָלָה הַפֹּרֵץ לִפְנֵיהֶם פָּרְצוּ וַיַּעֲבֹרוּ שַׁעַר וַיֵּצְאוּ בוֹ

(The one) who made the breach ‹Q.PTC› has gone up ‹Q.PFV› before them. They broke out ‹Q.PFV› and passed through ‹Q.PN› the gate and departed it. (Mic. 2:13)

Cf. "They will break through and go out." (*IBHS* §33.3.1d ex. 29)

142e

וַיֻּגַּד לְיוֹאָב הִנֵּה הַמֶּלֶךְ בֹּכֶה וַיִּתְאַבֵּל עַל־אַבְשָׁלֹם׃

It was told ‹HO.PN› to Joab, "Hey, the king (is) weeping ‹Q.PTC›, and he (?)mourned ‹HT.PN› over Absalom." (2 Sam. 19:2)

The prepositional phrase עַד־עָתָּה ("until now") in ex. 142a perhaps misled Waltke and O'Connor into glossing the PN as a present perfect, but a simple past is not incompatible with it. In ex. 142b the stative זָקֵן is ambiguous in form and semantics: it may be an adjective with null copula ("[was] old") or an inflected form that expresses either the same sense or a past perfect sense ("had become old"). In any case, the following PN is unaffected and should be interpreted as a past tense with perfective aspect. The verb כה״ה (Q) is not simple stative but inchoative, glossed with an unaccusative expression. The stative character of the PFV and PN in ex. 142c might be one reason to prefer the present habitual glossing in Joüon and others (e.g., NRSV, NJPS). However, it is not at all clear that a present tense interpretation is correct. The following clause, beginning with עַל־כֵּן ("therefore") followed by the PFV verb מְשָׁחֲךָ ("has anointed"), suggests that the king's *past* actions of loving/choosing righteousness and hating/rejecting wickedness is the basis for God's anointing. It is notable that examples of the PN in present and in future expressions all come from prophetic and poetic passages, whose temporal contours are far from agreed upon. For example, although Waltke and O'Connor (*IBHS* §33.3.1d ex. 29) gloss the PFV and PN verbs in Mic. 2:13 as future (ex. 142d above), Andersen and Freedman (2000: 341) comment on the verse as follows:

> We have from time to time mentioned the ambivalence of prefix verbs in time reference; a prefix verb may be past (archaic) or future (standard). No such ambivalence attaches to suffix verbs. Here, along with *waw*-consecutive forms, all the verbs are past tense.

Finally, in cases where the PN is actually unexpected (142e), Joüon (§118q) notes that the text may be suspect. Joosten (2012: 187–88) lists the passage as dubious, noting that "the example is unique [i.e., a PN following a PTC and exhibiting present progressive meaning]. It would be unwise to use this unique occurrence of present tense WAYYIQTOL as an argument against the preterite interpretation. Preferably, the passage should be explained in a different way." For example, McCarter (1984: 403) suggests reading וַיִּתְאַבֵּל as a PTC (וּמִתְאַבֵּל), which is in keeping with two medieval manuscripts and the Targum and Syriac (see *BHS*).[64]

3.4.3 Semantics and Discourse Pragmatics of the Past Narrative in Verse[65]

The PN is so labeled not only for its past semantics but also for its native narrative function. In contrast to prose narrative, the PN is notably rare in verse, which is evident from a cursory look at some of the statistics available in the Bible software. The prose narrative of Genesis, Judges–Kings, Ruth, and the narrative prophetic book of Jonah exhibits 51–77 PN forms per 1,000 words; in the books of mostly poetic verse—Psalms, Job, Song of Songs, and Lamentations—the average is 12 or less per 1,000 words.[66] Another way to consider the contrast is that in the prose-narrative books listed here, the

64. The Syriac evidence is significant here inasmuch as it departs from the LXX, which translates both the participle and past form as finite present tense. McCarter (1984: 403) observes that the MT as it stands suggests that Joab is the subject of the PN, "and he (Joab?) mourned," which is similar to Revell's (1989: 9) suggestion that the form could "begin the following narrative," but maintaining David as subject. See Joosten (2012: 188) for these and other suggested solutions.

65. This section draws heavily from my treatment in Cook (2012c: 298–304), which is based on an exhaustive study of the PN in the book of Psalms.

66. The book of Job has 20.98 PNs per 1,000 words, but more than half occur in the prose prologue and epilogue (149 of 261 occurrences).

PN form accounts for about 40 percent of the verbal forms, whereas in the poetic-verse books it is just a bit more than 5 percent.[67]

The unambiguously poetic-verse book of Psalms is instructive for how the PN functions on the rare occasions that it appears in verse. It is important to note that the distribution of PN in the book is uneven: 89 of the poems lack any PN form, only 11 poems contain 4 or more PN forms,[68] and 185 of the 332 PN forms cluster in five narrative poems (Pss. 18, 78, 105–7). The main function of the PN in poetic verse is to convey narrative sequences of events (i.e., past, temporally successive events)—notably in the five narrative poems and, rarely, in isolated sections of other poems, as in ex. 143.

143. Narrative Sequence of PNs in Poetry

קַוֹּה קִוִּיתִי יְהוָה וַיֵּט אֵלַי וַיִּשְׁמַע שַׁוְעָתִי׃ וַיַּעֲלֵנִי מִבּוֹר
שָׁאוֹן מִטִּיט הַיָּוֵן וַיָּקֶם עַל־סֶלַע רַגְלַי כּוֹנֵן אֲשֻׁרָי׃ וַיִּתֵּן בְּפִי
שִׁיר חָדָשׁ תְּהִלָּה לֵאלֹהֵינוּ

I waited ‹PI.PFV› patiently ‹PI.AINF› for Yhwh, and he turned ‹Q.PN› to me and he heard ‹Q.PN› my cry; then he brought me up ‹HI.PN› from the desolate pit, from the muddy mire, and he established ‹HI.PN› my feet upon a rock; he secured ‹POLEL.PFV› my steps, then he placed ‹Q.PN› a new song in my mouth—a song of praise to our God. (Ps. 40:2–4)[69]

The passage in ex. 143 illustrates the features of this "narrative" use of the PN in poetic verse. First, the PN is frequently preceded by a PFV verb with which it forms a narrative sequence, often consisting of just those two verbs (ex. 144a). When it is juxtaposed instead with a prefix verb, the contexts suggest in some cases that the prefix form is the preterite progenitor of the PN form (ex. 144b); in other cases, the prefix form is the IPFV expressing past imperfective aspect (ex. 144c). We must also allow for the possibility, especially if there is versional support, that some isolated occurrences of the PN form in poetic verse are incorrectly vocalized IPFV verbs (e.g., Pss. 34:8; 59:16).

67. These statistics are from Groves-Wheeler, searched in Accordance Bible Software.

68. Pss. 7:5, 13, 16 [2×]; 29:5, 6, 9, 10; 37:36 [2×], 40 [2×]; 40:2 [2×], 3 [2×], 4; 44:3 [2×], 10, 19–21; 50:1, 6, 16–18; 64:8–10 [2×]; 69:11 [2×], 12 [2×], 21 [2×], 22; 80:6, 9–10 [2×]; 109:3, 4, 16, 17 [3×], 18 [2×], 28; 119:26, 52, 55, 59–60, 106, 131, 147, 158, 167. Excluded from these statistics are the eight examples in the prose-narrative titles (i.e., Pss. 34:1 [2×]; 52:2 [2×]; 54:2; 59:1; 60:2 [2×]).

69. See also Ps. 69:11–12.

144. Narrative Functions of PNs in Poetry

144a

כִּי הוּא אָמַר וַיֶּהִי הוּא־צִוָּה וַיַּעֲמֹד׃

Because he spoke ‹Q.PFV› and it happened ‹Q.PN›; he commanded ‹Q.PFV› and it stood ‹Q.PN›. (Ps. 33:9)[70]

144b

גֶּפֶן מִמִּצְרַיִם תַּסִּיעַ תְּגָרֵשׁ גּוֹיִם וַתִּטָּעֶהָ׃

A vine from Egypt you pulled out ‹HI.PRET›; you drove out ‹PI.PRET› nations and planted it ‹Q.PN›. (Ps. 80:9)[71]

144c

עֶרֶב וָבֹקֶר וְצָהֳרַיִם אָשִׂיחָה וְאֶהֱמֶה וַיִּשְׁמַע קוֹלִי׃

Evening and morning and noonday I was lamenting ‹Q.IPFV› and I was moaning ‹Q.IPFV›; and he heard ‹Q.PN› my voice. (Ps. 55:18)[72]

Second, the passage in ex. 143 illustrates the assiduous avoidance of the PN with appositional lines: in verse 3b, "he established my feet upon a rock" (וַיָּקֶם עַל־סֶלַע רַגְלַי) and "he secured my steps" (כּוֹנֵן אֲשֻׁרָי) are appositional, referring to the same event rather than two distinct ones.[73] This illustrates the unique semantic-pragmatic character of the PN in verse. I argued above that temporal succession is the default interpretation of juxtaposed events in prose narrative and *not* a property of the PN verb; it seems reasonable to suppose that in nontemporally successive parallel/appositional verse form, the PN is employed to overtly signal temporal succession, which is an augmented pragmatic meaning from its high degree of correlation with temporally successive events in prose narrative. This analysis is confirmed by the avoidance of the PN form in the five narrative poems wherever events are not temporally ordered (e.g., Pss. 78:44–51; 105:16–18).

70. This pattern accounts for more than half of the PN occurrences outside of the five narrative poems. In addition to the verses in ex. 144, see Pss. 3:6; 7:13, 16; 20:9; 22:5, 30; 28:7 [2×]; 30:3, 12; 37:36 [2×]; 38:13; 39:12; 40:2 [2×], 3 [2×], 4; 41:13; 44:3, 10, 19–21; 45:8; 50:17–18; 55:7; 64:10 [2×]; 65:10; 66:12; 69:11 [2×], 12 [2×], 21 [2×]; 73:13, 16; 75:9; 77:11; 80:10 [2×]; 81:8, 13; 90:10; 94:23; 97:4, 8 [2×]; 102:5, 8, 11; 109:3, 5, 17 [2×], 18, 28; 114:3; 118:21; 119:26, 52, 59, 90, 131, 147, 158; 120:1; 136:4; 138:3; 139:1, 5; 143:4, 6.

71. See also Pss. 3:5 and 44:3.

72. See also Ps. 94:7.

73. On an appositional/nonappositional approach to Hebrew verse, see Holmstedt 2019.

In parts of the five narrative poems (Pss. 18, 78, 105–7), only the syntax of the lines (terse, balanced, and stichic) makes evident that it is verse form and not prose narrative (ex. 145).

145. Series of PNs in Narrative Poetry

וַיִּצָּמְדוּ לְבַעַל פְּעוֹר וַיֹּאכְלוּ זִבְחֵי מֵתִים׃
וַיַּכְעִיסוּ בְּמַעַלְלֵיהֶם וַתִּפְרָץ־בָּם מַגֵּפָה׃
וַיַּעֲמֹד פִּינְחָס וַיְפַלֵּל וַתֵּעָצַר הַמַּגֵּפָה׃

They attached themselves ‹NI.PN› to Baal Peor, and ate ‹Q.PN› sacrifices to the dead.

Thus they provoked ‹HI.PN› with their deeds, and a plague broke out ‹Q.PN› among them.

Then Phineas stood up ‹Q.PN› and interceded ‹PI.PN›, and the plague was halted ‹NI.PN›. (Ps. 106:28–30)

In other portions, the artistic skill of the PN's use in parallelistic poetry is more evident, where each PN clause advancing the narrative is succeeded by an appositional one that slows the forward motion of the narrative poem (ex. 146).

146. Temporally Successive PN Poetic Lines Alternating with Appositional Lines in Narrative Poetry

וַיִּקַץ כְּיָשֵׁן אֲדֹנָי כְּגִבּוֹר מִתְרוֹנֵן מִיָּיִן׃
וַיַּךְ־צָרָיו אָחוֹר חֶרְפַּת עוֹלָם נָתַן לָמוֹ׃
וַיִּמְאַס בְּאֹהֶל יוֹסֵף וּבְשֵׁבֶט אֶפְרַיִם לֹא בָחָר׃
וַיִּבְחַר אֶת־שֵׁבֶט יְהוּדָה אֶת־הַר צִיּוֹן אֲשֶׁר אָהֵב׃
וַיִּבֶן כְּמוֹ־רָמִים מִקְדָּשׁוֹ כְּאֶרֶץ יְסָדָהּ לְעוֹלָם׃

Then the Lord awoke ‹Q.PN›, as a sleeper; (he awoke) as a strongman shouting ‹HITHPOLEL.PTC› because of wine.

He routed ‹HI.PN› his enemies; he placed ‹Q.PFV› on them enduring disgrace.

He rejected ‹Q.PN› the tent of Joseph; he did not choose ‹Q.PFV› the tribe of Ephraim.

But he chose ‹Q.PN› the tribe of Judah, Mount Zion, which he loves ‹Q.PFV›.

> Then he built ‹Q.PN› his sanctuary like the heights, like the earth he founded ‹Q.PFV› forever. (Ps. 78:65–69)

The other, minority use of the PN in poetic verse notably lacks any pragmatic sense of temporal succession and instead employs the form simply for its past-tense semantics. This includes instances in which the PN is closely (or immediately) juxtaposed with a PFV form that is synonymous, antithetical, or otherwise forms a poetic word pair (exs. 147a–b)[74] or expresses an isolated past event (ex. 147c).[75]

147. Isolated PNs in Poetry

147a

קוֹל רַעַמְךָ בַּגַּלְגַּל הֵאִירוּ בְרָקִים תֵּבֵל רָגְזָה
וַתִּרְעַשׁ הָאָרֶץ׃

The sound of your thunder (was) in the wheel, lightning lit up ‹HI.PFV› the earth, the earth shook ‹Q.PFV› and quaked ‹Q.PN›. (Ps. 77:19)

147b

אָהַבְתָּ צֶּדֶק וַתִּשְׂנָא רֶשַׁע עַל־כֵּן מְשָׁחֲךָ אֱלֹהִים אֱלֹהֶיךָ
שֶׁמֶן שָׂשׂוֹן מֵחֲבֵרֶיךָ׃

You (have) loved ‹Q.PFV› righteousness and you hated ‹Q.PN› wickedness; therefore, God your God anointed ‹Q.PFV› you with the oil of gladness beyond your companions. (Ps. 45:8)

147c

אִסְפוּ־לִי חֲסִידָי כֹּרְתֵי בְרִיתִי עֲלֵי־זָבַח׃ וַיַּגִּידוּ שָׁמַיִם
צִדְקוֹ כִּי־אֱלֹהִים שֹׁפֵט הוּא סֶלָה׃ שִׁמְעָה עַמִּי וַאֲדַבֵּרָה
יִשְׂרָאֵל וְאָעִידָה בָּךְ אֱלֹהִים אֱלֹהֶיךָ אָנֹכִי׃

"Gather ‹Q.IMPV› to me my pious ones, (those who) cut ‹Q.PTC› my covenant over sacrifice." The heavens declared ‹HI.PN› his righteousness, that God, a judge (is) he. "Listen ‹Q.IMPV›, my people, and I will speak ‹PI.JUSS›, (listen) O Israel, and I will testify ‹HI.JUSS› against you. God your God (am) I." (Ps. 50:5–7)

74. Pss. 7:5, 16; 16:9; 29:10; 37:40; 38:3; 50:1; 73:13; 80:6; 89:20, 39; 90:2; 109:16; 119:55, 106, 167. See also ex. 137 and the accompanying note.

75. See also Pss. 8:6; 35:21; 64:8–9; 65:9; 76:3; 81:17; 92:11–12; 94:22; 109:17–18; 139:11; 148:14. See also ex. 135 and the accompanying note.

Although there are a handful of outlier examples that do not fit the above patterns (see Cook 2012c: 301), the evidence overwhelmingly supports the notion that the PN retains its past-tense semantics and, likely, foregrounding pragmatics in poetic verse and that in some cases it conveys temporal succession through a pragmatic sense acquired from prose narrative.[76]

3.5 The Perfective Conjugation

For the purposes of typological comparison, the BH PFV conjugation is appropriately classified as a perfective gram. However, to understand its particular range of functions, it is best described in terms of its dynamic development through time—especially given the diachronically diverse literature of the HB—and its oppositions to other forms in the BH verbal system. In §3.5 of this chapter, the development of the gram and its range of meanings are explained; in the next chapter, I illustrate its interactions with the other verbal forms in the context of various stretches of discourse.

3.5.1 Diachronic Development of the Perfective

Semitic scholars are widely agreed that the BH PFV is a reflex of the West Semitic suffixed conjugation, which developed from the BH STA cognate attested in Akkadian (see Cook 2012c: 203). As noted above (§3.3.2), this development follows a well-established grammaticalization path (ex. 125), which typologically supports both the stative classification of the originating form and the perfective aspect identification of the PFV and accounts for the variety of meanings exhibited by the PFV in BH. At the earliest stage, the Common Semitic stative was used in a copular expression as a predicate complement, as it is still employed in BH (ex. 148a). The innovation of West Semitic was its grammaticalization of this copular construction to create an inflected verbal conjugation (148b), a process that is evident from the morphological similarities between the independent pronouns and the inflectional endings on the conjugation (e.g., 2MS pronoun אַתָּה and תָּ- inflectional ending).

76. I have not listed foreground as a function of the past narrative in poetry because it is unclear whether the foreground/background distinction applies to poetry as it does in prose narrative. In parallelistic/appositional poetic discourse, lead lines might be interpreted as foreground and appositional lines as background. If this is valid, then it supports the contention that the PN retains its foregrounding function in poetic discourse, inasmuch as the form does not typically appear in appositional poetic lines.

148. Predicate Adjective → Inflected Verb

148a

אַתֶּם קְרֵבִים הַיּוֹם לַמִּלְחָמָה

You (are) drawn near ‹STA› today to war. (Deut. 20:3)

148b

הֵן קָרְבוּ יָמֶיךָ לָמוּת

Hey, your days have drawn near ‹Q.PFV› to die ‹Q.INF›. (Deut. 31:14)

After this new inflected form developed with STA predicates (ex. 148b), it likely spread initially to non-STA unaccusative predicates in which the subject "undergoes" the action (ex. 149a), then to unergative intransitive predicates (ex. 149b), and eventually to dynamic transitive predicates (ex. 149c).[77]

149. Spread of Suffix Conjugation

149a

אֵיךְ נָפְלוּ גִבֹּרִים בְּתוֹךְ הַמִּלְחָמָה

How are the mighty fallen ‹Q.PFV› in the midst of the battle! (2 Sam. 1:25 RSV)

149b

עַל נַהֲרוֹת בָּבֶל שָׁם יָשַׁבְנוּ גַּם־בָּכִינוּ

By the rivers of Babylon, there we sat ‹Q.PFV›, also we wept ‹Q.PFV›. (Ps. 137:1)

149c

בְּיָמָיו בָּנָה חִיאֵל בֵּית הָאֱלִי אֶת־יְרִיחֹה

In his days, Hiel the Bethelite built ‹Q.PFV› Jericho. (1 Kings 16:34)

Semantically, the stative resultative developed into a more dynamic meaning as a perfect, a shift that can be illustrated by the analogous shift of resultative → perfect in English Bible translations (ex. 150).

77. On unaccusative and unergative intransitive predicates, see §2.5.3.

150. Resultative → Perfect

150a. English Past Resultative

וְהָעָם לֹא יָדַע כִּי הָלַךְ יוֹנָתָן

The people knew ‹Q.PFV› not that Jonathan was gone ‹Q.PFV›. (1 Sam. 14:3 KJV, ASV)[78]

150b. English Past Perfect

The people did not know ‹Q.PFV› that Jonathan had gone ‹Q.PFV›. (1 Sam. 14:3 RSV, NRSV, NJPS, ESV)

The shift from perfect → perfective is more subtle and had already largely occurred by the biblical period: throughout the biblical corpus the PFV conjugation may be interpreted with either the earlier perfect sense or a perfective one, depending on whether the implied preceding dynamic event or the current state is in focus. In the first clause of ex. 151, Leah speaks of wages that she continues to retain in the time of speaking; in the second clause, the giving of her servant to her husband is a state of affairs that does not continue into a present state.

151. Perfective Expressing Perfect and Perfective Meanings

וַתֹּאמֶר לֵאָה נָתַן אֱלֹהִים שְׂכָרִי אֲשֶׁר־נָתַתִּי
שִׁפְחָתִי לְאִישִׁי

Leah said ‹Q.PN›, "God has given ‹Q.PFV› my wages, (I) who gave ‹Q.PFV› my servant to my husband." (Gen. 30:18)[79]

This same ambiguity can be found in the present perfect constructions of some modern languages, like the French *passé composé* and the German *Perfekt*.[80] The final shift from perfective → past is evident in the transition from

78. Cf. these versions for Num. 21:28; 1 Sam. 14:17; 2 Sam. 3:23; 1 Kings 1:25; 21:18; Isa. 15:8; 38:8; 45:23; 51:5; Jer. 4:7; 14:2; 23:19; Ezek. 7:10; 19:14; Mic. 2:13; Pss. 19:5; 88:17; Prov. 7:19; Ruth 1:13, 15; Song 6:2.

79. The parenthetical *I* is provided to smooth the English, as a resumption of the relative head, the clitic pronoun "my." On this identification of the relative clause head, see Holmstedt 2016: 112.

80. Linguists distinguish between perfects and "extended-now" perfects, noting that past temporal adverbials (e.g., *hier*/*gestern*/*yesterday*) are acceptable with perfects like French (e.g., *Marie a téléphoné hier*) and German (e.g., *Maria hat gestern angerufen*) but not extended-now perfects, as English has (**Mary has called yesterday*). Examples are from Grønn and Stechow 2016: 326.

BH to post-biblical Hebrew, at which stage, not coincidentally, the PN became obsolete. The key indicator that the conjugation has shifted from perfective to past tense is the gram's shift from a default present-time meaning with STAs to a past-time one (exs. 152a–b). This shift is already in its incipient stage in BH, triggering the new strategy to express present states of STAs by means of the active PTC pattern (ex. 152c).[81]

152. Perfect → Perfective → Past

152a

עַתָּה יָדַעְתִּי כִּי־יְרֵא אֱלֹהִים

Now I know ‹Q.PFV› that (you are) a fearer ‹STA› of God. (Gen. 22:12)

152b

כִּי־יָדְעוּ הָאֲנָשִׁים כִּי־מִלִּפְנֵי יְהוָה הוּא בֹרֵחַ

For the men knew ‹Q.PFV› that from before Yhwh he (was) fleeing ‹Q.PTC›. (Jon. 1:10)

152c

כִּי גַּם־יוֹדֵעַ אָנִי אֲשֶׁר יִהְיֶה־טּוֹב לְיִרְאֵי הָאֱלֹהִים

For also I know ‹Q.PTC› that goodwill ‹Q.IPFV› belongs to fearers of God. (Eccles. 8:12)

Alongside this gradual drift of the perfect conjugation through the realis mood resultative-to-past path, an irrealis meaning emerged for the form, likely through its use in conditional structures. As with other irrealis mood constructions, the IR-PFV is marked by V-S word order in contrast to S-V realis mood order. In the standard grammars, the IR-PFV is described as the waw-conversive or consecutive perfect. The oft-observed ultimate accent shift in the consecutive perfect is inconsistent and likely a late development, an attempt to analyze the form retrospectively (see Revell 1984; Cook 2012c: 210). The construction predominantly appears with a proclitic conjunction -וְ, which traditionally has been taken as a marker of the gram, analogous to the case of the PN. However, IR-PFV examples lacking the conjunction occur, albeit infrequently, suggesting that rather than being part of the inflection of the gram, the waw is due to the prevalent appearance of the gram at the

81. These developments are discussed in more detail in Cook 2012a and 2012c: 203–8.

clause or phrase's front boundary due to the V-S irrealis ordering and the ubiquitous use of the conjunction to mark such boundaries. Explaining it as a V-S irrealis form rather than the traditional consecutive based on ultimate accent and proclitic -וְ allows us to recognize that the IR-PFV and the so-called consecutive perfect do not completely overlap, a perspective that also accords better with the comparative evidence.

Irrealis mood presumably initially attached to the perfect by virtue of the conditional structure: the "if/when" event is postulated as a possible situation or "world" that will make the "then" event accessible or "real," categorizing both events as irrealis mood (see §3.2.3). This classification, therefore, differs from the traditional conversive or consecutive analysis not only in semantics but also in distribution. In ex. 153, both the PFV forms without any waw conjunction in the protases and the PFVs with proclitic -וְ in the apodoses are classified as IR-PFV (i.e., the PFV functioning with irrealis mood). Because the irrealis mood is broad and is effected by the conditional structure, TAM distinctions may still be effected by verb choices in the protasis and apodosis.

153. Conditional Constructions with Perfect Verbs

153a

אִם־אָמַרְנוּ נָבוֹא הָעִיר וְהָרָעָב בָּעִיר וָמַתְנוּ שָׁם וְאִם־יָשַׁבְנוּ פֹה וָמָתְנוּ

If we say ‹Q.IR-PFV›, "Let us enter ‹Q.JUSS› the city," the famine (is) in the city and we will die ‹Q.IR-PFV› there; if we remain ‹Q.IR-PFV› here, we will die ‹Q.IR-PFV›. (2 Kings 7:4)

153b

אִם־חָפֵץ בָּנוּ יְהוָה וְהֵבִיא אֹתָנוּ אֶל־הָאָרֶץ הַזֹּאת וּנְתָנָהּ לָנוּ

If Yhwh is pleased ‹STA/Q.IR-PFV› with us, then he will bring ‹HI.IR-PFV› us into this land and he will give ‹Q.IR-PFV› it to us. (Num. 14:8)

153c

אִם־גֻּלַּחְתִּי וְסָר מִמֶּנִּי כֹחִי וְחָלִיתִי וְהָיִיתִי כְּכָל־הָאָדָם

If I were shaven ‹PU.IR-PFV›, then my strength would depart ‹Q.IR-PFV› from me and I would become weak ‹Q.IR-PFV› and would become ‹Q.IR-PFV› like all men. (Judg. 16:17)

In ex. 153a both the protasis and apodosis PFV forms lack any perceptible "pastness." By contrast, the stative חָפֵץ in the protasis of ex. 153b has its default present-stative sense, while the apodosis has a clear nonpast meaning. The use of the PFV forms in ex. 153c within the context of the Samson and Delilah story suggests that they may express a past-for-counterfactual sense: Samson knows what would happen if his hair *were* shaven, but he expects it *won't* be.

Scholars have recognized a similar pattern in a number of ancient Semitic languages, where forms cognate to the BH PFV appear within conditional constructions in V-S order and sometimes with nonpast (i.e., irrealis) semantics (ex. 154). A perfective gram may occur in the protasis (ex. 154a), apodosis (exs. 154b–c), or both (ex. 154d).

154. West Semitic Perfect with Irrealis Semantics in Conditional Clauses (from Cook 2012c: 251)

154a. Imperial Aramaic

hn grynk dyn wdbb wgryn lbr bbrh lk wlmn zy ṣbyt lmntn ʾnḥn nntn lk ksp

If we institute against you suit or process or institute (suit) against son or[82] daughter of yours or (anyone) to whom you desire to give (it), we shall give you silver. Porten and Yardeni 1986: B3 4.14–15; see discussion in Folmer 1995: 395)

154b. El-Amarna Canaanite

allū paṭārima awīlūt ḫupšī u ṣabtū *lú.pl.*GAZ *āla*

Behold, if the serfs desert, then the Ḫapiru will capture the city. (Moran 2003: 31)

154c. Phoenician

wʾm mlk bmlkm wrzn brznm . . . ymḥ šm ʾztwd bšʿr z wšt šm . . . wmḥ bʿlšmm wʾl qn ʾrṣ . . . ʾyt hmmlkt hʾ wʾyt hmlk hʾ wʾyt ʾdm hʾ

And if a king among kings and ruler among rulers . . . erases the name of Azitawada on this gate and places his name . . . then Baalshamen and El, creator of the earth,

82. The text reads "in/with," but this is likely a scribal error.

will erase that kingdom and that king and that man.
(*KAI* 26 III.12–IV.1; see discussion in Krahmalkov 1986: 9–10)

154d. Arabic

ʾin qatalum ṣāḥibayya qataltu ṣāḥibaykum

If you kill my two friends, I will kill yours.
(from Peled 1992: 18; see also Wright 1962: 2.15)

The likely origin of the deontic function of the IR-PFV lies more specifically in conditional law codes, in which the apodosis verb expresses not only an irrealis contingent situation but a deontic one (ex. 155).

155. Conditional-Deontic Construction with Perfect Verbs

וְכִי־יִגֹּף שׁוֹר־אִישׁ אֶת־שׁוֹר רֵעֵהוּ וָמֵת וּמָכְרוּ אֶת־הַשּׁוֹר הַחַי וְחָצוּ אֶת־כַּסְפּוֹ

If/when the ox of a man gores ‹Q.IPFV› the ox of his neighbor and it dies ‹Q.IR-PFV›, they should/must sell ‹Q.IR-PFV› the living ox and should/must divide in two ‹Q.IR-PFV› its price. (Exod. 21:35)

Once the V-S-ordered PFV became associated with irrealis mood within the context of conditional law codes, we can surmise that its usage spread beyond the structure, taking the most prevalent functions with it, including expressing conditional structures without any conditional word (ex. 156a), and nonconditional expressions of deontic (ex. 156b, first clause) and contingent (ex. 156b, second clause) modality (see further §3.5.3 below).

156. Spread of Irrealis Meanings for Perfect Verb

156a. Unmarked Conditional Clause

וּדְפָקוּם יוֹם אֶחָד וָמֵתוּ כָּל־הַצֹּאן

If they drive ‹Q.IR-PFV› them one day, then the whole flock will die ‹Q.IR-PFV›. (Gen. 33:13)

156b. Nonconditional Deontic and Contingent Modalities

וְעָשׂוּ לִי מִקְדָּשׁ וְשָׁכַנְתִּי בְּתוֹכָם׃

They should make ‹Q.IR-PFV› for me a sanctuary, so that I might dwell ‹Q.IR-PFV› in their midst. (Exod. 25:8)

3.5.2 Realis Perfective

The wide divergence in the PFV's realis and irrealis functions warrant making mood the major division in treating the gram.[83] As described in the preceding section (§3.5.1), diachronically the BH PFV is at a transitional stage of development between perfect and perfective aspect, similar to the French *passé composé* or German *Perfekt*.[84] Semantically these two meanings are distinct (see above §3.3.1) and can be modeled as such based on whether perfect (PERF $= \text{RF} \subset \text{EF}_{\text{CODA}}$) or perfective (PFV $= \text{RF} \subset \text{EF}_{\text{NUCLEUS}}$) is assigned to the aspect phrase in the distributed morphology structure (fig. 3.7).[85] The perfect shows three temporal varieties, indicated by the optional values for the tense phrase (in curly brackets): past (RF<S), present (RF,S), or future (S<RF). By contrast, the perfective, although it can appear in all three temporal spheres, shows a strong implicature relationship with past-time event expression, indicated by the parenthetical (PAST) in the tense phrase.

83. The notable divergence is evident in the traditional approaches, which typically treat the two mood functions as expressed by two distinct verbal conjugations, the nonconversive/nonconsecutive and the conversive/consecutive form. Whether the PFV gram is polysemous (i.e., having both a realis and irrealis meaning) or if realis PFV and IR-PFV are homonyms (i.e., distinct conjugations) is unanswerable and a matter of the degree of distance between them (see the note in the paragraph preceding ex. 183). It makes no practical difference in the analysis of IR-PFV.

84. While Grønn and Stechow (2016: 326) distinguish between the "extended now semantics" of English and Scandinavian perfects versus the "relative past semantics" of German and French perfects (see the first note in the paragraph following ex. 151), Bybee, Perkins, and Pagliuca (1994: 78) use the term "old anteriors" to describe forms that "represent an intermediate stage between pure anterior [i.e., perfect] and past or perfective." For an argument that BH PFV belongs in this category, see Grasso 2021, though he uses the term "perfect" rather than "old anterior." I have consistently labeled the BH PFV as a perfective form on the basis of its furthest developed semantics (i.e., perfective aspect), while recognizing that it has retained its earlier perfect meaning. This approach has the advantage of clarifying the central opposition in the system as perfective/imperfective grams.

85. Constructions in which the perfect combines with another aspect, notably with the progressive (e.g., English *have been doing*), require separate perfect phrase (PerfP) and aspect phrase (AspP) heads in the tree. Because such constructions are rare in BH (e.g., 2 Sam. 3:17; 2 Kings 9:14; Isa. 9:15; Ezek. 34:2; 44:19; Ps. 122:2; Ezra 4:2; Neh. 5:11) and the perfect and perfective meanings are mutually exclusive for the PFV gram, I have simplified the model to include only an AspP, except in such cases (see fig. 3.10).

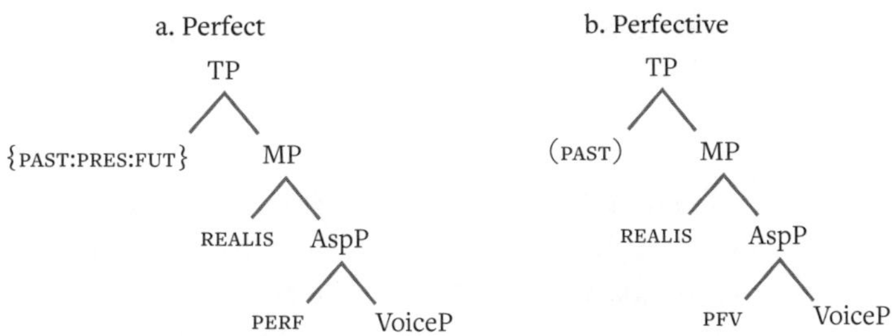

Figure 3.7. Perfect and Perfective Aspect (Realis Mood)

Despite these differences, perfective and perfect aspect are expressed by a single verbal form in some languages (e.g., German, French, BH), where the perfect aspect can be seen as a narrower, often optional, semantic meaning as determined by the context (see the discussion of this point generally in §3.3.1 above, and with respect to the PN, in §3.4.2). The free variation of the English simple past (= perfective past) and perfect verb glosses for the following examples illustrates the general optionality of the perfect interpretation for these PFVs. At the same time, there is a difference of "focus" between the perfective and perfect that is discernible in many passages. For example, in ex. 157, glossing the two PFV verbs as simple past adequately conveys the temporal-logical relationships among the reported events. A present perfect does not alter this interpretation but instead shifts the focus of Joab's concern to the resultant state of David's actions, to the fact that Abner is now gone (i.e., at the time of Joab's speaking). He underscores this concern by the PN וַיֵּלֶךְ, which is temporally successive with the PFV שִׁלַּחְתּוֹ and reinforces the resultant state of Abner's absence at the time of Joab's speech.

157. Semantic Contrast between Perfective and Perfect

וַיָּבֹא יוֹאָב אֶל־הַמֶּלֶךְ וַיֹּאמֶר מֶה עָשִׂיתָה הִנֵּה־בָא אַבְנֵר אֵלֶיךָ לָמָּה־זֶּה שִׁלַּחְתּוֹ וַיֵּלֶךְ הָלוֹךְ

Joab came ‹Q.PN› to the king and said ‹Q.PN›, "What did you do/have you done ‹Q.PFV›? Look, Abner came ‹Q.PFV› to you. Why is this (that) you dismissed/have dismissed ‹PI.PFV› him and he went ‹Q.PN› away ‹Q.AINF›?" (2 Sam. 3:24)[86]

86. Judg. 6:29; 15:6; 1 Kings 1:24; Esther 6:3.

Thus the interpretation of the PFV as perfective or as perfect depends semantically on whether the predicate in its context focuses the reader's attention more suitably on the event or on its implied resultant state. The latter, as a stative expression, correctly predicts that PFVs with a perfect sense form part of the background material in the discourse. This suggests that syntax may also aid in distinguishing between a perfective or perfect interpretation: while the perfect PFV predominates in subordinate clauses, which are categorically background information, the perfective interpretation is more frequently suitable for PFVs in independent or main clauses, as illustrated in the contrastive PFVs in ex. 158. However, this is no more than a general tendency.

158. Syntactic Contrast between Perfective and Perfect

וַיהוָה נָתַן חָכְמָה לִשְׁלֹמֹה כַּאֲשֶׁר דִּבֶּר־לוֹ

And Yhwh gave ‹Q.PFV› wisdom to Solomon just as he had said ‹PI.PFV› to him. (1 Kings 5:26)[87]

The tensed varieties of the perfect aspect are associated with discourse modes of the appropriate temporality: past perfect with past narrative (ex. 159); present perfect with speech, whose reference time is established by the speaker's "present" (ex. 160); and future perfect with future/irrealis discourse (ex. 161). The examples in ex. 159 illustrate the past perfect interpretation of the PFV in a subordinate and independent clause. In ex. 159a Rachel's earlier theft of the household gods is important background information that explains Laban's search and the ignorance of which accounts for Jacob's reaction in the context. The PFV verb in ex. 159b is also background information: it sets up the dilemma to which the people weepingly respond in the following foreground verse (Judg. 20:2) by referencing the oath previously sworn when the tribes assembled at Mizpah (see Judg. 20:1).

159. Past Perfect PFV

159a

לֹא־יָדַע יַעֲקֹב כִּי רָחֵל גְּנָבָתַם

Jacob did not know ‹Q.PFV› that Rachel stole/had stolen ‹Q.PFV› them. (Gen. 31:32)[88]

87. Deut. 34:9; Judg. 21:15; 1 Sam. 1:22; 2 Sam. 13:30; 1 Kings 2:28; 2 Kings 5:1; 2 Chron. 11:13–14; 26:20.

88. Gen. 1:31; 36:6; 39:13; 42:9; 43:2; Exod. 9:12; 18:1; 39:42–43; 40:27; Num. 22:2, 36; 23:30; Deut. 9:21; Josh. 2:7; 4:14; 8:31; Judg. 2:7; 14:9; 16:20; 20:22; 1 Sam. 10:26; 30:12; 2 Sam. 8:9; 11:27; 13:10; 1 Kings 2:27; 12:2; 13:5; 2 Kings 5:8; 7:17; 25:16; Isa. 37:8; Jer. 38:27; 41:18; Jon.

159b

וְאִישׁ יִשְׂרָאֵל נִשְׁבַּע בַּמִּצְפָּה לֵאמֹר אִישׁ מִמֶּנּוּ לֹא־יִתֵּן בִּתּוֹ לְבִנְיָמִן לְאִשָּׁה׃

Now (every) man of Israel swore/had sworn ‹NI.PFV› at Mizpah [COMP], "Every one of us will not give ‹Q.IPFV› his daughter to Benjamin for a wife." (Judg. 21:1; see 20:1)[89]

In the context of reported speech, the PFV verb may express the cause of the state that exists at the speech time, resulting in a present-perfect interpretation (ex. 160). In ex. 160b it is the state of Israel's current (to Moses's speech) numerousness. The copular statement that finishes the sentence clarifies and reinforces the implied resultant state expressed by the PFV verb, thus making the present-perfect interpretation of the PFV form felicitous.

160. Present Perfect PFV

160a

הַרְפֵּה־לָהּ כִּי־נַפְשָׁהּ מָרָה־לָהּ וַיהוָה הֶעְלִים מִמֶּנִּי וְלֹא הִגִּיד לִי

Leave her be ‹HI.IMPV›, for her soul is embittered ‹Q.PFV› for her and Yhwh has hidden ‹HI.PFV› (it) from me and has not told ‹HI.PFV› me. (2 Kings 4:27)[90]

160b

יְהוָה אֱלֹהֵיכֶם הִרְבָּה אֶתְכֶם וְהִנְּכֶם הַיּוֹם כְּכוֹכְבֵי הַשָּׁמַיִם לָרֹב

Yhwh your God multiplied/has multiplied ‹HI.PFV› you, and look, today you (are) as the stars of the heavens with respect to numerousness. (Deut. 1:10)[91]

1:10; 3:10; Ruth 1:6; 2:17; Esther 4:7; 6:14; Ezra 8:22; Neh. 2:1; 6:1; 9:23; 1 Chron. 10:11; 19:6; 2 Chron. 12:9; 33:22; 35:18.

89. Exod. 24:13; Deut. 9:16; Josh. 22:7; Judg. 4:11; 1 Sam. 4:18; 25:21; 30:14; 2 Sam. 17:14; 2 Kings 7:6–7, 17; 8:1; Ezek. 33:22; 37:8; Neh. 2:1; 2 Chron. 35:18.

90. Gen. 3:22; 39:8; 43:23; 44:16; Exod. 3:9; 4:11; 32:30; 33:12; Lev. 17:11; 20:18; Josh. 9:19; 22:2; 23:3; Judg. 6:29; 7:2; 15:18; 21:7; 1 Sam. 1:28; 12:20; 16:1; 21:3; 2 Sam. 1:16; 12:13; 24:17; 1 Kings 3:6–7; 8:53; 2 Kings 5:22; 19:11; Jer. 27:6; 44:26; Ezra 10:2, 10; Neh. 1:3; 2 Chron. 12:5; 13:11; 36:23.

91. Gen. 4:11; 5:29; 16:11; 18:19; 20:9; 31:15; Exod. 4:21; 5:21; 18:10; 32:21; Josh. 2:9, 17; 9:9; 23:3; Judg. 1:7; 4:14; 6:36; 1 Sam. 4:22; 20:8; 23:7; 2 Sam. 19:7, 21; 1 Kings 1:29; 2:24; 3:13; 8:36; 9:6; 19:10; 2 Kings 7:12; 17:38; 18:20; 20:3; 21:11; Ezra 9:2; 1 Chron. 17:5–6, 27; 22:18; 2 Chron. 6:4, 15, 18; 9:8; 34:21.

Future perfect expressions are less common than either present perfect or past perfect ones, and instances of the PFV with this sense are more dubious.[92] Almost all of the identified examples occur in subordinate clauses, frequently preceded by a temporal marker such as עַד אֲשֶׁר־אִם ,עַד אֲשֶׁר ,עַד אִם ,עַד ("until when"). Again, a future perfect English gloss is not required to correctly interpret the passage. In ex. 161a it is clear enough that the PFV event precedes the future/irrealis time set by the preceding predicates (IPFV, IR-PFV), and so a perfective past or present perfect gloss is equally acceptable (as most English versions reflect). The future perfect interpretation is less avoidable in ex. 161b, where the temporal בְּיוֹם makes it inevitable that the second PFV form be interpreted future of the time of speaking.[93] Yet the PFV expresses not simple future, as the IPFV might, but an event anterior to the future time of acquiring the field, implying that the field and Ruth are an inseparable "package deal" for the kinsman redeemers.

161. Future Perfect PFV

161a

וַאֲנִי אֶתֵּן אֶת־פָּנַי בָּאִישׁ הַהוּא וְהִכְרַתִּי אֹתוֹ מִקֶּרֶב עַמּוֹ
כִּי מִזַּרְעוֹ נָתַן לַמֹּלֶךְ

I will set ‹Q.IPFV› my face against that one so that I cut him off ‹HI.IR-PFV› from the midst of his people, because he gave (NJPS)/has given (RSV)/ will have given ‹Q.PFV› one of his offspring to Molech. (Lev. 20:3)[94]

161b

וַיֹּאמֶר בֹּעַז בְּיוֹם־קְנוֹתְךָ הַשָּׂדֶה מִיַּד נָעֳמִי וּמֵאֵת רוּת
הַמּוֹאֲבִיָּה אֵשֶׁת־הַמֵּת קָנִיתִי לְהָקִים שֵׁם־הַמֵּת עַל־נַחֲלָתוֹ׃

Boaz said ‹Q.PN›, "On the day you acquire ‹Q.INF› the field from Naomi, you will have acquired ‹Q.PFV *qere*› Ruth the Moabitess, wife of the dead ‹Q.PTC›, in order to raise up ‹HI.INF› the name of the dead ‹Q.PTC› on his inherited property." (Ruth 4:5)

92. A case in point, Joosten (2012: 205n16) notes that Gen. 24:14, אֹתָהּ הֹכַחְתָּ לְעַבְדְּךָ לְיִצְחָק ("you will have designated ‹HI.PFV› her for your servant, for Isaac"), is the "only certain case" of a future perfect PFV in a main/independent clause. A future perfect interpretation suggests that Yhwh has yet to designate Rebekah when the servant speaks. However, an equally acceptable interpretation is that Yhwh has already designated her, and the servant is merely requesting to be informed of Yhwh's choice. In that case, the PFV would be interpreted as present perfect or perfective past.

93. Notwithstanding, ASV and NJPS translate with a deontic sense "must buy." The future perfect interpretation is consonant with the translations in RSV and NRSV.

94. Gen. 24:19, 33; 28:15; Deut. 8:10; Num. 32:17; 1 Kings 8:47; 2 Kings 7:3; Isa. 6:11; 30:17; Jer. 8:3; 29:14, 18; 32:37; 46:28; Ezek. 29:13; Eccles. 2:16; Ruth 2:21; Dan. 11:36.

The future time frame of such PFVs raises the question of whether they should be classified as future tense or irrealis mood. A number of future perfect PFV examples appear in conditional structures (ex. 162), in which the structure itself imposes irrealis mood, and yet, as pointed out above (§3.5.1), tense-aspect distinctions may be preserved.

162. Future Perfect PFV in Conditional Protasis

וְאַתָּה כִּי־הִזְהַרְתָּ רָשָׁע מִדַּרְכּוֹ לָשׁוּב מִמֶּנָּה וְלֹא־שָׁב
מִדַּרְכּוֹ הוּא בַּעֲוֺנוֹ יָמוּת וְאַתָּה נַפְשְׁךָ הִצַּלְתָּ

But if/when you warn a wicked person from his way, to return from it, and he does not return from it, (then) he for his iniquity will die, but you your life will have saved ‹HI.PFV›. (Ezek. 33:9)[95]

Given the frequent coincidence of future tense and irreal mood in languages (e.g., English *will*), it might be suggested that the two are mutually implicating, similar to but stronger than is the case with perfective aspect and past tense. However, the meaning is infrequent enough to not require any further analysis here or in the following section on IR-PFV.

The perfective meaning of the PFV, due to its close association with past tense, occurs fairly frequently in past narrative discourse. However, since the PN form dominates in this discourse mode, and perfect interpretations are dominant in subordinate clauses, the PFV verb has a perfective past interpretation particularly at the head or near the conclusion of narrative episodes or scenes, as a means of avoiding the temporal succession associated with the foregrounding PN, and where syntactically the PN is precluded. A new episode in the Elisha narratives is introduced with a PFV (ex. 163a), and after Abram and Lot part ways, we find the summary statement with PFV verbs (ex. 163b).

163. Perfective Past PFV

163a

וְאִשָּׁה אַחַת מִנְּשֵׁי בְנֵי־הַנְּבִיאִים צָעֲקָה אֶל־אֱלִישָׁע

One wife from the wives of the sons of the prophets cried out ‹Q.PFV› to Elisha. (2 Kings 4:1)[96]

95. Gen. 43:9; 2 Kings 7:3; Ezek. 3:19; Ps. 127:1.

96. Gen. 11:27; 13:12, 14; 17:27; 18:33; 21:1; 22:1; 24:1; 36:2; Josh. 21:45; Judg. 3:5; 16:23; 1 Sam. 4:11; 5:1; 16:14; 19:18; 2 Sam. 2:30; 13:21; 17:23–24; 1 Kings 2:12, 46; 10:13; 13:1; 16:29; 20:1; 22:41, 52; 2 Kings 1:3; 3:1; 4:38; 9:1, 11, 27; 11:1; 14:7, 22; 15:13; Jer. 36:32; Job 42:10, 12;

163b

אַבְרָם יָשַׁב בְּאֶרֶץ־כְּנָעַן וְלוֹט יָשַׁב בְּעָרֵי הַכִּכָּר

(So) Abram settled ‹Q.PFV› in the land of Canaan and Lot settled ‹Q.PFV› among the cities of the plain. (Gen. 13:12)

This pattern applies equally to STA predicates, as illustrated in ex. 164; in such contexts, they may be interpreted as a past state or past inchoative event.

164. Perfective Past PFV with STA Predicates

164a. Past Stative STA

וְהָאָדָם יָדַע אֶת־חַוָּה אִשְׁתּוֹ

The man knew ‹Q.PFV› Eve, his wife. (Gen. 4:1)[97]

164b. Past Inchoative STA

וּמָרְדֳּכַי יָדַע אֶת־כָּל־אֲשֶׁר נַעֲשָׂה

Mordecai came to know ‹Q.PFV› all that had happened ‹NI.PFV›. (Esther 4:1)[98]

The PFV can express bounded, and so temporally successive, events just as the PN, but the predominance of the latter in foregrounded temporally successive narratives and the perfect meanings for the PFV make it the verb of choice for avoiding temporal succession. Whether a PFV is interpreted as temporally successive is thus dependent not solely on semantics but also on the discourse mode (see §§4.3–4). For example, it is impossible to avoid a temporally successive interpretation of the two PFV clauses in ex. 165a, whose orders if reversed make no sense: "went up ‹PN› . . . entered . . . took." By contrast, although out of context the three S-V PFV clauses in ex. 165b might be interpreted as successive (i.e., "rose . . . then entered . . . then rained"), the larger context lets us know that these are concurrent, because in the preceding verse (Gen. 19:22) the angels tell Lot that they cannot do anything until he reaches safety. Hence, the sunrise, arrival, and the decimation of Sodom and Gomorrah are reported as independent events that are understood to be temporally coordinated by the discourse.

Esther 7:10; 1 Chron. 29:26; 2 Chron. 9:1, 12; 24:20; 29:1; 36:21. This list consists of only clauses that do not preclude the option of a PN form, such as negated clauses (e.g., 2 Kings 10:31).

97. Gen. 24:1; Josh. 13:1; 1 Kings 1:1; 1 Chron. 23:1.

98. 1 Sam. 13:1; 2 Kings 3:1; 20:1.

165. Temporal Succession and the PFV

165a. PFVs in Temporal Succession

וַיַּעֲלוּ חֲמֵשֶׁת הָאֲנָשִׁים הַהֹלְכִים לְרַגֵּל אֶת־הָאָרֶץ בָּאוּ שָׁמָּה לָקְחוּ אֶת־הַפֶּסֶל וְאֶת־הָאֵפוֹד וְאֶת־הַתְּרָפִים וְאֶת־הַמַּסֵּכָה

The five men who (were) going ‹Q.PTC› to spy out the land went up ‹Q.PN›; they entered ‹Q.PFV› there and took ‹Q.PFV› the image and the ephod and the household gods and the molten image. (Judg. 18:17)[99]

165b. PFVs in Nontemporal Succession

הַשֶּׁמֶשׁ יָצָא עַל־הָאָרֶץ וְלוֹט בָּא צֹעֲרָה׃ וַיהוָה הִמְטִיר עַל־סְדֹם וְעַל־עֲמֹרָה גָּפְרִית וָאֵשׁ מֵאֵת יְהוָה מִן־הַשָּׁמָיִם׃

The sun rose ‹Q.PFV› over the land, and Lot entered ‹Q.PFV› Zoar, and Yhwh rained ‹HI.PFV› upon Sodom and Gomorrah brimstone and fire from Yhwh out of the heavens. (Gen. 19:23–24)[100]

The PFV with a perfective past sense equivalent to the PN is employed in narrative discourse whenever word-order constraints preclude the PN. This includes in negated clauses (ex. 166a), clauses with fronted constituents (ex. 166b), and subordinate clauses (ex. 166c). Many instances of the PFV in subordinate structures are susceptible to a perfect interpretation.

166. Word-Order Motivated PFVs

166a. Negated PFV

וְלֹא־שָׁמַע הַמֶּלֶךְ אֶל־הָעָם

The king did not listen ‹Q.PFV› to the people. (2 Chron. 10:15)[101]

166b. PFV Following Fronted Constituent

וּשְׁתֵּים עֶשְׂרֵה אֲבָנִים הֵקִים יְהוֹשֻׁעַ בְּתוֹךְ הַיַּרְדֵּן

Twelve stones Joshua set up ‹HI.PFV› in the midst of the Jordan. (Josh. 4:9)[102]

99. Gen. 4:18; Exod. 10:13; Esther 7:6–8; 8:14–15; 2 Chron. 2:10–13, 36–40; 5:30–40; 8:33, 36–37; 9:39, 42–43.

100. 2 Kings 17:30–31; Esther 3:5; 2 Chron. 35:8–9.

101. Gen. 8:9; 13:6; 42:4; Exod. 7:21; 14:20; 16:18; Josh. 8:17; 9:18; 10:14; Judg. 1:21; 3:29; 4:16; 1 Sam. 11:11; 13:8; 30:17; 2 Sam. 6:10; 17:19; 1 Kings 12:15; 18:21; 22:50; 2 Kings 3:9; 4:41; 24:4; 25:3; Jer. 40:14; 52:20; Neh. 8:17; 1 Chron. 2:34; 10:4; 11:18; 23:17, 22; 24:28; 27:24; 2 Chron. 5:14; 21:7; 32:25.

102. Gen. 1:5, 10, 27; 3:16; 9:19; 20:16; Exod. 12:28, 50; 14:6; 16:13, 22; Josh. 2:7; 3:16; 4:14; 6:10, 23; Judg. 2:10; 6:19; 8:30; 18:27; 1 Sam. 6:10, 14; 15:8; 25:14, 43; 2 Sam. 2:10; 3:22; 20:1;

166c. PFV in Subordinate Clause

וַיַּבֵּט הַפְּלִשְׁתִּי וַיִּרְאֶה אֶת־דָּוִד וַיִּבְזֵהוּ כִּי־הָיָה נַעַר

The Philistine looked ‹HI.PN› and saw ‹Q.PN› David and despised ‹Q.PN› him because he was ‹Q.PFV› a lad. (1 Sam. 17:42)[103]

Although the present-perfect interpretation of the PFV verb was described above as particularly associated with reported speech, a perfective-past sense also appears in speech, especially in independent clauses (disregarding subordination to the speech verb). Such clauses may constitute isolated events (ex. 167a) or, as in narrative discourse, the perfective past PFV may initiate a speech-embedded narrative episode that is continued by PNs (ex. 167b).

167. PFVs in Reported Speech

167a. For an Isolated Event

וַתָּבֹא הָאִשָּׁה וַתֹּאמֶר לְאִישָׁהּ לֵאמֹר אִישׁ הָאֱלֹהִים בָּא
אֵלַי וּמַרְאֵהוּ כְּמַרְאֵה מַלְאַךְ הָאֱלֹהִים נוֹרָא מְאֹד

The woman came ‹Q.PN› and said ‹Q.PN› to her husband [COMP], “A man of God came ‹Q.PFV› to me, and his appearance (was) like the appearance of a messenger of God—very fearsome ‹NI.PTC›.” (Judg. 13:6)[104]

167b. PFV at the Head of a Narrative Sequence

וַתֹּאמֶר שָׂרַי אֶל־אַבְרָם חֲמָסִי עָלֶיךָ אָנֹכִי נָתַתִּי שִׁפְחָתִי
בְּחֵיקֶךָ וַתֵּרֶא כִּי הָרָתָה וָאֵקַל בְּעֵינֶיהָ

Sarai said ‹Q.PN› to Abram, “May my wrong (be) upon you. I placed ‹Q.PFV› my servant in your embrace, and she saw ‹Q.PN› that she had conceived and I became trivial ‹Q.PN› in her eyes.” (Gen. 16:5)[105]

---

1 Kings 2:11; 3:5; 8:66; 11:2; 18:35; 2 Kings 15:37; 16:9; Esther 2:18; 7:8; 8:1; 9:11, 14; Dan. 1:2, 15; Ezra 1:11; 2:69; Neh. 11:3–4; 12:12; 1 Chron. 1:19; 9:38; 20:4; 2 Chron. 1:15; 4:17; 8:11.

103. Gen. 2:23; 5:5; 16:14; 19:30; 20:11; 21:16; 24:47; 49:28, 30; Exod. 1:21; 3:6; 8:11; 12:40; 32:1; 34:29; Deut. 5:15; Judg. 8:1, 20; 9:55; 1 Sam. 2:25; 14:18; 28:21; 2 Sam. 10:9; 13:22; 1 Kings 3:28; 8:64; 2 Kings 3:26; Esther 7:7; 2 Chron. 20:26.

104. Gen. 28:16; Josh. 14:8; 21:2; Judg. 17:2; 1 Sam. 4:16; 2 Sam. 19:10.

105. Gen. 3:12–13; 19:9; 24:35; 48:3; Josh. 14:8; 22:2; Judg. 6:8; 1 Sam. 10:18; 2 Sam. 1:6–7; 12:7; 2 Kings 1:6; 14:6; 2 Chron. 25:18.

In reported speech, STA predicates conjugated with the PFV frequently exhibit a present stative meaning (ex. 168) in contrast to their past stative sense in narrative (ex. 164), since the reference time is anchored in the speaker's "present" and the default interpretation of PFV with STAs is a present state.

168. PFV with STA Predicate in Reported Speech Expressing Present State

לָמָּה זֶּה צָחֲקָה שָׂרָה לֵאמֹר הַאַף אֻמְנָם אֵלֵד וַאֲנִי זָקַנְתִּי

"Why did Sarah laugh ‹Q.PFV› [lit. Why is this, Sarah laughed] [COMP], 'Shall even I really give birth ‹Q.IPFV› and I am old ‹Q.PFV›?'" (Gen. 18:13)[106]

Passive PFVs (especially Niphals) in reported speech may also at times be interpreted as stative when the context suggests a focus on the resultant state of the passive event rather than the event itself. In the passage in ex. 169, Elijah's concern seems to have little to do with *having been left alone* when the last other prophet of Yhwh died, judging from the less felicitous present-perfect gloss. Rather, his concern is *being left alone* at the moment of his speaking.

169. PFV Passive (NI) in Reported Speech Expressing Present State

וַיֹּאמֶר אֵלִיָּהוּ אֶל־הָעָם אֲנִי נוֹתַרְתִּי נָבִיא לַיהוָה לְבַדִּי

Elijah said ‹Q.PN› to the people, "I alone have been/am left ‹NI.PFV› a prophet of Yhwh." (1 Kings 18:22)[107]

Often the broader pragmatic context plays a role in deciding whether a past or present stative interpretation or even a present-perfect sense is most felicitous for a PFV with a stative predicate in reported speech. In ex. 170 the events recounted by the daughters of Zelophehad are somewhat removed in time and space from the speakers' reference point—in the plains of Moab anticipating entrance into the promised land—and so a past inchoative rather than a past stative interpretation makes the best sense (i.e., "our father died" rather than "our father is dead").

106. Gen. 18:12; 19:31; 20:6; 26:27; 30:29; 31:6; 44:19, 27; Exod. 3:19; 23:9; 32:22; Num. 20:14; Deut. 29:15; 31:27; Josh. 1:2; 13:1; 14:6; 23:2; 1 Sam. 8:5; 12:2; 28:9; 2 Sam. 7:20; 17:8; 1 Kings 1:51; 2:5, 15; 5:17; 12:11; 22:8; 2 Kings 2:5; 4:14; 6:1; 9:11; 2 Chron. 18:7.

107. Lev. 14:35; Josh. 13:1; Dan. 10:17; Neh. 1:3.

170. Contextual Interpretation of PFV with STA

אָבִינוּ מֵת בַּמִּדְבָּר וְהוּא לֹא־הָיָה בְּתוֹךְ הָעֵדָה הַנּוֹעָדִים
עַל־יְהוָה בַּעֲדַת־קֹרַח כִּי־בְחֶטְאוֹ מֵת וּבָנִים לֹא־הָיוּ לוֹ

Our father died ‹STA/Q.PFV› in the wilderness. He was ‹Q.PFV› not among the congregation that gathered themselves together against Yhwh with the congregation of Korah, but for his own sin he died ‹STA/Q.PFV›, and he did not have ‹STA/Q.PFV› sons. (Num. 27:3)[108]

The case with הי"ה is somewhat different, since a null copula strategy is available to express a present state: for example, the last clause in ex. 170 could have been expressed with the אַיִן existential with a present stative sense, וּבָנִים אֵין לוֹ, "he does not have sons." The fact that their father died sometime back suggests that the לֹא־הָיוּ was chosen expressly to mark his lack of male offspring as a past state, which nevertheless continues to the speaker's present time, because states are not "bounded" by perfective aspect.[109]

The range of interpretations of the PFV verb in prophetic speech and poetry parallels that of the form in reported speech within prose narrative. All four PFV verbs in ex. 171a can be interpreted as perfective past or present perfect. In ex. 171b the overt copular is employed to clearly mark a past (versus present) stative interpretation of the clause. By contrast, the temporal וְעַתָּה in ex. 171c forces an inchoative interpretation ("I have become") of the overt copular instead of a past state ("I was"). Finally, the STA predicates in ex. 171d are ambiguous between a present perfect and present stative interpretation.

171. PFV in Prophetic and Poetic Discourse

171a

שִׁמְעוּ שָׁמַיִם וְהַאֲזִינִי אֶרֶץ כִּי יְהוָה דִּבֵּר בָּנִים גִּדַּלְתִּי
וְרוֹמַמְתִּי וְהֵם פָּשְׁעוּ בִי

Listen ‹Q.IMPV›, heavens, and give ear ‹HI.IMPV›, earth, because Yhwh has spoken/spoke ‹PI.PFV›: "Sons I (have) raised ‹PI.PFV› and I (have) reared ‹POLEL.PFV›, but they (have) rebelled ‹Q.PFV› against me." (Isa. 1:2)[110]

108. Josh. 17:4; 21:2; Judg. 6:8; 11:23; 1 Sam. 10:18; 15:6; 2 Sam. 7:24; 12:7; 19:10; 1 Kings 1:17; 12:4, 10–11, 14; 2 Kings 9:25; 10:18; 2 Chron. 12:5. Often a temporal modifier like לְפָנִים ("previously, earlier") can be inserted into the clause without altering the sense of the temporal distance between the event and the time of speaking.

109. Gen. 1:2; 3:1; 4:2; Judg. 8:11; 11:1; 1 Sam. 3:16; 13:2; 1 Kings 15:16; Ezra 8:31; 2 Chron. 13:7.

110. Isa. 42:6; 45:12–13; 48:13; Jer. 2:21; 5:7; Ezek. 7:6; 11:24; Hosea 8:4; 11:3; Amos 4:6; Pss. 2:6; 124:7; Job 5:3; 6:3; 10:8; Prov. 4:2; 8:22.

171b

כִּי־בֵן הָיִיתִי לְאָבִי רַךְ וְיָחִיד לִפְנֵי אִמִּי

When a son was ‹Q.PFV› I to my father, a tender only (child) before my mother . . . (Prov. 4:3)[111]

171c

וְעַתָּה נְגִינָתָם הָיִיתִי וָאֱהִי לָהֶם לְמִלָּה

Now I have become ‹Q.PFV› their song, and I became ‹Q.PN› to them a byword. (Job 30:9)[112]

171d

אֲנִי יָדַעְתִּי אֶפְרַיִם וְיִשְׂרָאֵל לֹא־נִכְחַד מִמֶּנִּי

I know/have known ‹Q.PFV› Ephraim, and Israel is not hidden/has not been hidden ‹NI.PFV› from me. (Hosea 5:3)[113]

The realis PFV verb expressing perfective aspect in the sphere of present time is greatly restricted because of the close association of imperfective aspect and present tense (see Bybee, Perkins, and Pagliuca 1994: 141)—an association analogous and complementary to that between perfective aspect and past tense. The restriction is similar to the case of the English simple present, which is dispreferred to describe an event taking place at the speaker's reference time, apart from play-by-play sports announcing, where the description lags mere seconds or less behind the occurrence of each event (e.g., *he dribbles, he shoots, he scores*), and performative expressions, by which a speaker performs an action by stating the event (e.g., *I hereby pronounce/christen/resign . . .*). Semantically, the restriction of the simple present to these uses is due to the perfective character of the construction (versus imperfective/progressive, used to describe events ongoing at the speech time; e.g., *she is running* vs. *she runs*; see §3.3.2 and the first note in that section), which associates the "completion" of the event with the completion of the statement of the event.

Obviously, BH lacks any examples of play-by-play announcing, but it does have examples of the PFV verb used in performative expressions. The perfective character of the verb makes it more suitable than either the IPFV or progressive PTC, both of which are semantically more compatible with

111. Isa. 5:1; 38:17; 42:21; Jer. 5:8; 11:19; Ezek. 7:19; 16:31; 19:10; Nah. 3:9; Pss. 18:18; 73:22; 78:53; 99:8; Job 16:12; 29:10; 36:16; Song 8:10; Lam. 4:9, 18.

112. Isa. 1:14, 21; 44:12; Pss. 39:4; 83:10; 114:2; Eccles. 2:9.

113. Isa. 33:9; 37:27; 47:14; Jer. 5:27; Ezek. 9:9; 22:4; Pss. 96:10; 116:10; Job 7:6; 9:25; 23:2.

expressing events ongoing at the present speech time. Performative examples are not always unambiguous, such as the equivocal perfect/performative interpretation of examples like ex. 172a. Others are more clearly performative by virtue of appearing within a cultic "script," as is the case in ex. 172b. The most frequent structure associated with performative expressions appears to be clauses with הִנֵּה and a first-person PFV, sometimes accompanied by other indications of the instantaneous character of the event, such as הַיּוֹם in ex. 172c.

172. PFV for Performative Expressions

172a

אָז אָמַרְתִּי הִנֵּה־בָאתִי

Then I said ‹Q.PFV›, "Hey, I (have/hereby) come ‹Q.PFV›." (Ps. 40:8)[114]

172b

וְעַתָּה הִנֵּה הֵבֵאתִי אֶת־רֵאשִׁית פְּרִי הָאֲדָמָה

Now, hey, I bring ‹Q.PFV› the firstfruits of the ground. (Deut. 26:10)

172c

וְעַתָּה הִנֵּה פִתַּחְתִּיךָ הַיּוֹם מִן־הָאזִקִּים אֲשֶׁר עַל־יָדֶךָ

Now, hey, I release ‹PI.PFV› you today from the shackles that are on your hands. (Jer. 40:4)

There are a number of performative-like examples that tend toward a future rather than present temporal interpretation but might be understood as an extension of the performative meaning (cf. *IBHS* §30.5.1d, "perfect of resolve"). In these "commissive" expressions, the speaker commits to carrying out a specified action, though it may not occur immediately (Austin 1962: 156). The relationship between the performative and commissive is analogous to that between the present progressive and prospective aspects: the former of each pair (i.e., progressive and performative) describe an event occurring at the reference time; the latter of each pair (i.e., prospective and commissive) describe an event whose realization lies in the future but is presented as already underway, portrayed either as already in progress (prospective) or as committed to doing so (ex. 173a). Such examples are rare, even by comparison

114. Gen. 1:29; 19:21; 48:22; Exod. 31:6; Lev. 17:11; Num. 3:12; 18:6, 8, 21; Deut. 26:10; 30:18; Judg. 2:3; 1 Sam. 17:10; 2 Sam. 14:21; 1 Kings 3:12; Isa. 41:15; Jer. 1:9, 18; 40:4; 44:26; Ezek. 3:8; 4:5; 16:27; 22:13; Mic. 6:13.

with the infrequent performative. Moreover, it is perhaps preferable to analyze these few occurrences as cases of IR-PFV without the proclitic -וְ conjunction, considering that some of these examples are conjoined to unambiguous IR-PFVs (ex. 173b) and that unambiguous IR-PFVs may be employed for such expressions (ex. 173c).

173. PFV for Commissive Expressions

173a

וַיֹּאמֶר יְהוָה יְהוּדָה יַעֲלֶה הִנֵּה **נָתַתִּי** אֶת־הָאָרֶץ בְּיָדוֹ׃

Yhwh said ‹Q.PN›, "Judah shall go up ‹Q.IPFV›; hey, I give ‹Q.PFV› the land into his hand." (Judg. 1:2)[115]

173b

וּלְיִשְׁמָעֵאל שְׁמַעְתִּיךָ הִנֵּה **בֵּרַכְתִּי** אֹתוֹ **וְהִפְרֵיתִי** אֹתוֹ **וְהִרְבֵּיתִי** אֹתוֹ בִּמְאֹד מְאֹד

And regarding Ishmael, I have heard ‹Q.PFV› you. Look, I bless ‹PI.IR?-PFV› him and/so that I will make him fruitful ‹HI.IR-PFV› and multiply ‹HI.IR-PFV› him exceedingly much. (Gen. 17:20)

173c

וּבֵרַכְתִּיהָ וְהָיְתָה לְגוֹיִם מַלְכֵי עַמִּים מִמֶּנָּה יִהְיוּ׃

I will bless ‹PI.IR-PFV› her so that she becomes ‹Q.IR-PFV› nations; kings of peoples will come ‹Q.IPFV› from her. (Gen. 17:16)

Alongside this uncertain realis category of commissive, the PFV in counterfactual expressions, the so-called prophetic perfect, and the dubious optative/precative meaning all properly belong to the sphere of irrealis mood and are addressed in the following section (§3.5.3).

The PFV in generic expressions deserves further comment here. In a few cases, examples of the "gnomic perfect" (e.g., *IBHS* §30.4b) are likely IR-PFV expressing habituality, as illustrated by the clear V-S word order in ex. 174, which suggests that the verb is a habitual IR-PFV.

174. IR-PFV Expressing Habituality

אָמַר עָצֵל שַׁחַל בַּדָּרֶךְ אֲרִי בֵּין הָרְחֹבוֹת

115. Gen. 17:16 (the נָתַתִּי clause); 23:13; Num. 11:18; 1 Sam. 17:10; Jer. 13:26; 2 Chron. 12:5.

A lazy person is wont to say ‹Q.IR-PFV›, "A lion in the street! A lion in the square!" (Prov. 26:13)[116]

In general, however, the "gnomic perfect" is a bit of a misnomer, suggesting as it does (for English speakers at least) that it is semantically a present tense meaning for the form. Cross-linguistically, languages show a tendency toward "minimal marking" of generic expressions, and they rarely have a dedicated generic verb construction. Rather, generic expressions can be found in a variety of TAM forms: e.g., *A bird in hand is worth two in the bush* (present); *Boys will be boys* (future); *Curiosity killed the cat* (past). This is likely because generic expressions refer to kinds of events or universal situations rather than particular ones, however that distinction is understood.[117] Hence, the realis PFV in generic expressions is expected to retain its usual range of TAM. This includes perfect aspect (ex. 175a) and perfective past (ex. 175b). Especially in narrative combination with the PN, the generic PFV may convey an anecdotal form of wisdom saying (ex. 175c; see Cook 2005: 130–31).

175. PFV in Generic Expressions

175a

אֹזֶן שֹׁמַעַת וְעַיִן רֹאָה יְהוָה עָשָׂה גַם־שְׁנֵיהֶם

An ear that hears ‹Q.PTC› and an eye that sees ‹Q.PTC›—Yhwh (has) made ‹Q.PFV› both of them. (Prov. 20:12)[118]

175b

מָצָא אִשָּׁה מָצָא טוֹב וַיָּפֶק רָצוֹן מֵיְהוָה

He found ‹Q.PFV› a wife, he found ‹Q.PFV› good, and received ‹HI.PN› favor from Yhwh. (Prov. 18:22; cf. NJPS)

175c

עִיר גִּבֹּרִים עָלָה חָכָם וַיֹּרֶד עֹז מִבְטֶחָה

116. Num. 11:8; 1 Sam. 7:17; 8:1(?); Eccles. 12:9 (תִּקֵּן), 10.

117. Linguists have offered a number of approaches to try to account for the "kind-referring" or "universal" character of generic expressions, including inductivist, rules-and-regulations, and alternative-based theories (see Cook 2005: 120–21).

118. Prov. 11:7; 13:24; 14:7; 16:30; 20:16; 21:7, 25; 22:9; 27:13.

A wise man went up ‹Q.PFV› to a city of warriors and brought down ‹HI. PN› the strength of the stronghold. (Prov. 21:22; cf. RSV, ESV)[119]

3.5.3 Irrealis Perfective

The IR-PFV is distinct from the realis PFV in mood (fig. 3.8). Just as the realis PFV was associated with a default past-tense interpretation, so the IR-PFV is associated with future tense, which is closely associated with irrealis mood cross-linguistically. Since aspectual distinctions may be evident even in irrealis structures, the model provides for either a perfect or perfective aspectual head. Obviously, which of these occurs can affect tense marking, which otherwise defaults to future.

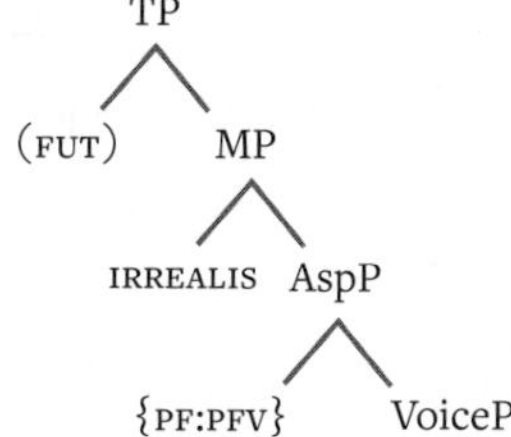

Figure 3.8. Irrealis Perfective (IR-PFV)

This categorization is not merely a departure of nomenclature from the traditional waw-conversive/consecutive perfect, which is a morphologically defined category based on the requisite waw conjunction and ultimate stress shift, despite the inconsistency of the latter (see §3.4.1). Rather, the IR-PFV can be identified with the morphological PFV form in expressions with overt lexical marking of irrealis mood, in irrealis mood constructions (e.g., protasis-apodosis conditionals), or with a proclitic -וְ. Thus, all three verbs in ex. 176 are IR-PFV, based on the irrealis context of the conditional clause, whose protasis is overtly marked by the counterfactual negative לוּלֵא.

119. Prov. 11:8; 22:12; Eccles. 9:14–15.

176. Lexically Marked IR-PFV

לוּלֵי יְהוָה צְבָאוֹת הוֹתִיר לָנוּ שָׂרִיד כִּמְעָט כִּסְדֹם הָיִינוּ לַעֲמֹרָה דָּמִינוּ׃

Had not Yhwh of Hosts left ‹NI.IR-PFV› for us a few survivors, as Sodom we would have become ‹Q.IR-PFV›; we would have become like ‹Q.IR-PFV› Gomorrah. (Isa. 1:9)[120]

Aside from appearing in irrealis syntactic structures or being preceded by an irrealis lexeme (e.g., לוּלֵא, "if not"; לוּ, "if"; אִם, "if"), the IR-PFV rarely lacks the proclitic -וְ, and if it does, the word order and/or context make clear the irrealis semantics, as in the habitual example in ex. 177 (see also ex. 174 and the accompanying note):[121] the preponderance of proclitic -וְ IR-PFVs in the verse makes it evident that both the initial V-S clause (minus the -וְ) and the דָּכוּ clause (no overt subject and אוֹ, "or," conjunction) should likewise be analyzed as IR-PFVs.

177. IR-PFV without Proclitic -וְ

שָׁטוּ הָעָם וְלָקְטוּ וְטָחֲנוּ בָרֵחַיִם אוֹ דָכוּ בַּמְּדֹכָה וּבִשְּׁלוּ בַּפָּרוּר וְעָשׂוּ אֹתוֹ עֻגוֹת

The people would go around ‹Q.IR-PFV› and gather ‹Q.IR-PFV› and grind with millstones or beat ‹Q.IR-PFV› with the mortar and boil ‹PI.IR-PFV› in the pot and make ‹Q.IR-PFV› it into cakes. (Num. 11:8)

The main semantic functions of the IR-PFV are three: to express contingent modality (i.e., conditional and temporal protasis-apodosis constructions and result or purpose clauses), deontic modality, habituality, and counterfactuality. These functions of the IR-PFV can be explained by a closer examination of the mechanism of context-induced reinterpretation responsible for the

120. The collocation כִּמְעַט + PFV can be interpreted as counterfactual (so irrealis mood) or as a realis PFV with adverbial phrasal "almost became." While the לוּלֵי protasis marker makes the latter reading less felicitous in this case (so also Ps. 94:17), in other cases the choice is less clear: כִּמְעַט כִּלּוּנִי בָאָרֶץ וַאֲנִי לֹא־עָזַבְתִּי פִקֻּדֶיךָ׃, "they almost made an end/would have made an end of me in the land, but I have not abandoned your statutes" (Ps. 119:87). The adverbial reading suggests that despite almost being destroyed, the psalmist has not abandoned the statutes; by contrast, the irrealis interpretation implies that not abandoning the statutes has saved the psalmist from destruction.

121. Joosten (2012: 218) contends that "most" cases of the IR-PFV without the proclitic -וְ "are text-critically or otherwise doubtful." In the case of Num. 11:8, he (2012: 218n41) notes that the Septuagint appears to attest to וְשָׁטוּ in its rendering of the form with an imperfect verb (διεπορεύετο).

development of the IR-PFV starting in conditional clauses (§3.5.1). Heine, Ulrike, and Hünnemeyer (1991: 71–72) describe this mechanism in three stages: stage 1, the development of an additional meaning(s) for a form within a specific context; stage 2, the spread of that new meaning(s) to structures other than the original one; stage 3, conventionalization of the new meaning(s) alongside the earlier one, creating a polysemous gram.

The first stage in this context-induced development of IR-PFV from the PFV likely occurred within conditional structures, as attested by cognate evidence (ex. 153). Presumably this process would have begun in clearly marked conditional structures, such as those headed by a conditional word such as אִם or כִּי for "real" conditions and לוּ or לוּלֵא for counterfactual ones (ex. 178). It is evident that the conditional structure imposes irrealis mood on these predicates, because an array of them appear in conditional clauses (see footnoted examples), and TAM distinctions are sometimes evident in the structure, despite the tendency to gloss such predicates with the English simple present (similar to the leveling of generic expressions), such as the present stative in the protasis of ex. 178a, the present perfect in the protasis of ex. 181a, or the dynamic modal sense of the irrealis IPFV in the protasis of ex. 181b.

178. Lexically Marked Conditional Structures with IR-PFV

178a

אִם־חָפֵץ בָּנוּ יְהוָה וְהֵבִיא אֹתָנוּ אֶל־הָאָרֶץ הַזֹּאת
וּנְתָנָהּ לָנוּ

If Yhwh is pleased ‹STA/Q.IR-PFV› with us, he will bring ‹HI.IR-PFV› us into this land and give ‹Q.IR-PFV› it to us. (Num. 14:8)[122]

178b

וְהָיָה כִּי־מָלְאוּ יָמֶיךָ לָלֶכֶת עִם־אֲבֹתֶיךָ וַהֲקִימוֹתִי
אֶת־זַרְעֲךָ אַחֲרֶיךָ אֲשֶׁר יִהְיֶה מִבָּנֶיךָ וַהֲכִינוֹתִי
אֶת־מַלְכוּתוֹ׃

[IRREALIS] When your days fill up ‹Q.IR-PFV› to go with your fathers, I will raise up ‹HI.IR-PFV› your seed after you who will be ‹Q.IPFV› one of your sons and I will establish ‹HI.IR-PFV› his kingdom. (1 Chron. 17:11)[123]

122. Gen. 38:9; 40:14; 43:9; 47:6, 16; Lev. 6:21; Num. 15:24; 21:9; Judg. 6:3; 14:12–13; 16:17; 1 Sam. 12:14; 17:9; 2 Sam. 15:33; 1 Kings 9:4–5; 2 Kings 7:4; Isa. 4:4–5; Ps. 78:34; Job 7:4; 10:14; 21:6.

123. Josh. 15:19; Judg. 2:18; Ezek. 18:11.

178c

לוּ חָפֵץ יְהוָה לַהֲמִיתֵנוּ לֹא־לָקַח מִיָּדֵנוּ עֹלָה וּמִנְחָה
וְלֹא הֶרְאָנוּ אֶת־כָּל־אֵלֶּה

If Yhwh had desired ‹STA/Q.IR-PFV› to kill ‹HI.INF› us, he would not have taken ‹Q.IR-PFV› from our hand burnt offering and meal offering and would not have shown ‹HI.IR-PFV› us all these things. (Judg. 13:23)[124]

178d

לוּלֵא חֲרַשְׁתֶּם בְּעֶגְלָתִי לֹא מְצָאתֶם חִידָתִי׃

If you had not plowed ‹Q.IR-PFV› with my heifer, you would not have discovered ‹Q.IR-PFV› my riddle. (Judg. 14:18)[125]

Conditional structures like these imposed the requisite irrealis sense that facilitated the development of three distinct meanings for the IR-PFV that could then spread beyond the structure: result/purpose, habitual, and deontic. A resultative sense naturally attaches to many conditional apodoses and some protases conjuncts (ex. 179). The close semantic relationship between result and purpose may have allowed the latter sense to eventually emerge for the gram (ex. 182a), though it is much less frequent than the resultative sense.

179. IR-PFV in Conditional Apodosis with Resultative Sense

179a

אִם־לֹא הֲבִיאֹתִיו אֵלֶיךָ וְהִצַּגְתִּיו לְפָנֶיךָ וְחָטָאתִי לְךָ
כָּל־הַיָּמִים

If I do not bring ‹HI.IR-PFV› him to you and stand ‹HI.IR-PFV› him before you, then (as a result) I will be guilty ‹Q.IR-PFV› to you all the days. (Gen. 43:9)

179b

אִשָּׁה כִּי תַזְרִיעַ וְיָלְדָה זָכָר וְטָמְאָה שִׁבְעַת יָמִים

If a woman should conceive ‹HI.IPFV› and (as a result) bears ‹Q.IR-PFV› a male child, she is unclean ‹Q.IR-PFV› seven days. (Lev. 12:2)

124. Gen. 23:13; Num. 22:29; Deut. 32:29; Josh. 7:7; Judg. 8:19; Isa. 14:30; 18:12; 19:7; 48:18; 63:19; Ezek. 14:15; Mic. 2:11; Ps. 81:14–15; Job 6:1–2; 16:4.

125. Gen. 31:42; 43:10; 1 Sam. 25:34; 2 Sam. 2:27; Isa. 1:9; Pss. 94:17; 106:23; 119:92; 124:1–2.

A habitual meaning arises particularly in conditional-temporal structures that refer to multiple events, as illustrated by ex. 180: Yhwh would from time to time raise up judges and would (habitually) be with them.[126]

180. IR-PFV in Conditional Clause with Habitual Sense

וְכִי־הֵקִים יְהוָה לָהֶם שֹׁפְטִים וְהָיָה יְהוָה עִם־הַשֹּׁפֵט
וְהוֹשִׁיעָם מִיַּד אֹיְבֵיהֶם כֹּל יְמֵי הַשּׁוֹפֵט

Whenever Yhwh would raise up ‹HI.IR-PFV› for them judges, Yhwh would be ‹Q.IR-PFV› with the judge and would deliver ‹HI.IR-PFV› them from the power of their enemies all the days of the judge. (Judg. 2:18)[127]

Finally, a deontic sense is pervasive in conditional law code apodoses, which provide cultic direction and remedies for civil and cultic missteps, as illustrated in ex. 181.

181. IR-PFV in Conditional Law Code with Deontic Sense[128]

181a

אִם־זָרְחָה הַשֶּׁמֶשׁ עָלָיו דָּמִים לוֹ שַׁלֵּם יְשַׁלֵּם אִם־אֵין
לוֹ וְנִמְכַּר בִּגְנֵבָתוֹ׃

If the sun has risen ‹Q.IR-PFV› on him, (then) bloodguilt (belongs) to him; he absolutely must recompense ‹PI.IPFV›. If he has nothing, then he should be sold ‹NI.IR-PFV› in exchange for his theft. (Exod. 22:2)

181b

אִם־יָקוּם וְהִתְהַלֵּךְ בַּחוּץ עַל־מִשְׁעַנְתּוֹ וְנִקָּה הַמַּכֶּה

If he can stand up ‹Q.IPFV› so that he walks around ‹HT.IR-PFV› outside on his staff, then the one who struck ‹HI.PTC› has been cleared ‹NI.IR-PFV›. (Exod. 21:19)

126. Whether the protasis is interpreted as "if" or "when" depends on whether the situation involves a possibility or inevitability: if the situation is something that may or may not occur, or especially one that should not occur (e.g., theft, as in ex. 181a), then "if" is appropriate; if the situation is one that regularly occurs (or is expected to), it has a temporal sense. Either sense is appropriate in cases where societal expectations dictate that the situation is generally expected but not inevitable (e.g., Deut. 24:1, כִּי־יִקַּח אִישׁ אִשָּׁה; cf. NIV/ESV: "if/when a man takes a wife").

127. Gen. 31:8; 38:9; Num. 21:9; Judg. 6:3; Ps. 78:34.

128. Exod. 1:16; 12:4; 29:34; Lev. 13:21, 26, 56; 15:28; 26:21; 27:20; Num. 5:20–21; 27:3, 7–14, 18–23; 30:6; 32:21, 29; Deut. 19:8–9; 20:8; 21:14; 23:10.

The second stage of development is when these meanings—conditional, final, habitual, and deontic—begin to appear in new contexts that are compatible with the new meanings (exs. 182a–c) but exclude conflation with the earlier one (i.e., conditional protasis/apodosis). I would also place at this stage of development the expansion of the form to express conditional clauses without any overt marking of them as such (ex. 182d).

182. IR-PFV Expanded Meanings beyond Original Context

182a. Purpose

הִנֵּה שָׁלַחְתִּי אֵלֶיךָ אֶת־נַעֲמָן עַבְדִּי וַאֲסַפְתּוֹ מִצָּרַעְתּוֹ

Hey, I have sent ‹Q.PFV› to you Naaman my servant so that you might heal ‹Q.IR-PFV› him [lit., gather him from his affliction]. (2 Kings 5:6)[129]

182b. Habitual

וּבֵרַךְ עֵלִי אֶת־אֶלְקָנָה וְאֶת־אִשְׁתּוֹ וְאָמַר יָשֵׂם יְהוָה לְךָ
זֶרַע מִן־הָאִשָּׁה הַזֹּאת תַּחַת הַשְּׁאֵלָה אֲשֶׁר שָׁאַל לַיהוָה
וְהָלְכוּ לִמְקֹמוֹ׃

And Eli would bless ‹PI.IR-PFV› Elkanah and his wife and would say ‹Q.IR-PFV›, "May Yhwh grant ‹Q.JUSS› to you offspring from this woman in exchange for the request that she asked ‹Q.PFV› of Yhwh." Then they would go ‹Q.IR-PFV› home [lit., to his place]. (1 Sam. 2:20)[130]

182c. Deontic

וְאָהַבְתָּ אֵת יְהוָה אֱלֹהֶיךָ וְשָׁמַרְתָּ מִשְׁמַרְתּוֹ וְחֻקֹּתָיו
וּמִשְׁפָּטָיו וּמִצְוֺתָיו כָּל־הַיָּמִים׃

You should love ‹Q.IR-PFV› Yhwh your God and should keep ‹Q.IR-PFV› his charge and his statutes and his laws and his commandments always. (Deut. 11:1)[131]

129. Gen. 3:5; 13:16; 18:25; 29:15; 39:9; Exod. 5:7; 11:5; 16:12; Judg. 5:26; 11:8; Isa. 49:26; Ezek. 11:10.

130. Gen. 2:6; 30:41–42; Judg. 6:2; 19:30; 1 Sam. 1:4; 2:13–16; 16:23; 27:9–11; 2 Sam. 15:2–5; Amos 4:7–8; Job 1:4; Eccles. 1:13; 8:10; 2 Chron. 24:11.

131. Exod. 25:8; 36:1; Lev. 11:44; Deut. 6:5; 10:16, 19; 29:8; 30:19; 2 Kings 5:10; 9:7; 10:3; Jer. 2:2; 17:19; 19:1.

182d. Unmarked Conditional

וּבִקַּשְׁתֶּם מִשָּׁם אֶת־יְהוָה אֱלֹהֶיךָ וּמָצָאתָ

If/when you seek ‹PI.IR-PFV› from there Yhwh your God, you will find ‹Q.IR-PFV› him. (Deut. 4:29)[132]

The third and final stage of context-induced reinterpretation is the conventionalization of the new meaning(s), resulting in a polysemous form—in this case realis PFV and IR-PFV—which may eventually lead toward a complete separation as homonyms.[133] It is possible to discern multiple of these alternative meanings associated with the IR-PFV in a given instance, as evident from the above examples and ex. 183.

183. Ambiguity among New Meanings for IR-PFV

עַתָּה שַׁבְנוּ אֵלֶיךָ וְהָלַכְתָּ עִמָּנוּ וְנִלְחַמְתָּ בִּבְנֵי עַמּוֹן וְהָיִיתָ לָּנוּ לְרֹאשׁ לְכֹל יֹשְׁבֵי גִלְעָד

Honestly, we have now turned back ‹Q.PFV› to you. If you come ‹Q.IR-PFV› with us and fight ‹NI.IR-PFV› the Ammonites, you shall be ‹Q.IR-PFV› our commander over all the inhabitants of Gilead. (Judg. 11:8 NJPS)

Nevertheless, we have now turned back ‹Q.PFV› to you, so that you may go ‹Q.IR-PFV› with us and fight ‹NI.IR-PFV› with the Ammonites, and become ‹Q.IR-PFV› head over us, over all the inhabitants of Gilead. (NRSV)

Nevertheless, we are turning ‹Q.PFV› to you now; come ‹Q.IR-PFV› with us to fight ‹NI.IR-PFV› the Ammonites, and you will be ‹Q.IR-PFV› head over all of us who live in Gilead. (NIV)

On the one hand, such ambiguity may help explain why the traditional "consecutive" approach continues to be endorsed (e.g., Joosten 2012: 293), which neatly levels it all to a simple "and then" meaning.[134] On the other hand, that these meanings may appear interchangeable lends support to this

132. Exod. 12:13; 16:21; Num. 10:17; Deut. 30:8–9; 1 Sam. 27:9; 2 Kings 9:2–3.

133. I conservatively assume that the PFV is polysemous in BH and that the context and word order along with the increasingly conventionalized waw conjunction sufficiently distinguish the two foci of meaning—the (REALIS) PFV and the IR-PFV. However, treating these as homonyms makes no practical difference to the analysis of individual examples.

134. The weakness of this approach lies, of course, in its inability to account for how or why the IR-PFV became essentially a TAM-underspecified "sequential" verb (see Cook 2004).

reconstruction of their emergence from a single construction and their association with a single gram.

Although the counterfactual meaning (exs. 178c–d) is properly classified as irrealis mood, it is associated in the grammars with the realis PFV (e.g., GKC §106p). There is some justification for this because the counterfactual expressions can be explained by the past-unreal correlation, whereby events are portrayed as past so as to express them as unreal, as is the case also in English: *If I had driven (but I didn't)* versus noncounterfactual *If I drove (and I may)*. However, the question of how the irrealis counterfactual meaning came to be attached to the IR-PFV is largely a moot question since most cases appear in conditional structures, although the apodosis is sometimes missing (ex. 184).

184. IR-PFV in Counterfactual Conditional Clause

וְלוּ גָוַעְנוּ בִּגְוַע אַחֵינוּ לִפְנֵי יְהוָה׃

If (only) we had perished ‹Q.IR-PFV› when our brothers perished ‹Q.INF› before Yhwh (*then we would not be experiencing what we are). (Num. 20:3)[135]

While the above examples and discussion illustrate well the functions of the IR-PFV and their development from conditional clauses, they also evince that with respect to lexical and verbal choice much remains to be understood about BH's irrealis mood and particularly conditional clauses:[136] Is there a meaningful distinction (besides frequency) between אִם and כִּי in marking conditional protases? Is there a semantic difference between IR-PFV and irrealis IPFV in conditional or other irrealis contexts? Are there regular TAM distinctions within irrealis mood constructions and contexts that dictate verb choice? A long-standing suggestion with regard to IR-PFV and IPFV is that they are positional variants: the IR-PFV is clause initial and the IPFV is not (e.g., Joosten 2012: 263–64). However, in light of arguments that this word-order distinction holds for IPFV itself—irrealis IPFV is clause initial and realis IPFV is not (Revell 1989)—such an approach seems insufficiently explanatory. It has been suggested that BH irrealis mood verbs are indifferent to tense and aspect distinctions (so Joosten 2012: 276, 280), and that future tense, which semantically is closely related to irrealis mood, exhibits "neutral" aspect

135. Gen. 17:18; Num. 14:2; Ps. 27:13.

136. It is noteworthy that, to my knowledge, no large-scale study of lexical (i.e., אִם, כִּי, or -וְ) and verb choice in protasis-apodosis constructions in BH has appeared since Ferguson 1882.

(Smith 1997: 62). Given that plausible TAM explanations may be offered for verb choice in some of the above cases, it seems premature to deny that there is a meaning distinction between the IR-PFV and IPFV in conditional and other irrealis contexts, even if we are hard pressed to determine it at times. It is noteworthy that while IR-PFV was being conventionalized with a proclitic -וְ, the IPFV is frequently lexically marked to indicate its modal function: for example, כִּי or אִם in conditional protases and לְמַעַן in purpose and result clauses. It also seems evident that the ability of the PFV (in contrast to the IPFV) to create bounded situations is responsible for the preponderance of IR-PFV forms in the foreground of procedural passages—both in directive discourse where the actions are prescribed to be done in order and each completed before the other is begun (ex. 185a) and in habitual passages to describe the customary order in which something is done (ex. 185b).

185a. IR-PFV in Foreground of Procedural Discourse

נֶפֶשׁ כִּי־תֶחֱטָא בִשְׁגָגָה מִכֹּל מִצְוֹת יְהוָה אֲשֶׁר לֹא
תֵעָשֶׂינָה וְעָשָׂה מֵאַחַת מֵהֵנָּה׃ אִם הַכֹּהֵן הַמָּשִׁיחַ יֶחֱטָא
לְאַשְׁמַת הָעָם וְהִקְרִיב עַל חַטָּאתוֹ אֲשֶׁר חָטָא פַּר
בֶּן־בָּקָר תָּמִים לַיהוָה לְחַטָּאת׃ וְהֵבִיא אֶת־הַפָּר אֶל־פֶּתַח
אֹהֶל מוֹעֵד לִפְנֵי יְהוָה וְסָמַךְ אֶת־יָדוֹ עַל־רֹאשׁ הַפָּר וְשָׁחַט
אֶת־הַפָּר לִפְנֵי יְהוָה׃

If/when a person sins ‹Q.IPFV› unintentionally out of any of the commands of Yhwh that should not be committed ‹NI.IPFV› so that he commits ‹Q.IR-PFV› any one of them, if the anointed priest sins ‹Q.IPFV›, to the guilt of the people, he should offer ‹HI.IR-PFV› for his sin that he committed ‹Q.PFV› a bull of the herd without blemish to Yhwh for a sin offering. He should bring ‹HI.IR-PFV› the bull to the tent of meeting before Yhwh and lay ‹Q.IR-PFV› his hand upon the head of the bull and slaughter ‹Q.IR-PFV› the bull before Yhwh. (Lev. 4:2–4)[137]

137. Exod. 25–31; Lev. 1–6.

185b. IR-PFV in Foreground of Habitual Procedural Discourse

וַיַּרְא וְהִנֵּה בְאֵר בַּשָּׂדֶה וְהִנֵּה־שָׁם שְׁלֹשָׁה עֶדְרֵי־צֹאן
רֹבְצִים עָלֶיהָ כִּי מִן־הַבְּאֵר הַהִוא יַשְׁקוּ הָעֲדָרִים וְהָאֶבֶן
גְּדֹלָה עַל־פִּי הַבְּאֵר׃ וְנֶאֶסְפוּ־שָׁמָּה כָל־הָעֲדָרִים וְגָלְלוּ
אֶת־הָאֶבֶן מֵעַל פִּי הַבְּאֵר וְהִשְׁקוּ אֶת־הַצֹּאן וְהֵשִׁיבוּ
אֶת־הָאֶבֶן עַל־פִּי הַבְּאֵר לִמְקֹמָהּ׃

He looked ‹Q.PN› and, hey, (there was) a well in a field and, hey, there three flocks of sheep (were) lying ‹Q.PTC› beside it, because from that well they would water ‹HI.IPFV› the flocks, and the stone (was) large upon the mouth of the well: all the flocks would gather ‹NI.IR-PFV› there, then they would roll ‹Q.IR-PFV› the stone from upon the mouth of the well, then they would water ‹HI.IR-PFV› the flock, then they would replace ‹HI.IR-PFV› the stone upon the mouth of the well. (Gen. 29:2–3)[138]

Notably missing from this discussion are the optative/precative and prophetic perfect, which appear in some of the grammars, though these are usually associated with the PFV rather than the waw-conversive/consecutive form (= IR-PFV). Semantically, wishes/curses and future prophetic pronouncements belong to the irrealis mood realm. However, as semantic meanings of the IR-PFV, these are suspect. Cases of optative (IR-)PFV are dubious and have been dismissed long ago by some scholars (see Cook 2012c: 250n87). The prophetic perfect, in those few cases where the (IR-)PFV appears to refer to the future but excludes either a future perfect interpretation or irrealis analysis (e.g., Isa. 5:13), is best understood as a rhetorical employment of the realis PFV to highlight the certainty of the future rather than interpreted as a semantic property of the PFV or IR-PFV (so Joüon §112h; cf. Carver 2017; see further in chap. 4).

3.6 The Participle Used Predicatively

The PTC and STA were analyzed in §2.2.3 as dual-categorized verbal adjectives (fig. 2.3), meaning that they are a special type of adjective that can encode event predicates. Whereas the STA exhibits a split encoding—sometimes as an adjective and sometimes as a verb—the PTC remains adjectival. However, the predicative construction of the PTC (i.e., as the adjectival complement of a copula, whether overt or null) entered into the TAM system as a progressive gram. In this section the diachronic development is briefly treated (§3.6.1),

138. Exod. 33:7–11; 34:34–35; Num. 9:21; Judg. 2:18–19.

followed by a discussion of the PTC in its adjectival function and its relationship with the *qotel* noun pattern (§3.6.2), and then its predicative functions as a progressive → continuous gram are discussed (§3.6.3).

3.6.1 Diachronic Development of the Participle

Little can or need be said about the diachronic development of the PTC within the context of the Semitic language family. Both the active and passive verbal adjectives are reconstructed as part of the Proto-Semitic inventory (Lipiński 2001: 419). However, a word needs to be said about the placement of the BH PTC on its diachronic path (ex. 186, repeated from ex. 126).

186. Progressive to Imperfective/Present Grammaticalization Path

Progressive → Continuous → Imperfective/Present

It was noted above (§3.2.2) that continuous represents a broadening distribution compared with progressives: whereas progressives, as their name implies, require a process-like predicate, continuous aspect may be applied to static situations including stative predicates and generic and habitual expressions. However, some languages show a continuous-like behavior at the earliest stages before becoming prototypical progressives and subsequently broadening into imperfectives/presents (see the note in the section preceding ex. 110; Bertinetto, Ebert, and de Groot 2000: 538–40). The early stages of English and Romance progressives (see examples of Old English and Latin progressives expressing habitual events in Bertinetto, Ebert, and de Groot 2000: 531; and Bertinetto 2000: 563) seem to be paralleled by the early Semitic participle in Akkadian, which Kouwenberg (2010: 204–5) describes as frequently referring in literary texts to "a permanent quality" and being employed for habitual expressions. It seems safe to assume that this early behavior belongs to a stage in the gram's development prior to it having become a "grammaticalized aspectual indicator in the verbal system," as Rissanen (1992: 216) describes the English progressive, which he notes "goes back to Old English" but is only "fully developed around the end of the eighteenth century." Thus, at the earliest stages a gram along this development path (ex.186) may reflect the static qualities of emerging from an adjectival construction, and this stage may extend for an appreciable time. This very tentative reconciliation of the arguments and data presented by Bertinetto, Ebert, and de Groot (2000: 538–40) and Bybee, Pekins, and Pagliuca (1994: 139–41) suggests that uses of the PTC that are more adjectival, particularly in relative clause constructions, preserve some of the earliest stages of the verbal adjective, whereas the PTC's increasing appropriation of functions from the IPFV and PFV forms is indicative of its broadening meaning toward a continuous gram.[139] In post-biblical Hebrew, in the context of an increasingly tense-prominent TAM system, the PTC has become a present tense gram (so Geiger 2013; see Bybee, Perkins, and Pagliuca 1994: 141).

3.6.2 Adjectival Aspects of the Participle

Due to its adjectival character and entrance into the TAM system, the function of the PTC in context can be ambiguous in two respects. First, BH has a *qotel* noun pattern that is homonymous with the Qal PTC (see Fox 2003: chap. 29). The roots of some of these nouns are *never* inflected verbally, so it is easy to classify them unambiguously as nouns (e.g., בּוֹקֵר, "herdsman," Amos 7:14; כֹּרֵם, "vinedresser," 2 Kings 25:12; Isa. 61:5; Jer. 52:16; Joel 1:11; 2 Chron. 26:10; for others, see Joüon §88Fb). Others of these roots, however, are verbally inflected, suggesting that they may appear in the PTC form, thereby creating ambiguity between a nominal or adjectival function, as illustrated with respect to שׁמ"ר (ex. 187): Is this the null copula predicative PTC with overt subject אָנֹכִי and object complement אָחִי, "(Am) I watching my brother?" or is this a copula clause involving a subject pronoun אָנֹכִי and a predicative noun bound to (i.e., in construct with) its semantic patient אָחִי, "(Am) I a watcher of my brother?" The answer relies on determining which analysis makes the best sense in the context, and most versions and commentators treat שֹׁמֵר here nominally even though none would classify it as a *qotel* noun (e.g., "my brother's keeper" NRSV, ESV, NJPS, etc.).

187. Ambiguity between Adjectival and Nominal Functions of PTC

הֲשֹׁמֵר אָחִי אָנֹכִי

(Am) I watching ‹Q.PTC› my brother? *or* (Am) I a watcher ‹Q.PTC› of my brother? (Gen. 4:9)

The second ambiguity is between the predicative PTC as a progressive gram and its adjectival function in a relative clause. Although in many cases the PTC is marked by the relative ה, which is homonymous with the article (Holmstedt

139. Joosten (2012: 392) observes that "in LBH [Late Biblical Hebrew], the process of verbalization has not yet run its full course, but it has progressed further than in CBH [Classical Biblical Hebrew]." In particular, he points to third-person null-subject PTCs expressing progressive aspect as evidence for this verbal development (e.g., Ezra 10:6; Eccles. 1:5).

2016: 69–77),[140] in a good number of cases the PTC may be unmarked or even unmarked and headless (i.e., without an overt nominal head to modify), creating ambiguity. For example, whereas the ה-marked PTC in ex. 188a unambiguously composes a relative clause modifying יְהוָה, the bare PTC in ex. 188b can be analyzed either as a predicate complement of a null copula clause with יְהוָה as its subject or as an unmarked relative clause modifying יְהוָה.

188. PTC in Relative Clause and Ambiguity with Predicate Function

188a. ה-Marked PTC in Relative Clause

אֲנִי יְהוָה הַקּוֹרֵא בְשִׁמְךָ

I (am) Yhwh who summons ‹Q.PTC› by your name. (Isa. 45:3)

188b. PTC in Unmarked Relative Clause or as Predicate Complement

אֲנִי יְהוָה עֹשֶׂה כָל־אֵלֶּה

I the LORD do ‹Q.PTC› all these things. (Isa. 45:7 NRSV, NJPS)[141]

or I (am) the LORD, (who) does ‹Q.PTC› all these things. (ESV)

Although the versions do not agree on which analysis is best, the decision between these two analyses makes only a slight interpretive difference. In other cases there are more significant meaning differences, as illustrated in ex. 189. While the first two PTCs are fairly easily recognizable as unmarked headless relatives due to their appearance in clauses lacking any alternative subject for the finite verb, the PTC in Ps. 121:5 could be treated as the main predicate, "Yhwh guards you." The latter analysis shifts the focus considerably from pronouncing Yhwh as one's guardian to describing Yhwh as guarding the blessing's recipient at the time the blessing is pronounced. In this case, the immediate context disambiguates the meaning, pointing clearly toward an adjectival function rather than as the main predicate.

189. Illustration of Interpretive Significance of Ambiguous PTC Construction

אַל־יִתֵּן לַמּוֹט רַגְלֶךָ אַל־יָנוּם שֹׁמְרֶךָ׃ הִנֵּה לֹא־יָנוּם וְלֹא
יִישָׁן שׁוֹמֵר יִשְׂרָאֵל׃ יְהוָה שֹׁמְרֶךָ יְהוָה צִלְּךָ עַל־יַד יְמִינֶךָ׃

May he not allow ‹Q.JUSS› your foot to slip, may (he who) guards ‹Q.PTC› you not slumber ‹Q.JUSS›. Hey, (he who) guards ‹Q.PTC› Israel will not

140. The ה-relative is the preferred relative marker with the PTC, and other relative words (e.g., אֲשֶׁר) are comparatively infrequent with the form.

141. Isa. 44:24; 45:19; 61:8; Jer. 17:10.

slumber ‹Q.IPFV› and will not sleep ‹Q.IPFV›. Yhwh (is he who) guards ‹Q.PTC› you, (he is) your shade at your right hand. (Ps. 121:3–5)[142]

While I have glossed all three PTCs in ex. 189 as unmarked headless relatives, they may also be treated nominally, as the NJPS does, which translates all three instances as "guardian" nominally bound to its semantic patient. This suggests that the decision between a nominal rendering and a headless relative one is a target language issue: that is, except for unambiguous *qotel* nouns,[143] PTC forms that function in NP positions can be analyzed as headless NP modifiers (i.e., headless relative clauses), as I have glossed them in ex. 189. On this analysis, the purported nominal function of the PTC can be merged with its adjectival functions. Moreover, following Holmstedt (2016: 74–75), they can be analyzed as part of a single system of NP modification spanning the cline of internal complexity (Holmstedt 2016: 11). At the one end are adjectival (ex. 190a) and monovalent STA and PTC forms (exs. 190b–c) that lack any internal modification, so a full clause structure need not be projected—though it could be, as illustrated by the relative-clause alternative glosses. Syntactically, however, these are all adjectival constructions (i.e., NP modifiers); the alternate glosses are a target-language issue.

190. NP Modification with Lesser Internal Complexity

190a. Adjective

אִישׁ־צַדִּיק

a righteous man *or* a man (who is) righteous (2 Sam. 4:11)

190b. Stative (Monovalent)

הָאִישׁ הַזָּקֵן

the old man *or* the man who (is) old (Judg. 19:17)[144]

142. Gen. 7:16; 9:18; 12:3; 14:10; 18:25; 27:29; Exod. 15:7; Lev. 2:3, 10; 5:9; 7:17, 29; 14:46; 18:25; Num. 2:3, 5; 10:35; 15:29; Deut. 7:20; 13:2, 6, 16; 18:3; 19:6, 18, 20; Josh. 3:15; 4:18; 9:3, 23; 15:15; 17:7; 20:5; Judg. 21:7, 18; 1 Sam. 14:7; 2 Sam. 14:6; 15:13; 18:24; 22:18, 40; 1 Kings 5:7; 14:28; 18:29; 2 Kings 9:8, 10; 22:5; Isa. 1:28, 31; 3:12; 46:6; 47:15; 49:17, 26; Jer. 15:9; 17:18; 19:9; 20:11; 38:2; Ezek. 11:15; 12:27; 13:6; 20:32; 27:8, 26; 34:4; 38:13; Hosea 5:14; Amos 1:8; 3:10; 5:10; Mic. 2:13; 6:12, 16; Nah. 1:11; 2:2; Zech. 8:20; 11:6; Pss. 31:16; 33:15; 35:4, 19; 36:11; 38:12; 44:6; 66:7; 74:4; 87:4; 88:5; 120:6; 147:6; Job 8:22; 31:3; 34:17; 36:3; Prov. 6:32; 10:5; 11:18–19; 14:2; 17:5; 20:19; 21:15; 24:25; 27:18; 31:6; Song 6:9; Eccles. 10:8; Lam. 1:7; Dan. 11:16; Ezra 8:35; Neh. 3:13, 32; 7:7; 13:20; 1 Chron. 21:12; 2 Chron. 12:11; 20:7; 22:1; 24:13; 32:22; 33:9.

143. Of course the fragmentary character of the BH data leaves this "unambiguous" determination uncertain: perhaps a root like כר״ם was used to form both a *qotel* noun (כֹּרֵם, "vinedresser") and a verb (?כָּרַם, "dress vines") in ancient Hebrew, and we simply lack any instances of the latter.

144. Gen. 41:7; Deut. 20:8; Judg. 8:15; Jer. 19:13; Ezek. 37:4; Eccles. 11:5.

190c. Participle (Monovalent)

הָעָם הָרָצִים

the running ‹Q.PTC› people *or* the people who (were) running ‹Q.PTC› (2 Chron. 23:12)[145]

At the other end of the spectrum stand relative PTC and STA clauses with modifiers (exs. 191a–b) as well as relative clauses with finite verbs (ex. 191c). In these cases a full relative clause is projected as required by the relative clause's internal modifiers.

191. NP Modification with Greater Internal Complexity

191a. Participle (Bivalent)

הָאִישׁ הָעֹשֶׂה זֹאת

the man who (he) did ‹Q.PTC› this (2 Sam. 12:5)[146]

191b. Stative (Bivalent)

מִי־הָאִישׁ הֶחָפֵץ חַיִּים

Who is the man who is desirous (of)/desires (STA/Q.PFV) life? (Ps. 34:13)[147]

191c. Finite Verb

וַיִּשְׂמַח יְחִזְקִיָּהוּ וְכָל־הָעָם עַל הַהֵכִין הָאֱלֹהִים לָעָם

Hezekiah and all the people rejoiced ‹Q.PN› over (that) which God established ‹HI.PFV› for the people. (2 Chron. 29:36)[148]

145. Gen. 1:21; 41:35; Exod. 16:23; 26:12; Lev. 11:43; 14:14; 27:8; Num. 5:19; 25:15; Deut. 8:15; 10:17; 25:5–6; Josh. 21:16; Judg. 20:4, 48; 2 Sam. 21:13; 1 Kings 14:28; 2 Kings 11:3; 14:6; 22:13; Isa. 2:13; 6:4; 55:3; Jer. 34:7; 50:16; Ezek. 1:22; 8:3; 9:4; 18:4, 32; 28:14; 33:6; Zech. 12:14; Eccles. 2:16; Dan. 9:26; Ezra 2:62; 3:5; 8:25; Neh. 3:31; 4:8; 11:22; 1 Chron. 6:55; 25:7; 26:28; 2 Chron. 12:10; 29:28.

146. Gen. 7:21; 31:12; 32:20; Exod. 3:9; 4:19; 25:33; 29:13, 37; 31:15; Lev. 11:20–21; 25:28; Num. 4:37; 19:13; 32:13; Deut. 2:4; 11:30; 20:11; 25:18; Josh. 5:4; 8:25; 17:16; Judg. 20:46; 1 Sam. 2:14; 6:5; 10:18; 30:24; 2 Sam. 2:23; 18:31; 19:6; 22:31; 1 Kings 8:5; 15:18; 2 Kings 10:11; 14:14; 18:21; 21:24; Isa. 41:11; Jer. 7:2; 12:14; 19:10; 24:8; 29:16; 40:15; Ezek. 8:3; 9:4; 17:16; 28:24; 34:27; Zeph. 1:5; Zech. 2:4; 4:14; 14:16; Pss. 18:31; 31:25; 103:3–5; Eccles. 4:15; Lam. 4:13; Esther 1:5; 8:11; Dan. 1:13; Ezra 3:8; Neh. 4:11; 8:17; 1 Chron. 1:46; 9:16; 27:1; 2 Chron. 5:6; 7:11; 11:16; 15:9; 29:29; 31:1.

147. Exod. 9:20; Deut. 4:4; Jer. 9:13; Amos 2:13. Groves-Wheeler and *HALOT* classify חָפֵץ in this passage as an adjective, while ETCBC and *DCH* classify it as a verb.

148. Holmstedt (2016: 303–4) identifies the following as the only possible cases of the ה-relative on a non-participial/non-adjectival constituent: Gen. 18:21; 21:3; 46:27; Josh. 10:24; 1 Sam. 9:24; 1 Kings 11:9; Isa. 51:10; 56:3; Jer. 5:13; Ezek. 26:17; Job 2:11; Ruth 1:22; 2:6; 4:3; Dan. 8:1; Ezra 8:25; 10:14, 17; 1 Chron. 26:28; 29:8, 17; 2 Chron. 4:1.

The PTC as NP modifier likely represents the earliest function of the form for a number of reasons. First, as demonstrated by the unified analysis of NP modification above, the relative PTC function stands closest to its adjectival origins. Second, the ה-relative is the second most frequent relative word in BH (after אֲשֶׁר) and most often is attached to a PTC that functions as the complement of a null copula relative clause whose subject is the null resumption of the relative clause head (e.g., ex. 191a; see Holmstedt 2016: 69). This is significant because of the static character of null copula clauses and because this subordinating function of the ה has been identified as one of its earliest functions (see Holmstedt 2016: 77). Third, relative PTCs do not exhibit their own TAM distinctions; rather, these are determined from the main clause and discourse context. For example, in ex. 191a the PTC predicate refers to the man in Nathan's parable, and because David takes the events of this parable as having already occurred, a perfective past (NJPS) or present perfect (NRSV) translation is appropriate.

3.6.3 Predicative Behavior of the Participle

The PTC enters into the TAM system as a progressive gram constructed of a copula (null or overt) and a complementary PTC (fig. 3.9, with simplified VoiceP and omitted optional CauseP). While the PTC in this structure is associated with progressive aspect, the copula carries the tense and mood marking.

Despite treating the adjectival function and the predicative functions in separate sections, it is impossible to draw a clear demarcation between these uses, as illustrated by ex. 192a, which might be glossed as a "static" adjectival "in whose land I (am) an inhabitant," or as a progressive "in whose land I (am) dwelling." This is especially true in the case of the PTC in subordinate clauses and with null copula, which is frequent. In such cases the TAM is derived from other predicates in the context, and the PTC may or may not be obviously progressive. For example, the temporality of the PTC clause is set by the speech time in exs. 192a, d, the temporal adverbial PP in ex. 192b, and the leading PN verb in ex. 192c.

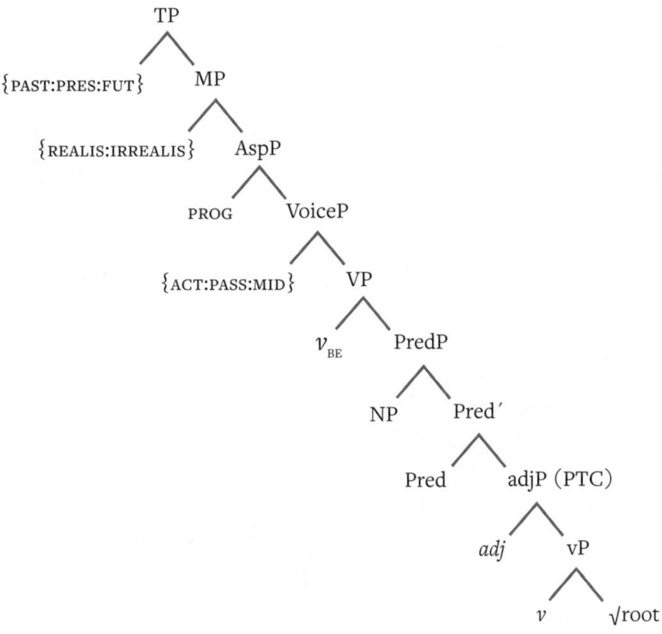

Figure 3.9. Predicative Participle

192. Determination of TAM in Predicative PTC Constructions with Covert/Null Copula

192a

לֹא־תִקַּח אִשָּׁה לִבְנִי מִבְּנוֹת הַכְּנַעֲנִי אֲשֶׁר אָנֹכִי יֹשֵׁב בְּאַרְצוֹ׃

You must not take ‹Q.IPFV› a wife for my son from the daughters of the Canaanites, in whose land I dwell/(am) dwelling ‹Q.PTC›. (Gen. 24:37)

192b

וּבָעֵת הַהִיא פְּלִשְׁתִּים מֹשְׁלִים בְּיִשְׂרָאֵל׃

At that time the Philistines (were) ruling ‹Q.PTC› over Israel. (Judg. 14:4)

192c

וַיִּפְנוּ מִשָּׁם הָאֲנָשִׁים וַיֵּלְכוּ סְדֹמָה וְאַבְרָהָם עוֹדֶנּוּ עֹמֵד
לִפְנֵי יְהוָה׃

The men turned ‹Q.PN› from there and went ‹Q.PN› to Sodom; but Abraham, he (was) still standing ‹Q.PTC› before Yhwh. (Gen. 18:22)

192d

בְּזֹאת תֵּדַע כִּי אֲנִי יְהוָה הִנֵּה אָנֹכִי מַכֶּה בַּמַּטֶּה אֲשֶׁר־
בְּיָדִי עַל־הַמַּיִם אֲשֶׁר בַּיְאֹר

By this you will know ‹Q.IPFV› that I (am) Yhwh: hey, I (am) striking/going to strike ‹HI.PTC› with the rod that (is) in my hand the waters that (are) in the Nile. (Exod. 7:17)

The last example, ex. 192d, can be glossed with a present progressive anchored by the speech time ("am striking") or as prospective aspect ("am going to strike"). The free alternation of these glosses suggests the prospective aspect is actually a pragmatically derived interpretation of the progressive gram in a context in which the described event—frequently a telic one—cannot be interpreted as actually occurring at the reference time. In this case, the preceding predicate stating that they "will know" expressed by the IPFV suggests that Moses is not *at that moment of speaking* striking the waters, but that he intends to do so shortly.[149]

An overt copula may be used to disambiguate the tense-aspect of the PTC or more clearly integrate it with the surrounding discourse. For example, an overt PN copula may support the PTC within a series of PNs (ex. 193a). The progressive PTC can co-occur with a PN or PFV copula to mark past time (exs. 193a–b), with an IPFV to mark future (ex. 193c), with an IR-PFV for irrealis mood (ex. 193d), or with a JUSS or IMPV for directive-volitive modality (exs. 193e–f).

149. For this reason a prospective aspect phrase head is not included in the model in fig. 3.7; a prospective sense might be modeled by the combination a PROG head with a telic situation type (i.e., achievement or accomplishment).

193. Determination of TAM in Predicative PTC Constructions with Overt Copula

193a

יִמְלֹךְ דָּוִד עַל־כָּל־יִשְׂרָאֵל וַיְהִי דָוִד עֹשֶׂה מִשְׁפָּט
וּצְדָקָה לְכָל־עַמּוֹ׃

David ruled ‹Q.PN› over all Israel and David was ‹Q.PN› administering ‹Q.PTC› justice and righteousness for all his people. (2 Sam. 8:15; cf. 1 Chron. 18:14)[150]

193b

וְגַם־אִישׁ הָיָה מִתְנַבֵּא בְּשֵׁם יְהוָה

Also, a man was ‹Q.PFV› prophesying ‹HT.PTC› in the name of Yhwh. (Jer. 26:20)[151]

193c

יְהוָה יִהְיֶה שֹׁמֵעַ בֵּינוֹתֵינוּ אִם־לֹא כִדְבָרְךָ כֵּן נַעֲשֶׂה

Yhwh will be ‹Q.IPFV› listening ‹Q.PTC› between us if not according to your word thus we act ‹Q.IPFV›. (Judg. 11:10)[152]

193d

וְהָיוּ בְמִקְדָּשִׁי מְשָׁרְתִים פְּקֻדּוֹת אֶל־שַׁעֲרֵי הַבַּיִת
וּמְשָׁרְתִים אֶת־הַבָּיִת

They shall be ‹Q.IR-PFV› in my sanctuary serving ‹PI.PTC› watch at the gates of the temple and serving ‹PI.PTC› (in) the temple. (Ezek. 44:11)[153]

150. Judg. 19:1; 1 Sam. 7:10; 18:9, 14; 23:26; 2 Sam. 4:3; 2 Kings 17:25, 28–29, 32; 21:15; Esther 2:7, 15; 6:1; Ezra 4:4–5; Neh. 1:4; 2:13, 15; 1 Chron. 6:17; 2 Chron. 9:26; 20:25; 24:12, 14; 30:10; 36:16.

151. Gen. 39:22; 1 Sam. 2:11; 17:34; 2 Sam. 3:6, 17; 1 Kings 5:1; 12:6; 2 Kings 9:14; 18:4; Isa. 59:2; Jer. 32:30; Ezek. 16:22; 27:9; 34:2; 43:6; 44:11; Job 1:14; Dan. 8:5; 10:2; Neh. 3:26; 6:14; 13:5; 2 Chron. 10:6; 26:10.

152. Gen. 4:12; Exod. 26:3; Lev. 15:2; Num. 14:33; Deut. 19:11; Ezek. 13:13; Neh. 13:22. This list includes examples of IPFV in conditional law and directive clauses.

153. Gen. 4:14; Exod. 25:20; Deut. 28:29; 1 Sam. 25:20; 2 Sam. 6:16; Isa. 28:4; 30:20; 49:23; Jer. 47:2; Hosea 9:17; Zech. 10:5.

193e

יְהִי רָקִיעַ בְּתוֹךְ הַמָּיִם וִיהִי מַבְדִּיל בֵּין מַיִם לָמָיִם׃

Let a firmament be ‹Q.JUSS› in the midst of the waters and let it be ‹Q.JUSS› dividing between waters and waters. (Gen. 1:6)

193f

וַיֹּאמֶר אֶל־הָעָם הֱיוּ נְכֹנִים לִשְׁלֹשֶׁת יָמִים אַל־תִּגְּשׁוּ אֶל־אִשָּׁה׃

He said to the people, "Be ‹Q.IMPV› preparing ‹NI.PTC› for the third day; do not approach ‹Q.JUSS› a woman." (Exod. 19:15)[154]

An overt copula is required with the negative לֹא (ex. 194a). More frequently, the PTC employs the negative existential אַיִן (ex. 194b). The positive existential יֵשׁ is used less frequently as a copula with the PTC (ex. 194c).

194. Negative and Existentials with Predicative PTCs

194a

וְלֹא הָיָה נֹדֵד כָּנָף

A wing was ‹Q.PFV› not moving ‹Q.PTC›. (Isa. 10:14)[155]

194b

תֶּבֶן אֵין נִתָּן לַעֲבָדֶיךָ

Straw is not (NEG-EXIST) being given ‹NI.PTC› to your servants. (Exod. 5:16)[156]

194c

וְעַתָּה אִם־יֶשְׁכֶם עֹשִׂים חֶסֶד וֶאֱמֶת אֶת־אֲדֹנִי הַגִּידוּ לִי

Now, if you are (EXIST) doing/going to do ‹Q.PTC› loyalty and truth with my master, tell ‹HI.IMPV› me. (Gen. 24:49)[157]

154. Exod. 34:2; Ps. 30:11.

155. Gen. 42:31; Exod. 23:26; 1 Kings 10:3; 2 Kings 2:21; Isa. 3:7; Jer. 50:3.

156. Gen. 39:23; 42:31; Exod. 3:2; 5:10–11; 8:17; 23:26; 33:15; Deut. 21:18, 20; Josh. 6:1; Judg. 3:25; 19:15, 18; 1 Sam. 3:1; 11:7; 19:11; 2 Sam. 19:8; 1 Kings 10:3; 21:5; 2 Kings 12:8; 17:26, 34; Isa. 1:15; 3:7; 57:1; Jer. 4:29; 14:12; 50:3; Ezek. 3:7; 8:12; 9:9; 20:39; Mal. 2:2; Ps. 33:16; Eccles. 4:17; 5:11; 8:7; 9:1–2, 5, 16; 11:5–6; Esther 2:20; 3:5; 5:13; 7:4; Neh. 2:2; 13:24; 2 Chron. 18:7.

157. Gen. 24:42; 43:4; Deut. 13:4; 29:14; Judg. 6:36.

The PTC rarely appears in constructions that combine progressive and perfect aspects and is usually supported by an overt PFV copula (ex. 195).

195. Perfect Progressive Participle[158]

195a

לֹא כֵן לְכוּ־נָא הַגְּבָרִים וְעִבְדוּ אֶת־יְהוָה כִּי אֹתָהּ אַתֶּם
מְבַקְשִׁים

Not so! Let the men go ‹Q.IMPV› now and worship ‹Q.IMPV› Yhwh, because that you (have been) seeking ‹PI.PTC›. (Exod. 10:11)

195b

כִּי אִם־עֲוֺנֹתֵיכֶם הָיוּ מַבְדִּלִים בֵּינֵכֶם לְבֵין אֱלֹהֵיכֶם

But rather your iniquities have been ‹Q.PFV› causing a separation ‹HI.PTC› between you and your God. (Isa. 59:2)

195c

וַיִּשְׁלַח דָּוִד מַלְאָכִים וַיִּקָּחֶהָ וַתָּבוֹא אֵלָיו וַיִּשְׁכַּב עִמָּהּ
וְהִיא מִתְקַדֶּשֶׁת מִטֻּמְאָתָהּ וַתָּשָׁב אֶל־בֵּיתָהּ׃

David sent ‹Q.PN› messengers and he took ‹Q.PN› her and she came ‹Q.PN› to him and he lay ‹Q.PN› with her—she (had been) purifying herself ‹HT.PTC› from her ceremonial impurity—and she returned ‹Q.PN› to her house. (2 Sam. 11:4)

195d

וְיוֹרָם הָיָה שֹׁמֵר בְּרָמֹת גִּלְעָד הוּא וְכָל־יִשְׂרָאֵל מִפְּנֵי
חֲזָאֵל מֶלֶךְ־אֲרָם

Joram had been ‹Q.PFV› guarding ‹Q.PTC› at Ramoth Gilead, he and all Israel, against Hazael king of Aram. (2 Kings 9:14)

Modeling examples like these requires an additional perfect phrase (PerfP) along with the aspect phrase (AspP) in the distributed morphology tree (fig. 3.10).

158. Deut. 9:7, 22, 24; 31:27; 1 Kings 12:6; 2 Kings 9:14; 18:4; Ezek. 34:2; 36:13; Ps. 122:2; 2 Chron. 10:6.

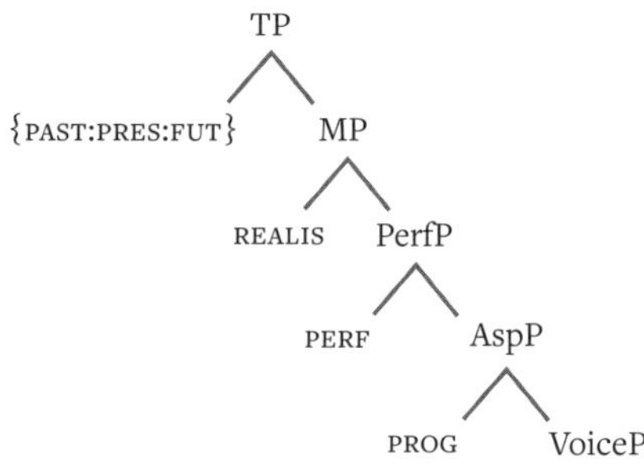

Figure 3.10. Perfect Progressive Participle

Two or three emerging functions of the PTC point to its development toward the continuous and imperfective stages of the path. The first of these is its expanded use in generic expressions, judging from the earlier wisdom sayings in Proverbs to later ones in Ecclesiastes (ex. 196; Cook 2005; 2013).

196. Generic IPFV and PTC

196a

כָּל־עָרוּם יַעֲשֶׂה בְדָעַת וּכְסִיל יִפְרֹשׂ אִוֶּלֶת׃

Every prudent (person) will act/acts ‹Q.IPFV› with knowledge, but a fool will spread/spreads ‹Q.IPFV› folly. (Prov. 13:16)[159]

196b

הַכְּסִיל חֹבֵק אֶת־יָדָיו וְאֹכֵל אֶת־בְּשָׂרוֹ׃

The fool folds ‹Q.PTC› his hands and eats ‹Q.PTC› his flesh. (Eccles. 4:5)[160]

The second emerging function for the PTC is with STA predicates to express a present state. Despite STAs being characterized as lacking an active PTC form, a number of highly used STA predicates appear in the PTC form (ex. 197a). It is difficult to know whether the stative character of these is merely a target language issue, as the combination of progressive and stative is avoided in some languages, such as English (see §3.2.2 above). The same case might be made about passive statives with the PTC (ex. 197b).

159. Prov. 10:1; 11:6; 12:25; 14:17; 15:1, 2; 16:23; 18:1; 26:24; 29:2, 8.
160. Eccles. 1:4–7; 2:14; 3:20; 5:9, 11; 6:6, 10, 11; 8:1, 12; 9:1, 5, 16, 17; 10:19.

197. Participle with Stative Predicates

197a

כִּי מְנַסֶּה יְהוָה אֱלֹהֵיכֶם אֶתְכֶם לָדַעַת הֲיִשְׁכֶם אֹהֲבִים אֶת־יְהוָה אֱלֹהֵיכֶם בְּכָל־לְבַבְכֶם וּבְכָל־נַפְשְׁכֶם

For Yhwh your God (is) testing ‹PI.PTC› you to know ‹Q.INF› whether you are (EXIST) loving ‹Q.PTC› Yhwh your God with all your heart and with all your soul. (Deut. 13:4; cf. English "whether you love")[161]

197b

שַׁעַר הֶחָצֵר הַפְּנִימִית הַפֹּנֶה קָדִים יִהְיֶה סָגוּר שֵׁשֶׁת יְמֵי הַמַּעֲשֶׂה

The gate of the inner court that faces ‹Q.PTC› east will be ‹Q.IPFV› closed ‹Q.PPTC› (after) six days of work. (Ezek. 46:1)[162]

However, a more notable pattern can be discerned in some cases, such as the stative יד"ע, for which the PFV is employed to express a present state in earlier parts of the BH corpus but later shifts to the PTC for these present stative expressions (ex. 198; see Cook 2012a). The data attest to a broadening of the PTC beyond a strictly progressive gram, allowing it to be employed in new strategies to express present states as the PFV gram becomes increasingly confined to past temporal reference.

198. Development from PFV with STA to Express a Present State to PTC

198a

הַיּוֹם יָדַע עַבְדְּךָ כִּי־מָצָאתִי חֵן בְּעֵינֶיךָ

Today your servant knows ‹Q.PFV› that I have found ‹Q.PFV› favor in your eyes. (2 Sam. 14:22)[163]

161. Deut. 4:42; 19:11; Josh. 20:5; 1 Sam. 18:16; 2 Sam. 13:4; Isa. 61:8; Pss. 33:5; 87:2; 146:8; Prov. 29:24.

162. Gen. 4:11; 14:19; Deut. 28:29; 1 Sam. 1:28; 5:4; 30:16; 2 Sam. 6:14; 1 Kings 2:45; 22:35; 2 Kings 11:3; Isa. 5:25; 65:6; Jer. 3:21; 4:29; 5:8; 36:30; Ezek. 8:10; 19:13; Hosea 13:12; Pss. 18:31; 45:6; 99:3; Job 18:10; Prov. 30:5; Eccles. 5:12; Neh. 6:5; 8:10; 2 Chron. 1:12.

163. Gen. 4:9; 12:11; 18:19; Exod. 3:7, 19; 4:14; Num. 10:31; 11:16; Deut. 1:39; 34:6; Josh. 14:6; 22:31; Judg. 15:11; 1 Sam. 17:28; 28:9; 29:9; 2 Sam. 1:5; 17:8. For a full list of examples for this verb, see Cook 2012a: 92.

198b

וּמִי יוֹדֵעַ פֵּשֶׁר דָּבָר

Who knows ‹Q.PTC› the interpretation of a matter? (Eccles. 8:1)[164]

A third possible developing use of the PTC that I previously tentatively identified is its employment in the performative-like statement in ex. 199 (see Cook 2013: 333). In this context we might reasonably expect the PFV (i.e., מָצָאתִי, "I find"), so finding the PTC here instead may indicate that it is beginning to appropriate this function from the PFV. Although this is just one example, the possibility of this development is bolstered by the fact that the PTC is increasingly used for performative statements in Rabbinic Hebrew (Dobbs-Allsopp 2004–7: 65–66) and is employed in this manner in the Biblical Aramaic corpus (Cook 2019: 9–10).

199. PTC for Performative Expression

וּמוֹצֶא אֲנִי מַר מִמָּוֶת אֶת־הָאִשָּׁה אֲשֶׁר־הִיא מְצוֹדִים וַחֲרָמִים לִבָּהּ אֲסוּרִים יָדֶיהָ

I find ‹Q.PTC› more bitter than death "the woman," who (is) snares, and her mind (is) nets, her hands (are) fetters. (Eccles. 7:26; trans. Holmstedt, Cook, and Marshall 2017: 220)

3.7 The Imperfective Conjugation

The imperfective (IPFV) stands in opposition to the perfective (PFV), together constituting the core opposition in the TAM system in BH (fig. 3.11; cf. fig. 3.7b). However, the system has been affected by diachronic changes to individual grams that have left this inner core somewhat "skewed." This is seen particularly in the broad range of meanings associated with the IPFV, which has led some to suggest that it be called the "non-perfective" form, in privative opposition with the perfective (so *IBHS* §29.6e–f). While they rightly note that the IPFV is "more than opposite" the PFV, the imperfective label for the form remains convenient for the purposes of typological comparison, though it should not be considered a straitjacket definition in which to fit

164. Gen. 3:5; 33:13; Josh. 22:22; 1 Sam. 23:17; 2 Sam. 12:22; 17:10; 2 Kings 17:26; Isa. 29:15; Jer. 29:23; Joel 2:14; Jon. 1:12; 3:9; Nah. 1:7; Zeph. 3:5; Pss. 1:6; 37:18; 44:22; 90:11; 94:11; 139:14; Prov. 12:10; 14:10; 24:22; Eccles. 2:19; 3:21; 4:17; 6:12; 8:7, 12; 9:1, 5; 11:5–6; Esther 4:11, 14; 2 Chron. 2:7.

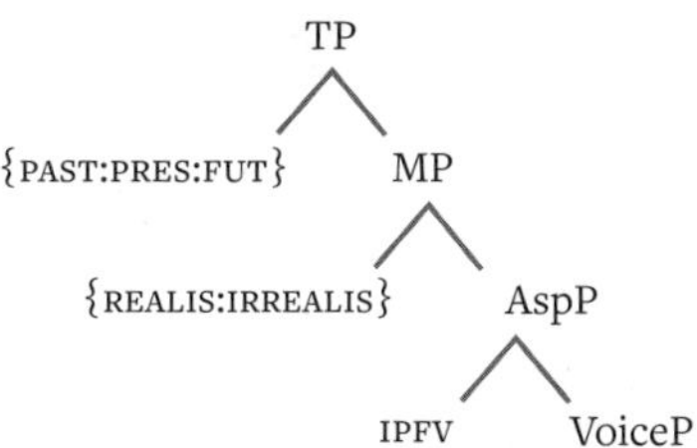

Figure 3.11. Imperfective

the conjugation. Typologically, TAM systems develop perfective grams in opposition to existing imperfective ones (Bybee, Perkins, and Pagliuca 1994: 91), which means that the above arguments in favor of the BH PFV being a perfective gram support the classification of the IPFV as imperfective (ex. 200a). Further, the main source for IPFV grams is progressive constructions (Bybee, Perkins, and Pagliuca 1994: 174), which accounts for both semantic overlap between the IPFV and the predicative PTC and the relatively wider semantic functionality of the IPFV in contrast to the PTC (ex. 200b).

200. Comparison of IPFV and Related Grams

200a. IPFV and PFV

אוֹי לָנוּ כִּי־פָנָה הַיּוֹם כִּי יִנָּטוּ צִלְלֵי־עָרֶב

Woe to us because the day has turned ‹Q.PFV›; because the shadows of evening are lengthening ‹NI.IPFV›. (Jer. 6:4)

200b. IPFV and PTC

וַיִּשְׁאָלֵהוּ הָאִישׁ לֵאמֹר מַה־תְּבַקֵּשׁ׃ וַיֹּאמֶר אֶת־אַחַי אָנֹכִי מְבַקֵּשׁ

The man asked ‹Q.PN› him [COMP], "What are you seeking ‹PI.IPFV›?" He said ‹Q.PN›, "My brothers I (am) seeking ‹PI.PTC›." (Gen. 37:15–16; see also Ps. 19:2–3)

3.7.1 Diachronic Development of the Imperfective

Unlike the consensus surrounding the origins of BH PFV (see §3.5.1), there is much uncertainty about the prehistory of the IPFV. What is striking is that the prefix form **yaqtulu* is distinctive of Central Semitic (i.e., Northwest Semitic, Ancient Arabian, North Arabian), in contrast to a geminated form

**yaqattal* with similar semantics in East Semitic (i.e., Akkadian) and South Semitic (i.e., Ethio-Semitic, Modern South Arabian; see Huehnergard and Pat-El 2019: 3). As Kouwenberg (2010: 98) states, "The fundamental issue is whether the similarity between East Semitic and South Semitic imperfectives justifies the reconstruction of a geminated imperfective in Proto-Semitic, or whether Proto-Semitic instead had an imperfective based on the 'simple' prefix conjugation." After surveying the problems with assuming either of the imperfectives to be "innovations," Kouwenberg (2010: 97–100, 584–89) concludes that the geminated **yaqattal* is a "replacement" of the Afroasiatic **yaqtulu* derived from a Proto-Semitic pluractional gram, while the Central Semitic system represents a "reduction of an older, more comprehensive system" (i.e., one with both an imperfective **yaqtulu* and pluractional **yaqattal*).

Prior to the West Semitic innovation of the suffixed verb, Semitic had the contrast of perfective **yaqtul* (of which BH *wayyiqtol* is a reflex) and imperfective **yaqtulu*.[165] In BH the reflex of the **yaqtulu* retains its prototypical imperfective meanings (e.g., ongoing action in the past and present), but these meanings have become marginalized for the form, which is becoming increasingly associated with irrealis mood. As mentioned above (§3.3.2), during the BH period, competition from the adjectival PTC in a predicatively constructed progressive gram was slowly displacing the prototypical imperfective functions of the IPFV form and relegating it to a "miscellaneous set of functions" such as are found likewise with "old presents" (Bybee, Perkins, and Pagliuca 1994: 277; Haspelmath 1998).[166] This miscellaneous collection of functions can be classified as belonging to the realm of irrealis or subjunctive mood, which Bybee, Perkins, and Pagliuca (1994: 230) identify as developing from imperfective grams, among other sources. They point out that "out-of-focus and more marginal uses can retain the older gram long after the new gram has taken over the central, focused functions" (235).[167] The partial homonymy between the IPFV and irrealis JUSS likely also aided in this shift toward irrealis functions as the identical form could be freely used for realis imperfective or irrealis jussive

165. Various explanations have been offered for the final *-u* vowel (see Kouwenberg 2010: 230n65; Cook 2012c: 220) but with no consensus. Kouwenberg's (2010: 228) agnostic approach seems best.

166. Bybee, Perkins, and Pagliuca (1994: 126) note the close association between imperfective and present grams: "An imperfective restricted to the present is simply a present."

167. Kouwenberg's (2010: 227–32) explanation of the Akkadian subjunctive provides an interesting parallel to the BH development of the IPFV and PTC. While some scholars have argued that the **yaqtulu* gram owes its origin to the Akkadian subjunctive, whose *-u* termination spread from subordinate expressions to main clauses, Kouwenberg avers that competition with the **yaqattal* conjugation resulted in a reanalysis of the final *-u* in **yaqtulu* as a marker of subordination.

meanings. The syntactic and semantic distinctions between IPFV and the JUSS are already breaking down in the Dead Sea Scrolls (Reymond 2023), and by the period of Rabbinic Hebrew, the IPFV has fully shifted into an irrealis gram and the PTC has displaced it for ongoing action and general present.

3.7.2 Form and Functions of the Imperfective

I noted above (§3.5.2) that the wide divergence in meaning between the realis PFV and IR-PFV warranted treating the gram under that major division. The situation with the IPFV is the reverse: categories of meaning for the IPFV often blur the divide between realis and irrealis mood for a number of reasons. The first of these is the partial homonymy between the IPFV and the irrealis JUSS, which are distinct in only three cases: the Hiphil binyan, roots with a middle or final glide, and when negated (Kummerow 2007: 71–74). In the Hiphil, the IPFV 3MS, 3FS, and 2MS forms show a hireq-yod theme vowel, whereas the JUSS of these persons shows a tsere (ex. 201).

201. Morphological Contrast between IPFV and JUSS in Hiphil Binyan

201a

וְיַפְקֵד הַמֶּלֶךְ פְּקִידִים בְּכָל־מְדִינוֹת מַלְכוּתוֹ

Let the king appoint ‹HI.JUSS› officers throughout all the provinces of his kingdom. (Esther 2:3)

201b

לְמִכְמָשׂ יַפְקִיד כֵּלָיו

At Michmash he is storing ‹HI.IPFV› his baggage. (Isa. 10:28)

Roots having a middle or final glide (i.e., semivowels ו or י) are contrastive in their 3MS, 3FS, and 2MS forms with respect to their theme vowels in the IPFV and JUSS (ex. 202).

202. Morphological Contrast between IPFV and JUSS in Roots with Middle or Final Glide

202a

וּבָבֶל תָּבוֹא וְשָׁם תָּמוּת וְשָׁם תִּקָּבֵר

(To) Babylon you will go ‹Q.IPFV› and there you will die ‹Q.IPFV› and there you will be buried ‹IPFV›. (Jer. 20:6)

202b

תָּמֹת נַפְשִׁי מוֹת יְשָׁרִים

Let me [lit., my soul] die ‹Q.JUSS› the death of upright ones. (Num. 23:10)

202c

כִּי־נְזִיר אֱלֹהִים יִהְיֶה הַנַּעַר מִן־הַבָּטֶן

Because a Nazarite of God the lad will be ‹Q.IPFV› from the womb. (Judg. 13:5)

202d

עַתָּה בְנִי יְהִי יְהוָה עִמָּךְ

Now, my son, may Yhwh be ‹Q.JUSS› with you. (1 Chron. 22:11)

Third, the אַל negator is employed with JUSS, whereas the IPFV uses לֹא, providing a lexical indicator of the conjugation (ex. 203).

203. Negators of JUSS and IPFV

203a

וְאַל־תַּעַשׂ לוֹ מְאוּמָה

Do not do ‹Q.JUSS› anything to him. (Gen. 22:12)

203b

וְכֵן לֹא יֵעָשֶׂה

And such (a thing) must not be done ‹NI.IPFV›. (Gen. 34:7)

A second way in which the categories of meaning for the IPFV blur is in the relationship between future tense and irrealis mood. The use of *will* in English for both future tense and (irrealis) expressions of volition is illustrative of the close relationship between them that makes speaking of a "realis future" problematic (see McCawley 1993: 432–34). Cross-linguistically, a good many languages employ irrealis mood marking for future, or else their future tense marking selects irrealis (in contrast to past tense selecting realis), so that "on the whole, the connection between future and irrealis prevails, for obvious semantic reasons: future events are non-factual, hence naturally belong to the domain of irrealis" (Malchukov and Xrakovskij 2016: 206). Many first- and second-person IPFV predicates may be interpreted as either realis future or irrealis volitional, even in cases with S-V order: the overt fronted subject pronoun in ex. 204a can be attributed to focus (i.e., I and not another), while the preceding IMPV suggests that the IPFV here expresses Yhwh's intent and not a realis predication of the future. Similarly, in ex. 204b the overt second-person pronouns serve to single out David as a focus element, while leaving the verbs ambiguous between future predication and Yhwh's directive for David.

204. Ambiguity between Realis Future or Irrealis Volition

204a

וְעַתָּה לֵךְ וְאָנֹכִי אֶהְיֶה עִם־פִּיךָ

And now, go ‹Q.IMPV› and I will be ‹Q.IPFV› with your mouth. (Exod. 4:12)[168]

204b

וַיֹּאמֶר יְהוָה לְךָ אַתָּה תִרְעֶה אֶת־עַמִּי אֶת־יִשְׂרָאֵל וְאַתָּה תִּהְיֶה לְנָגִיד עַל־יִשְׂרָאֵל

Yhwh said ‹Q.PN› to you, "You will shepherd ‹Q.IPFV› my people Israel and you will be ‹Q.IPFV› a prince over Israel." (2 Sam. 5:2)[169]

Nevertheless, a *realis* future meaning for the IPFV is arguably present in cases where there is no obvious place for volition (ex. 205). The volitional expression in ex. 205a ("be willing") derives from the verbal lexeme, making clear that the future "will" is realis tense and not to be conflated with volition. The future adverbial מָחָר ("tommorow") in ex. 205b makes an irrealis volitional interpretation unlikely.

168. Exod. 4:21; 7:3; Lev. 20:3; Num. 6:27; 2 Sam. 12:12; Isa. 41:17–19; 45:2; Jer. 4:12; Mic. 7:7; 1 Chron. 28:6.

169. Exod. 14:14; Lev. 20:24; Josh. 18:6; 2 Sam. 9:7; 1 Kings 8:30; Jer. 1:17; Ezek. 11:11; Hosea 12:7; Ps. 12:8.

205. Unambiguous Realis IPFVs

205a

וּבֵית יִשְׂרָאֵל לֹא יֹאבוּ לִשְׁמֹעַ אֵלֶיךָ כִּי־אֵינָם אֹבִים לִשְׁמֹעַ אֵלָי

The house of Israel will not be willing ‹Q.IPFV› to listen ‹Q.INF› to you, because they are not ‹NEG-EXIST› willing ‹Q.PTC› to listen ‹Q.INF› to me. (Ezek. 3:7)[170]

205b

הִתְקַדָּשׁוּ כִּי מָחָר יַעֲשֶׂה יְהוָה בְּקִרְבְּכֶם נִפְלָאוֹת׃

Sanctify ‹HT.IMPV› yourselves, because tomorrow Yhwh will perform ‹Q.IPFV› wonders in your midst. (Josh. 3:5)[171]

Two places where lack of volition is especially evident are (1) wisdom literature's generic and habitual statements (ex. 206a), which frequently show S-V word order and for which irrealis mood is only infrequently found (see ex. 174 in §3.5.2 above), and (2) future-in-the-past expressions, which are relatively rare (ex. 206b).

206. Expressions with Unambiguous Realis IPFVs

206a. Generic Expressions

בֵּית רְשָׁעִים יִשָּׁמֵד וְאֹהֶל יְשָׁרִים יַפְרִיחַ׃

A house of wicked (ones) will be demolished ‹NI.IPFV›, but a tent of upright (ones) will flourish ‹HI.IPFV›. (Prov. 14:11)[172]

206b. Future-in-the-Past Expressions

אֲנִי טֶרֶם אֲכַלֶּה לְדַבֵּר אֶל־לִבִּי וְהִנֵּה רִבְקָה יֹצֵאת

I, before I would finish ‹PI.IPFV› speaking ‹PI.INF› to myself, hey, Rebekah (was) coming out ‹Q.PTC›. (Gen. 24:45; cf. v. 15)[173]

170. Gen. 24:5; Deut. 29:19; Josh. 22:22; Isa. 7:16; 8:4; 52:6; Jer. 40:15; Neh. 4:5.

171. Exod. 6:1; 8:19; 9:5; Num. 22:4; 1 Sam. 11:9; 13:12; 23:11; 1 Kings 11:26; Isa. 40:10, 31; 41:11, 15–16; Jer. 14:10; Ezek. 7:13; Ps. 121:1; Ruth 3:4; 2 Chron. 32:11.

172. Job 11:12, 20; 14:10–11; 15:35; 18:5; 27:19; 32:8; 41:13; Prov. 10:1; 11:6; 12:25; 14:17; 16:23; 17:2; 19:9; 27:18; 28:18; 29:23; Eccles. 3:15; 7:19, 26; 8:1; 9:18; 10:12, 14, 19.

173. Other future-in-the-past following טֶרֶם include Gen. 2:5; 37:18; 41:50; Exod. 12:34; Num. 11:33; Josh. 2:8; 3:1; Judg. 14:18; 1 Sam. 2:15; 3:3, 7; 2 Kings 6:32; Jer. 47:1; Ruth 3:14 (see discussion in Cook 2012c: 260–63). Other IPFV future-in-the-past examples are Gen. 43:7; 1 Kings 7:8; 2 Kings 3:27; 13:14; Isa. 43:17.

A third source of the blurring of meaning in the IPFV, related to the problem of the future and irrealis, is that some occurrences of the IPFV are genuinely ambiguous between a realis and irrealis mood interpretation. Is the IPFV in ex. 207a a realis future, as the NASB suggests, or an irrealis dynamic, as the NRSV translates it? Does the IPFV in ex. 207b express realis past imperfective (ESV) or habitual (NRSV), which meaning some scholars analyze as modal (e.g., Joosten 2012: 26; Boneh and Doron 2008; 2010)?

207. Realis-Irrealis Ambiguity in the Interpretation of IPFV

207a

גַּם אֶת־הָעֹלָם נָתַן בְּלִבָּם מִבְּלִי אֲשֶׁר לֹא־יִמְצָא הָאָדָם
אֶת־הַמַּעֲשֶׂה אֲשֶׁר־עָשָׂה הָאֱלֹהִים מֵרֹאשׁ וְעַד־סוֹף

He has also set ‹Q.PFV› eternity in their heart, yet so that man will not find out ‹Q.IPFV› the work which God has done ‹Q.PFV› from the beginning even to the end. (Eccles. 3:11 NASB)[174]

Moreover he has put ‹Q.PFV› a sense of past and future into their minds, yet they cannot find out ‹Q.IPFV› what God has done ‹Q.PFV› from the beginning to the end. (NRSV)

207b

וְאֵד יַעֲלֶה מִן־הָאָרֶץ וְהִשְׁקָה אֶת־כָּל־פְּנֵי־הָאֲדָמָה

And a mist was going up ‹Q.IPFV› from the land and was watering ‹HI.IR-PFV› the whole face of the ground. (Gen. 2:6 ESV)[175]

But a stream would rise ‹Q.IPFV› from the earth, and water ‹HI.IR-PFV› the whole face of the ground. (Gen. 2:6 NRSV)

As was true of the future (ex. 205), so also here a case can be made that habitual is not inevitably modal (so A. Cohen 2018). While habitual expressions frequently employ IR-PFV, instances of the IPFV with S-V order and the PTC without an overt copula (to mark mood) also appear (ex. 208). That both realis and irrealis mood constructions can express habituality makes sense given that the realis mood predominates in generic statements, to which habitual is closely related (see the note in the paragraph preceding ex. 115). It also makes sense in light of A. Cohen's (2018) analysis of the habitual as intensional (see §1.2.2): "All modal [i.e., irrealis] expressions are intensional,

174. See ex. 215b and the accompanying note.
175. Exod. 19:19; Judg. 17:6; 21:25.

of course, but not all intensional expressions are modal" (A. Cohen 2018: 2). Thus, irrealis grams, which are modal, can express habituality, which is intensional, but habituality can also be expressed by nonmodal grams, such as the PTC.

208. Habitual Expressions

208a

וְעָלָה הָאִישׁ הַהוּא מֵעִירוֹ מִיָּמִים יָמִימָה

That man would go up ‹Q.IR-PFV› from his city periodically. (1 Sam. 1:3)[176]

208b

וְהֶעָרִים יַהֲרֹסוּ וְכָל־חֶלְקָה טוֹבָה יַשְׁלִיכוּ אִישׁ־אַבְנוֹ וּמִ־
לְאוּהָ וְכָל־מַעְיַן־מַיִם יִסְתֹּמוּ וְכָל־עֵץ־טוֹב יַפִּילוּ

The cities they would overthrow ‹Q.IPFV› and every good field each his stone would throw ‹HI.IPFV› so as to fill ‹PI.IR-PFV› it, and every spring of water they would stop up ‹Q.IPFV› and every good tree they would fell ‹HI.IPFV›. (2 Kings 3:25)[177]

208c

וּבְכָל־יוֹם וָיוֹם מָרְדֳּכַי מִתְהַלֵּךְ לִפְנֵי חֲצַר בֵּית־הַנָּשִׁים

Every day Mordecai (was) walking ‹HT.PTC› before the court of the harem. (Esther 2:11)[178]

These considerations suggest that rather than attempting to neatly separate realis IPFV from irrealis IPFV, one needs to approach the data in terms of a continuum: at the one end are unambiguous realis uses of the IPFV and at the other end unambiguous irrealis meanings. In between are ambiguous cases such as those discussed above. This range of functions is presented here with the label IPFV, which covers the full range of possible realis and irrealis meanings. At the realis end of the spectrum are the prototypical imperfective expressions of past imperfective (ex. 209a) and present imperfective (ex. 209b).

176. See other examples at ex. 182b and the accompanying note.

177. Judg. 6:5; 1 Sam. 26:23; 2 Sam. 9:10; 17:17; 22:29; 2 Kings 12:17; 13:20; 14:6.

178. Joosten (2012: 394–95) notes that the habitual PTC appears more frequently in LBH than in early parts of the corpus, in line with the above reconstruction (§3.7.1), which suggests that this function belongs to the emerging continuative meaning of the form. Other examples of habitual PTCs in LBH that he lists include Esther 2:14; 4:3; 8:17; 9:19; Neh. 4:10, 11, 12, 15; 5:2–4; 6:9, 17; 9:3; 12:47; 1 Chron. 12:40–41; 15:24; 16:5; 23:5; 2 Chron. 3:11–12; 4:3; 9:14, 24, 28; 17:11; 30:21; 32:23; 33:17.

While other possible realis examples might be listed, these include those least susceptible to alternate interpretations as habitual, though as explained above that would not thereby classify them as irrealis mood.[179]

209. Prototypical Imperfective Expressions with IPFV

209a. Past Imperfective IPFV

וְהָאֲנָשִׁים יְנַחֲשׁוּ וַיְמַהֲרוּ וַיַּחְלְטוּ הֲמִמֶּנּוּ וַיֹּאמְרוּ אָחִיךָ בֶּן־הֲדַד

The men were seeking an omen ‹PI.IPFV› and they quickly ‹PI.PN› seized ‹PI.PN› upon it[180] and said ‹Q.PN›, "Your brother (is) Ben Hadad." (1 Kings 20:33; cf. 2 Sam. 18:24 with יוֹשֵׁב ‹Q.PTC› instead of IPFV)[181]

209b. Present Imperfective IPFV

שְׁבָה אִתִּי אַל־תִּירָא כִּי אֲשֶׁר־יְבַקֵּשׁ אֶת־נַפְשִׁי יְבַקֵּשׁ אֶת־נַפְשֶׁךָ

Stay ‹Q.IMPV› with me; do not be afraid ‹Q.JUSS›, because (the one) who is seeking ‹PI.IPFV› my life is seeking ‹PI.IPFV› your life. (1 Sam. 22:23)[182]

Analogous to the general restriction of the English progressive to dynamic predicates, the BH IPFV appears less frequently with statives—at least in past time—than with dynamic predicates (ex. 210).[183]

179. Even less so would interpreting any of these as iterative actions make them irrealis, contra Joosten (2012: 33–34, 63). As Langacker (1997: 196) explains, "In contrast to habituals, which express some kind of generalization, repetitives [or iteratives] describe actual multiple instances of a basic event type."

180. This gloss is based on redividing הֲמִמֶּנּוּ so as to interpret the ה as the 3FS pronoun attached to the preceding verb, referring back to the king's words in the previous verse (see *BHS* for support).

181. Gen. 2:6; 37:7; Exod. 8:20; 13:22; 19:19; Judg. 9:38; 1 Sam. 1:10; 13:17–18; 2 Sam. 2:28; 15:37; 23:10; 1 Kings 6:8; 21:6; Isa. 1:21; 6:4; 42:14, 17; 43:9; Hosea 2:1; Pss. 32:5; 55:18; 77:17; 94:7; 116:3; 139:13; Song 2:6; 8:3; Eccles. 10:6; Esther 4:3.

182. Gen. 16:8; 24:31; 32:30; 37:15; 42:1; 44:7; Exod. 5:4, 15; Josh. 9:8; 1 Sam. 1:8; 11:5; 2 Sam. 16:9; 2 Kings 20:14; Isa. 41:5, 6; 42:1; Jer. 36:18; Pss. 2:2; 5:3; 19:2–3; 27:7; 82:1; 83:6; 142:2; Job 16:14; Eccles. 8:4.

183. The stative יכ״ל ("be able") would appear to be an exception, occurring over twice as often in the IPFV than the PFV conjugation, even occasionally in past temporal contexts (e.g., Gen. 43:32; 48:10; 1 Sam. 3:2). However, these forms might be parsed better as Qal passive PFVs, despite having an active sense (Bauer and Leander 1922: 386m′).

210. IPFV with STA Predicate in Past Time

כִּי יוֹמָם וָלַיְלָה תִּכְבַּד עָלַי יָדֶךָ

Because day and night your hand was heavy ‹Q.IPFV› on me. (Ps. 32:4)[184]

The IPFV with stative predicates in present time is more frequent (ex. 211a) and may indicate that the IPFV was employed alongside the PTC as another strategy for expressing present states in reaction to the PFV's drift toward being more "tensed" with its concomitant increased restriction to past-time interpretation (Cook 2012a; see ex. 198, §3.6.3 above). At the same time, in a number of such cases, the choice of the IPFV appears to be motivated by irrealis mood, as the contrast to the PFV in ex. 211b suggests.

211. IPFV with STA Predicate in Present Time

211a

כִּי־פְשָׁעַי אֲנִי אֵדָע וְחַטָּאתִי נֶגְדִּי תָמִיד׃

Indeed my transgressions I know ‹Q.IPFV› and my sin (is) continually before me. (Ps. 51:5)[185]

211b

מַה־יָּדַעְתָּ וְלֹא נֵדָע תָּבִין וְלֹא־עִמָּנוּ הוּא׃

What do you know ‹Q.PFV› that we might not/cannot know ‹Q.IPFV›? (What) do/can you understand ‹HI.IPFV› and it (is) not with us? (Job 15:9)

Future and habitual expressions with IPFV have been illustrated above (exs. 205–8) as classifiable under either realis or irrealis mood, depending on elements such as what person the predicate is and what other TAM grams appear in the discourse context. For example, first and second person are more readily associated with speaker volition. The IPFV expressing habituality outside of wisdom sayings typically occurs in isolation or is followed by an IR-PFV if the events form a bounded series (e.g., ex. 207b, read as habitual; see other examples in the note accompanying ex. 208b). However, in the few times that habitual IPFVs cluster (ex. 208b), a clear contrast can be observed, with habitual passages featuring a series of IR-PFVs (ex. 212). While the IPFV habitual events show no boundedness, which would result in a temporal successive interpretation, the IR-PFVs create bounded situations and a temporally

184. Gen. 2:25.

185. Gen. 24:50; 31:35; 1 Kings 3:7; Isa. 1:13; 40:21; 41:5; Ps. 61:3; Prov. 3:12; 15:9; 16:13; 39:7; Song 8:7; Eccles. 1:15; 8:17.

successive habitual passage. This suggests that even in irrealis contexts, the aspectual distinction of IPFV and PFV, respectively, is maintained.

212. IR-PFV Expressing Habitual Bounded Events

וַיַּ֗רְא וְהִנֵּ֨ה בְאֵ֜ר בַּשָּׂדֶ֗ה וְהִנֵּה־שָׁ֞ם שְׁלֹשָׁ֤ה עֶדְרֵי־צֹאן֙
רֹבְצִ֣ים עָלֶ֔יהָ כִּ֚י מִן־הַבְּאֵ֣ר הַהִ֔וא יַשְׁק֖וּ הָעֲדָרִ֑ים וְהָאֶ֥בֶן
גְּדֹלָ֖ה עַל־פִּ֥י הַבְּאֵֽר׃ **וְנֶאֶסְפוּ**־שָׁ֣מָּה כָֽל־הָעֲדָרִ֗ים **וְגָלֲל֤וּ**
אֶת־הָאֶ֨בֶן֙ מֵעַל֙ פִּ֣י הַבְּאֵ֔ר **וְהִשְׁק֖וּ** אֶת־הַצֹּ֑אן **וְהֵשִׁ֧יבוּ** אֶת־
הָאֶ֛בֶן עַל־פִּ֥י הַבְּאֵ֖ר לִמְקֹמָֽהּ׃

He looked ‹Q.PN› and, hey, (there was) a well in a field and, hey, there three flocks of sheep (were) lying ‹Q.PTC› beside it, because from that well they would water ‹HI.IPFV› the flocks, and the stone (was) large upon the mouth of the well: all the flocks would gather ‹NI.IR-PFV› there, then they would roll ‹Q.IR-PFV› the stone from upon the mouth of the well, then they would water ‹HI.IR-PFV› the flock, then they would replace ‹HI.IR-PFV› the stone upon the mouth of the well. (Gen. 29:2–3)[186]

This reasoning applies likewise to procedural directive discourse, in which the IR-PFV expresses the bounded procedural steps while the IPFV is used to express unbounded events, which are not temporally successive with the surrounding discourse events. In ex. 213, the IR-PFV marks the temporally successive events, while the detail that the overlaying should be done to the inside and outside of the ark is independent of the temporal sequence and so is expressed nontemporally by the unbounded IPFV predicate.

213. IPFV Expressing Unbounded Event in Procedural Discourse

וְעָ֥שׂוּ לִ֖י מִקְדָּ֑שׁ וְשָׁכַנְתִּ֖י בְּתוֹכָֽם׃ כְּכֹ֗ל אֲשֶׁ֤ר אֲנִי֙ מַרְאֶ֣ה
אוֹתְךָ֔ אֵ֚ת תַּבְנִ֣ית הַמִּשְׁכָּ֔ן וְאֵ֖ת תַּבְנִ֣ית כָּל־כֵּלָ֑יו וְכֵ֖ן תַּעֲשֽׂוּ׃
וְעָשׂ֖וּ אֲר֣וֹן עֲצֵ֣י שִׁטִּ֑ים אַמָּתַ֨יִם וָחֵ֜צִי אָרְכּ֗וֹ וְאַמָּ֤ה וָחֵ֨צִי֙
רָחְבּ֔וֹ וְאַמָּ֥ה וָחֵ֖צִי קֹמָתֽוֹ׃ וְצִפִּיתָ֤ אֹתוֹ֙ זָהָ֣ב טָה֔וֹר מִבַּ֥יִת
וּמִח֖וּץ **תְּצַפֶּ֑נּוּ** וְעָשִׂ֧יתָ עָלָ֛יו זֵ֥ר זָהָ֖ב סָבִֽיב׃

And they should make ‹Q.IR-PFV› for me a sanctuary so that I may dwell ‹Q.IR-PFV› in your midst. According to all that I (am) showing ‹HI.PTC›

186. This passage also appears above as ex. 185b at the end of the section on the irrealis perfective (§3.5.3).

you—the pattern of the sanctuary and the pattern of all its furniture—thus you should make ‹Q.IPFV› it. They should make ‹Q.IR-PFV› an ark of acacia wood; and its length (should be) two and a half cubits, its width a cubit and a half, and its height a cubit and a half. You should overlay ‹PI.IR-PFV› it with pure gold; inside and outside you should overlay ‹PI.IPFV› it, and you should make ‹Q.IR-PFV› a molding of gold upon it all around. (Exod. 25:8–11)[187]

It stands to reason that the bounded character of the (IR-)PFV gram is also the motive behind its predominance in conditional apodoses, even while the IPFV predominates in protases (ex. 214a; see also ex. 181). If *x* is the case, then *y* follows; that is, a relationship that is logically/temporally successive is established. By contrast, if an IPFV appears in the apodosis, it may be motivated by word-order issues (e.g., a negator or other fronted element) or may carry some additional irrealis nuance (ex. 214b). However, this is just a generalized tendency, and as mentioned above (§3.5.3), the various explanations of verb choice in conditional structures still need to be fully elucidated by a focused study of them.

214. PFV and IPFV in Conditional Apodoses

214a

אִם־יַעֲלֶה שׁוּעָל וּפָרַץ חוֹמַת אַבְנֵיהֶם׃

If a fox goes up ‹Q.IPFV›, he would breach ‹Q.IR-PFV› the wall of their stones. (Neh. 3:35)[188]

214b

אִם־תַּעְצְרֵנִי לֹא־אֹכַל בְּלַחְמֶךָ וְאִם־תַּעֲשֶׂה עֹלָה לַיהוָה תַּעֲלֶנָּה

If you detain ‹Q.IPFV› me, I will not eat ‹Q.IPFV› your food, and if you make ‹Q.IPFV› a burnt offering, to Yhwh you should offer ‹HI.IPFV› it. (Judg. 13:16)[189]

187. Exod. 25:15, 18–20, 27, 29, 31, 36, 39; etc.; see Exod. 25–31; Lev. 1–6.

188. Josh. 2:20; Judg. 4:8; 1 Sam. 3:9; 12:14; 17:9; 2 Sam. 10:11; 1 Kings 6:12; 9:4–5; 11:38; Hosea 9:12; Eccles. 4:11; 1 Chron. 19:12; 2 Chron. 7:17–20.

189. Gen. 31:8; 44:23; Judg. 4:8; 15:7; 2 Sam. 18:3; 1 Kings 1:52; 2:4; 13:8; 2 Kings 7:4; Isa. 1:18–20; Jer. 4:1; 15:19; Amos 9:2–4; Hag. 2:13; Pss. 27:3; 50:12; 132:12; Job 14:7–9; Prov. 2:4–5; Eccles. 11:3; 2 Chron. 15:2.

It is noteworthy that the unambiguous irrealis meanings expressed by the IPFV are often (in comparison with IR-PFV) highly marked by syntactic construction (e.g., conditional clauses), lexically (e.g., כִּי or אִם in conditional protases, יכ״ל for dynamic modality, אוּלַי for epistemic modality, and פֶּן and לְמַעַן for final modality), or by genre (e.g., prohibitions in legal corpus). This suggests that just as the IR-PFV range of meanings emerged from a context-induced reinterpretation, these lexical, syntactic, and genre indicators of irrealis mood helped drive the broadening of meanings of the IPFV into the irrealis realm.

Dynamic modality is regularly expressed lexically by יכ״ל in the IPFV conjugation with a complementary INF (ex. 215a; however, see the note above between exs. 209b and 210). However, the IPFV by itself often has a dynamic modal meaning determined by the context, in which ability is at stake in the situation. In ex. 215b the near occurrence of יכ״ל signals a dynamic interpretation of the conjoined IPFV.

215. IPFV Expressing Dynamic Modality

215a

וַיֹּאמְרוּ אֲלֵיהֶם לֹא נוּכַל לַעֲשׂוֹת הַדָּבָר הַזֶּה

They said ‹Q.PN› to them, "We cannot ‹Q.IPFV› do ‹Q.INF› this thing." (Gen. 34:14)[190]

215b

כַּסְפָּם וּזְהָבָם לֹא־יוּכַל לְהַצִּילָם בְּיוֹם עֶבְרַת יְהוָה נַפְשָׁם
לֹא יְשַׂבֵּעוּ וּמֵעֵיהֶם לֹא יְמַלֵּאוּ

Their silver and gold will not be able ‹Q.IPFV› to rescue ‹HI.INF› them on the day of the wrath of Yhwh; their life they cannot satisfy ‹PI.IPFV› and their bellies they cannot fill ‹PI.IPFV›. (Ezek. 7:19)[191]

190. Gen. 15:5; 19:19; 31:35; 44:1, 26; Exod. 10:5; 18:18; 33:20; Num. 13:31; 22:11; 24:13; Deut. 7:17; 12:17; 28:35; Josh. 7:13; 9:19; 24:19; Judg. 11:35; 14:13; 21:18; 1 Sam. 6:20; 17:33, 39; 2 Sam. 12:23; 17:17; 1 Kings 3:9; 13:16; 20:9; 2 Kings 18:23, 29; Isa. 56:10; 59:14; Jer. 6:10; 11:11; 14:9; 18:6; 19:11; 36:5; Ezek. 7:19; 33:12; 47:5; Hosea 5:13; Zeph. 1:18; Pss. 18:39; 78:20; Prov. 30:21; Ruth 4:6; Song 8:7; Eccles. 1:15; 6:10; 7:13; 8:17; Lam. 1:14; Neh. 4:4; 6:3.

191. Gen. 16:10; 32:13; Lev. 5:7, 11; 12:8; Num. 31:23; 1 Sam. 12:21; 2 Sam. 5:6; 14:14; 1 Kings 8:27; Isa. 30:5–6; 33:23; 44:20; 45:20; Jer. 4:19; 10:4–5; 23:24; Ezek. 3:6, 25; Hosea 2:1, 8; Pss. 33:17; 77:5; 88:9; 125:1; Job 9:15; 10:15; 14:5; Prov. 8:11; Lam. 3:7; 2 Chron. 13:12; 24:20.

The situation is similar for epistemic modality: אוּלַי ("perhaps") lexically marks epistemic possibility followed by an IPFV (ex. 216a),[192] but a given IPFV may express epistemic possibility (ex. 216b) or epistemic necessity (ex. 216c) by itself as appropriate to the context.

216. IPFV Expressing Epistemic Modality

216a

אוּלַי תִּסָּתְרוּ בְּיוֹם אַף־יְהוָה

Perhaps you will be hidden ‹NI.IPFV› on the day of the wrath of Yhwh. (Zeph. 2:3)[193]

216b

יֵשׁ דָּבָר שֶׁיֹּאמַר רְאֵה־זֶה חָדָשׁ הוּא

A thing exists ‹EXIST› about which one might say ‹Q.IPFV›, "See ‹Q.IMPV› this—it (is) new!" (Eccles. 1:10; trans. Holmstedt, Cook, and Marshall 2017: 64)[194]

216c

וְשָׂנֵאתִי אֲנִי אֶת־כָּל־עֲמָלִי שֶׁאֲנִי עָמֵל תַּחַת הַשָּׁמֶשׁ
שֶׁאַנִּיחֶנּוּ לָאָדָם שֶׁיִּהְיֶה אַחֲרָי׃

I came to hate ‹Q.PFV›, I, all my toil, (in) which I (was) burdened under the sun, which I must leave ‹HI.IPFV› it to the man who will come ‹Q.IPFV› after me. (Eccles. 2:18)[195]

192. אוּלַי appears 35 times with IPFV but just 2 times with PFV (Num. 22:33; Job 1:5), which in both verses exhibits (past/present) perfect semantics.

193. Gen. 16:2; 18:28–32; 27:12; 32:21; Num. 22:6, 11; 23:3, 27; 1 Sam. 6:5; 9:6; 14:6; 2 Sam. 14:15; 16:12; 1 Kings 18:5; 20:31; 2 Kings 19:4; Isa. 37:4; 47:12; Jer. 20:10; 21:2; 26:3; 36:3, 7; 51:8; Ezek. 12:3; Hosea 8:7; Amos 5:15; Jon. 1:6.

194. Isa. 40:30; 54:17; Eccles. 2:3; 5:11, 14; 10:9.

195. Eccles. 2:21. Cases of epistemic necessity are uncommon and ambiguous with deontic necessity. While deontic necessity imposes obligation on the event (i.e., *I of necessity must leave*), epistemic necessity expresses certainty about a state of affairs (i.e., *It is necessarily the case that I will leave*). The epistemic interpretation seems plausible in these instances in which the sage is contemplating the state of human existence and not reflecting on, for example, human obligations in relation to God.

The construction לְמַעַן ("so that") strongly prefers the IPFV (see *BHRG* §40.36).[196] Typically it expresses positive final (purpose) modality (ex. 217a) but appears a number of times with a לֹא-negated predicate to provide a negative final sense (ex. 217b). Rarely, a resultative sense better fits this construction (ex. 217c), which otherwise is more frequently expressed with לְמַעַן followed by an INF (e.g., Lev. 20:3; 2 Kings 22:17; Jer. 7:18; 25:7 [*qere*]; 27:10; 32:29, 35; Amos 2:7; 2 Chron. 34:25).

217. IPFV with לְמַעַן

217a

דִּרְשׁוּ־טוֹב וְאַל־רָע לְמַעַן תִּחְיוּ

Seek ‹Q.IMPV› good and not evil in order that you might live ‹Q.IPFV›. (Amos 5:14)[197]

217b

בְּלִבִּי צָפַנְתִּי אִמְרָתֶךָ לְמַעַן לֹא אֶחֱטָא־לָךְ׃

In my heart I have hidden ‹Q.PFV› your word so that I might not sin ‹Q.IPFV› against you. (Ps. 119:11)[198]

217c

וְהָרַע בְּעֵינֶיךָ עָשִׂיתִי לְמַעַן תִּצְדַּק בְּדָבְרֶךָ

(That which is) evil in your sight I have done ‹Q.PFV› so that you are/will be justified ‹Q.IPFV› when you speak ‹Q.INF›. (Ps. 51:6)[199]

As with dynamic and epistemic modality, the IPFV may express a final meaning apart from a lexical marker, given the appropriate context, such as in the immediate context of the lexical marker לְמַעַן (ex. 218a) or conjoined to some other irrealis mood gram (ex. 218b). All these instances of

196. The construction appears only twice with a PFV form, though the *qere* of Jer. 25:7 has the better reading of an INF, and the same INF reading is suggested for Josh. 4:24 (see *BHS*).

197. Gen. 12:13; 27:25; Exod. 4:5; 8:6, 18; 9:29; 10:2; 11:7; 13:9; 16:4, 32; 20:12; 23:12; 33:13; Lev. 23:43; Num. 15:40; 27:20; 36:8; Deut. 4:1, 40; 5:14, 16, 29, 33; 6:2, 18; 8:1; 11:8–9, 21; 12:25, 28; 13:18; 14:23, 29; 16:3, 20; 17:19–20; 22:7; 23:21; 24:19; 25:15; 29:5, 8; 30:19; 31:12, 19; Josh. 1:7–8; 4:6; 1 Kings 2:3–4; 8:40, 43; Isa. 5:19; 23:16; 28:13; 41:20; 43:10, 26; 45:3, 6; 66:11; Jer. 4:14; 7:23; 10:18; 32:14; 35:7; 36:3; 44:29; 51:39; Ezek. 4:17; 6:6; 12:16, 19; 16:54, 63; 24:11; Amos 9:12; Hab. 2:2; Pss. 9:15; 30:13; 48:14; 60:7; 68:24; 78:6; 108:7; 119:71, 101; 130:4; Job 19:29; 40:8; Prov. 2:20; 19:20; Ezra 9:12; Neh. 6:13; 1 Chron. 28:8; 2 Chron. 6:31, 33; 31:4; 32:18.

198. Num. 17:5; Deut. 20:18; Ezek. 14:11; 19:9; 25:10; 26:20; 31:14; 46:18; Zech. 12:7; Pss. 119:80; 125:3.

199. Isa. 44:9; Hosea 8:4; Obad. 9.

"unmarked" IPFVs expressing dynamic, epistemic, or final modality are more a target-language issue than a question of semantic nuance to the IPFV form. That is, the IPFV in all these instances expresses irrealis mood, which may be glossed or interpreted any number of ways within a given context and as the target language may allow.

218. IPFV with a Final (Purpose) Meaning

218a

הוֹדִעֵנִי נָא אֶת־דְּרָכֶךָ וְאֵדָעֲךָ לְמַעַן אֶמְצָא־חֵן בְּעֵינֶיךָ

Please show ‹HI.IMPV› me your way that I might know ‹Q.IPFV› you in order that I might find ‹Q.IPFV› favor in your eyes. (Exod. 33:13)

218b

וְעַתָּה הַנִּיחָה לִּי וְיִחַר־אַפִּי בָהֶם וַאֲכַלֵּם וְאֶעֱשֶׂה אוֹתְךָ לְגוֹי גָּדוֹל

Now, let me be ‹HI.IMPV› that my anger might burn ‹Q.IPFV› and I might consume ‹Q.IPFV› them so that I may make ‹Q.IPFV› you into a great nation. (Exod. 32:10)[200]

More frequently than לְמַעַן with negator לֹא, negative purpose is expressed by the dedicated negative final word פֶּן ("lest"), which is almost always paired with the IPFV (see *BHRG* §41.11).[201]

219. IPFV with פֶּן

הָאִירָה עֵינַי פֶּן־אִישַׁן הַמָּוֶת

Lighten ‹HI.IMPV› my eyes lest I sleep ‹Q.IPFV› the death. (Ps. 13:4)[202]

200. Gen. 20:7; 35:3; Exod. 2:7; 5:9; Num. 14:12; Deut. 9:14; 30:13; 1 Sam. 17:46–47; Isa. 41:12, 23, 26, 28; 43:9–10; 53:2.

201. פֶּן appears twice with the PFV. In one occurrence two manuscripts have an IPFV (2 Sam. 20:6; see *BHS*), and in the other the PFV has a past meaning (2 Kings 2:16). Otherwise it appears just a handful of times with other predicates (see Gen. 44:34; Deut. 29:17; 2 Kings 10:23) and twice as a simple negator (Jer. 51:46; Prov. 5:6). By contrast, the negative-purposive בִּלְתִּי ("lest") occurs just twice with the IPFV (Exod. 20:20; 2 Sam. 14:14). It typically negates the INF, which is another strategy for expressing negative purpose (see ex. 5).

202. Gen. 3:3, 22; 11:4; 19:15, 17, 19; 24:6; 26:7, 9; 31:24, 31; 32:12; 38:11, 23; 42:4; 44:34; 45:11; Exod. 1:10; 5:3; 13:17; 19:21–22, 24; 20:19; 23:29, 33; 33:3; 34:12, 15; Lev. 10:7; Num. 16:26, 34; Deut. 4:9, 16, 19, 23; 6:12, 15; 7:22, 25; 8:11–12; 9:28; 11:16; 12:13, 19, 30; 15:9; 19:6; 20:5–7; 22:9; 25:3; 32:27; Josh. 2:16; 6:18; 24:27; Judg. 7:2; 9:54; 14:15; 15:12; 18:25; 1 Sam. 4:9; 9:5; 13:19; 15:6; 20:3; 27:11; 31:4; 2 Sam. 1:20; 12:28; 15:14; 17:16; Isa. 6:10; 27:3; 28:22; 36:18;

As discussed above, the IPFV is partially homonymous with the JUSS, and they overlap in their directive-volitive functions, as illustrated by the *ketiv-qere* variations (ex. 220; for prohibitions, see ex. 203). This homonymy undoubtedly helped reinforce the irrealis mood character of the IPFV.

220. *Ketiv-Qere* Preservation of IPFV-JUSS Variations

220a

לֵכְנָה שֹּׁבְנָה אִשָּׁה לְבֵית אִמָּהּ יַעֲשֶׂה יְהוָה עִמָּכֶם חֶסֶד

Go ‹Q.IMPV›, return ‹Q.IMPV› each to the house of her mother; may Yhwh deal (*ketiv* Q.IPFV; *qere* Q.JUSS) loyally with you. (Ruth 1:8)[203]

220b

הֲשִׁיבֵנוּ יְהוָה אֵלֶיךָ וְנָשׁוּבָ

Restore ‹HI.IMPV› us, Yhwh, to you, so that we are restored (*ketiv* Q.JUSS; *qere* Q.IPFV). (Lam. 5:21)[204]

Nevertheless, a distinction can be seen between the negated IPFV employed for prohibitive expressions and the negated JUSS, because they employ distinct negators (ex. 203). While often there is an instinctually felt semantic difference between these grams in prohibitive statements, scholars have struggled to find appropriate categories to describe it. They have used descriptives like "urgency" of the JUSS versus IPFV (for both positive and negative deontic expressions; e.g., Shulman 1996: 128, 187). Shulman (2000: 180) has suggested a deontic (JUSS) versus epistemic (IPFV) distinction, but as she explains it, this is more of a distributional description than a semantic one (i.e., IPFV are "typically used for epistemic modality" although they "may be used for either deontic or epistemic modality").

A better way to express the distinction between JUSS and IPFV in deontic expressions is Verstraete's (2007: 32–35) division between subjective and objective deontic: whereas subjective deontics have their source of obligation in the speaker, objective deontics have a source of obligation outside the

48:5, 7; Jer. 1:17; 4:4; 6:8; 10:24; 21:12; 38:19; Hosea 2:5; Amos 5:6; Mal. 3:24; Pss. 2:12; 7:3; 13:4–5; 28:1; 38:17; 50:22; 59:12; 91:12; Job 32:13; 36:18; Prov. 5:9–10; 9:8; 20:13; 22:25; 24:18; 25:8, 10, 16–17; 26:4–5; 30:6, 9–10; 31:5; Ruth 4:6; 1 Chron. 10:4.

203. Prov. 23:6; 24:1.

204. Hag. 1:8; Ruth 4:4. While these *ketiv-qere* examples illustrate the interchangeability of first-person prefix forms with and without a final ה with an irrealis sense, the ה is not related to modality (see §3.8.1).

speaker—whether expressed or left unexpressed. Thus, if we were to imagine Abraham asking who is telling him not to harm Isaac (ex. 203a), the answer from heaven would be "I am." By contrast, the answer to such a question about the rape of Dinah (ex. 203b) would be less forthcoming and notably non-agentive and inanimate: customs, morality, and the like say this should not be done. A good case can be made that the directive-volitive subsystem (see §3.8) as a whole is associated with subjective deontic modality, whereas deontic modality as expressed by the IPFV as well as the IR-PFV may be either subjective or objective. As a privative opposition, this subjective-objective distinction only partially distinguishes between the JUSS and IPFV in prohibitive as well as other volitive expressions. For example, a good number of IPFV prohibitions appear in legal code, most notably in the decalogue (ex. 221). These might be explained as subjective (i.e., Yhwh says so) or objective (i.e., so it is written in the covenant stipulations). The point is simply that the IPFV in prohibitive and directive deontic expressions does not specify the locus of authority for the obligation.

221. Deontic IPFV

לֹא תַעֲשֶׂה־לְךָ פֶסֶל

You shall not make ‹Q.IPFV› for yourself an image. (Exod. 20:4)[205]

3.8 The Directive-Volitive Irrealis Subsystem: Imperative and Jussive

Scholars are largely agreed on the volitive character of the IMPV, JUSS, and "cohortative" (e.g., Joosten 2012: 17; Dallaire 2014: 15). These are characterized by directive-volitive modality and show invariability of both tense and aspect. To the extent that future tense is conflated with irrealis mood, the forms are invariably "future" oriented. And as with future expressions generally, which only rarely diverge from perfective aspect, the IMPV and JUSS forms do not exhibit an imperfective variation of the general directive-volitive sense. Hence both the TP (FUT) and AspP (PFV) values are placed in parentheses in fig. 3.12.

In an effort to be more transparent in their range of meanings, the compound label directive-volitive is employed here, since volitive itself in common parlance is associated with wishes more than with commands. What unifies this subsystem of irrealis mood is that these grams invariably express the will of the speaker (i.e., subjective deontic modality), in contrast to other deon-

205. Exod. 20:3, 5, 7, 10, 13–17, 23, 25–26; Deut. 5:7–9, 11, 14, 17–21; etc.

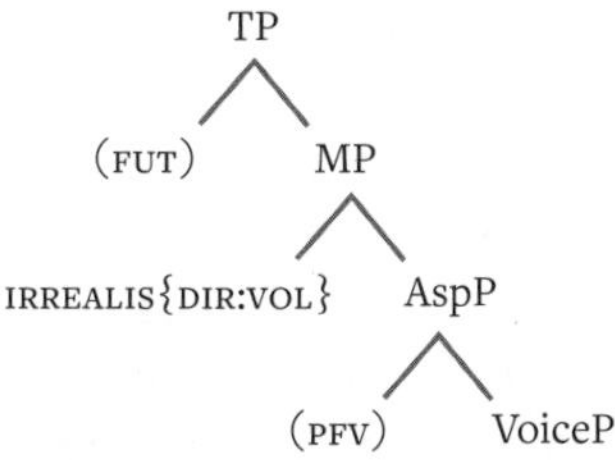

Figure 3.12. Directive-Volitive Irrealis Subsystem

tic modal constructions that may express objective or subjective modality—notably, the IPFV and IR-PFV (see §3.7.2).

3.8.1 Diachronic Development of the Directive-Volitive Subsystem

Whereas discussion of the IR-PFV and irrealis IPFV revolved around plausible paths by which these realis forms developed irrealis functions, the irrealis status of the directive-volitive forms is not in question. However, the analysis of the paragogic ָה- that often appears on the "long" imperative and on the cohortative forms has been disputed. Proposals include that it is a reflex of a West Semitic *yaqtulan(na)* modal verb or a Canaanite *yaqtula* modal verb or that it is related to the Akkadian ventive *-am* termination (Dallaire 2014: 63, 108).

Although Dallaire (2014) entertains the Akkadian ventive explanation for only the long imperative and not the cohortative, there are good reasons for analyzing the paragogic ָה- as a unified morpheme that occurs with multiple conjugations. For one, the ָה- is not invariably associated with the cohortative (cf. various explanations for the "cohortative ָה-" in Ewald 1879: 17; S. Driver 1998: 51; Joüon §117c), as thirteen apocopated, or "short," first-person "cohortative" forms appear in the Hebrew Bible.[206] For another, a paragogic ָה- appears on more than one hundred PN forms, the vast majority of which are first person,[207] suggesting that it is the same morpheme that appears on both

206. Deut. 18:16; 1 Sam. 14:36; Isa. 41:23, 28; Ezek. 5:16; Hosea 9:15; 11:4; Zeph. 1:2, 3; Job 23:9; Neh. 1:4 (as identified by Dallaire 2014: 92n172). Apart from Hosea 9:15, these are all tagged as cohortative (in form or both form and meaning) in Groves-Wheeler (accessed within Accordance Bible Software).

207. Gentry (1998: 24n67) lists 99 occurrences, varying from McFall's (1982: 211–14) list; Groves-Wheeler (accessed within Accordance Bible Software) tag 103 occurrences, including 95 first-person-singular forms (Gen. 32:6; Num. 8:19; Josh. 24:8 [*ketiv*]; Judg. 6:9–10; 10:12; 12:3 [2×]; 1 Sam. 2:28; 28:15; 2 Sam. 4:10; 7:9; 12:8 [2×]; 22:24; Jer. 11:18; 32:9; Ezek. 3:3; 9:8; 16:11; Zech. 11:13; Pss. 3:6; 7:5; 69:12, 21; 73:16; 119:55, 59, 106, 131, 147, 158; Job 1:15–17, 19; 19:20;

the PN and on the cohortative forms. If this is the case, then the morpheme cannot be a marker of irrealis mood or modality, appearing as it does on both realis and irrealis mood forms. Finally, similar nonmodal explanations have been offered for the paragogic ה ָ- on the PN form and the “long” imperative forms: namely, the morpheme is analogous to the Akkadian ventive, and it expresses a reflexive-benefactive sense (Gentry 1998: 24; Shulman 1996: 66; Fassberg 1999: 13). Dallaire’s (2014: 67–68) dismissal of this latter analysis of the long imperative begs the question of the morpheme’s function, since she simply suggests that it is more associated with modality than reflexivity. Since the IMPV form is always modal, of course ה ָ- with the IMPV may appear to be associated with modality.

The paragogic ה ָ- with first-person PN forms increases in frequency largely in Late Biblical Hebrew and is ubiquitous in many of the Dead Sea Scrolls (Qimron 1997: 177), suggesting that as the paragogic ה ָ- is conventionalized, it is simultaneously increasingly bleached of semantic meaning, which may account for a reflexive-benefactive sense not always being immediately apparent. While the same argument cannot be made about the paragogic ה ָ- on the imperative, the fact that the contrast between the long and short imperative has been deemed mere stylistic variation by some scholars (e.g., *IBHS* §34.4a) indicates that the original semantic function of the morpheme may have become obscured by the time of the biblical period. All this suggests a simpler analysis of the directive-volitive subsystem of irrealis mood: it consists of a first- and third-person JUSS, the former of which usually appears with a paragogic ה ָ- expressing an increasingly conventionalized reflexive-benefactive sense; a second-person IMPV limited to positive directive expressions; and a second-person JUSS that is limited to negative directives using the distinctive אַל negator.[208]

3.8.2 Semantics of the Directive-Volitive Subsystem

As the label directive-volitive indicates, the IMPV and JUSS forms express directive and volitive modalities, both of which are subcategories of deontic modality. Directives are commands, whereby the speaker imposes his/her will on another person. The IMPV and second-person JUSS appear in complementary

29:17; Eccles. 1:17; Dan. 8:13, 15, 17; 9:3, 4 [2×]; 10:16 [2×], 19; 12:8; Ezra 7:28; 8:15–16, 17 [*ketiv*], 24–26, 28; 9:3 [2×], 5 [2×], 6; Neh. 1:4; 2:1, 6, 9, 13; 5:7 [2×], 8, 13; 6:3, 8, 11–12; 7:5; 12:31; 13:7–8, 9 [2×], 10, 11 [2×], 13, 17 [2×], 19 [2×], 21 [2×], 22, 30); 6 first-person-plural forms (Gen. 41:11; 43:21; Ps. 90:10; Ezra 8:23 [2×], 31); and 2 non-first-person forms (Ezek. 23:16 [*qere*], 20).

208. Only three unambiguous JUSS second-person forms without אַל occur (1 Sam. 10:8; Ezek. 3:3; Ps. 71:12). The two examples with אֶל in the Leningrad Codex (Exod. 10:8; Deut. 2:9) are spelling errors for אַל (see *BHS*).

distribution, largely limited to the expression of positive commands and negative prohibitions, respectively (ex. 222).

222. IMPV and Negated Second-Person JUSS for Positive and Negative Commands

קְנֵה חָכְמָה קְנֵה בִינָה אַל־תִּשְׁכַּח וְאַל־תֵּט מֵאִמְרֵי־פִי׃

Acquire ‹Q.IMPV› wisdom, acquire understanding; do not forget ‹Q.JUSS.2S› and do not turn ‹Q.JUSS.2S› from the words of my mouth. (Prov. 4:5)[209]

In contrast to the IMPV and second-person JUSS forms, the first-person singular JUSS is largely limited to volitive expressions (wishes and intentions), since self-imposed directives and first-person volitives are semantically indistinguishable (ex. 223a). In the plural the form may express the joint volition of the speaker and addressee, or it may impose the will of the speaker on the addressee (i.e., directive), who is urged to join the speaker in a common action (ex. 223b).

223. First-Person JUSS Expressing Volitive and Directive Modality

223a

אָקוּמָה נָּא וַאֲסוֹבְבָה בָעִיר בַּשְּׁוָקִים וּבָרְחֹבוֹת אֲבַקְשָׁה אֵת שֶׁאָהֲבָה נַפְשִׁי

I will arise ‹Q.JUSS.1S› and I will circle around ‹POEL.JUSS.1S› through the city in the streets and in the squares; I will seek ‹PI.JUSS.1S› the (one) whom my soul loves ‹Q.PFV›. (Song 3:2)[210]

223b

אִם־יֹאמְרוּ לְכָה אִתָּנוּ נֶאֶרְבָה לְדָם נִצְפְּנָה לְנָקִי חִנָּם׃ נִבְלָעֵם כִּשְׁאוֹל חַיִּים

If they say ‹Q.IPFV› to you, "Come ‹Q.IMPV› with us. Let us lie in wait ‹Q.JUSS.1P› for blood; let us hide ‹Q.JUSS.1P› for the innocent for no

209. Other verses showing positive IMPV and negative JUSS contrast include Deut. 9:27; Jer. 39:12; Ezek. 2:8; Job 36:21; 40:32; Eccles. 11:6; Esther 6:10; Neh. 3:36–37; 13:14. Verses with multiple IMPVs include Judg. 5:12; Jer. 29:5–6; 46:3–4; 51:27–28; Joel 1:13–14; 2:15–16; Job 40:11–13; 1 Chron. 16:8–10, 28–30. Verses with multiple JUSSs include Deut. 20:3; Jer. 7:16; 14:21; 16:5; 22:3; Ezek. 2:6; 20:18; Hosea 4:15; Obad. 13–14; Prov. 4:6.

210. Gen. 12:2; 18:21; 30:31–32; 46:31; 50:5; Exod. 4:18; 2 Sam. 3:21; 17:1–2; 19:27; Isa. 1:24–26; Jer. 46:8; Mic. 1:8; Hab. 2:1; Pss. 55:7–9; 60:8; 108:8; Job 9:27; 16:4–5; 23:3–5; 32:20–21.

reason. Let us swallow ‹Q.JUSS.1P› them like Sheol, alive. . . ." (Prov. 1:11–12)[211]

In contrast to the second-person JUSSs, which appear predominantly in prohibitions, the first-person JUSSs are usually positive and appear negated with אַל only a handful of times (ex. 224).

224. Negated First-Person JUSS

224a

יֵבֹשׁוּ רֹדְפַי וְאַל־אֵבֹשָׁה אָנִי יֵחַתּוּ הֵמָּה וְאַל־אֵחַתָּה אָנִי

Let (those that are) pursuing ‹Q.PTC› me be put to shame ‹Q.JUSS.3MP›, but may I not be put to shame ‹Q.JUSS.1CS›; let them be terrified ‹NI.JUSS.3MP›, but may I not be terrified ‹NI.JUSS.1CS›. (Jer. 17:18)[212]

224b

לְכוּ וְנַכֵּהוּ בַלָּשׁוֹן וְאַל־נַקְשִׁיבָה אֶל־כָּל־דְּבָרָיו

Come ‹Q.IMPV› and let us strike ‹HI.JUSS.1P› him with the tongue and do not let us pay attention ‹HI.JUSS.1P› to any of his words. (Jer. 18:18)

Finally, the third-person JUSS is more varied in its functions, expressing positive and negative directive (ex. 225a) and volitional (ex. 225b) modalities.

225. Third-Person JUSS

225a

וַיַּזְעֵק וַיֹּאמֶר בְּנִינְוֵה מִטַּעַם הַמֶּלֶךְ וּגְדֹלָיו לֵאמֹר הָאָדָם
וְהַבְּהֵמָה הַבָּקָר וְהַצֹּאן אַל־יִטְעֲמוּ מְאוּמָה אַל־יִרְעוּ וּמַיִם
אַל־יִשְׁתּוּ׃ וְיִתְכַּסּוּ שַׂקִּים הָאָדָם וְהַבְּהֵמָה וְיִקְרְאוּ אֶל־
אֱלֹהִים בְּחָזְקָה וְיָשֻׁבוּ אִישׁ מִדַּרְכּוֹ הָרָעָה וּמִן־הֶחָמָס
אֲשֶׁר בְּכַפֵּיהֶם׃

He proclaimed ‹HI.PN+Q.PN› [lit., cried and said] through Nineveh, "From decree of the king and his nobles [COMP]: No human or beast—the herd or the flock—shall taste ‹Q.JUSS.3MP› anything nor graze ‹Q.JUSS.3MP›. And water they shall not drink ‹Q.JUSS.3MP›. But human and beast shall cover ‹HT.JUSS.3MP› themselves in sackcloths and call

211. Gen. 19:32; 43:8; 2 Kings 6:2; Isa. 7:6; Song 1:4; 7:12–13; Neh. 5:2.
212. 2 Sam. 24:14; Pss. 25:2; 31:2, 18; 69:15; 71:1.

‹Q.JUSS.3MP› to God with strength. Each shall turn back ‹Q.JUSS.3MP› from his wicked way and from the violence that (is) in his hands." (Jon. 3:7–8)[213]

225b

יֹאבַד יוֹם אִוָּלֶד בּוֹ וְהַלַּיְלָה אָמַר הֹרָה גָבֶר׃ הַיּוֹם הַהוּא יְהִי חֹשֶׁךְ אַל־יִדְרְשֵׁהוּ אֱלוֹהַּ מִמָּעַל וְאַל־תּוֹפַע עָלָיו נְהָרָה׃ יִגְאָלֻהוּ חֹשֶׁךְ וְצַלְמָוֶת תִּשְׁכָּן־עָלָיו עֲנָנָה יְבַעֲתֻהוּ כִּמְרִירֵי יוֹם׃ הַלַּיְלָה הַהוּא יִקָּחֵהוּ אֹפֶל אַל־יִחַדְּ בִּימֵי שָׁנָה בְּמִסְפַּר יְרָחִים אַל־יָבֹא׃ הִנֵּה הַלַּיְלָה הַהוּא יְהִי גַלְמוּד אַל־תָּבֹא רְנָנָה בוֹ׃ יִקְּבֻהוּ אֹרְרֵי־יוֹם הָעֲתִידִים עֹרֵר לִוְיָתָן׃

May the day (that) I was born ‹NI.PRET› perish ‹Q.JUSS.3MS› and the night (that) said ‹Q.PFV›, "A man is conceived ‹PU.PFV›!" May that day be ‹Q.JUSS.3MS› darkness; may God not seek ‹Q.JUSS.3MS› it from above, and may light not shine ‹HI.JUSS.3FS› upon it. May darkness and deep darkness redeem ‹Q.JUSS.3MP› it; may a cloud settle ‹Q.JUSS.3FS› upon it; may eclipses of the day terrify ‹PI.JUSS.3MP› it. May darkness seize ‹Q.JUSS.3MS› that night; may it not rejoice ‹Q.JUSS.3MS› in the days of the year; into the numbers of the months may it not enter ‹Q.JUSS.3MS›. Hey, may that night be ‹Q.JUSS.3MS› barren; may a cry of joy not enter ‹Q.JUSS.3FS› into it. May the cursers of day curse ‹Q.JUSS.3MP› it, those (who are) ready to rouse ‹POLEL.INF› Leviathan. (Job 3:3–7)[214]

It is noteworthy that many of the above forms of the JUSS are morphologically indistinct from the IPFV. In many cases, the presence of one or more distinctly JUSS forms in the context dictates that the ambiguous forms should be parsed likewise as JUSS. Frequently the decision of IPFV or JUSS parsing depends on the general interpretation of the passage in question. The three morphological databases all take different approaches to the issue: ECBTC treats all the prefix forms under a single label, regardless of whether or not they are apocopated; Andersen-Forbes parse strictly on the basis of semantics (e.g., both the short וַיְהִי and long יִהְיֶה in Judg. 6:39 are labeled imperfect/*yiqtol*, while the short יְהִי and indistinct prefix forms in Job 3:3–7, above,

213. Gen. 41:33; Josh. 7:3–4; Judg. 6:39; 7:3; 13:14; 1 Kings 18:23; 2 Kings 1:10, 12; Isa. 55:7; Jer. 9:16–17, 22–23; Hosea 4:4; Esther 2:2–4.

214. Gen. 9:26–27; 28:3; Num. 6:24–26; Deut. 33:6; 1 Sam. 18:17, 21; 1 Kings 1:47; 8:57; 2 Kings 16:16; Job 3:8; 6:9–10; 21:19–20; 31:8, 10; Ruth 1:8; 1 Chron. 16:31–32.

are parsed as jussives); finally, Groves-Wheeler take a via media, grouping all prefix forms under the imperfect/*yiqtol* label but then further distinguishing some as jussive/cohortative in form, in meaning, or in both.

Nothing of the above description is in any serious dispute across the grammars. However, a point of disagreement is whether these forms conjoined to another irrealis form express final (i.e., purpose/result) modality. Joüon (§116; 1923: 290) introduced the label "indirect volitive" (Fr. *volitif indirect*) for these examples, in contrast to "direct volitives" (Fr. *volitif direct*; see also Dallaire 2014: 102, 118; for a list of others who use these labels, see Muraoka 1997: 229n6).[215] Both Shulman and Muraoka have questioned this final meaning for directives. Shulman (1996: 221) claims that the meanings in these cases are implicated or contextual; more strongly and clearly, Muraoka (1997: 240) concludes:

> In summing up we would say that the syntagm in question does not have a function of normally indicating purpose. A sequence of volitive verb forms is a series of so many expressions of the speaker's or writer's wish and will. The fact that in some cases the second verb can be more elegantly translated as indicating a purpose of the first is essentially a question of pragmatics and translation techniques, and not of descriptive grammar and syntax.

This sketch of the directive-volitive subsystem is deceptively simple in that many levels of directive and volitional are possible, from direct commands to consent to advisement to intent to counterfactual wish (see Austin 1962). None of these levels are clearly indicated grammatically, and the import of the נָא morpheme that is often appended to the directive-volitive forms is far from clear (on נָא, see Shulman 1999; Dallaire 2014). While the interpretation of this clitic lies somewhat beyond this volume's focus on the TAM system, I suggest that the נָא is a lexical reinforcement of the illocutionary force (i.e., the purpose or intention) of the directive-volitive form it accompanies, whatever the nature of that illocutionary force might be. Determining what it might be is heavily dependent on the pragmatic context in a given passage.

215. Consistent with their strong semantics-based approach, Andersen-Forbes parse out "sequential" varieties of the perfect/*qatal* (e.g., IR-PFV), imperfect/*yiqtol*, and cohortative.

Chapter 4

DYNAMIC SYNTAX AND THE BIBLICAL HEBREW VERB IN CONTEXT

4.1 Introduction

Much has been said in the previous chapters about context and its significance in correctly interpreting the TAM grams. Too often appeals are made to context in a rather general and vague way, which is something to be avoided. This chapter treats the question of how the TAM grams interact with their context. I will examine the discourse function of isolated ה״יה (§4.2) and the temporal structure of discourse (§4.3), and I will illustrate the BH verb in context by examining representative passages from select genres: prose narrative, legal code, prophetic speech, and poetic verse (§4.4).

4.2 Discourse ה״יה

As discussed in §2.4.2, ה״יה can function as a copula, an existential, and as a full verb expressing an inchoative (–stages, +telic) event. However, the 3MS PN (וַיְהִי), IR-PFV (וְהָיָה), and rarely the JUSS (וִיהִי) forms of ה״יה also appear isolated as the only constituent in the clause, which semantic contribution I have indicated within square brackets (ex. 226).

226. הי״ה Discourse

226a. Past Narrative

וַיְהִי אַחֲרֵי הַדְּבָרִים הָאֵלֶּה וַיֻּגַּד לְאַבְרָהָם לֵאמֹר הִנֵּה
יָלְדָה מִלְכָּה גַם־הִוא בָּנִים לְנָחוֹר אָחִיךָ׃

[PAST] After these things (it) was told ‹HO.PN› to Abraham [COMP], "Hey, Milcah has borne ‹Q.PFV›—also she—children to Nahor your brother." (Gen. 22:20)

Other examples of discourse וַיְהִי are as follows: Gen. 4:3, 8; 6:1; 7:10; 8:6, 13; 11:2; 12:11, 14; 14:1; 15:17; 19:17, 29, 34; 20:13; 21:22; 22:1, 20; 24:22, 30, 52; 25:11; 26:8, 32; 27:1, 30; 29:10, 13, 23, 25; 30:25; 31:10; 34:25; 35:18, 22; 37:23; 38:1, 24, 27–29; 39:7, 10–11, 13, 15, 18–19; 40:1, 20; 41:1, 8, 13; 42:35; 43:2, 21; 44:24; 48:1; Exod. 1:21; 2:11, 23; 4:24; 6:28; 12:29, 41, 51; 13:15, 17; 14:24; 16:10, 13, 22, 27; 18:13; 19:16; 32:19, 30; 34:29; 40:17; Lev. 9:1; Num. 7:1; 10:11, 35; 11:25; 16:31; 17:7, 23; 22:41; 25:19; Deut. 1:3; 2:16; 5:23; 9:11; 31:24; Josh. 1:1; 3:2, 14; 4:1, 11, 18; 5:1, 8, 13; 6:8, 15–16, 20; 8:14, 24; 9:1, 16; 10:1, 11, 20, 24, 27; 11:1; 15:18; 23:1; 24:29; Judg. 1:1, 14, 28; 2:4; 3:18, 27; 6:7, 25, 27; 7:9, 15; 8:33; 9:42; 11:4–5, 35, 39; 13:20; 14:11, 15, 17; 15:1, 17; 16:4, 16, 25; 19:1, 5; 21:4; 1 Sam. 1:20; 3:2; 4:5, 18; 5:9–10; 7:2; 8:1; 9:26; 10:11; 11:11; 13:10; 14:1, 19; 16:6; 18:1, 6, 9–10, 19, 30; 20:27, 35; 23:6; 24:2, 6, 17; 25:2, 37–38; 28:1; 30:1, 25; 31:8; 2 Sam. 1:1–2; 2:1, 23; 3:6; 4:4; 6:13; 7:1, 4; 8:1; 11:1–2, 14, 16; 12:18; 13:1, 23, 36; 15:1–2, 7, 32; 16:16; 17:21, 27; 19:26; 21:18; 1 Kings 2:39; 3:18; 5:21; 6:1; 8:10, 17, 54; 9:1, 10; 11:4, 15, 29; 12:2, 20; 13:4, 20, 23, 31; 14:6, 25, 28; 15:21, 29; 16:11, 18, 31; 17:7, 17; 18:1, 4, 7, 17, 27, 29, 36, 44–45; 19:13; 20:12, 26, 29, 39; 21:1, 15–16, 27; 22:2, 32–33; 2 Kings 2:1, 9, 11; 3:5, 20; 4:6, 8, 25, 40; 5:7–8; 6:5, 20, 24, 26, 30; 7:18; 8:3, 5, 15, 21; 9:22; 10:7, 9, 25; 12:7, 11; 13:21; 14:5; 17:25; 18:1, 9; 19:1, 35, 37; 20:4; 22:3, 11; 25:1, 25, 27; Isa. 7:1; 22:7; 36:1; 37:1, 38; Jer. 13:6; 20:3; 26:8; 28:1; 35:11; 36:1, 9, 16, 23; 39:4; 41:1, 4, 6–7, 13; 42:7; 43:1; 52:4, 31; Ezek. 1:1; 3:16; 8:1; 9:8; 10:6; 11:13; 16:23; 20:1; 26:1; 29:17; 30:20; 31:1; 32:1, 17; 33:21; Jon. 4:8; Zech. 7:1, 13; Job 1:5; 42:7; Ruth 1:1, 19; 3:8; Esther 1:1; 2:8; 3:4; 5:1–2; Dan. 8:2, 15; Neh. 1:1, 4; 2:1; 3:33; 4:1, 6, 9; 6:1, 16; 7:1; 13:3, 19; 1 Chron. 10:8; 17:3; 18:1; 19:1; 20:1; 2 Chron. 5:11, 13; 8:1; 10:2; 12:1–2, 11; 13:15; 16:5; 18:31–32; 20:1; 21:9, 19; 22:8; 24:4, 11, 23; 25:3, 14, 16; 34:19.

226b. Irrealis Perfective

וְהָיָה בִּקְרָב־אִישׁ לְהִשְׁתַּחֲוֺת לוֹ וְשָׁלַח אֶת־יָדוֹ וְהֶחֱזִיק לוֹ וְנָשַׁק לוֹ׃

[IRREALIS] Whenever a person would draw near ‹Q.INF› to bow down ‹HISHTAPHEL.INF› to him, he would stretch out ‹Q.IR-PFV› his hand and grasp ‹HI.IR-PFV› him and kiss ‹IR-PFV› him. (2 Sam. 15:5)

Other examples of discourse וְהָיָה are as follows: Gen. 9:14; 12:12; 24:14, 43; 27:40; 30:41; 38:9; 44:31; 46:33; 47:24; Exod. 1:10; 3:21; 4:8, 16; 12:26; 13:5, 11, 14; 17:11; 18:22; 22:26; 33:7–9, 22; Lev. 5:5, 23; 14:9; 27:10, 33; Num. 10:32; 15:19, 24; 16:7; 17:20; 21:8–9; 33:56; Deut. 6:10; 7:12; 8:19; 11:13, 29; 12:11; 15:16; 17:18; 18:19; 20:2, 9, 11; 21:3, 14, 16; 23:12, 14; 24:1; 25:2, 6, 19–26:1; 27:2, 4; 28:1, 15, 63; 29:18; 30:1; 31:21; Josh. 2:14, 19; 3:13; 6:5; 7:14–15; 8:5, 8; 22:18; 23:15; Judg. 2:19; 4:20; 6:3; 7:4, 17; 9:33; 11:31; 12:5; 19:30; 21:22; 1 Sam. 1:12; 2:36; 3:9; 10:7, 9; 13:22; 16:16, 23; 17:25, 48; 23:23; 25:30; 2 Sam. 11:20; 14:26; 15:5, 35; 17:9; 1 Kings 1:21; 2:37; 11:38; 17:4; 18:12, 24; 19:17; 20:6; 2 Kings 3:15; 4:10; Isa. 3:24; 4:3; 7:18, 21–23; 8:21; 10:12, 20, 27; 11:10–11; 13:14; 14:3; 16:2, 12; 17:4; 22:20; 23:15, 17; 24:18, 21; 27:12–13; 65:24; 66:23; Jer. 3:9, 16; 4:9; 5:19; 12:15–16; 15:2; 16:10; 17:24; 25:12, 28; 27:8; 30:8; 31:28; 37:11; 38:28; 42:4; 49:39; 51:63; Ezek. 21:12; 38:10, 18; 39:11; 43:27; 44:17; 47:10, 22–23; Hosea 1:5; 2:1, 18, 23; 4:9; Joel 3:1; 4:18; Amos 6:9; 7:2; 8:9; Mic. 4:1; 5:9; Nah. 3:7; Zeph. 1:8, 10, 12; Zech. 8:13; 12:3, 9; 13:2–4, 8; 14:6–7, 13, 16–17; 1 Chron. 17:11.

226c. Jussive

וִיהִי כְּשָׁמְעֲךָ אֶת־קוֹל הַצְּעָדָה בְּרָאשֵׁי הַבְּכָאִים אָז תֵּצֵא בַמִּלְחָמָה

[DIR-VOL] When you hear ‹Q.INF› the sound of the march at the heads of the balsam trees, then you should go forth ‹Q.IPFV› into the battle. (1 Chron. 14:15)[1]

The isolated form of the verb in such cases is due not merely to a lack of *overt* constituents. There is no semantic role for a subject or VP complement; nor is there any antecedent available to suggest a null subject or object. These constructions may be analyzed in two ways. Wilson (2018: 131–42; 2019; 2020) argues that these are cases of an "isolated verb" that defaults to 3MS, "mirrors" the TAM of the verb in the main clause (i.e., the PN, IR-PFV, and directive

1. 1 Sam. 10:5; 2 Sam. 5:24, 18:22–23; Ruth 3:4.

IPFV in the above examples), and appears in the highest of the left-periphery domain of the clause; that is, it occupies the front-most position in the tree structure, the complementizer phrase (CP; fig. 4.1).

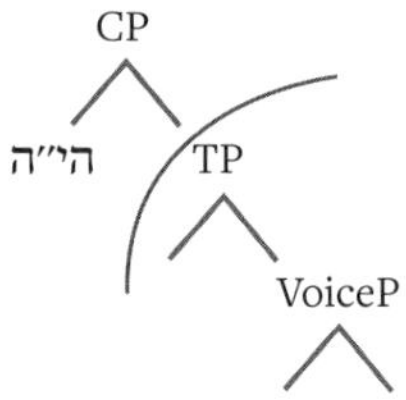

CP
הי"ה TP
VoiceP

Figure 4.1. The Complementizer Phrase Left-Periphery Domain

He produces the following points in support of these three aspects of his analysis (i.e., the form is isolated, mirrors the main verb, and is located in left periphery): (1) cases in which, if the form were a copula, it would exhibit gender/number mismatch with the subject (e.g., Gen. 39:5; Exod. 17:12); (2) cases in which the isolated verb agrees in TAM with the main verb; and (3) cases in which the form precedes even left (initial) dislocated constituents (ex. 227).

227. Discourse הי"ה Preceding Left-Dislocated Constituent

227a

וַיְהִי כָּל־הָאִישׁ אֲשֶׁר־יִהְיֶה־לּוֹ־רִיב לָבוֹא אֶל־
הַמֶּלֶךְ לַמִּשְׁפָּט וַיִּקְרָא אַבְשָׁלוֹם אֵלָיו

[PAST] Any man that there would be ‹Q.IPFV› to him a case to come ‹Q.INF› to the king for judgment, Absalom called ‹Q.PN› to him. (2 Sam. 15:2)

227b

וְהָיָה הָאֱלֹהִים אֲשֶׁר־יַעֲנֶה בָאֵשׁ הוּא הָאֱלֹהִים

[IRREALIS] The god that will answer ‹Q.IPFV› in fire, he (is) the god. (1 Kings 18:24)[2]

The other analysis of these occurrences is as independent avalent clauses (i.e., without a subject or VP complements) that function discourse-pragmatically

2. Gen. 24:14, 43; Num. 16:7; 17:20; Deut. 12:11; 18:19; 21:3; Josh. 2:19; 1 Sam. 17:25; Jer. 27:8; Zech. 13:8.

with respect to a following clause. This alternative analysis cannot account for the lack of gender/number agreement in some cases, but such disagreement appears likewise with instances of the homonymous copular forms, which cannot be explained.[3] This avalent clausal analysis would make Wilson's observations about the isolated verb and the left periphery moot (fig. 4.1), since it is not on the periphery of any clause. Rather, it stands as an independent clause pragmatically rather than syntactically connected to the following clause. This avalent analysis avoids the weakness of Wilson's linking the TAM of the isolated verb to the verb in the main clause: on the one hand, his approach requires equating the TAM values of different grams (e.g., PN and PFV in Gen. 22:1; IR-PFV and PFV in Gen. 24:14; JUSS and IPFV in 1 Chron. 14:15 [ex. 226c]); on the other hand, it begs the question of why—if the verb "mirrors" the TAM of the main verb—other conjugations, such as the IPFV וְיִהְיֶה, are not employed in this manner.

Wilson provides an "exhaustive" list (2019: 111–14) and tally (2020: 327) of the more than seven hundred discourse היה forms. His and my lists above (see the Scripture references accompanying exs. 226a–c) diverge because of cases like the initial וַיְהִי in ex. 228. While he treats this as an isolated verb, I analyze it as a copula and the following two constituents as the subject and predicate complement, respectively. Compare the second and third וַיְהִי forms in the verse, which we agree function as copulas (see Wilson 2019: 106–7).

228. Discourse and Copular Functions of היה

וַיְהִי יְהוָה אֶת־יוֹסֵף וַיְהִי אִישׁ מַצְלִיחַ וַיְהִי בְּבֵית אֲדֹנָיו הַמִּצְרִי׃

Yhwh was ‹Q.PN› with Joseph and he was/became ‹Q.PN› a man of success ‹HI.PTC› and he was ‹Q.PN› in the house of his master the Egyptian. (Gen. 39:2)

To treat any of these three וַיְהִי forms as an avalent/isolated verb requires positing a null copula for the following constituents, which is not as linguistically elegant as a copular analysis. As Wilson (2019: 107) admits with respect to his copular analysis of the second וַיְהִי in this verse, "this decision is mostly

3. Gen. 30:42; 32:9; 35:5, 16; 39:5; 47:28; Exod. 17:12; Num. 9:6; 20:2; 33:14; Josh. 5:1; 8:20; 17:9, 18; 19:1, 33; 21:20; 1 Sam. 1:2; 25:20; 1 Kings 10:5; 11:3; 2 Kings 3:9; Ezek. 47:9; Mic. 5:6–7; Job 8:7; 1 Chron. 2:34; 23:17; 24:28 2 Chron. 9:4. Of these, Wilson (2019: 112) identifies the following as instances of the isolated verb: Gen. 32:9; 35:16; 39:5; Exod. 17:12; Josh. 19:1; 1 Sam. 25:20; Ezek. 47:9.

contextual rather than grammatical." Given that scholars are not agreed on the function of the discourse הי"ה in context (even Wilson's thinking has altered slightly among his three publications), a syntax-based analysis of the structure is preferable to a decision based on the uncertain semantic and/or discourse-pragmatic function of the construction.

A good number of suggestions have been advanced to explain the function of these avalent occurrences of הי"ה (see Wilson 2019: 91–93). In Cook (2012c: 309–12) I argued closely in line with van der Merwe (1999) that these forms semantically reassert the reference time and organize episodes and scenes in the discourse according to discourse-pragmatics. Wilson (2018: 131–42; 2019; 2020) enriches such suggestions by identifying this construction with thetic statements. In contrast to a categorical statement, which comments on (i.e., predicates something about) a topic, a thetic statement "either introduces an entity in the discourse or points to a state of affairs as a whole (i.e., not establishing a syntactic subject-predicate distinction)" (Macías 2016: 51; cited approvingly in Wilson 2020: 314). A number of thetic subtypes are suggested in the literature, such as existentials (e.g., *There are books on the table*) and weather statements (e.g., *It is snowing*; Macías 2016: iv; Wilson 2020: 324), both of which notably show a "dummy" subject in English, indicating that rather than predicating something about a topic (as a categorical statement does), the state-of-affairs as a whole is being asserted.[4] Wilson (2020: 324–25) helpfully compares the function of this thetic marking structure to pseudo-cleft structures like *What happened was . . .* , which is recognizably similar to the traditional English gloss of this discourse הי"ה structure—*And it was/shall come to pass*—which features a dummy *it* subject.

Wilson (2020) places this thetic marking analysis within the context of a semantics of information structure approach, explaining that such an approach sees each new assertion as "updating" the "common ground"—the shared information among interlocutors, whether speakers/hearers or writers/readers. In this context, Wilson (2020: 322) contends that "a thetic sentence is a spontaneous common ground *creator*." That is, thetic sentences introduce as presupposition a new common ground on which the subsequent discourse is based. This explains why in prose narrative, וַיְהִי is frequently followed by

4. Wilson (2019: 99; 2020: 315) notes that theticity correlates with Lambrecht's (1994) "sentence focus" and (2020: 324) that dummy subjects have been classified as a type of "detopicalization" strategy (Lambrecht and Polinksy 1997: 4). Wilson (2019) adopts Sasse's (1996) five functions of thetic expressions (annuntiative, introductive, interruptive, descriptive, and explanatory) and applies them to Gen. 39. However, I find these functions unhelpfully indiscrete. How do "introductive" and "descriptive" differ when both appear to be equally applicable to scene-opening thetic statements? What is the semantic distinction between "annuntiative" and "interruptive," both of which seem equally to apply to "out-of-the-blue" statements?

a topicalized scene-setting clause subordinated to the following main clause, as illustrated in ex. 229.[5] After the discussion among the brothers of what to do with Joseph, the thetic expression with a topicalized scene-setting clause sets ups a new common ground—the brother's action toward Joseph—and so introduces a new temporal/spatial scene in the story.

229. Discourse וַיְהִי with Topicalized Scene-Setting Clause

וַיְהִי כַּאֲשֶׁר־בָּא יוֹסֵף אֶל־אֶחָיו וַיַּפְשִׁיטוּ אֶת־יוֹסֵף
אֶת־כֻּתָּנְתּוֹ

[PAST] When Joseph came ‹Q.PFV› to his brothers, they stripped ‹HI.PN› Joseph of his tunic. (Gen. 37:23)

While we might conclude on the basis of such examples that the discourse הי״ה is strictly a pragmatic device, "frozen" in form, passages such as ex. 230 suggest that וְהָיָה is an avalent clause that semantically sets or "updates" the reference time for the discourse that follows, which it pragmatically introduces by marking the initial thetic sentences: both occurrences of וְהָיָה in ex. 230 disambiguate that the following clauses, respectively, are irrealis mood, conveying the habitual occurrence of a snake biting and the victim looking and living.

230. Discourse וְהָיָה Establishing Irrealis Mood

וַיֹּאמֶר יְהוָה אֶל־מֹשֶׁה עֲשֵׂה לְךָ שָׂרָף וְשִׂים אֹתוֹ עַל־נֵס
וְהָיָה כָּל־הַנָּשׁוּךְ וְרָאָה אֹתוֹ וָחָי׃ וַיַּעַשׂ מֹשֶׁה נְחַשׁ נְחֹשֶׁת
וַיְשִׂמֵהוּ עַל־הַנֵּס וְהָיָה אִם־נָשַׁךְ הַנָּחָשׁ אֶת־אִישׁ וְהִבִּיט
אֶל־נְחַשׁ הַנְּחֹשֶׁת וָחָי׃

Yhwh said to Moses, "Make ‹Q.IMPV› for yourself a serpent, and place ‹Q.IMPV› it on a standard. [IRREALIS] Everyone who (is) bitten ‹Q.PPTC› should look ‹Q.IR-PFV› at it and live ‹Q.IR-PFV›." Moses made ‹Q.PN› a bronze snake and placed ‹Q.PN› it on the standard. [IRREALIS] When the snake bit a person, he would gaze ‹HI.IR-PFV› at the bronze snake and live ‹Q.IR-PFV›. (Num. 21:8–9)

5. Wilson (2020: 327) states that 85 percent of his tally of 748 examples feature a following temporal adverbial expression, as in ex. 229.

If the discourse הי"ה seems to make only a slight contribution to the structure of BH discourse, it must be borne in mind that the use of this avalent TAM-asserting, thetic-marking structure is optional, as illustrated by the following contrastive examples (ex. 231).

231. Optionality of Discourse הי"ה

231a

אַחַר הַדְּבָרִים הָאֵלֶּה הָיָה דְבַר־יְהוָה אֶל־אַבְרָם

After these things, the word of Yhwh came ‹Q.PFV› to Abram. (Gen. 15:1)[6]

231b

וַיְהִי אַחַר הַדְּבָרִים הָאֵלֶּה וְהָאֱלֹהִים נִסָּה אֶת־אַבְרָהָם

[PAST] After these things, God tested ‹PI.PFV› Abraham. (Gen. 22:1)

231c

בַּיּוֹם הַהוּא יְגַלַּח אֲדֹנָי בְּתַעַר הַשְּׂכִירָה בְּעֶבְרֵי נָהָר

On that day the Lord will shave ‹PI.IPFV› with a razor that (is) hired beyond the river. (Isa. 7:20)[7]

231d

וְהָיָה בַּיּוֹם הַהוּא יְחַיֶּה־אִישׁ עֶגְלַת בָּקָר וּשְׁתֵּי־צֹאן׃

[IRREALIS] On that day, a man will keep alive ‹PI.IPFV› a young cow and two sheep. (Isa. 7:21)

4.3 The Temporal Structure of Discourse

Reichenbach's (1947) idea of the "permanence" of the R-point (i.e., reference point) in multiclause expressions led tense-aspect studies to the idea that the R-point "shifts" from clause to clause as the discourse unfolds (see §3.2.2). Dynamic semantics, which encompasses several linguistic theories, analyzes meaning at the discourse level (i.e., beyond individual clauses) in terms of the accumulation of information and/or "updating" contexts. Discourse

6. Compare the parallel passages 1 Kings 8:54 and 2 Chron. 7:1; 2 Kings 12:11 and 2 Chron. 24:11; 2 Kings 22:3 and 2 Chron. 34:8. See other examples in *IBHS* §33.2.4.

7. Compare Isa. 2:2 and 2:20; Isa. 7:18, 20 and 7:21, 23; Isa. 17:4 and 17:7.

representation theory is one of the earliest dynamic semantic theories to adopt Reichenbach's R-point. Unlike Reichenbach, however, discourse representation theory posited a moveable R-point to analyze how clausal predicates instruct the reader/listener to incorporate additional information into the existing context. Kamp and Rohrer (1983: 250) illustrated their claim of a moveable R-point with the sentences in ex. 232, contrasting the semantics of the French *imparfait* and *passé simple*, which correspond analogously to the English past progressive and simple past as imperfective and perfective aspects, respectively (from Kamp and Rohrer 1983: 254; see Cook 2012c: 37–38).

232. Movement of R-Point Effected by Verbal Aspect

232a. [$_{e1}$Quand Pierre entra (***passé simple***)], [$_{e2}$Maria téléphona (***passé simple***)].

When Pierre entered (perfective), Marie telephoned (perfective)

232b. [$_{e1}$Quand Pierre entra (***passé simple***)], [$_{e2}$Marie téléphonait (***imparfait***)].

When Pierre entered (perfective), Marie was telephoning (imperfective).

They explain that the perfective *passé simple* in the second clause in ex. 232a "transfers" the reference point to the second event, so that the latter is interpreted as taking place *after* the first event is completed. By contrast, the imperfective *imparfait* does not transfer the reference point, resulting in the interpretation that the second event in ex. 232b temporally overlaps with the first event.

The idea that some events "advance" the reference time has since become widespread, but early studies struggled to identify precisely what semantic feature(s) was/were responsible for this interpretative effect. While Kamp and Rohrer (1983) attributed the distinction to viewpoint aspect (at least in French), others have argued that situation aspect is the mechanism; specifically, achievements and accomplishments advance the reference time, whereas states and activities do not (e.g., Dry 1981; see Cook 2012c: 38). By the end of the twentieth century, a consensus emerged that the movement of the R-point is effected by boundedness, defined as an event having reached a temporal boundary (Depraetere 1995: 2–3). The property of (un)boundedness is determined by various factors, including viewpoint and situation aspect, adverbial modification, syntax, and pragmatics (see Cook 2004: 250–53).

To understand the significance of (un)boundedness and the temporal movement of the reference time between events, we need to revisit situation aspect (§2.3) and analyze its interaction with viewpoint aspect (§3.2.2).

Accomplishments and achievements were described in chapter 2 as sharing the property of [+telic] (table 2.1 and fig. 2.5 in §2.3). That is, they have a conclusion or endpoint that is built in or "natural" to the event itself. When such situations are presented with the "wide-angle" perfective viewpoint, that final event boundary is visible or explicit, presenting the events as "bounded." When multiple such perfective accomplishments and/or achievements are presented in sequence, they are understood to "move" the reference time, or R-point, forward from event to event, as illustrated in ex. 233.

233. Movement of R-Point by Bounded Perfective Accomplishments and Achievements

וַיֵּרֶד אַשְׁקְלוֹן וַיַּךְ מֵהֶם שְׁלֹשִׁים אִישׁ וַיִּקַּח אֶת־חֲלִיצוֹתָם
וַיִּתֵּן הַחֲלִיפוֹת לְמַגִּידֵי הַחִידָה

He went down ‹Q.PN› (to) Ashkelon and struck down ‹HI.PN› from them thirty men and took ‹Q.PN› their gear and gave ‹Q.PN› the garments to those (who) guessed ‹HI.PTC› the riddle. (Judg. 14:19)

Each of these four events is an accomplishment or an achievement with the [+telic] property. Two are [+telic] by virtue of the event itself: "take" (לָקַח) and "give" (נָתַן), which are both achievements (i.e., the transfer of possession is more or less instantaneous). The other two are [+telic] based on their valency. "Strike" (הִכָּה) can be an achievement with a singular complement, because making contact with something is instantaneous. However, with a plural complement, as here (שְׁלֹשִׁים אִישׁ), it is an accomplishment—the event takes time and has not reached its endpoint until the thirtieth man has been struck. "Go down" (יָרַד) is not instantaneous and in isolation could be construed as a directional activity, but with a locative goal, as here (אַשְׁקְלוֹן), it is an accomplishment that reaches its endpoint at the arrival at that goal. In each of these cases, the event can be "stopped" before the endpoint is reached but only "finished" once it has been reached. Thus, combined with the perfective viewpoint of the PN, each event is completed before the next one begins, creating a temporally successive string of bounded events, wherein the narrative reference time is transferred from one event to the next in turn.

Contrast this with ex. 234 in which the events are presented with the narrow-lens imperfective viewpoint. The effect of the narrow scope is that the event times overlap, although one might be interpreted as an accomplishment ("doing the work," עֹשֶׂה בַמְּלָאכָה) and another as an achievement ("grasping the weapon," מַחֲזֶקֶת הַשָּׁלַח):[8] while they were "laboring" (an activity), they were *at the same time* "doing the work" and "grasping the weapon." These are unbounded events, because the narrow scope of the progressive PTC (like the imperfective) excludes the natural endpoint of the [+telic] situations.

234. Non-movement of R-Point by Progressive/ Imperfective Aspect (Unbounded)

וְהַנֹּשְׂאִים בַּסֶּבֶל עֹמְשִׂים בְּאַחַת יָדוֹ עֹשֶׂה בַמְּלָאכָה וְאַחַת מַחֲזֶקֶת הַשָּׁלַח

(Those) who (were) carrying ‹Q.PTC› baskets (were) laboring ‹Q.PTC›.[9] With one of his hands (he was) doing ‹Q.PTC› the work, and one (was) grasping ‹HI.PTC› a weapon. (Neh. 4:11)

Both activities and states behave differently than accomplishments and achievements. With imperfective aspect, activities (like accomplishments and achievements) are unbounded, as "laboring" (עֹמְשִׂים) and "carrying" (וְהַנֹּשְׂאִים) above (ex. 234). With perfective aspect, however, activities have been described as having an "implicit temporal bound" (Smith 1999: 488). That is, depending on the pragmatic context, activities with a perfective viewpoint may be interpreted as advancing the reference time in some cases and not in others (ex. 235). The activity of offering burnt offerings and peace offerings in ex. 235a might be understood as concluding before making a feast, but it is not absolutely certain. The possibility of ambiguity about the temporal boundary of an activity is indicated by the fact that in ex. 235b a temporal boundary is expressly given by the pragmatic context of the following clause, which states that David "ceased" from the activity.

235. R-Point Movement and Activities with Perfective Aspect (Bounded or Unbounded)

235a

וַיַּעַל עֹלוֹת וַיַּעַשׂ שְׁלָמִים וַיַּעַשׂ מִשְׁתֶּה לְכָל־עֲבָדָיו

He offered up ‹HI.PN› burnt offerings and made ‹Q.PN› peace offerings and made ‹Q.PN› a feast for all his servants. (1 Kings 3:15)

8. However, it seems more natural in this context to interpret these as activities: cf. English "working *at* it"; not "grasping" as in "grabbing hold of," but "holding on to" the weapons for the duration of their work.

9. On the translation of the first clause, see Williamson 1985: 220.

235b

וַיַּעַל דָּוִד עֹלוֹת לִפְנֵי יְהוָה וּשְׁלָמִים׃ וַיְכַל דָּוִד מֵהַעֲלוֹת הָעוֹלָה וְהַשְּׁלָמִים

David offered up ‹HI.PN› burnt offerings before Yhwh and peace offerings. David ceased ‹PI.PN› from offering ‹HI.INF› the burnt offering and peace offerings. (2 Sam. 6:17–18)

States, by contrast, remain unbounded regardless of viewpoint aspect: for example, whether with the perfective PFV or the imperfective predicative PTC, the STA ידע״ temporally "overlaps" the adjoining events (ex. 236): in ex. 236a, God's state of knowing precedes both the serpent's speaking and the woman's assessment of the fruit; in ex. 236b, the sons' knowledge of Jacob's younger two sons persists even after the one, Joseph, departed.

236. Non-movement of R-Point with States (Unbounded)

236a

וַיֹּאמֶר עַבְדְּךָ אָבִי אֵלֵינוּ אַתֶּם יְדַעְתֶּם כִּי שְׁנַיִם יָלְדָה־לִּי אִשְׁתִּי׃ וַיֵּצֵא הָאֶחָד מֵאִתִּי

Your servant, my father, said ‹Q.PN› to us, "You know ‹Q.PTC› that two sons my wife bore ‹Q.PFV› for me, and the one left ‹Q.PN› me." (Gen. 44:27–28)

236b

וַיֹּאמֶר הַנָּחָשׁ אֶל־הָאִשָּׁה לֹא־מוֹת תְּמֻתוּן׃ כִּי יֹדֵעַ אֱלֹהִים כִּי בְּיוֹם אֲכָלְכֶם מִמֶּנּוּ וְנִפְקְחוּ עֵינֵיכֶם . . . וַתֵּרֶא הָאִשָּׁה כִּי טוֹב הָעֵץ לְמַאֲכָל

And the serpent said ‹Q.PN› to the woman, "You will not really die ‹Q.AINF+Q.IPFV›, because God knows ‹Q.PTC› that on the day you eat ‹Q.INF› from it your eyes will be opened ‹N.IR-PFV›. . . ." The woman saw ‹Q.PN› that the tree was good for food. (Gen. 3:4–6)

States—or any situation type—regardless of which viewpoint aspect they appear with, can be unambiguously bounded by lexically indicating a boundary: while וַיְהִי חֹשֶׁךְ־אֲפֵלָה ("was pitch-dark") is stative, it is bounded by the temporal phrase שְׁלֹשֶׁת יָמִים ("three days"; ex. 237a).[10] Similarly, although

10. The PN וַיְהִי may also be translated as a dynamic inchoative ("became dark"), but this does not change the fact that the state of "being dark" continues temporally beyond the point

the activity "doing" is unbounded with the IPFV (יִפְעַל), the adjunct phrase פַּעֲמַיִם שָׁלוֹשׁ ("twice, three [times]") delimits it, creating a temporal bound to the event.

237. States Bounded by Lexical Expressions

237a

וַיֵּט מֹשֶׁה אֶת־יָדוֹ עַל־הַשָּׁמָיִם וַיְהִי חֹשֶׁךְ־אֲפֵלָה בְּכָל־אֶרֶץ מִצְרַיִם שְׁלֹשֶׁת יָמִים׃ . . . וַיִּקְרָא פַרְעֹה אֶל־מֹשֶׁה

Moses stretched ‹Q.PN› his hand over the heavens and pitch-darkness was ‹Q.PN› over all the land of Egypt (for) three days. . . . Pharaoh summoned ‹Q.PN› Moses. (Exod. 10:22, 24)

237b

הֶן־כָּל־אֵלֶּה יִפְעַל־אֵל פַּעֲמַיִם שָׁלוֹשׁ עִם־גָּבֶר

Hey, all these (things) God does ‹Q.IPFV› twice, three (times) with man. (Job 33:29)

Conversely, any situation type, regardless of the viewpoint aspect with which it is combined, can be syntactically signaled as temporally overlapping another by means of a temporal subordinate clause. In ex. 238, the temporal protasis is expressed by the INF with ב preposition to express that the dislocating of Jacob's hip did not precede or follow the wrestling, but the accomplishment situation occurred *during* one or more temporal intervals of the activity of wrestling.

238. Unbounded/Temporal Overlay Effected by Subordinate Clause

וַתֵּקַע כַּף־יֶרֶךְ יַעֲקֹב בְּהֵאָבְקוֹ עִמּוֹ

He dislocated ‹Q.PN› Jacob's hip socket while he wrestled ‹NI.INF› with him. (Gen. 32:26)

The above observations about how (un)boundedness is effected through combinations of situation and viewpoint aspect, lexical and syntactic signals, as well as pragmatic factors are summarized in table 4.1.

---

that the next event of summoning Moses begins. The text is unclear when the darkness lifts, but my use of it is merely illustrative.

Table 4.1. Determination of (Un)boundedness (Based on Cook 2012c: 282)

Bounded situations (temporally successive)	Unbounded situations (not temporally successive)
perfective viewpoint + accomplishment or achievement (ex. 233)	any viewpoint + state (default interpretation) (ex. 236)
perfective viewpoint + activity ("implicitly bound") (ex. 235)	imperfective viewpoint + any situation type (ex. 234)
any combination of viewpoint and situation aspects with lexically asserted temporal boundary (ex. 237)	any combination of viewpoint and situation aspects with syntactically signaled temporal overlay (ex. 238)

This discussion of (un)boundedness has aimed to lay bare the complexities of interpreting the movement of time and interrelationships of events within discourse, which is a central focus of dynamic semantic theories. These theories stand in contrast to both traditional semantics, which focuses on meaning at the clause or lower level (e.g., phrase, word, etc.), and discourse linguistics, which due to its all-encompassing character sometimes comes across as literary study more than linguistic theory. Although discourse representation theory is highly formalized, Smith (2003) models how its insights can be translated into a less formalized version, which I have adapted and applied to BH discourse (Cook 2012c: 312–38). Smith (2003: 93–99) identifies three types of "temporal location" that clauses may exhibit in discourse: continuity, deixis, and anaphora. Based on Smith, I have developed a model of four discourse modes, each of which can occur in realis or irrealis mood (summarized in table 4.2).

Continuous mode in realis mood is typified by prose narrative; that is, it refers to the default discourse of narration in which each successively reported event advances the reference time and is interpreted as occurring after the previously reported event. In irrealis mood, continuous mode answers most readily to procedural instructions, in which the reader/listener is guided step by step through a procedure that obliges one to carry out each action in the order in which it is directed. The contrast between these two continuous discourse modes highlights the fundamental distinction between events in realis and irrealis mood. Events in realis mood are temporally related to each other in terms of the order in which they occur in time (temporal precedence). By contrast, since irrealis mood describes potential events, they are described in terms of accessibility relationships. Thinking again of step-by-step directions, a later step can be carried out (be accessible) only after the previous step has

Table 4.2. Interpretations of Interclausal Relationships (Based on Cook 2012c: 319)

	Realis Mood: Temporal Relations (Precedence)	Irrealis Mood: Modal Relations (Accessibility)
Continuous	One event temporally follows another.	One alternative event is accessible after another.
Deictic	An event is temporally anchored in a personal deictic center (speaker or narrator).	An event is modally anchored in a personal deictic center (obligation, wish, volition, etc.).
Anaphoric	An event is temporally anchored by a preceding event in the discourse context.	An event is modally anchored by a preceding event in the discourse context.
Generic	An event is true at all times; it is temporally "unanchored."	An event is accessible across all situations; it is modally "unanchored."

been completed (bounded). Compare the two passages in ex. 239. The first gives the irrealis procedural directions for making the ark of the covenant, and the second presents the realis narrative account of the same. Note that the IR-PFV carries forward the procedural events while the PN similarly moves the realis narrative account forward, and either sequence is departed from in clauses that are not continuous, such as elaborating on dimensions of the ark and how it is to be overlayed. The null copula clauses are interpreted in keeping with the mood of the continuous mode structure—irrealis and realis, respectively. (On these noncontinuous predicates, see the discussion of the anaphoric mode below.)

239a. Continuous Irrealis Mode

10 וְעָשׂוּ אֲרוֹן עֲצֵי שִׁטִּים אַמָּתַיִם וָחֵצִי אָרְכּוֹ וְאַמָּה וָחֵצִי
רָחְבּוֹ וְאַמָּה וָחֵצִי קֹמָתוֹ׃ 11 וְצִפִּיתָ אֹתוֹ זָהָב טָהוֹר מִבַּיִת
וּמִחוּץ תְּצַפֶּנּוּ וְעָשִׂיתָ עָלָיו זֵר זָהָב סָבִיב׃ 12 וְיָצַקְתָּ לּוֹ
אַרְבַּע טַבְּעֹת זָהָב וְנָתַתָּה עַל אַרְבַּע פַּעֲמֹתָיו וּשְׁתֵּי טַבָּעֹת
עַל־צַלְעוֹ הָאֶחָת וּשְׁתֵּי טַבָּעֹת עַל־צַלְעוֹ הַשֵּׁנִית׃

10 They should make ‹Q.IR-PFV› an ark of acacia wood; its length (should be) two and a half cubits, its width (should be) a cubit and a half, and its height (should be) a cubit and a half. 11 You should overlay ‹PI.IR-PFV› it with pure gold—inside and outside you should overlay ‹PI.IPFV› it—and

you should make ‹Q.IR-PFV› for it a gold border around (it). [12]You should cast ‹Q.IR-PFV› four rings of gold and should put ‹Q.IR-PFV› (them) on its four feet—two rings on its one side and two rings upon its other side. (Exod. 25:10–12)

239b. Continuous Realis Mode

[1]וַיַּעַשׂ בְּצַלְאֵל אֶת־הָאָרֹן עֲצֵי שִׁטִּים אַמָּתַיִם וָחֵצִי אָרְכּוֹ
וְאַמָּה וָחֵצִי רָחְבּוֹ וְאַמָּה וָחֵצִי קֹמָתוֹ׃ [2]וַיְצַפֵּהוּ זָהָב טָהוֹר
מִבַּיִת וּמִחוּץ וַיַּעַשׂ לוֹ זֵר זָהָב סָבִיב׃ [3]וַיִּצֹק לוֹ אַרְבַּע
טַבְּעֹת זָהָב עַל אַרְבַּע פַּעֲמֹתָיו וּשְׁתֵּי טַבָּעֹת עַל־צַלְעוֹ
הָאֶחָת וּשְׁתֵּי טַבָּעוֹת עַל־צַלְעוֹ הַשֵּׁנִית׃

[1]Bezalel made ‹Q.PN› the ark of acacia wood; its length (was) two and a half cubits, its width (was) a cubit and a half, and its height (was) a cubit and a half. [2]He overlayed ‹PI.PN› it with pure gold inside and outside and made ‹Q.PN› for it a border of gold around (it). [3]He cast ‹Q.PN› for it four rings of gold for its four feet; two rings (were) on its one side and two rings (were) on its other side. (Exod. 37:1–3)

Deictic mode in realis mood most clearly contrasts with the continuous mode in the distinction between direct reported speech and prose narrative. The temporality of narrative concerns not just the temporal relationship between the speaker and the events but between the successive events themselves. By contrast, direct reported speech (excepting narrative embedded within speech) temporally anchors each event independently to the deictic center, which is the speaker's "present" by default. In contrast to deictic mode in realis mood, in which events are temporally anchored to the speaker's deictic center, in irrealis mood the deictic mode anchors events in the speaker's *modal* deictic center—the source of obligation, volition, or qualification of knowledge. The distinction between continuous realis narrative and deictic mode, both realis and irrealis mood, is illustrated by the passage in ex. 240. The continuous mode realis narrative events are indicated by the subscripted number events (e_1, e_2, etc.). These structure the narrative and advance the reference time. By contrast, the reported speech is in deictic mode, anchored by the speaker Jacob's deictic center, both temporally ("I have heard," שָׁמַעְתִּי) and modally—deontic ("go down . . . buy grain," רְדוּ . . . וְשִׁבְרוּ), epistemic ("we might live and not die," וְנִחְיֶה וְלֹא נָמוּת),[11] and final ("lest harm encounter him," פֶּן־יִקְרָאֶנּוּ אָסוֹן). (On the noncontinuous, nondeictic events in this passage, see below on anaphoric discourse mode.)

240. Continuous Realis Mode with Embedded Deictic Realis and Irrealis Modes

1וַיַּרְא יַעֲקֹב כִּי יֶשׁ־שֶׁבֶר בְּמִצְרָיִם וַיֹּאמֶר יַעֲקֹב לְבָנָיו
לָמָּה תִּתְרָאוּ׃ 2וַיֹּאמֶר הִנֵּה שָׁמַעְתִּי כִּי יֶשׁ־שֶׁבֶר בְּמִצְרָיִם
רְדוּ־שָׁמָּה וְשִׁבְרוּ־לָנוּ מִשָּׁם וְנִחְיֶה וְלֹא נָמוּת׃ 3וַיֵּרְדוּ
אֲחֵי־יוֹסֵף עֲשָׂרָה לִשְׁבֹּר בָּר מִמִּצְרָיִם׃ 4וְאֶת־בִּנְיָמִין אֲחִי
יוֹסֵף לֹא־שָׁלַח יַעֲקֹב אֶת־אֶחָיו כִּי אָמַר פֶּן־יִקְרָאֶנּוּ אָסוֹן׃
5וַיָּבֹאוּ בְּנֵי יִשְׂרָאֵל לִשְׁבֹּר בְּתוֹךְ הַבָּאִים כִּי־הָיָה הָרָעָב
בְּאֶרֶץ כְּנָעַן׃

1 $_{e1}$Jacob saw ‹Q.PN› that grain was ‹EXIST› in Egypt. $_{e2}$Jacob said ‹Q.PN› to his sons, "Why are you looking ‹HT.IPFV› at each other?" 2 $_{e3}$He said ‹Q.PN›, "Hey, I have heard ‹Q.PFV› that grain is ‹EXIST› in Egypt. Go down ‹Q.IMPV› there and buy grain ‹Q.IMPV› for us from there and we might live ‹Q.IPFV› and not die ‹Q.IPFV›." 3 $_{e4}$The ten brothers of Joseph went down ‹Q.PN› to buy ‹Q.INF› grain from Egypt. 4 Benjamin, the brother of Joseph, Jacob did not send ‹Q.PFV› with his brothers, because he (had) said ‹Q.PFV›, "Lest harm encounter ‹Q.IPFV› him." 5 $_{e5}$The sons of Israel came ‹Q.PN› to buy grain ‹Q.INF› in the midst of (others) who (were) coming ‹Q.PTC›, because the famine was ‹Q.PFV› in the land of Canaan. (Gen. 42:1–5)

Anaphoric mode contrasts with continuous just as still pictures contrast with video: anaphora portrays situations all anchored to a certain time (and often place), with the shift from one situation to another being more spatial than temporal (so Smith 2003: 95). In anaphoric mode, temporality (realis) and modality (irrealis) are anchored to the temporal-spatial topic. In ex. 241 all the (realis) descriptions are tied to "the rebellious, defiled, and oppressive city," whether they are descriptions of what she has thus far done or not done, what her leadership is like, or what Yhwh does. The static character of

11. These epistemic clauses are typically interpreted as expressing a final sense (e.g., ESV, NJPS "that we might live and not die"), being classifiable in Joüon's (1923) "indirect volitive" category. As that categorization has been rejected (§3.8.2), any final sense here is a result of the logical relationship of the events and the choice of IPFV for the expression of epistemic modality. To paraphrase, *in that case—of your procuring grain—we might live and might not die.*

anaphoric mode is evident in this passage, full of static adjectival participles and null copula clauses.

241. Anaphoric Realis Mode

[1]הוֹי מֹרְאָה וְנִגְאָלָה הָעִיר הַיּוֹנָה׃ [2]לֹא שָׁמְעָה בְּקוֹל לֹא
לָקְחָה מוּסָר בַּיהוָה לֹא בָטָחָה אֶל־אֱלֹהֶיהָ לֹא קָרֵבָה׃
[3]שָׂרֶיהָ בְקִרְבָּהּ אֲרָיוֹת שֹׁאֲגִים שֹׁפְטֶיהָ זְאֵבֵי עֶרֶב לֹא
גָרְמוּ לַבֹּקֶר׃ [4]נְבִיאֶיהָ פֹּחֲזִים אַנְשֵׁי בֹּגְדוֹת כֹּהֲנֶיהָ חִלְּלוּ־
קֹדֶשׁ חָמְסוּ תּוֹרָה׃ [5]יְהוָה צַדִּיק בְּקִרְבָּהּ לֹא יַעֲשֶׂה עַוְלָה
בַּבֹּקֶר בַּבֹּקֶר מִשְׁפָּטוֹ יִתֵּן לָאוֹר לֹא נֶעְדָּר וְלֹא־יוֹדֵעַ עַוָּל
בֹּשֶׁת׃

[1]Woe the rebellious ‹Q.PTC›, defiled ‹NI.PTC›, and oppressive ‹Q.PTC› city. [2]She has not heeded ‹Q.PFV›, she has not accepted ‹Q.PFV› discipline, in Yhwh she has not trusted ‹Q.PFV›, to her God she has not drawn near ‹Q.PFV›. [3]Her princes in her midst (are) roaring ‹Q.PTC› lions; her judges (are) evening wolves; they have gnawed ‹Q.PFV› until the morning. [4]Her prophets (are) reckless ‹Q.PTC› men of treachery; her priests have profaned ‹PI.PFV› (the) holy, they have committed violence ‹Q.PFV› (to the) law. [5]Yhwh (is) righteous in her midst. He will not commit iniquity ‹Q.IPFV›; every morning his justice he brings ‹Q.IPFV› to light, (which) has not failed ‹NI.PFV›. But the godless (does) not know ‹Q.PTC› shame. (Zeph. 3:1–5)[12]

In ex. 242, the temporal phrase בַּיּוֹם הַהוּא ("on that day") anchors what follows in the irrealis-future mood, to which the JUSS forms are anaphorically linked: "On that day . . . I will gather (אֹסְפָה) . . . I will assemble (אֲקַבֵּצָה)." The PFVs that follow are ambiguous in their relationship to the preceding. If interpreted as promissory PFVs, they might be taken as anaphorically anchored like the JUSSs. More likely, however, they are IR-PFVs that express continuity with the preceding, adding final (purposive) clauses to the JUSS actions. The relative clauses—both the unmarked PTCs and marked PFV—are all likewise anchored in the leading temporal phrase, but temporally and not modally: these groups are described as having been afflicted prior to Yhwh's actions "on that day."

12. In verse 5, I have interpreted לֹא נֶעְדָּר as an unmarked relative clause, on which see Berlin 1994: 130.

242. Anaphoric Irrealis and Continuous Irrealis Modes

[6]בַּיּוֹם הַהוּא נְאֻם־יְהוָה אֹסְפָה הַצֹּלֵעָה וְהַנִּדָּחָה אֲקַבֵּצָה
וַאֲשֶׁר הֲרֵעֹתִי׃ [7]וְשַׂמְתִּי אֶת־הַצֹּלֵעָה לִשְׁאֵרִית וְהַנַּהֲלָאָה
לְגוֹי עָצוּם וּמָלַךְ יְהוָה עֲלֵיהֶם בְּהַר צִיּוֹן מֵעַתָּה וְעַד־עוֹלָם׃

On that day—declaration of Yhwh—I will gather ‹Q.JUSS› (those) who (are) lame ‹Q.PTC›, and (those) that (are) driven out ‹NI.PTC› I will assemble ‹PI.JUSS›, and (those) that I afflicted ‹HI.PFV›, so that/and I will make ‹Q.IR-PFV› (those) who (are) lame ‹Q.PTC› into a remnant and (those) who (are) outcasts ‹NI.PTC› into a mighty nation, and/so that Yhwh will reign ‹Q.IR-PFV› over them on Mount Zion from then until forever. (Mic. 4:6–7)

Anaphoric mode is also illustrated by the noncontinuous, nondeictic clauses in the preceding passages (exs. 239–40). The IPFV (תְּצַפֶּנּוּ) and null copula clauses in ex. 239a are interpreted as irrealis deontic because they are anaphorically anchored by the preceding irrealis deontic IR-PFVs. Similarly, the null copula clauses in ex. 239b are interpreted as realis past by virtue of their anaphoric anchoring in their respective preceding PN forms. The anaphoric mode is substantiated by the contrastive interpretations given to the existential clauses in ex. 240: the first occurrence of יֶשׁ־שֶׁבֶר is interpreted as past tense ("grain was") because it is anaphorically anchored to the leading PN (וַיַּרְא). By contrast, in Jacob's speech, the same predicate is anaphorically anchored to the deictically anchored שָׁמַעְתִּי ("I have heard"), and so it is interpreted as present tense ("grain is"). Likewise, the narrative PFV forms in ex. 240, "did not send . . . (had) said" (לֹא־שָׁלַח . . . אָמַר), are anaphoric, being anchored as past and past-in-the-past (optionally expressed by English past perfect) with respect to the PN-established reference time, "went down" (וַיֵּרְדוּ). Finally, both the relative PTC (הַבָּאִים) and PFV STA (הָיָה) toward the end of the passage are anaphorically anchored to the leading PN וַיָּבֹאוּ, effecting the past overlapping situations: others "(were) coming" and the famine "was" at the same time as the sons of Jacob "came" to Egypt.

Generic is a mode that I posited alongside the three Smith (2003: 93–99) identifies. It is motivated by the generic expressions we find in BH, which are clearly not continuous, deictic, or anaphoric. Instead, their "universal" quality comes from their "unanchored" character, whether temporally (realis) or modally (irrealis). Consider the realis generic mode passage in ex. 243. While these verses contain an array of predicates, temporality has little to do with their interpretation as sayings with universal validity. Some linguists have suggested that such expressions describe the way the world works rather than referring to particular situations (see Cook 2005: 120–21). In contrast to the other discourse modes, this deserves to be thought of as temporally "unanchored," even while the contrast of TAM among the individual expressions is respected (see §3.5.2).

243. Generic Realis Mode

[1]חַכְמוֹת נָשִׁים בָּנְתָה בֵיתָהּ וְאִוֶּלֶת בְּיָדֶיהָ תֶהֶרְסֶנּוּ׃ [2]הוֹלֵךְ
בְּיָשְׁרוֹ יְרֵא יְהוָה וּנְלוֹז דְּרָכָיו בּוֹזֵהוּ׃ [3]בְּפִי־אֱוִיל חֹטֶר
גַּאֲוָה וְשִׂפְתֵי חֲכָמִים תִּשְׁמוּרֵם׃

[1]A wise (woman) built ‹Q.PFV› her house, but a foolish (woman) with her hands will tear ‹Q.IPFV› hers down. [2](One who) walks ‹Q.PTC› in his integrity (is) a fearer of Yhwh, but (one who is) perverse ‹NI.PTC› (in) his ways despises ‹Q.PTC› him. [3]In the mouth of a fool (is) the rod of pride, but the lips of the wise will guard ‹Q.IPFV› them. (Prov. 14:1–3)

This example of realis generic mode makes clear that this mode is more pragmatically dependent than the other modes. That is, the generic expression is only identifiable as such because the pragmatics of the discourse in which it appears suggest this interpretation. This is true whether the expression appears in the context of a collection of such sayings, as in ex. 243, or if it appears embedded in another sort of mode, as in ex. 244a. In the latter, the lack of definiteness and terseness of the speech points to its generic quality, indicating that the JUSS (indicated by the directive-volitive אַל negator) is not anchored in the speaker, the king of Israel, but is modally unanchored. Other irrealis generic expressions, outside of proverbial sayings, are found in contexts suggesting a source of obligation in the way the world works, as in ex. 244b, where God seems to suggest to Jonah that it is simply "right" that he pity the people of Nineveh.

244. Generic Irrealis Mode

244a

וַיַּעַן מֶלֶךְ־יִשְׂרָאֵל וַיֹּאמֶר דַּבְּרוּ אַל־יִתְהַלֵּל חֹגֵר כִּמְפַתֵּחַ׃

The king of Israel answered ‹Q.PN› and said ‹Q.PN›, "Say ‹PI.IMPV›, '(One who) girds ‹Q.PTC› himself should not boast ‹HT.JUSS› as (one who) ungirds ‹PI.PTC› himself.'" (1 Kings 20:11)

244b

וַאֲנִי לֹא אָחוּס עַל־נִינְוֵה הָעִיר הַגְּדוֹלָה

And should I not pity ‹Q.IPFV› Nineveh, the great city? (Jon. 4:11)

These four modes in their realis and irrealis forms provide a way to clarify what we mean when we talk about the "contextual" interpretation of the verbal system. In some cases, there are strong ties between certain modes and moods (e.g., PN and realis continuous or the PTC and anaphoric), but the generic mode demonstrates that the determination of meaning is not so simplistic as one-to-one correspondences between form and mode. Rather, the entire context from verb form, syntax, and discourse-pragmatics must be taken into account.

4.4 The Biblical Hebrew Verb in Context

This section draws together all the insights of the preceding chapters and the previous sections and applies them to some sample passages to illustrate how the BH verb functions as a system in various contexts. What I said in the introduction bears repeating here since it is even more evident in these longer passages. The English translations I have provided are awkwardly literal at times, but this is done to make the syntax and semantics of the Hebrew text more apparent; I do not intend them as elegant translations. A constant danger of working with a corresponding gloss language and analytical metalanguage is that the approach veers into an analysis of the translation rather than the text in question. Perhaps the awkwardness of the English gloss translation will remind us that the Hebrew text is the focus of our analysis.

4.4.1 Prose Narrative: Genesis 18

Genesis 18 provides a good example of classical Hebrew prose narrative, whose storyline is structured by PN forms, interspersed with reported speech and unbounded events. The foregrounded storyline is marked in each paragraph as e_1, e_2, and so on.

245. Genesis 18:1–2

1 וַיֵּרָא אֵלָיו יְהוָה בְּאֵלֹנֵי מַמְרֵא וְהוּא יֹשֵׁב פֶּתַח־הָאֹהֶל
כְּחֹם הַיּוֹם׃ 2 וַיִּשָּׂא עֵינָיו וַיַּרְא וְהִנֵּה שְׁלֹשָׁה אֲנָשִׁים נִצָּבִים
עָלָיו וַיַּרְא וַיָּרָץ לִקְרָאתָם מִפֶּתַח הָאֹהֶל וַיִּשְׁתַּחוּ אָרְצָה׃

1 $_{e1}$Yhwh appeared ‹NI.PN› to him at the oaks of Mamre; he (was) sitting ‹Q.PTC› at the opening of the tent in the heat of the day. 2 $_{e2}$(He) lifted ‹Q.PN› his eyes $_{e3}$and looked ‹Q.PN›, and hey, three men (were) standing ‹NI.PTC› before him. $_{e4}$(He) saw ‹Q.PN› and $_{e5}$ran ‹Q.PN› to meet ‹Q.INF› them from the opening of the tent $_{e6}$and (he) bowed ‹HISHTAPHEL.PN› to the ground.

Genesis 18 opens a new scene in which Abraham is visited by three men. However, the connection to the preceding chapter is evident from the use of anaphoric pronominal references to Abraham (אֵלָיו and הוּא). The storyline represents realis continuous discourse mode, structured by six bounded (i.e., temporally successive) realis events, including two paired events (וַיִּשָּׂא עֵינָיו וַיַּרְא and וַיַּרְא וַיָּרָץ). The two other clauses feature the progressive (predicative) PTC to express unbounded static situations that "overlap" with the surrounding storyline events: Abraham "(was) sitting (יֹשֵׁב) at the opening of the tent" both before the three men appeared and shortly afterward, before he got up to go meet them. Likewise, the men "(were) standing (נִצָּבִים) before him" both before he looked up to see them and as he ran to meet them.

246. Genesis 18:3–5

3 וַיֹּאמַר אֲדֹנָי אִם־נָא מָצָאתִי חֵן בְּעֵינֶיךָ אַל־נָא תַעֲבֹר
מֵעַל עַבְדֶּךָ׃ 4 יֻקַּח־נָא מְעַט־מַיִם וְרַחֲצוּ רַגְלֵיכֶם וְהִשָּׁעֲנוּ
תַּחַת הָעֵץ׃ 5 וְאֶקְחָה פַת־לֶחֶם וְסַעֲדוּ לִבְּכֶם אַחַר תַּעֲבֹרוּ
כִּי־עַל־כֵּן עֲבַרְתֶּם עַל־עַבְדְּכֶם וַיֹּאמְרוּ כֵּן תַּעֲשֶׂה כַּאֲשֶׁר
דִּבַּרְתָּ׃

3 $_{e1}$(He) said ‹Q.PN›, "My lords, if please (I) have found ‹Q.PFV› favor in your eyes, do not pass ‹Q.JUSS› by your servant. 4 Please let a little water be fetched ‹QPASS.JUSS› and wash ‹Q.IMPV› your feet and recline ‹NI.IMPV› under the tree. 5 (I) will take ‹Q.JUSS› a piece of bread, and sustain ‹Q.IMPV› yourselves; afterward (you) may pass on ‹Q.JUSS›, seeing that (you) have passed by ‹Q.PFV› your servant." $_{e2}$(They) said, "Do ‹Q.IPFV› so, just as (you) have said ‹PI.PFV›."

This paragraph consists of reported speech embedded in the narrative storyline, which consists of just the two speech frames (וַיֹּאמַר and וַיֹּאמְרוּ). The reported speech shifts from the realis continuous mode of narration to a deictic one consisting of both realis and irrealis events tied to the speaker's present. Abraham's proposal of hospitality consists of four JUSS and three IMPV expressions bookended by stative perfect clauses, which describe the context of the invitation: "have found favor" (מָצָאתִי) and "have passed by" (עֲבַרְתֶּם).[13] Just as the PFV forms are anchored temporally in Abraham's personal deictic center, so the JUSS and IMPV forms are modally anchored so as to create a modal deictic mode of discourse. Although the directive-volitive events logically demand a certain order—water and food must precede washing and eating—the events are not continuous, but each is independently anchored in the speaker's deictic center. The response, featuring the distinctly IPFV תַּעֲשֶׂה (vs. JUSS), clearly expresses irrealis mood but may be interpreted as permission ("you may do so") or command ("do so"). The stative perfect PFV provides the static backdrop to the irrealis IPFV, just as the bookend PFVs operate in Abraham's speech.

247. Genesis 18:6–8

6 וַיְמַהֵר אַבְרָהָם הָאֹהֱלָה אֶל־שָׂרָה וַיֹּאמֶר מַהֲרִי שְׁלֹשׁ
סְאִים קֶמַח סֹלֶת לוּשִׁי וַעֲשִׂי עֻגוֹת׃ 7 וְאֶל־הַבָּקָר רָץ
אַבְרָהָם וַיִּקַּח בֶּן־בָּקָר רַךְ וָטוֹב וַיִּתֵּן אֶל־הַנַּעַר וַיְמַהֵר
לַעֲשׂוֹת אֹתוֹ׃ 8 וַיִּקַּח חֶמְאָה וְחָלָב וּבֶן־הַבָּקָר אֲשֶׁר עָשָׂה
וַיִּתֵּן לִפְנֵיהֶם וְהוּא־עֹמֵד עֲלֵיהֶם תַּחַת הָעֵץ וַיֹּאכֵלוּ׃

6 $_{e1}$Abraham hurried ‹PI.PN› to the tent to Sarah, $_{e2}$and (he) said ‹Q.PN›, "Hurry ‹PI.IMPV›, three *seahs* of fine flour. Knead ‹Q.IMPV› (them) and make ‹Q.IMPV› cakes." 7 $_{e3}$To the flock Abraham ran ‹Q.PFV› $_{e4}$and took ‹Q.PN› a tender and good calf $_{e5}$and gave ‹Q.PN› (it) to the servant, $_{e6}$and (he) hurried ‹PI.PN› to prepare ‹Q.INF› it. 8 $_{e7}$(He) took ‹Q.PN› curds and milk and the calf that (he) had prepared ‹Q.PFV› $_{e8}$and placed ‹Q.PN› (them) before them—he (was) standing ‹Q.PTC› beside them under the tree—$_{e9}$and (they) ate ‹Q.PN›.

13. Although עָבַר is an achievement predicate, and a literal English gloss suggests that the men have already gone past Abraham (cf. NJPS "have come your servant's way"), the pragmatics of the situation demand the interpretation that they are now paused in the act of passing by, otherwise Abraham could not speak with them at all.

Abraham's hospitality is reported as carried out by him, Sarah, and the servant in realis continuity mode marked by PNs with the exception of the shift to PFV in e_3. This shift, with the focus-fronted locative PP, ties Abraham's two "trips" together, with the PFV event anaphorically anchored to the first PN event: he went to the tent (e_1), and he went to the flock (e_3). The order of the two events does not matter; rather, they represent the initiation of two tasks, the making of bread and the cooking of a calf. The series of three IMPVs in the reported speech represent modal deixis, the directives being anchored to Abraham's modal deictic center. The verb "to knead" (לוּשׁ) appears with an overt object elsewhere (Jer. 7:18; Hosea 7:4), but the indefiniteness of "three *seahs* of fine flour" (שְׁלֹשׁ סְאִים קֶמַח סֹלֶת) allows for the null object here (cf. 1 Sam. 28:24). Similarly, the indefinite character of "a tender and good calf" (בֶּן־בָּקָר רַךְ וָטוֹב) and "curds and milk and the calf" (חֶמְאָה וְחָלָב וּבֶן־הַבָּקָר) account for the null objects in e_5 "he gave (it)" (וַיִּתֵּן), e_8 "he placed (them)" (וַיִּתֵּן), and e_9 "they ate (them)" (וַיֹּאכֵלוּ)—this despite the definiteness of וּבֶן־הַבָּקָר in the latter list (cf. בֶּן־בָּקָר in v. 7). By contrast, preparing the calf in e_6 employs the object marker (אֹתוֹ).

While indefiniteness and inanimacy are key factors licensing null objects, prototypical transitive predicates like עשׂ"ה that involve a change of state are far less likely to allow null objects (see Bekins 2014: 81–82), versus verbs involving the transfer of an object, like נת"ן. The case of אכ"ל is similar to English *eat* in that it seems to freely alternate between intransitive and transitive constructions (see §2.5.4 and Cook 2020). The situation is different with regard to the lack of an object in the relative clause (אֲשֶׁר עָשָׂה): here "accessibility" of the NP indicates how susceptible it is to relativization and in turn how likely it is to be overtly resumed. The direct object is second only to the subject in the accessibility hierarchy, allowing it to be resumed by a null (see Holmstedt 2016: 173–75).[14] The predicative PTC construction interrupts the storyline just before the final PN verb, situating Abraham in his static position as background activity to the foreground event of the men eating.

248. Genesis 18:9–15

9 וַיֹּאמְרוּ אֵלָיו אַיֵּה שָׂרָה אִשְׁתֶּךָ וַיֹּאמֶר הִנֵּה בָאֹהֶל׃
10 וַיֹּאמֶר שׁוֹב אָשׁוּב אֵלֶיךָ כָּעֵת חַיָּה וְהִנֵּה־בֵן לְשָׂרָה
אִשְׁתֶּךָ וְשָׂרָה שֹׁמַעַת פֶּתַח הָאֹהֶל וְהוּא אַחֲרָיו׃

14. The "Noun Phrase Accessibility Hierarchy" employed by Holmstedt (2016) is from Keenan and Comrie (1977: 66): Subject > Direct Object > Indirect Object > Oblique > Genitive > Object of Comparison.

11 וְאַבְרָהָם וְשָׂרָה זְקֵנִים בָּאִים בַּיָּמִים חָדַל לִהְיוֹת לְשָׂרָה
אֹרַח כַּנָּשִׁים׃ 12 וַתִּצְחַק שָׂרָה בְּקִרְבָּהּ לֵאמֹר אַחֲרֵי בְלֹתִי
הָיְתָה־לִּי עֶדְנָה וַאדֹנִי זָקֵן׃ 13 וַיֹּאמֶר יְהוָה אֶל־אַבְרָהָם
לָמָּה זֶּה צָחֲקָה שָׂרָה לֵאמֹר הַאַף אֻמְנָם אֵלֵד וַאֲנִי זָקַנְתִּי׃
14 הֲיִפָּלֵא מֵיְהוָה דָּבָר לַמּוֹעֵד אָשׁוּב אֵלֶיךָ כָּעֵת חַיָּה
וּלְשָׂרָה בֵן׃ 15 וַתְּכַחֵשׁ שָׂרָה לֵאמֹר לֹא צָחַקְתִּי כִּי יָרֵאָה
וַיֹּאמֶר לֹא כִּי צָחָקְתְּ׃

9 $_{e1}$(They) said ‹Q.PN› to him, "Where (is) Sarah your wife?" 10 $_{e2}$(He) said
‹Q.PN›, "There, in the tent." $_{e3}$(He) said ‹Q.PN›, "(I) certainly ‹Q.AINF›
shall return ‹Q.IPFV› to you next year and, hey, Sarah your wife (will
have) a son." Sarah (was) listening ‹Q.PTC› at the opening of the tent,
and it (was) behind him. 11 Abraham and Sarah (were) old, advancing
‹Q.PTC› in days. The way of women had ceased ‹Q.PFV› to belong ‹Q.INF›
to Sarah. 12 $_{e4}$Sarah laughed ‹Q.PN› to herself [COMP], "After my wearing
out ‹Q.INF› will pleasure have become ‹Q.PFV› mine, and my lord is/has
become old ‹STA/Q.PFV›?" 13 $_{e5}$Yhwh said ‹Q.PN› to Abraham, "Why did
Sarah laugh ‹Q.PFV› [COMP], 'Will (I) really indeed bear ‹Q.IPFV› (a child)
and I have become old ‹Q.PFV›?' 14 Is (any)thing (too) wondrous ‹NI.IPFV›
for Yhwh? At the appointed time (I) shall return ‹Q.IPFV› to you, next
year, and Sarah (will have) a son." 15 $_{e6}$Sarah lied ‹PI.PN› [COMP], "I did not
laugh ‹Q.PFV›," because she was afraid ‹Q.PFV›. $_{e7}$He said ‹Q.PN›, "No, but
you did laugh ‹Q.PFV›."

This section of the narrative is structured by the seven PN events (e_1–e_7) that exhibit realis continuity and frame the dialogue and monologue. By contrast, the speech predicates are all tied to the respective speakers' deictic center, whether it be modal (irrealis) or temporal (realis). Thus, the null copula in Yhwh's initial question, "Where (is) Sarah your wife?" (**אַיֵּה שָׂרָה אִשְׁתֶּךָ**), defaults to the speaker's present time of speaking. By contrast, Yhwh's following statement is modally anchored in Yhwh's deictic center, as he assures with the AINF-IPFV focus structure (**שׁוֹב אָשׁוּב**) that he intends to return. This irrealis-future statement and the temporal PP (**כָּעֵת חַיָּה**) dictate that the following null copula be interpreted as future: "Hey, Sarah your wife (will have) a son" (**וְהִנֵּה־בֵן לְשָׂרָה אִשְׁתֶּךָ**).

At this point the narrator intrudes with backgrounded unbounded predicates to explain the situation that leads to Sarah's laughter. Both "Sarah (was) listening" (**וְשָׂרָה שֹׁמַעַת**) and "Abraham and Sarah (were) old, advancing in days" (**וְאַבְרָהָם וְשָׂרָה זְקֵנִים בָּאִים בַּיָּמִים**) feature null copulas that are interpreted as past based on the narrative reference time set by the PN framing. The STA זְקֵנִים is unambiguously adjectival here and is most elegantly analyzed with the unambiguous participle בָּאִים as the compound complement of the null copula. Although the combination of the dynamic unergative בו״א with the stative adjective may appear odd, consider similar stative-like gerundive expressions in colloquial English like *they're getting up there in years*. The shift from unbounded PTC and STA predicates to the PFV demands a similarly stative expression rooted in an event preceding the narrative reference time, so a past perfect interpretation of חָדַל is called for ("had ceased").

The PFVs in Sarah's monologue are also stative perfects, but her question casts the first event into the irrealis-future, suggesting a future perfect interpretation, "After my wearing out will pleasure have become mine?" (אַחֲרֵי בְלֹתִי הָיְתָה־לִּי עֶדְנָה). The gloss of the INF here preserves the fundamental nominal character of the dual-classified nominal verb form. The predicate of the second clause of Sarah's monologue is an ambiguously encoded STA. The construction וַאדֹנִי זָקֵן could be analyzed as the adjectival encoding with default present null copula ("and my lord [is] old") or as a 3MS PFV encoding with a present perfect inchoative sense ("and my lord has become old"). The interpretive (rather than grammatical) decision rests on whether the focus of the expression lies in Abraham's being in current state or his having attained his current state. Given the temporal focus of Sarah's remarks, the latter may be more appropriate to the context: she might have had this pleasure earlier in life, but her lord Abraham not only *is* old but *has become* old.

Yhwh's reply continues in the deixis mode of reported speech, in which PFV forms receive a perfective past ("Why did Sarah laugh?" לָמָּה זֶּה צָחֲקָה שָׂרָה) and present perfect ("I have become old," וַאֲנִי זָקַנְתִּי), which might alternatively be interpreted as a present state ("I am old"). The stative passive Niphal הֲיִפָּלֵא might be interpreted as a realis generic statement cast as a rhetorical question, "Is anything too wondrous?"; but it might alternatively be interpreted as having an irrealis dynamic modal sense: "*Can* anything be too wondrous?" The following IPFV mirrors the irrealis-future meaning of the preceding AINF-IPFV structure, and as with the previous instance, the following null copula receives a future interpretation following the volitive-future IPFV. The final brief exchange between Sarah and Yhwh features PNs to frame the reported speech and perfective past PFVs. The narrator's causal comment on Sarah's response ("because [she was] afraid," כִּי יָרֵאָה) features a STA that is interpreted as a past state based on the narrative reference time.[15]

15. The adjectival form of this STA, if it occurred, would be vocalized the same way but with ultimate stress. The form here is in pause (atnach accent) with penultimate stress, which

249. Genesis 18:16–21

16וַיָּקֻמוּ מִשָּׁם הָאֲנָשִׁים וַיַּשְׁקִפוּ עַל־פְּנֵי סְדֹם וְאַבְרָהָם
הֹלֵךְ עִמָּם לְשַׁלְּחָם׃ 17וַיהוָה אָמָר הַמְכַסֶּה אֲנִי מֵאַבְרָהָם
אֲשֶׁר אֲנִי עֹשֶׂה׃ 18וְאַבְרָהָם הָיוֹ יִהְיֶה לְגוֹי גָּדוֹל וְעָצוּם
וְנִבְרְכוּ בוֹ כֹּל גּוֹיֵי הָאָרֶץ׃ 19כִּי יְדַעְתִּיו לְמַעַן אֲשֶׁר יְצַוֶּה
אֶת־בָּנָיו וְאֶת־בֵּיתוֹ אַחֲרָיו וְשָׁמְרוּ דֶּרֶךְ יְהוָה לַעֲשׂוֹת
צְדָקָה וּמִשְׁפָּט לְמַעַן הָבִיא יְהוָה עַל־אַבְרָהָם אֵת אֲשֶׁר־
דִּבֶּר עָלָיו׃ 20וַיֹּאמֶר יְהוָה זַעֲקַת סְדֹם וַעֲמֹרָה כִּי־רָבָּה
וְחַטָּאתָם כִּי כָבְדָה מְאֹד׃ 21אֵרֲדָה־נָּא וְאֶרְאֶה הַכְּצַעֲקָתָהּ
הַבָּאָה אֵלַי עָשׂוּ כָּלָה וְאִם־לֹא אֵדָעָה׃

16 $_{\text{e1}}$The men rose ‹Q.PN› from there $_{\text{e2}}$and looked down ‹HI.PN› upon the face of Sodom. Abraham (was) walking ‹Q.PTC› with them to send ‹PI.INF› them off. 17Yhwh had said ‹Q.PFV›, "(Am) I going to hide ‹PI.PTC› from Abraham (that) which I (am) going to do ‹Q.PTC›? 18Abraham certainly ‹Q.AINF› will become ‹Q.IPFV› a great and vast nation so that through him all nations of the earth will be blessed ‹NI.IR-PFV›, 19because (I) have known ‹Q.PFV› him, in order that (he) might command ‹PI.IPFV› his sons and his household after him (that they) should keep ‹Q.IR-PFV› the way of Yhwh by doing ‹Q.INF› righteousness and justice in order that Yhwh bring ‹HI.INF› upon Abraham (that) which (he) has spoken ‹PI.PFV› concerning him." 20 $_{\text{e3}}$Yhwh said ‹Q.PN›, "The cry of Sodom and Gomorrah indeed is great ‹Q.PFV›, and their sin indeed is very grave ‹Q.PFV›. 21(I) will go down ‹Q.JUSS› now that (I) may see ‹Q.IPFV› whether according to the cry that (has) come ‹Q.PFV› to me (they) have altogether done ‹Q.PFV›; and if not, (I) will know ‹Q.JUSS›."

This section of the narrative is dominated by Yhwh's reported speeches, first an inner monologue then an aloud speech for Abraham to hear. The first two PNs shift the scene by the movement of the men away from Abraham's place, and the only other PN in the section is the framing of Yhwh's second speech. The first speech, Yhwh's inner monologue, is introduced by a PFV instead of PN (וַיהוָה אָמָר), suggesting that this reflects Yhwh's *earlier* contemplation about whether to share his intent with Abraham, making it possible to interpret it as a past perfect "had said" rather than perfective past "said." The latter would imply that Yhwh began thinking about the matter

---

retains the tsere. When not in pause, the verbal encoding is spelled יֵרָאֶה, with ultimate stress and penultimate vowel reduction (e.g., Jer. 3:8).

after having already gotten up and looked upon Sodom, which is possible but unduly compresses the speech times and begs the question of why the PFV is employed here instead of the PN. Yhwh's inner monologue begins with two PTC predicates, both expressing prospective aspect, as demanded by the fact that he is contemplating but not yet engaged in these activities. The first of these (הַמְכַסֶּה אֲנִי) might be understood as simple progressive, with the logical idea of "continuing to hide." However, since the preceding PFV has cast this inner monologue earlier than this narrative reference time, it is reasonable to see Yhwh as having earlier contemplated action against Sodom and at the same time contemplated keeping it from Abraham, which he will now not do. Since function words (like the interrogative) do not trigger V-S with null copula clauses, and the pronoun can host the interrogative (e.g., Isa. 66:9), I conclude that the PTC must be fronted for focus, contrasting the option of hiding his plans with the option Yhwh chooses, that of disclosing them to Abraham.

Yhwh's inner monologue continues with a complex description of his vision for Abraham as the basis for his consideration of whether or not to hide his intent. It begins with a predicate focusing AINF-IPFV construction. The copular predicate frequently receives an inchoative interpretation when combined with a ל PP, as here: "Abraham certainly will become a great and vast nation" (וְאַבְרָהָם הָיוֹ יִהְיֶה לְגוֹי גָּדוֹל וְעָצוּם). The focus AINF underscores the definitiveness of God's promises (Gen. 12:1–3) and removes any implication that his current contemplation calls into question these earlier stated intentions. The following IR-PFV (וְנִבְרְכוּ) is often interpreted as a simple future, continuing the IPFV; however, in this context of Yhwh's stated intentions, a final or resultative sense ("so that") fits well. This joint statement of Abraham's future and its outcome is adjoined by a causal clause with a present perfect PFV, since Yhwh's acquaintance with/choosing of Abraham is still valid. To this causal clause are attached two stacked לְמַעַן purpose clauses, the first with an אֲשֶׁר-marked complement clause with IPFV (לְמַעַן אֲשֶׁר יְצַוֶּה) and the second with an INF clause (לְמַעַן הָבִיא יְהוָה). The IR-PFV (וְשָׁמְרוּ) heads the logical content of what Abraham is to command his offspring—"(that) they should keep . . . by doing" (לַעֲשׂוֹת). The last clause in the monologue (אֵת אֲשֶׁר־דִּבֶּר עָלָיו) is embedded within the direct object complement of the INF הָבִיא. The relative head is null and marked by אֵת, while the relative clause PFV predicate ambiguously expresses perfective past or present perfect.

The third PN (וַיֹּאמֶר) introduces Yhwh's aloud speech. Yhwh begins by describing the state of affairs with Sodom and Gomorrah using two PFV STA forms, both preceded by an asseverative כִּי, underscoring the severity of the situation. Both are interpreted as present stative, their default value and fitting with the deixis discourse mode, which anchors these to the speech time. The two verbally encoded STAs show only slight differences when compared with their adjectival counterparts: compare רָבָּה, with penultimate-stress vowel lengthening in pause (atnach accent), and adjective רַבָּה, with ultimate stress; כָּבְדָה, with penultimate-vowel reduction, and adjective כָּבֵדָה. Yhwh's intent is expressed by a JUSS (אֵרֲדָה־נָּא), whose identification is made sure by the conventionalized paragogic הָ- and the clitic נָא, and an IPFV (וְאֶרְאֶה), with a final-epistemic sense ("that I might see"). The object complement of the IPFV is the indirect question clause with PFV verb (עָשׂוּ), which is slightly better understood as present perfect rather than perfective past, if we assume that the bad acting has not stopped. The word order is somewhat confusing because the subject-object complement (עָשׂוּ כָּלָה) is preceded by the adjunct כ PP, which hosts the interrogative -הֲ and is modified by a ה-relative PFV clause. The PFV הַבָּאָה is distinguished by the penultimate accent versus the ultimate-accented PTC.[16] The final clause (וְאִם־לֹא אֵדָעָה) is a reduced conditional clause, in which the preceding clause is gapped in the protasis: "If not (according to the cry that has come before me they have altogether done), I will know." The apodosis is likely JUSS because of the conventionalized paragogic הָ- expressing Yhwh's wish to know the situation accurately. However, since it was argued in §3.8.1 that the paragogic הָ- is not invariably attached to the first-person JUSS or inherently modal in meaning, it is possible to interpret this as a final-epistemic IPFV with a reflexive/benefactive הָ-: "that I may know for myself," rather than via the cry.

250. Genesis 18:22–33

22 וַיִּפְנוּ מִשָּׁם הָאֲנָשִׁים וַיֵּלְכוּ סְדֹמָה וְאַבְרָהָם עוֹדֶנּוּ עֹמֵד
לִפְנֵי יְהוָה׃ 23 וַיִּגַּשׁ אַבְרָהָם וַיֹּאמַר הַאַף תִּסְפֶּה צַדִּיק עִם־
רָשָׁע׃ 24 אוּלַי יֵשׁ חֲמִשִּׁים צַדִּיקִם בְּתוֹךְ הָעִיר הַאַף תִּסְפֶּה
וְלֹא־תִשָּׂא לַמָּקוֹם לְמַעַן חֲמִשִּׁים הַצַּדִּיקִם אֲשֶׁר בְּקִרְבָּהּ׃
25 חָלִלָה לְּךָ מֵעֲשֹׂת כַּדָּבָר הַזֶּה לְהָמִית צַדִּיק עִם־רָשָׁע
וְהָיָה כַצַּדִּיק כָּרָשָׁע חָלִלָה לָּךְ הֲשֹׁפֵט כָּל־הָאָרֶץ לֹא
יַעֲשֶׂה מִשְׁפָּט׃ 26 וַיֹּאמֶר יְהוָה אִם־אֶמְצָא בִסְדֹם חֲמִשִּׁים

16. Holmstedt (2016: 69–71) discusses the fact that the ה-relative strongly prefers the PTC, which has led to suggested emendations of forms like this to read them as PTCs. However, even if cases like this were emended, there remain a handful of unambiguously non-PTC verbal forms with the ה-relative, which clearly identifies the ה as a relative marker and indicates its grammaticality with a finite verb.

צַדִּיקִם בְּתוֹךְ הָעִיר וְנָשָׂאתִי לְכָל־הַמָּקוֹם בַּעֲבוּרָם׃ [27]וַיַּעַן
אַבְרָהָם וַיֹּאמַר הִנֵּה־נָא הוֹאַלְתִּי לְדַבֵּר אֶל־אֲדֹנָי וְאָנֹכִי
עָפָר וָאֵפֶר׃ [28]אוּלַי יַחְסְרוּן חֲמִשִּׁים הַצַּדִּיקִם חֲמִשָּׁה
הֲתַשְׁחִית בַּחֲמִשָּׁה אֶת־כָּל־הָעִיר וַיֹּאמֶר לֹא אַשְׁחִית
אִם־אֶמְצָא שָׁם אַרְבָּעִים וַחֲמִשָּׁה׃ [29]וַיֹּסֶף עוֹד לְדַבֵּר אֵלָיו
וַיֹּאמַר אוּלַי יִמָּצְאוּן שָׁם אַרְבָּעִים וַיֹּאמֶר לֹא אֶעֱשֶׂה
בַּעֲבוּר הָאַרְבָּעִים׃ [30]וַיֹּאמֶר אַל־נָא יִחַר לַאדֹנָי וַאֲדַבֵּרָה
אוּלַי יִמָּצְאוּן שָׁם שְׁלֹשִׁים וַיֹּאמֶר לֹא אֶעֱשֶׂה אִם־אֶמְצָא
שָׁם שְׁלֹשִׁים׃ [31]וַיֹּאמֶר הִנֵּה־נָא הוֹאַלְתִּי לְדַבֵּר אֶל־אֲדֹנָי
אוּלַי יִמָּצְאוּן שָׁם עֶשְׂרִים וַיֹּאמֶר לֹא אַשְׁחִית בַּעֲבוּר
הָעֶשְׂרִים׃ [32]וַיֹּאמֶר אַל־נָא יִחַר לַאדֹנָי וַאֲדַבְּרָה אַךְ־הַפַּעַם
אוּלַי יִמָּצְאוּן שָׁם עֲשָׂרָה וַיֹּאמֶר לֹא אַשְׁחִית בַּעֲבוּר
הָעֲשָׂרָה׃ [33]וַיֵּלֶךְ יְהוָה כַּאֲשֶׁר כִּלָּה לְדַבֵּר אֶל־אַבְרָהָם
וְאַבְרָהָם שָׁב לִמְקֹמוֹ׃

[22] $_{e1}$The men turned ‹Q.PN› from there $_{e2}$and went ‹Q.PN› to Sodom. As for Abraham, he (was) still standing ‹Q.PTC› before Yhwh. [23] $_{e3}$Abraham approached ‹Q.PN› $_{e4}$and said ‹Q.PN›, "Will (you) sweep away ‹Q.IPFV› righteous with wicked? [24]Perhaps fifty righteous are ‹EXIST› in the midst of the city. Will (you) sweep away ‹Q.IPFV› (them) and not forgive ‹Q.IPFV› the place for the sake of the fifty righteous who (are) in it? [25]Far be it for you from acting ‹Q.INF› like this thing—to kill ‹HI.INF› righteous with wicked, (that) like the righteous like the wicked are ‹Q.IR-PFV›; far be it for you! Should not the judge of the whole earth perform ‹Q.IPFV› justice?" [26] $_{e5}$Yhwh said ‹Q.PN›, "If (I) find ‹Q.IPFV› in Sodom fifty righteous in the midst of the city, then (I) will forgive ‹Q.IR-PFV› the whole place on account of them." [27] $_{e6}$Abraham answered ‹Q.PN› and said ‹Q.PN›, "Hey, please, (I) have undertaken ‹HI.PFV› to speak ‹PI.INF› to the Lord, (though) I (am) dust and ashes. [28]Perhaps the fifty righteous lack ‹Q.IPFV› five. Will (you) destroy ‹HI.IPFV› for five the whole city?" $_{e7}$(He) said ‹Q.PN›, "(I) will not destroy ‹HI.IPFV› (it) if (I) find ‹Q.IPFV› there forty-five (righteous)." [29] $_{e8}$(He) yet again ‹HI.PN› spoke ‹PI.INF› to him and said ‹Q.PN›, "Perhaps forty (righteous) will be found ‹NI.IPFV› there." $_{e9}$(He) said ‹Q.PN›, "(I) will not do ‹Q.IPFV› (this) for the sake of the forty (righteous)." [30] $_{e10}$(He) said ‹Q.PN›, "Please do not let the Lord become angry ‹Q.IPFV›, and (I) will speak ‹PI.JUSS›. Perhaps thirty (righteous) will be found ‹NI.IPFV› there." $_{e11}$(He) said ‹Q.PN›, "(I) will not do ‹Q.IPFV›

(this) if (I) find ‹Q.IPFV› there thirty (righteous)." [31] $_{\text{e12}}$(He) said ‹Q.PN›,
"Hey, please, (I) have undertaken ‹HI.PFV› to speak ‹PI.INF› to the Lord.
Perhaps twenty (righteous) will be found ‹NI.IPFV› there." $_{\text{e13}}$(He) said
‹Q.PN›, "(I) will not destroy ‹HI.IPFV› (it) on account of the twenty
(righteous)." [32] $_{\text{e14}}$(He) said ‹Q.PN›, "Please do not let the Lord become
angry ‹Q.IPFV›, and (I) will speak ‹PI.JUSS› only once (more). Perhaps ten
(righteous) will be found ‹NI.IPFV› there." $_{\text{e15}}$(He) said ‹Q.PN›, "(I) will
not destroy ‹HI.IPFV› (it) on account of the ten (righteous)." [33] $_{\text{e16}}$Yhwh
went ‹Q.PN› when (he) had finished ‹PI.PFV› speaking ‹PI.INF› to Abraham,
$_{\text{e17}}$and Abraham returned ‹Q.PFV› to his place.

This last section is a lengthy and repetitive dialogue between Abraham and Yhwh. The dialogue is bookended by a handful of non-speech PNs, recounting the men turning (וַיִּפְנוּ) and heading (וַיֵּלְכוּ) to Sodom and Abraham approaching (וַיִּגַּשׁ) to speak at the beginning, and Yhwh's departure (וַיֵּלֶךְ) at the end, which is paired with the return (שָׁב) of Abraham to his place. This last PFV is anaphorically anchored in the PN event of Yhwh's departure, which occur in no particular order. The dialogue itself is narratively structured by eleven PN speech frames, nine of which are simply PNs of אמ"ר. The other two speech frames end with PNs of אמ"ר that do not constitute their own events but combine with the other predicates in the speech frames to create a more nuanced speech introduction: "Abraham answered and said" (וַיַּעַן אַבְרָהָם וַיֹּאמַר) and "he again spoke to him and said" (וַיֹּסֶף עוֹד לְדַבֵּר אֵלָיו וַיֹּאמַר).

The dialogue begins with Abraham's intercession for the people of Sodom and Gomorrah by raising the question of Yhwh's justice in sweeping away both righteous and wicked expressed by an irrealis-future IPFV (הַאַף תִּסְפֶּה צַדִּיק עִם־רָשָׁע). Without awaiting an answer, Abraham follows this up by raising the prospect of how many righteous might be in the city and the positive-negative interrogative pair of irrealis-future IPFV clauses (הַאַף תִּסְפֶּה וְלֹא־תִשָּׂא). The object complement of תִּסְפֶּה is null, and its antecedent is "fifty righteous" rather than "the city" in light of Abraham's next statement about treating the righteous and wicked alike—that is, he is concerned with the people, not the city. Abraham continues his plea with a double חָלִלָה לְּךָ expression bookending the INF clause (מֵעֲשֹׂת), whose object complement is כַּדָּבָר הַזֶּה ("as this thing"), which is appositionally modified by the לְהָמִית INF clause. The וְהָיָה is evidently an IR-PFV, because although the STA can express a present state, it makes good sense connected to the INF with a resultative sense: "(that) like the righteous like the wicked are" (i.e., so that the judgment of the righteous becomes no different than that of the wicked). Abraham's initial plea ends with an interrogative IPFV clause expressing deontic obligation on the "judge of the whole earth" to "perform justice" (הֲשֹׁפֵט כָּל־הָאָרֶץ לֹא יַעֲשֶׂה מִשְׁפָּט). Yhwh's initial reply is the longest, just as Abraham's initial speech is his longest, expressed by a conditional clause with an אִם-marked IPFV protasis and an IR-PFV apodosis (אִם־אֶמְצָא בִסְדֹם חֲמִשִּׁים צַדִּיקִם בְּתוֹךְ הָעִיר וְנָשָׂאתִי לְכָל־הַמָּקוֹם בַּעֲבוּרָם).

The ensuing exchanges are variations on a theme and tend to become more reduced as they go on. Twice each Abraham ingratiates himself with "Hey, please, I have undertaken to speak to the Lord" (הִנֵּה־נָא הוֹאַלְתִּי לְדַבֵּר אֶל־אֲדֹנָי) and "Please do not let the Lord become angry, and I will speak" (אַל־נָא יִחַר לַאדֹנָי וַאֲדַבֵּרָה). The Hiphil of יא"ל in verse 27 takes a complementary INF, and the PFV as present perfect is suitable to the speech context. The Qal of חר"ה is usually monovalent with אַף (lit., "nose"; fig., "wrath") as the subject (e.g., Gen. 30:2; Deut. 6:15), but it can be avalent with no semantic agent and the person to whom the "burning (anger)" belongs expressed by a PP (usually a לְ PP as here) but also בְּעֵינֵי ("in the eyes of [someone]"; Gen. 31:35). Abraham's requests are all headed by the epistemic marker אוּלַי followed by an IPFV; the main variation is between the transitive יַחְסְרוּן ("lack") and intransitive passive יִמָּצְאוּן ("be found"). After the first exchange, "righteous (people)" is left null and only numbers are employed, shortening the dialogue. Yhwh's subsequent responses vary between the negated IPFV לֹא אַשְׁחִית ("[I] will not destroy [it]") three times and לֹא אֶעֱשֶׂה ("[I] will not do [this]") twice, all with null complement referring to the persistent topic, the destruction of the city. The other variation is the expression of the protasis, which follows the apodosis after Yhwh's first response: two times he replies with "If I find there . . ." (אִם־אֶמְצָא שָׁם) followed by the number and three times with "on account of" (בַּעֲבוּר) followed by the number.

4.4.2 Legal Code: Leviticus 16:1–28

Leviticus 16 is a narratively framed complex of cultic legislation regarding the Day of Atonement. The main legislation is given to Moses to convey to Aaron (vv. 1–2) and details the cultic service to be carried out by Aaron in several discrete acts: the requisite materials (vv. 3–5), preliminaries and overview of rites (vv. 6–10), blood sprinkling in the sanctuary (vv. 11–19), the scapegoat (vv. 20–22), and cleansing of participants (vv. 23–28).[17] As with the narrative passage, continuity mode dominates here (although irrealis mood

17. I have omitted verses 29–34 from this discussion since they are widely viewed as an appendix that alters the original rite, which has been read as a response to the deaths of Aaron's sons (Lev. 10) and involves an "emergency measure" (Milgrom 1991: 1061) that the high priest could utilize whenever he thought it was needed.

and embedded within the reported-speech deictic mode) as Aaron is instructed to carry out the cultic acts in a specific order. The foregrounded procedural acts are therefore indicated by the notations e_1, e_2, and so on, as was done for narrative foreground in §4.4.1.

251. Leviticus 16:1–5

[1] וַיְדַבֵּר יְהוָה אֶל־מֹשֶׁה אַחֲרֵי מוֹת שְׁנֵי בְּנֵי אַהֲרֹן
בְּקָרְבָתָם לִפְנֵי־יְהוָה וַיָּמֻתוּ׃ [2] וַיֹּאמֶר יְהוָה אֶל־מֹשֶׁה דַּבֵּר
אֶל־אַהֲרֹן אָחִיךָ וְאַל־יָבֹא בְּכָל־עֵת אֶל־הַקֹּדֶשׁ מִבֵּית
לַפָּרֹכֶת אֶל־פְּנֵי הַכַּפֹּרֶת אֲשֶׁר עַל־הָאָרֹן וְלֹא יָמוּת כִּי
בֶּעָנָן אֵרָאֶה עַל־הַכַּפֹּרֶת׃ [3] בְּזֹאת יָבֹא אַהֲרֹן אֶל־הַקֹּדֶשׁ
בְּפַר בֶּן־בָּקָר לְחַטָּאת וְאַיִל לְעֹלָה׃ [4] כְּתֹנֶת־בַּד קֹדֶשׁ יִלְבָּשׁ
וּמִכְנְסֵי־בַד יִהְיוּ עַל־בְּשָׂרוֹ וּבְאַבְנֵט בַּד יַחְגֹּר וּבְמִצְנֶפֶת
בַּד יִצְנֹף בִּגְדֵי־קֹדֶשׁ הֵם וְרָחַץ בַּמַּיִם אֶת־בְּשָׂרוֹ וּלְבֵשָׁם׃
[5] וּמֵאֵת עֲדַת בְּנֵי יִשְׂרָאֵל יִקַּח שְׁנֵי־שְׂעִירֵי עִזִּים לְחַטָּאת
וְאַיִל אֶחָד לְעֹלָה׃

[1]Yhwh spoke ‹PI.PN› to Moses after the death of the two sons of Aaron when they approached ‹Q.INF› before Yhwh and died ‹Q.PN›. [2]Yhwh said ‹Q.PN› to Moses, "Speak ‹PI.IMPV› to Aaron your brother. (He) must not enter ‹Q.JUSS› at any time into the sanctuary inside the curtain before the propitiation (place) that is upon the ark, and (he) will not die ‹Q.IPFV›, for in a cloud (I) (may) appear ‹Q.IPFV› over the propitiation (place). [3]With this Aaron may enter ‹Q.IPFV› the sanctuary: with a bull of the herd for a sin offering and a ram for a burnt offering. [4]A holy linen tunic (he) shall wear ‹Q.IPFV› and linen undergarments shall be ‹Q.IPFV› on his body and with a linen belt (he) shall gird ‹Q.IPFV› (himself) and with a linen turban (he) shall wrap ‹Q.IPFV› (his head)—holy garments (are) they. (He) shall bathe ‹Q.IR-PFV› his body with water and put them on ‹Q.IR-PFV›. [5]From the congregation of the people of Israel (he) shall take ‹Q.IR-PFV› two male goats for a sin offering and one ram for a burnt offering."

The opening section begins with a speech frame of several PN forms. The first (וַיְדַבֵּר) and third (וַיֹּאמֶר) create a double speech frame, but the second (וַיָּמֻתוּ) is conjoined to the temporal INF בְּקָרְבָתָם, putting it out of narrative order with the speech frame predicates. The reported speech begins with an IMPV to speak to Aaron and the details of what Moses is to say in the form of indirect reported speech. As indirect (versus direct) speech, the deictic center does not shift from that of the irrealis deictic IMPV (cf. indirect "he shall" versus direct "you shall"). The indirect reported speech begins with an unambiguous negated JUSS (וְאַל־יָבֹא) that is conjoined to an unambiguous negated IPFV (וְלֹא יָמוּת). Logically the latter can be interpreted as a negative purpose clause because it is anaphorically anchored to the JUSS, expressing the outcome of following the JUSS prohibition: "He must not enter . . . and (in such case) he will not die." The causal clause is similarly anaphorically anchored to the preceding negative clause. It explains the risk of death if Aaron does not enter with suitable precautions in place: there Yhwh "appears" or "shows himself" in/by a cloud over the propitiation (place).[18] This IPFV (אֵרָאֶה) may be interpreted as either epistemic possibility ("may") or generic/habitual depending on how one understands the abiding presence of Yhwh's glory in the sanctuary. The latter interpretation constitutes a one-event realis generic mode discourse, which is temporally unanchored.

The remaining verses of this paragraph outline the accoutrements with which he may (permissive) enter the sanctuary. This permissive reading of יָבֹא makes sense of the legislation as an "emergency measure" the high priest could carry out at any time (Milgrom 1991: 1061). By contrast, a directive sense "shall enter" is demanded when read in light of the appendix (vv. 29–34, not treated here), which transforms the formerly ad hoc rite into an annual one (see Milgrom 1991: 1065). All five IPFV forms in this section are preceded by fronted elements: a topic-fronted cataphoric "with this" (בְּזֹאת), which is modified appositionally in the second part of the verse, and focus-fronted clothing elements. The irrealis deictic mode and the clearly fronted PPs indicates that the S-V order in וּמִכְנְסֵי־בַד יִהְיוּ עַל־בְּשָׂרוֹ is not indicative of the normal order but indicates focus-fronting of the subject NP before the irrealis verb, which would otherwise exhibit V-S order. These items of clothing are in no particular order and are qualified as a whole by the following parenthetical null clause. For continuity, the writer shifts to IR-PFVs that may be interpreted as an unmarked protasis-apodosis: "(When) he has bathed . . . (then) he should put on." The final IPFV shifts via a topic-fronted PP to the directive to take sacrificial animals from the congregation.

18. The term כַּפֹּרֶת is translated "mercy seat" (NRSV) or "cover" (NJPS), but there is little agreement on what it means, only that it refers to the place where propitiation rites are performed. Haggard (2022: 187) suggests that the noun is derived from כִּפֶּר ("propitiate") and metonymically indicates "the place of propitiation."

252. Leviticus 16:6–10

6 וְהִקְרִיב אַהֲרֹן אֶת־פַּר הַחַטָּאת אֲשֶׁר־לוֹ וְכִפֶּר בַּעֲדוֹ
וּבְעַד בֵּיתוֹ׃ 7 וְלָקַח אֶת־שְׁנֵי הַשְּׂעִירִם וְהֶעֱמִיד אֹתָם לִפְנֵי
יְהוָה פֶּתַח אֹהֶל מוֹעֵד׃ 8 וְנָתַן אַהֲרֹן עַל־שְׁנֵי הַשְּׂעִירִם
גֹּרָלוֹת גּוֹרָל אֶחָד לַיהוָה וְגוֹרָל אֶחָד לַעֲזָאזֵל׃ 9 וְהִקְרִיב
אַהֲרֹן אֶת־הַשָּׂעִיר אֲשֶׁר עָלָה עָלָיו הַגּוֹרָל לַיהוָה וְעָשָׂהוּ
חַטָּאת׃ 10 וְהַשָּׂעִיר אֲשֶׁר עָלָה עָלָיו הַגּוֹרָל לַעֲזָאזֵל יָעֳמַד־
חַי לִפְנֵי יְהוָה לְכַפֵּר עָלָיו לְשַׁלַּח אֹתוֹ לַעֲזָאזֵל הַמִּדְבָּרָה׃

6 $_{e1}$Aaron shall present ‹HI.IR-PFV› the bull of sin offering that (is) for him $_{e2}$and (he) shall make propitiation ‹PI.IR-PFV› for him and his house. 7 $_{e3}$(He) shall take ‹Q.IR-PFV› the two goats $_{e4}$and (he) shall station ‹HI.IR-PFV› them before Yhwh at the entrance of the tent of meeting. 8 $_{e5}$Aaron shall cast ‹Q.IR-PFV› lots over the two goats—one lot for Yhwh and the other lot for Azazel. 9 $_{e6}$Aaron shall present ‹HI.IR-PFV› the goat for which the lot came up ‹Q.PFV› for Yhwh $_{e7}$and (he) shall make ‹Q.IR-PFV› it a sin offering. 10 The goat for which the lot came up ‹Q.PFV› for Azazel shall be stationed ‹HO.IPFV› alive before Yhwh to make atonement ‹PI.INF› over it, to send it away ‹PI.INF› to Azazel into the wilderness.

In these verses the procedural directions begin with a summary of the cultic acts to be performed in the complex rite. Bounded IR-PFV forms predominate, marking the procedural foregrounded events (marked by e_1, e_2, etc.) of the irrealis continuous mode discourse. The only departure from the IR-PFV in main clauses is the IPFV יָעֳמַד in 16:10, which is employed in the clause with focus-fronted subject, drawing together in contrast the treatment of the two goats. Because of this contrast, the IPFV clause presents irrealis anaphoric discourse anchored to the preceding clause. Similarly, the two realis PFV forms (עָלָה), which both appear in relative clauses, are anaphorically anchored to their respective main clauses. In these two cases, however, the anaphoric mode is realis mood, placing these two events temporally prior to the predicates in their main clauses.

253. Leviticus 16:11–14

11 וְהִקְרִיב אַהֲרֹן אֶת־פַּר הַחַטָּאת אֲשֶׁר־לוֹ וְכִפֶּר בַּעֲדוֹ
וּבְעַד בֵּיתוֹ וְשָׁחַט אֶת־פַּר הַחַטָּאת אֲשֶׁר־לוֹ׃ 12 וְלָקַח
מְלֹא־הַמַּחְתָּה גַּחֲלֵי־אֵשׁ מֵעַל הַמִּזְבֵּחַ מִלִּפְנֵי יְהוָה וּמְלֹא
חָפְנָיו קְטֹרֶת סַמִּים דַּקָּה וְהֵבִיא מִבֵּית לַפָּרֹכֶת׃ 13 וְנָתַן
אֶת־הַקְּטֹרֶת עַל־הָאֵשׁ לִפְנֵי יְהוָה וְכִסָּה עֲנַן הַקְּטֹרֶת אֶת־
הַכַּפֹּרֶת אֲשֶׁר עַל־הָעֵדוּת וְלֹא יָמוּת׃ 14 וְלָקַח מִדַּם הַפָּר
וְהִזָּה בְאֶצְבָּעוֹ עַל־פְּנֵי הַכַּפֹּרֶת קֵדְמָה וְלִפְנֵי הַכַּפֹּרֶת יַזֶּה
שֶׁבַע־פְּעָמִים מִן־הַדָּם בְּאֶצְבָּעוֹ׃

11 $_{e1}$Aaron shall present ‹HI.IR-PFV› the bull of sin offering that (is) for him $_{e2}$and (he) shall make atonement ‹PI.IR-PFV› for him and his house. $_{e3}$(He) shall slaughter ‹Q.IR-PFV› the bull of sin offering that (is) for him,
12 $_{e4}$and (he) shall take ‹Q.IR-PFV› a full censer (with) coals of fire from the altar from before Yhwh and two handfuls of spiced ground incense $_{e5}$and bring ‹HI.IR-PFV› (them) inside the veil.
13 $_{e6}$(He) shall place ‹Q.IR-PFV› the incense on the fire before Yhwh $_{e7}$and the cloud of incense shall cover ‹PI.IR-PFV› the propitiation (place) that (is) over the testimony, and (he) will not die ‹Q.IPFV›.
14 $_{e8}$(He) shall take ‹Q.IR-PFV› some of the blood of the bull $_{e9}$and sprinkle ‹HI.IR-PFV› (it) with his finger upon the face of the propitiation (place) on its east side [lit., eastward]. Before the propitiation (place) (he) shall sprinkle ‹HI.IPFV› seven times some of the blood with his finger.

The first half of verse 11 is a verbatim repetition of verse 6, signaling the "resumption" of the cultic act whose details follow here (see §3.4.2 for cases of resumptive repetition with the PN). The second IR-PFV (וְכִפֶּר) denotes the ritual act that is explicated by the following actions, which are "temporally included subevents" (Cook 2004: 259). As such, these latter IR-PFVs (e_3–e_9) exhibit continuity with the first IR-PFV (וְהִקְרִיב) and among themselves, but not with וְכִפֶּר. The only departures from the IR-PFV structured irrealis continuous mode are the two IPFV forms. The first (וְלֹא יָמוּת) is identical in form and function to the expression in verse 2. Logically it can be construed as a purpose clause linked to the preceding IR-PFV, but that is because it is anaphorically anchored to the preceding two IR-PFVs: if Aaron takes the precaution of burning incense, the cloud of incense will shield him from seeing the glory of Yhwh above the place of propitiation, and he will not die. The second IPFV, which is the same verb as the preceding IR-PFV, has prompted debates since antiquity over whether there are seven total sprinklings or one plus seven (see Milgrom 1991: 1032). The shift from the IR-PFV suggests that this is a shift out of continuous mode to anaphoric and that the IPFV clause provides additional details regarding the sprinkling expressed by the IR-PFV: "He shall sprinkle (IR-PFV). . . he must sprinkle (IPFV) seven times." This would be similar to the IR-PFV followed by IPFV seen in Exod. 25:11 (ex. 213) and in keeping with the sevenfold sprinkling of the altar in verse 18. However, verse 15 suggests that there are two distinct locations for sprinkling in the sanctuary: "upon" the propitiation place and "before" the propitiation place. This latter interpretation is in keeping with the seven-plus-one pattern found elsewhere in the book (e.g., Lev. 8–9; see Haggard 2022: 193). In this case, the IPFV is still anaphoric, but rather than elaborating on the preceding act of sprinkling, it pairs it with an adjoining act, making them an inseparable pair (cf. the similar function of PN-PFV sequence in prose narrative at the end of ex. 250 above).

254. Leviticus 16:15–19

15 וְשָׁחַט אֶת־שְׂעִיר הַחַטָּאת אֲשֶׁר לָעָם וְהֵבִיא אֶת־דָּמוֹ
אֶל־מִבֵּית לַפָּרֹכֶת וְעָשָׂה אֶת־דָּמוֹ כַּאֲשֶׁר עָשָׂה לְדַם הַפָּר
וְהִזָּה אֹתוֹ עַל־הַכַּפֹּרֶת וְלִפְנֵי הַכַּפֹּרֶת׃ 16 וְכִפֶּר עַל־הַקֹּדֶשׁ
מִטֻּמְאֹת בְּנֵי יִשְׂרָאֵל וּמִפִּשְׁעֵיהֶם לְכָל־חַטֹּאתָם וְכֵן יַעֲשֶׂה
לְאֹהֶל מוֹעֵד הַשֹּׁכֵן אִתָּם בְּתוֹךְ טֻמְאֹתָם׃ 17 וְכָל־אָדָם
לֹא־יִהְיֶה בְּאֹהֶל מוֹעֵד בְּבֹאוֹ לְכַפֵּר בַּקֹּדֶשׁ עַד־צֵאתוֹ
וְכִפֶּר בַּעֲדוֹ וּבְעַד בֵּיתוֹ וּבְעַד כָּל־קְהַל יִשְׂרָאֵל׃ 18 וְיָצָא
אֶל־הַמִּזְבֵּחַ אֲשֶׁר לִפְנֵי־יְהוָה וְכִפֶּר עָלָיו וְלָקַח מִדַּם הַפָּר
וּמִדַּם הַשָּׂעִיר וְנָתַן עַל־קַרְנוֹת הַמִּזְבֵּחַ סָבִיב׃ 19 וְהִזָּה עָלָיו
מִן־הַדָּם בְּאֶצְבָּעוֹ שֶׁבַע פְּעָמִים וְטִהֲרוֹ וְקִדְּשׁוֹ מִטֻּמְאֹת
בְּנֵי יִשְׂרָאֵל׃

15 $_{e1}$(He) shall slaughter ‹Q.IR-PFV› the goat of the sin offering that is for the people, $_{e2}$and bring ‹HI.IR-PFV› its blood inside the curtain, $_{e3}$and treat ‹Q.IR-PFV› the blood just as (he) treated ‹Q.PFV› the blood of the bull—$_{e4}$sprinkle ‹HI.IR-PFV› it upon the propitiation (place) and before the propitiation (place), 16 so that (he) makes propitiation ‹PI.IR-PFV› for the sanctuary because of the impurities of the people of Israel and because of their transgressions—for all their sins. So (he) shall do ‹Q.IPFV› for the tent of meeting, which dwells ‹Q.PTC› with them in the midst of their impurities. 17 No one shall be ‹Q.IPFV› in the tent of meeting when he

> enters ‹Q.INF› to make atonement ‹PI.INF› in the sanctuary until he comes out ‹Q.INF›. $_{e5}$When (he) has made atonement ‹PI.IR-PFV› for himself and for his house and for all the congregation of Israel, [18] $_{e6}$(he) shall come out ‹Q.IR-PFV› to the altar that is before Yhwh $_{e7}$and make atonement ‹PI.IR-PFV› for it: $_{e8}$(he) shall take ‹Q.IR-PFV› some of the blood of the bull and some of the blood of the ram $_{e9}$and place ‹Q.IR-PFV› (it) on the horns of the altar (all) around, [19] $_{e10}$and (he) shall sprinkle ‹HI.IR-PFV› upon it some of the blood with his finger seven times, so that (he) purifies ‹PI.IR-PFV› and sanctifies ‹PI.IR-PFV› (it) because of the impurities of the people of Israel.

This section shifts from the bull sacrificed for Aaron and his house to the goat that is sacrificed on the people's behalf. The continuous mode with IR-PFVs provides the structure, as in the last paragraph. However, the IR-PFV is less dominant here because the ritual is both condensed due to its repetitiveness and expanded on by explanations of the purpose of the procedures. The procedure begins with sacrificing the goat, bringing its blood in, and "treating" it in the same manner as the bull offering—sprinkling it on and toward the place of propitiation. The act of sprinkling (וְהִזָּה) thus elaborates on the preceding (וְעָשָׂה) as a temporal "subevent" of it. This means that both the comparative relative PFV עָשָׂה clause and the וְהִזָּה clause are anaphorically anchored to וְעָשָׂה. Similarly, the clauses in verse 16 are both anaphorically anchored in the preceding procedures for the goat: the first must be a purpose statement, as it once again employs the umbrella term כִּפֶּר to describe what Aaron will have accomplished in the preceding goat ritual. The anaphoric וְכֵן ("and thus") likewise links the IPFV יַעֲשֶׂה to the preceding procedures, indicating that they should be applied likewise to the "tent of meeting."[19] The IPFV of verse 17 warns against anyone else being in the tent of meeting when Aaron performs his duties, thus anaphorically linking, once again, to the aforementioned ritual procedure.

The continuous mode resumes with the וְכִפֶּר in verse 17 and the following two IR-PFVs. This וְכִפֶּר may function as a summation of what Aaron has accomplished, but the rendering of this by NJPS as temporal protasis (present perfect) and וְיָצָא as the directive apodosis makes better sense of transitioning from the previous propitiation rite to the next, described by וְכִפֶּר in verse 18. As seen in previous instances, this event, e_7 (וְכִפֶּר), is continuous with the preceding (e_6) but temporally includes the following IR-PFVs (e_8–e_{10}), "take

19. In this context, the אֹהֶל מוֹעֵד ("tent of meeting") must refer to the outer sanctum (versus the sanctuary, which refers to the inner sanctum or holiest place) rather than the larger complex (so Milgrom 1991: 1035).

. . . place . . . sprinkle," which explain the steps in the act of propitiation for the altar. The last two IR-PFVs (וְטִהֲרוֹ וְקִדְּשׁוֹ) describe what is effected by the propitiation rite, suggesting a purposive meaning perhaps as a verbal hendiadys (so Haggard 2022: 194).

255. Leviticus 16:20–25

[20]וְכִלָּה מִכַּפֵּר אֶת־הַקֹּדֶשׁ וְאֶת־אֹהֶל מוֹעֵד וְאֶת־הַמִּזְבֵּחַ
וְהִקְרִיב אֶת־הַשָּׂעִיר הֶחָי׃ [21]וְסָמַךְ אַהֲרֹן אֶת־שְׁתֵּי יָדָו עַל
רֹאשׁ הַשָּׂעִיר הַחַי וְהִתְוַדָּה עָלָיו אֶת־כָּל־עֲוֺנֹת בְּנֵי יִשְׂרָאֵל
וְאֶת־כָּל־פִּשְׁעֵיהֶם לְכָל־חַטֹּאתָם וְנָתַן אֹתָם עַל־רֹאשׁ
הַשָּׂעִיר וְשִׁלַּח בְּיַד־אִישׁ עִתִּי הַמִּדְבָּרָה׃ [22]וְנָשָׂא הַשָּׂעִיר
עָלָיו אֶת־כָּל־עֲוֺנֹתָם אֶל־אֶרֶץ גְּזֵרָה וְשִׁלַּח אֶת־הַשָּׂעִיר
בַּמִּדְבָּר׃ [23]וּבָא אַהֲרֹן אֶל־אֹהֶל מוֹעֵד וּפָשַׁט אֶת־בִּגְדֵי
הַבָּד אֲשֶׁר לָבַשׁ בְּבֹאוֹ אֶל־הַקֹּדֶשׁ וְהִנִּיחָם שָׁם׃ [24]וְרָחַץ
אֶת־בְּשָׂרוֹ בַמַּיִם בְּמָקוֹם קָדוֹשׁ וְלָבַשׁ אֶת־בְּגָדָיו וְיָצָא
וְעָשָׂה אֶת־עֹלָתוֹ וְאֶת־עֹלַת הָעָם וְכִפֶּר בַּעֲדוֹ וּבְעַד הָעָם׃
[25]וְאֵת חֵלֶב הַחַטָּאת יַקְטִיר הַמִּזְבֵּחָה׃

[20] $_{e1}$When (he) has finished ‹PI.IR-PFV› making atonement ‹PI.INF› for the sanctuary, the tent of meeting, and the altar, $_{e2}$(he) shall present ‹HI.IR-PFV› the live goat. [21] $_{e3}$Aaron shall lay ‹Q.IR-PFV› his two hands upon the head of the live goat $_{e4}$and confess ‹HT.IR-PFV› over it all the iniquities of the people of Israel and all their transgressions and all their sins $_{e5}$and place ‹Q.IR-PFV› them upon the head of the goat $_{e6}$and send (it) away ‹PI.IR-PFV› by the hand of a ready person into the wilderness, [22]so that the goat carries ‹Q.IR-PFV› upon it all their iniquities into an inaccessible land. $_{e7}$When (he) has sent away ‹PI.IR-PFV› the goat into the wilderness, [23] $_{e8}$Aaron shall enter ‹Q.IR-PFV› into the tent of meeting $_{e9}$and strip off ‹Q.IR-PFV› the linen garments that (he) wore ‹Q.PFV› when he entered ‹Q.INF› into the sanctuary $_{e10}$and leave ‹HI.IR-PFV› them there. [24] $_{e11}$(He) shall bathe ‹Q.IR-PFV› himself with water in a holy place $_{e12}$and put on ‹Q.IR-PFV› his garments $_{e13}$and come out ‹Q.IR-PFV› $_{e14}$and perform ‹Q.IR-PFV› his burnt offering and the burnt offering of the people so that he makes propitiation ‹PI.IR-PFV› for him and for the people. [25] $_{e15}$The fat of the sin offering (he) shall burn ‹HI.IR-PFV› on the altar.

This paragraph is dominated by IR-PFVs. Apart from the INF, the only TAM form is the anaphorically anchored PFV in the relative clause in verse 23. Two pairs of IR-PFVs are best taken as temporal protasis-apodosis, anaphorically anchoring the second of each pair in the first: verse 20, "when (he) has finished . . . then (he) shall present" (וְכִלָּה . . . וְהִקְרִיב); and verses 22–23, "when he has sent . . . then (he) shall enter" (וְשִׁלַּח . . . וּבָא). In the first instance, interpreting וְכִלָּה as a continuous mode directive ("[he] shall finish") seems less felicitous to the context than a temporal interpretation that anchors the following event. In the second case, the awkwardness of repeating וְשִׁלַּח (vv. 21, 22) suggests that the second instance is a temporal protasis that resumes the main line of procedurals through resumptive repetition after the final IR-PFV in verse 22, "so that the goat carries" (וְנָשָׂא הַשָּׂעִיר; see discussion in Milgrom 1991: 1046). The difference between anaphoric protasis-apodosis mode and the continuous mode is slight in the case of these constructions since with either interpretation the order of events is iconic (i.e., they are to occur in the order in which they are prescribed). However, the protasis-apodosis interpretation interprets the two events as more closely related, the first providing a temporal anchoring event for the following one.

256. Leviticus 16:26–28

[26]וְהַמְשַׁלֵּחַ אֶת־הַשָּׂעִיר לַעֲזָאזֵל יְכַבֵּס בְּגָדָיו וְרָחַץ אֶת־
בְּשָׂרוֹ בַּמָּיִם וְאַחֲרֵי־כֵן יָבוֹא אֶל־הַמַּחֲנֶה׃ [27]וְאֵת פַּר
הַחַטָּאת וְאֵת שְׂעִיר הַחַטָּאת אֲשֶׁר הוּבָא אֶת־דָּמָם לְכַפֵּר
בַּקֹּדֶשׁ יוֹצִיא אֶל־מִחוּץ לַמַּחֲנֶה וְשָׂרְפוּ בָאֵשׁ אֶת־עֹרֹתָם
וְאֶת־בְּשָׂרָם וְאֶת־פִּרְשָׁם׃ [28]וְהַשֹּׂרֵף אֹתָם יְכַבֵּס בְּגָדָיו
וְרָחַץ אֶת־בְּשָׂרוֹ בַּמָּיִם וְאַחֲרֵי־כֵן יָבוֹא אֶל־הַמַּחֲנֶה׃

[26](The one) who sent away ‹PI.PTC› the goat for Azazel $_{e1}$shall wash ‹PI.IPFV› his garments $_{e2}$and bathe ‹Q.IR-PFV› himself with water, and after this (he) may enter ‹Q.IPFV› into the camp. [27]The bull of sin offering and the goat of sin offering whose blood was brought in ‹HO.PFV› to make atonement for the sanctuary $_{e3}$(he) shall bring out ‹HI.IPFV› to outside of the camp $_{e4}$and burn ‹Q.IR-PFV› with fire their skin, their flesh, and their dung. [28](The one) who burns ‹Q.PTC› them $_{e5}$shall wash ‹PI.IPFV› his clothing $_{e6}$and bathe ‹Q.IR-PFV› his body with water, and after this (he) may enter ‹Q.IPFV› into the camp.

The last paragraph of procedural instruction treats the "cleanup" following the ritual acts themselves. As such, the topic shifts from the actions performed by Aaron—hence the suitability of the modally fronted IR-PFV and null subject in the previous verses—to the other actors and elements engaged in the ritual work. We therefore find here null-head PTC forms as subjects of directive IPFVs in S-V order (וְהַמְשַׁלֵּחַ . . . יְכַבֵּס, v. 26; וְהַשֹּׂרֵף . . . יְכַבֵּס, v. 28) and a fronted object in verse 27 (וְאֵת פַּר הַחַטָּאת וְאֵת שְׂעִיר הַחַטָּאת) also with a directive IPFV (יוֹצִיא). In all three cases, the IPFV is followed in continuity mode by an IR-PFV. Thus the e_2, e_4, and e_6 designated IR-PFVs exhibit continuity only with their leading IPFV and not among each other. This suggests that the writer is uninterested in ordering the cleanup of the two actors and the blood, though the second two cannot occur in the reverse order since the burning is what makes cleaning up from it necessary. The remaining three predicates are all anaphorically anchored to their respective leading predicate: the perfective past הוּבָא appears in a relative clause, anchoring it to the main clause (יוֹצִיא), and the two וְאַחֲרֵי־כֵן יָבוֹא clauses (vv. 26, 28) overtly signal the anaphoric mode through the anaphoric use of כֵּן. Since there is no inherent reason why the two actors *must* return to the camp, it seems best to understand the final verb not as a directive but as expressing permission.

4.4.3 Prophetic Speech: Zephaniah 1

Although the prophetic books contain a wide variety of literary forms, reported speech—divine and prophetic—is dominant in most of them. Therefore, deictic mode, which is the default speech mode, is the most frequent. Problematically, interpreters often proceed with the assumption that prophetic speech is inherently future oriented, even to the point of giving up on attempting to discern any semantic contrasts in verb choice, as Barton (2001: 88) points out: "Little notice was taken of the tenses in prophetic books, since it was assumed that everything, even narrative, had also a future reference." Such an assumption lies behind categorizations of some PFV forms in prophecy as "prophetic perfects" and "precative perfects" (see Rogland 2003; Carver 2017). Such an approach misses the fact that prophets may describe future events as immediately present to them, as in visionary passages such as Joel 2:3–11 or Hab. 3 (on the latter, see Cook 2012b: 315–16). In such cases, alternations between the PFV, IPFV, and PN are fully expected to describe events witnessed to as they unfold.

Another problem with a future-leveling approach arises even when prophets appear to speak unambiguously of the future. It can be difficult to determine whether they are *predicting* what will happen in realis mood or *warning* of

God's intentions in irrealis mood discourse. The ambiguity between future tense and irrealis mood is the root cause of this uncertainty. The frequency of unambiguous irrealis forms like the IR-PFV as well as the nature of prophetic speech as described in passages such as Jer. 18:1–11 suggests that rather than defaulting to a future tense (realis) interpretation, prophetic judgment speeches should be assumed to be cast in irrealis mood as a warning of what Yhwh plans to do if people's behavior does not change (see Carver 2023). Here Zeph. 1 (excluding the prefatory v. 1) provides a good example of a prophetic announcement of coming judgment, including a description of what things will be like on the day of judgment.

257. Zephaniah 1:2–6

[2]אָסֹף אָסֵף כֹּל מֵעַל פְּנֵי הָאֲדָמָה נְאֻם־יְהוָה׃ [3]אָסֵף אָדָם
וּבְהֵמָה אָסֵף עוֹף־הַשָּׁמַיִם וּדְגֵי הַיָּם וְהַמַּכְשֵׁלוֹת אֶת־
הָרְשָׁעִים וְהִכְרַתִּי אֶת־הָאָדָם מֵעַל פְּנֵי הָאֲדָמָה נְאֻם־
יְהוָה׃ [4]וְנָטִיתִי יָדִי עַל־יְהוּדָה וְעַל כָּל־יוֹשְׁבֵי יְרוּשָׁלִָם
וְהִכְרַתִּי מִן־הַמָּקוֹם הַזֶּה אֶת־שְׁאָר הַבַּעַל אֶת־שֵׁם
הַכְּמָרִים עִם־הַכֹּהֲנִים׃ [5]וְאֶת־הַמִּשְׁתַּחֲוִים עַל־הַגַּגּוֹת לִצְבָא
הַשָּׁמָיִם וְאֶת־הַמִּשְׁתַּחֲוִים הַנִּשְׁבָּעִים לַיהוָה וְהַנִּשְׁבָּעִים
בְּמַלְכָּם׃ [6]וְאֶת־הַנְּסוֹגִים מֵאַחֲרֵי יְהוָה וַאֲשֶׁר לֹא־בִקְשׁוּ
אֶת־יְהוָה וְלֹא דְרָשֻׁהוּ׃

[2](I) really ‹Q.AINF› will end ‹HI.IPFV›[20] everything from upon the face of
the land—declaration of Yhwh. [3](I) will end ‹HI.IPFV› human and beast,
(I) will end ‹HI.IPFV› (the) bird of the heavens and fishes of the sea and
the stumbling blocks with the wicked,[21] so that (I) will cut off ‹HI.IR-
PFV› human from upon the face of the land—declaration of Yhwh. [4]If/
when (I) stretch out ‹Q.IR-PFV› my hand against Judah and against all
(those who are) dwelling ‹Q.PTC› (in) Jerusalem, then (I) will cut off ‹HI.
IR-PFV› from this place the remnant of the Baal and the name of the
idolatrous priests along with the priests, [5]and (those) who bow down

20. The first two words are a well-known crux. As vocalized, the AINF is a Qal of אס״ף and the IPFV is a Hiphil of סו״ף. Typically the focus-AINF-with-finite-verb pattern employs the same verb, or at least the same root (i.e., not necessarily the same binyan; see §2.2.2). The finite verb seems well established by its repetition in the following verse, which points to the AINF as the real crux. The form might be explained as an AINF of סו״ף vocalized as Aramaic Aphel (instead of BH Hiphil; see Sweeney 2003: 59), which is euphonically motivated (cf. Isa. 28:28, אָדוֹשׁ יְדוּשֶׁנּוּ).

21. The expression וְהַמַּכְשֵׁלוֹת אֶת־הָרְשָׁעִים is another crux, on which see the commentaries.

> ‹HISHTAPHEL.PTC› upon the roofs to the host of the heavens and (those) who bow down ‹HISHTAPHEL.PTC› (and) who swear ‹NI.PTC› to Yhwh and who swear ‹NI.PTC› by their king,[22] 6and (those) who turn back ‹NI.PTC› from after Yhwh and who have not sought ‹PI.PFV› Yhwh and have not inquired ‹Q.PFV› (of) him.

This first section of the chapter reports Yhwh's intention to punish the people of Judah and Jerusalem, particularly for their unorthodox syncretistic worship practices. As such, IPFV first-person forms dominate, in which future and volitive converge: Is Yhwh declaring what he inevitably *will* do or what he *intends* to do? In light of Zeph. 2:3, I conclude that irrealis volitive modality is expressed by these verbs.[23] As a report of Yhwh's proclamation, all these IPFV verbs are in the deictic mode, anchored by the deictic center of Yhwh's speech. The AINF focus structure, the repetition of אָסֵף, and the hyperbolic and merism-like complements of the verb all add to the heightened drama of the threatened punishment. The shift to IR-PFV in verse 3 (וְהִכְרַתִּי) calls for an explanation. It cannot be attributed to simple word-order variation with the IPFVs, because they are all clause initial with a null subject in these two verses. Assuming that the change is semantically motivated, the IR-PFV might be interpreted with a final sense, expressing the goal of bringing everything to an end. The repetition of מֵעַל פְּנֵי הָאֲדָמָה נְאֻם־יְהוָה bookends verses 2 and 3, suggesting that verse 4 begins a new subsection.

The expression וְנָטִיתִי יָדִי ("stretch out my hand") refers to preparing to act, which is often conjoined with an IR-PFV verb expressing the action taken (e.g., Exod. 3:20; 7:5; Jer. 51:25; Ezek. 6:14; 14:9, 13; 35:3). In this case, the following verb is a second occurrence of וְהִכְרַתִּי. Together, these two verbs (וְנָטִיתִי . . . וְהִכְרַתִּי), which also appear in combination in Ezek. 25:13, 16, can be interpreted as a simple sequence (continuous mode) but are perhaps better understood as a protasis-apodosis ("if/when I stretch out . . . I will cut off") or with a final sense for the second verb ("I will stretch out . . . so that I cut off"). Though the semantics are ambiguous, either of these latter two understandings draws the two verbs more closely together and shifts the discourse from deictic to anaphoric: the apodosis is anchored in the protasis. Further, the protasis-apodosis interpretation is ambiguous as to whether it is

22. So reads the MT, followed by some ancient versions (e.g., LXX). Other ancient versions read the proper name of the Ammonite deity "Milcom" (e.g., Peshitta), and others have suggested the deity Moloch, associated with child sacrifice (e.g., Lev. 18:21 et al.; see Berlin 1994: 76–77; Sweeney 2003: 70).

23. A more accurate gloss in present-day English would be *intend to* (*OED* s.v. "will" #12a), because the modal/tensed distinction of *will/shall* has broken down, leaving *will* ambiguous.

a strict conditional ("if") or a temporal conditional ("when"). The determination depends on the larger interpretive question of whether the prophetic judgment speech is a threat or a statement of certain future events.

Apart from the relative PTC in verse 4, the rest of the verse as well as verses 5–6a contain a lengthy compound complement of וְהִכְרַתִּי. These consist of nouns, null-head relative PTCs, and an אשר-marked compound relative clause composed of two negated PFV forms. The null-head PTCs are best interpreted as generic mode habituals, describing events unanchored to any specific time but occurring "regularly." If these were interpreted as anaphorically linked to the speech time, they would receive a progressive interpretation, describing events ongoing at the reference time. This generic mode habitual interpretation rather than the anaphoric-mode progressive interpretation applies to the multiple other mostly null-head PTCs in the passage that describe behaviors prompting Yhwh's planned punishment. The two negated PFV forms may be interpreted as stative present perfect in the immediate context of the generic mode PTCs and the larger context of the deixis mode passage.

258. Zephaniah 1:7–13

7 הַס מִפְּנֵי אֲדֹנָי יְהוִה כִּי קָרוֹב יוֹם יְהוָה כִּי־הֵכִין יְהוָה
זֶבַח הִקְדִּישׁ קְרֻאָיו׃ 8 וְהָיָה בְּיוֹם זֶבַח יְהוָה וּפָקַדְתִּי עַל־
הַשָּׂרִים וְעַל־בְּנֵי הַמֶּלֶךְ וְעַל כָּל־הַלֹּבְשִׁים מַלְבּוּשׁ נָכְרִי׃
9 וּפָקַדְתִּי עַל כָּל־הַדּוֹלֵג עַל־הַמִּפְתָּן בַּיּוֹם הַהוּא הַמְמַלְאִים
בֵּית אֲדֹנֵיהֶם חָמָס וּמִרְמָה׃ 10 וְהָיָה בַיּוֹם הַהוּא נְאֻם־
יְהוָה קוֹל צְעָקָה מִשַּׁעַר הַדָּגִים וִילָלָה מִן־הַמִּשְׁנֶה וְשֶׁבֶר
גָּדוֹל מֵהַגְּבָעוֹת׃ 11 הֵילִילוּ יֹשְׁבֵי הַמַּכְתֵּשׁ כִּי נִדְמָה כָּל־עַם
כְּנַעַן נִכְרְתוּ כָּל־נְטִילֵי כָסֶף׃ 12 וְהָיָה בָּעֵת הַהִיא אֲחַפֵּשׂ
אֶת־יְרוּשָׁלִַם בַּנֵּרוֹת וּפָקַדְתִּי עַל־הָאֲנָשִׁים הַקֹּפְאִים עַל־
שִׁמְרֵיהֶם הָאֹמְרִים בִּלְבָבָם לֹא־יֵיטִיב יְהוָה וְלֹא יָרֵעַ׃
13 וְהָיָה חֵילָם לִמְשִׁסָּה וּבָתֵּיהֶם לִשְׁמָמָה וּבָנוּ בָתִּים וְלֹא
יֵשֵׁבוּ וְנָטְעוּ כְרָמִים וְלֹא יִשְׁתּוּ אֶת־יֵינָם׃

7 Hush before the Lord Yhwh, because near (is) the day of Yhwh, because Yhwh has prepared ‹HI.PFV› a sacrifice, (he) has sanctified ‹HI.PFV› (those who have been) summoned ‹Q.PPTC›. 8 [IRREALIS] On the day of the sacrifice of Yhwh (I) will punish ‹Q.IR-PFV› the princes and the sons of the king and all who wear ‹Q.PTC› foreign clothing. 9 (I)

> will punish ‹Q.IR-PFV› all who leap ‹Q.PTC› upon the threshold on that day, (those) who fill ‹PI.PTC› their master's house with violence and deceit. [10]On that day—declaration of Yhwh—will be ‹Q.IR-PFV› a voice of cry from the Fish Gate, and a howl from the Mishneh, and a great break from the hills. [11]Howl ‹HI.IMPV›,[24] (you who) inhabit ‹Q.PTC› the Machtesh, because all the people of Canaan will have been destroyed ‹NI.PFV›, all the weighers of silver will have been cut off ‹NI.PFV›. [12][IRREALIS] At that time (I) will search ‹PI.IPFV› Jerusalem with lamps so that (I) might punish ‹Q.IR-PFV› the men who (are) thickening ‹Q.PTC› upon their dregs, who (are) saying ‹Q.PTC› in their heart, "Yhwh will not do good ‹HI.IPFV› and will not do evil ‹HI.IPFV›," [13]so that their wealth becomes ‹Q.IR-PFV› plunder and their houses (become) a desolation. Although (they) build ‹Q.IR-PFV› houses, (they) will not dwell ‹Q.IPFV› in them. Although (they) plant ‹Q.IR-PFV› vineyards, (they) will not drink ‹Q.IPFV› their wine.

The theme of verses 7–18, which I have split into two parts for convenience,[25] is the day of Yhwh (v. 7). The present time interpretation of the copula is established by the deictic mode of this speech by the prophet, which is indicated by the third-person references to Yhwh. The following two PFV forms interpreted as present perfect fit well with the leading present stative null copula expression, as does the null-head relative PPTC קְרֻאָיו. The prophet returns in verse 8 to reporting Yhwh's intent with the thetic-marking discourse וְהָיָה and repeated IR-PFV form וּפָקַדְתִּי. The targets of Yhwh's punishment are expressed by NPs and several null-head relative PTC clauses (הַלֹּבְשִׁים . . . הַדּוֹלֵג . . . הַמְמַלְאִים). As mentioned in the discussion of the previous example (ex. 257), these are better interpreted as generic mode habituals rather than anaphorically anchored progressives. In contrast to the וְהָיָה in verse 8, the form at the head of verse 10 is an existential, which is followed by a locative adjunct (בַּיּוֹם הַהוּא) and three-part compound subject phrase.

24. The form is identified as IMPV in the lexica (see *HALOT*, *DCD* s.v. ילל) and treated as such by LXX, Targum Jonathan, and Peshitta. However, some versions analyze it as a PFV form, which is morphologically identical (e.g., NRSV, NJPS). The IMPV better fits the pattern of prophetic speech, in which the prophet calls on the inhabitants to "howl," followed by a כִּי clause indicating the reason for the call (Isa. 13:6; 14:31; 23:1, 14; Jer. 4:8; 25:34; 48:20; 49:3; Ezek. 21:17; Joel 1:5, 11, 13; Zech. 11:2).

25. The chapter is divided up variously: e.g., vv. 1–6, 7–18 (Sweeney 2003: 51); vv. 2–9, 10–18 (Berlin 1994: 1–2).

The IMPV הֵילִילוּ is followed by two PFV forms that are anaphorically anchored in the temporal PP בַּיּוֹם הַהוּא and are therefore glossed as future perfects.[26]

The pattern in verse 12 is very similar to that in verses 8–9: the discourse IR-PFV, a temporal PP (here בָּעֵת הַהִיא), first-person volitive verbs (אֲחַפֵּשׂ . . . וּפָקַדְתִּי), and NPs whose complements with relative PTCs (הַקֹּפְאִים . . . הָאֹמְרִים) express habituality or progressive aspect.[27] In this case, however, the latter are conjoined relative modifiers of an overt head, הָאֲנָשִׁים. Another departure from the pattern set in verses 8–9 is the presence in verse 12 of an IPFV (אֲחַפֵּשׂ) instead of two IR-PFVs. The searching is clearly preparatory to the purpose of punishment, suggesting that the TAM shift is to express a volitive-purpose sequence: "I will search . . . so that I might punish." The וְהָיְתָה in verse 13 is copular, expressing the consequences of Yhwh's punishment (so Sweeney 2003: 95). The copula with the לְ PP complement often, as here, indicates an inchoative interpretation: "become" versus "be." Hence the two IR-PFVs in these two verses are both anaphoric mode linked to the preceding predicates. The IPFVs in the embedded speech (לֹא־יֵיטִיב יְהוָה וְלֹא יָרֵעַ) express epistemic certainty—they surmise that Yhwh will not act to their betterment or detriment. The final two pairs of IR-PFVs and IPFVs are analyzed here as concessive protasis-apodosis constructions, in which the future predictive IPFVs are anaphorically anchored in the IR-PFVs of the protases.

259. Zephaniah 1:14–18

14קָרוֹב יוֹם־יְהוָה הַגָּדוֹל קָרוֹב וּמַהֵר מְאֹד קוֹל יוֹם יְהוָה
מַר צֹרֵחַ שָׁם גִּבּוֹר׃ 15יוֹם עֶבְרָה הַיּוֹם הַהוּא יוֹם צָרָה
וּמְצוּקָה יוֹם שֹׁאָה וּמְשׁוֹאָה יוֹם חֹשֶׁךְ וַאֲפֵלָה יוֹם עָנָן
וַעֲרָפֶל׃ 16יוֹם שׁוֹפָר וּתְרוּעָה עַל הֶעָרִים הַבְּצֻרוֹת וְעַל
הַפִּנּוֹת הַגְּבֹהוֹת׃ 17וַהֲצֵרֹתִי לָאָדָם וְהָלְכוּ כַּעִוְרִים כִּי
לַיהוָה חָטָאוּ וְשֻׁפַּךְ דָּמָם כֶּעָפָר וּלְחֻמָם כַּגְּלָלִים׃ 18גַּם־
כַּסְפָּם גַּם־זְהָבָם לֹא־יוּכַל לְהַצִּילָם בְּיוֹם עֶבְרַת יְהוָה
וּבְאֵשׁ קִנְאָתוֹ תֵּאָכֵל כָּל־הָאָרֶץ כִּי־כָלָה אַךְ־נִבְהָלָה יַעֲשֶׂה
אֵת כָּל־יֹשְׁבֵי הָאָרֶץ׃

26. The *temporality* dictates this understanding even though English grammar does not demand the future perfect construction.

27. The accomplishment of "thickening" is perhaps amenable to a progressive interpretation, as it envisions a drawn-out process, whereas "saying" is an activity that presumably happens periodically (habitual) not incessantly (progressive).

[14]Near (is) the great day of Yhwh; (it is) near and hastening ‹PI.INF› quickly. The sound of the day of Yhwh (is) bitter. A warrior shrieks ‹Q.PTC› there. [15]A day of wrath (is) that day, a day of trouble and distress, a day of devastation and desolation, a day of darkness and gloom, a day of cloud and thick darkness, [16]a day of trumpet and alarm against fortified cities and high corner towers. [17](I) will bring distress ‹HI.IR-PFV› to humanity and (they) will walk ‹Q.IR-PFV› like blind (people), because against Yhwh (they) have sinned ‹Q.PFV›. Their blood will be spilt ‹QPASS.IR-PFV› like dust and their flesh (will be spilt) like dung. [18]Even their silver and even their gold will not be able ‹Q.IPFV› to save ‹HI.INF› them on the day of the wrath of Yhwh. In the fire of his vengeance, the whole land will be consumed ‹NI.IPFV›, because a complete, indeed terrifying, (end) (he) will make ‹Q.IPFV› all (who) inhabit ‹PTC› the land.

Verses 15–16 describe the day of Yhwh with null copula clauses that default to the present deictic center of the prophet's speech. The PTC in verse 14 expresses anaphoric mode, set in the day of Yhwh. Verse 17 resumes the first-person IR-PFV that has dominated Yhwh's speech. The following IR-PFVs (וְהָלְכוּ . . . וְשֻׁפַּךְ) are treated consecutively (i.e., in temporal succession with וַהֲצֵרֹתִי), introducing briefly continuous mode. However, the latter verbs might alternatively be interpreted as resultative, shifting it to anaphoric mode, anchored by וַהֲצֵרֹתִי. The realis PFV חָטָאוּ in the causal clause is anaphorically anchored to its main clause, with a present perfect stative sense suitable to expressing the people's present and abiding guilt. The chapter ends with three IPFVs again in deictic mode expressing negatively (לֹא־יוּכַל לְהַצִּילָם) and positively (תֵּאָכֵל . . . יַעֲשֶׂה) the ultimate fate of the land and its inhabitants (a null-head relative PTC) if Yhwh carries out his threat.

4.4.4 Poetic Verse: Psalm 33

Like prophecy, poetry exhibits a wide variety of discourse modes and is often associated with deictic mode as performance "speech." This is evident from the higher incidence of directive-volitive forms in the poetry of Psalms versus prose narrative. These forms are invariably deictic because their irrealis anchor is the speaker's volition (i.e., subjective deontic versus objective deontic; see §3.8). Traditionally, biblical scholars have treated the verbal system in Hebrew poetry as operating in a way that is distinctly different from prose, and as recently as 2006 any claims to the contrary still seemed novel (Niccacci

2006).[28] Taken to an extreme, such a view is of course nonsense, as it would suggest that an understanding of BH prose would contribute nothing to our understanding of Hebrew poetry. Instead, the point is that poetry is palpably more difficult grammatically and more ambiguous with respect to the distribution and meaning of the verbal forms. But this is to be expected of poetry, properly understood as "verbal art," since a central technique of art is to make things "unfamiliar" (see Fabb 2002: 2; Hanson 2012). As such, poetry comes to us as the unfamiliar, which constitutes its poetic aesthetic. This does not mean it employs a distinct "poetic grammar" over and against "prose grammar." Rather, the dominant grammatical patterns in prose are the foil against which poetic creations are recognizable as more "unfamiliar" through their employment of grammatically, syntactically, and lexically challenging and/or ambiguous constructions. Practically, this means that analyzing the TAM and discourse mode in poetry presents more challenges than in prose. Psalm 33, a praise psalm, is analyzed here, but the English glosses misleadingly provide just one interpretation of a given verb form, whose range of meanings are explicated in the discussion.

260. Psalm 33:1–5

1רַנְּנוּ צַדִּיקִים בַּיהוָה לַיְשָׁרִים נָאוָה תְהִלָּה׃ 2הוֹדוּ לַיהוָה
בְּכִנּוֹר בְּנֵבֶל עָשׂוֹר זַמְּרוּ־לוֹ׃ 3שִׁירוּ־לוֹ שִׁיר חָדָשׁ הֵיטִיבוּ
נַגֵּן בִּתְרוּעָה׃ 4כִּי־יָשָׁר דְּבַר־יְהוָה וְכָל־מַעֲשֵׂהוּ בֶּאֱמוּנָה׃
5אֹהֵב צְדָקָה וּמִשְׁפָּט חֶסֶד יְהוָה מָלְאָה הָאָרֶץ׃

1Rejoice ‹PI.IMPV›, righteous (ones), in Yhwh; to the upright praise (is) fitting. 2Praise ‹HI.IMPV› Yhwh with lyre, with ten-stringed harp sing ‹PI.IMPV› to him. 3Sing ‹Q.IMPV› to him a new song, play music ‹PI.INF› well ‹HI.IMPV› with a shout, 4because the word of Yhwh (is) upright and all his works (are) in steadfastness. 5(He) loves ‹Q.PTC› righteousness and justice; the earth is full ‹Q.PFV› of the steadfast love of Yhwh.

As is typical of the hymns of praise, this psalm opens with the poet calling for praise of Yhwh, expressed by IMPVs. The three stative predicates in verses 1 and 4 provide the justification for the directive to praise Yhwh. While IMPV clauses are unambiguously irrealis deictic mode, the mode of the null copula stative expression is less clear. On the one hand, these might be treated as

28. The sharp division between the TAM system in BH prose and poetry arises in part from the dual treatment of prose and poetry in Ugaritic, where the distribution of the verbal forms in poetry "has thus far defied description" (Pardee 2004: 304).

simple statives, temporally anchored in the speech time. While this seems likely for the stative in verse 1, the two null copula expressions of verse 4 come across more like characterizing expressions, suggesting a realis generic mode. The PTC and stative PFV in verse 5 are also generic mode, expressing characteristics of Yhwh and his created order. The lack of a relative ה makes a relative analysis of the PTC somewhat less likely, but not grammatically impossible ("who loves"). Similarly, a null-head relative is possible, "the one who loves" (DeClaissé, Jacobson, and Tanner 2014: 311), but in that case probably as the predicate of a null copula clause: "He is the one loving . . ." (Craigie 1983: 269).

261. Psalm 33:6–9

[6]בִּדְבַר יְהוָה שָׁמַיִם נַעֲשׂוּ וּבְרוּחַ פִּיו כָּל־צְבָאָם׃ [7]כֹּנֵס כַּנֵּד
מֵי הַיָּם נֹתֵן בְּאֹצָרוֹת תְּהוֹמוֹת׃ [8]יִירְאוּ מֵיְהוָה כָּל־הָאָרֶץ
מִמֶּנּוּ יָגוּרוּ כָּל־יֹשְׁבֵי תֵבֵל׃ [9]כִּי הוּא אָמַר וַיֶּהִי הוּא־צִוָּה
וַיַּעֲמֹד׃

[6]By the word of Yhwh the heavens were made ‹NI.PFV› and by the breath of his mouth all the hosts (were made)— [7]gathering ‹Q.PTC› as a heap the waters of the sea, placing ‹Q.PTC› (them) in storehouses the deeps. [8]Let the whole earth fear ‹Q.IPFV› Yhwh; let all the inhabitants of the earth dread ‹Q.IPFV› him, [9]because he spoke ‹Q.PFV› and (it) came to be ‹Q.PN›, he commanded ‹PI.PFV› and (it) stood ‹Q.PN›.

The reference to the earth in verse 5 transitions to the praise of Yhwh's establishment of the created order, with the deictic-mode, passive perfective past נַעֲשׂוּ. The PTCs in verse 7 suggest generic or progressive, but in the context they appear to refer to Yhwh's past actions—whether creative or salvific (see Ps. 78:13). English versions render them either as past tense (NRSV) or general presents (NJPS). Logically they may refer to the means of establishing the heavens, by gathering up the waters and confining them (see Gen. 1:6–8). The glossing of them as nonfinite adjunct small clauses is an attempt to convey this latter understanding of the verse. Directives return with the ambiguous IPFV/JUSS forms in verse 8. The context and V-S word order indicate irrealis mood, with the complement of the second verb (מִמֶּנּוּ) focus fronted before both verb and subject. Verse 9 provides the justification for the directives in two narrative pairings featuring PFVs and PN to convey continous mode temporal succession (see §3.4.3).

262. Psalm 33:10–19

[10]יְהוָה הֵפִיר עֲצַת־גּוֹיִם הֵנִיא מַחְשְׁבוֹת עַמִּים׃ [11]עֲצַת
יְהוָה לְעוֹלָם תַּעֲמֹד מַחְשְׁבוֹת לִבּוֹ לְדֹר וָדֹר׃ [12]אַשְׁרֵי הַגּוֹי
אֲשֶׁר־יְהוָה אֱלֹהָיו הָעָם בָּחַר לְנַחֲלָה לוֹ׃ [13]מִשָּׁמַיִם הִבִּיט
יְהוָה רָאָה אֶת־כָּל־בְּנֵי הָאָדָם׃ [14]מִמְּכוֹן־שִׁבְתּוֹ הִשְׁגִּיחַ
אֶל כָּל־יֹשְׁבֵי הָאָרֶץ׃ [15]הַיֹּצֵר יַחַד לִבָּם הַמֵּבִין אֶל־כָּל־
מַעֲשֵׂיהֶם׃ [16]אֵין־הַמֶּלֶךְ נוֹשָׁע בְּרָב־חָיִל גִּבּוֹר לֹא־יִנָּצֵל
בְּרָב־כֹּחַ׃ [17]שֶׁקֶר הַסּוּס לִתְשׁוּעָה וּבְרֹב חֵילוֹ לֹא יְמַלֵּט׃
[18]הִנֵּה עֵין יְהוָה אֶל־יְרֵאָיו לַמְיַחֲלִים לְחַסְדּוֹ׃ [19]לְהַצִּיל
מִמָּוֶת נַפְשָׁם וּלְחַיּוֹתָם בָּרָעָב׃

[10]Yhwh has frustrated ‹HI.PFV› (the) decision of nations; (he) has brought to naught ‹HI.PFV› plans of peoples. [11]The decision of Yhwh forever will stand ‹Q.IPFV›; the plans of his mind generation to generation (stand). [12]Happy (is) the nation that Yhwh (is) their God, the people (that he) has chosen ‹Q.PFV› for an inheritance for himself. [13]From heaven Yhwh has looked ‹HI.PFV› down, (he) has seen ‹Q.PFV› all the children of mankind. [14]From the place of his sitting (he) has gazed ‹HI.PFV› at all the inhabitants of the earth, [15]who fashions ‹Q.PTC› the mind of them all, who understands ‹HI.PTC› all their works. [16]A king is not ‹NEG-EXIST› victorious ‹NI.PTC› through an abundance of military; a warrior will not save himself ‹NI.IPFV› through an abundance of strength. [17]A horse (is) vain hope for victory, and through the abundance of its might (it) will not deliver ‹PI.IPFV›. [18]Hey, the eye of Yhwh (is) on (those who are) fearful of him, on those (who) hope ‹PI.PTC› for his steadfast love, [19]to rescue ‹HI.INF› from death their life and to preserve ‹PI.INF› them in famine.

The poet moves from the created order to Yhwh's governance of the world. The PFV-IPFV contrast in verses 10–11 contrasts Yhwh's defeat of human usurpation and the lasting establishment of his own governing plans. There is no definitive event referenced in these PFVs, so it is best to take them as anecdotal generics (cf. *Curiosity killed the cat*, where no particular *cat* or *killing* is in view), which serves to create the past-future contrast with the generic IPFVs. Verse 12 returns to deictic mode with the declaration of happiness for the nation that Yhwh chose as his people (present perfect PFV). Verses 13–14 return to generic mode, with the anecdotal generic PFVs paired with the generic relative PTCs in verse 15. In verses 16–19 Yhwh's power is compared with the impotence of king, warrior, and horse to provide victory. Again, the generic mode dominates, expressed with a negated PTC, null copula, and IPFV clauses. The IPFV clauses emphasize the inevitability of the failure of these stratagems (see Cook 2005: 128).

263. Psalm 33:20–22

[20]נַפְשֵׁנוּ חִכְּתָה לַיהוָה עֶזְרֵנוּ וּמָגִנֵּנוּ הוּא׃ [21]כִּי־בוֹ יִשְׂמַח
לִבֵּנוּ כִּי בְשֵׁם קָדְשׁוֹ בָטָחְנוּ׃ [22]יְהִי־חַסְדְּךָ יְהוָה עָלֵינוּ
כַּאֲשֶׁר יִחַלְנוּ לָךְ׃

[20]Our life has waited ‹PI.PFV› for Yhwh. Our strength and shield (is) he. [21]Indeed, in him our heart will rejoice ‹Q.IPFV›, for in his holy name (we) have trusted ‹Q.PFV›. [22]May your steadfast love, Yhwh, be ‹Q.JUSS› upon us just as (we) have waited ‹PI.PFV› for you.

The hymn of praise ends with a deictic mode statement of confidence and a return to directives. The NRSV treats all the predicates in verses 20–21 as general presents. But the variation of PFV–null copula–IPFV–PFV is temporally significant: the congregation "has waited" because Yhwh continues to be strength and shield to them, and as such "indeed" they "will rejoice," because they "have trusted" in him. A similar future-irrealis + past pattern occurs again in the final directive with a comparative PFV clause: may you do accordingly in the future as we have done in the past and present.

GLOSSARY OF LINGUISTIC TERMS

Like all technical fields, linguistics thrives on specialized terms and shorthand expressions. Unfortunately, this terminology often results in some opacity, if not confusion, for students and scholars in biblical and textual studies who have not been trained in linguistics. And yet it is often not desirable to avoid all technical terminology. Doing so would not only result in unwieldy descriptions but remove studies like this from their explicit grounding in a linguistic theory and/or specific linguistic studies.

To facilitate the reading of this volume, I provide here a list of linguistic terms used in this volume. For convenience and to point the reader to one of the most useful linguistic tools for the nonlinguist, many definitions are quoted from or based on David Crystal, *A Dictionary of Linguistics and Phonetics* (6th ed.; Oxford: Blackwell, 2008). The number in brackets after an entry is the page number in Crystal 2008 where a more expansive definition can be found.

absolute tense. *See* tense-aspect-mood/modality: tense.

accomplishment. *See* tense-aspect-mood/modality: aspect: situation aspect.

achievement. *See* tense-aspect-mood/modality: aspect: situation aspect.

active-causative. When a cause produces a patient to engage in an activity, such as *lead* (i.e., *make someone follow*).

activity. *See* tense-aspect-mood/modality: situation aspect.

adjectival. *See* adjective.

adjective [11]. A word specifying the attribute of a noun.

adjunct [12]. An "optional or secondary element in a construction." Removing an adjunct will not affect the structural integrity of the rest of the construction.

adverb(ial) [14]. "A term used in the grammatical classification of words to refer to a heterogeneous group of items whose most frequent function is to specify the mode of action of the verb. . . . Syntactically, one can relate adverbs to such questions as *how*, *where*, *when* and *why*, and classify them accordingly, as adverbs of 'manner,' 'place,' 'time,' etc."

agreement [18]. The "formal relationship between elements, whereby a form of one word requires a corresponding form of another (i.e., the forms agree)."

anaphora [25]. The process or result of a linguistic item (e.g., pronoun) deriving its interpretation from some previously expressed unit of meaning (the antecedent). Anaphoric reference is one way of marking the identity between what is being expressed and what has already been expressed. In such a sentence as *He did that there*, the interpretation of each word is dependent on a corresponding referent in the preceding context. Anaphoric discourse mode refers to interpretation of tense-aspect-mood/modality of one clause based on its anaphoric relationship to another (see §4.3).

anterior. *See* tense-aspect-mood/modality: viewpoint aspect.

anticausative. An intransitive verb in which the event affects the subject and lacks any indication of the cause of the event (e.g., English *fall, break*, etc.). It is a subcategory of unaccusative verb (*see* unaccusative).

apocopation [30]. "The deletion of the final element in a word," in contrast to aphaeresis (omission of a beginning element) and syncope (omission of an interior element).

apodosis. *See* clause: conditional clause.

aspect. *See* tense-aspect-mood/modality.

asseverative כִּי. The use of כִּי to reinforce an affirmation. Translatable by English as "certainly, indeed."

autocausative. An intransitive verb that expresses a spontaneous (i.e., no conceivable agent) event (e.g., *The ground <u>split open</u>*).

auxiliary verb [46]. A verb that is subordinate to and supportive of the main lexical verb that helps to express tense-aspect-mood/modal distinctions.

avalent. *See* valency.

bivalent. *See* valency.

bound construction [59]. A morpheme is bound if it "cannot occur on its own as a separate word." The so-called construct state of nouns in BH involves a variant form of the noun that is bound to the following noun (bound construction).

bounded(ness). Describes an event as having reached a temporal boundary, versus unbounded(ness), which describes an event as having *not* reached a temporal boundary (see Depraetere 1995). This contrasts with telicity (see below): both telic and atelic events can be bounded or unbounded.

casus pendens. Latin for "hanging case." *See* dislocation.

clause [78]. A syntactical unit that is "smaller than the sentence but larger than phrases, words, or morphemes."

complement clause. A subordinate clause that serves as complement of a predicate, typically an infinitive clause or a finite clause introduced by כִּי or אֲשֶׁר.

conditional clause [99]. A clause expressing a hypothesis or condition; sometimes used of the two-part construction consisting of the condition (protasis) and the main clause (apodosis).

equative clause [171]. A clause that places two noun phrases in an identity relationship; i.e., it equates the two, as in *Rob is a professor*.

existential clause [178]. A clause that expresses the existence or presence of something. In English, existential clauses are composed with a "dummy" (nonreferential) subject, as in *It is raining* or *There is bread (on the table)*.

null copula clause. *See* copula.

purpose clause. A clause expressing the reason for the action in the main clause.

relative clause. A subordinate clause that modifies a noun phrase.

headless relative. A relative clause whose head is null (covert).

relative head. The relative head, or pivot, is the word modified by the relative clause.

unmarked relative. A relative clause that is not introduced by a relative pronoun.

result clause [415]. A clause expressing consequence or effect.

small clause [440]. A "clause that contains neither a finite verb nor an infinitival *to*," as *Becca smart* in *Jared finds Becca smart*.

specificational clause. A copular clause that identifies a subject by an alternate designation, as in *Frankfort is the capital of Kentucky*.

subordinate clause. A clause (of any kind) that is subordinated to a larger clause. *See* subordination.

temporal clause. A subordinate clause indicating when the events of the main clause occur.

clitic [80]. "A term used in grammar to refer to a form which resembles a word, but which cannot stand on its own as a normal utterance, being phonologically dependent upon a neighboring word (its host) in a construction."

complement [92]. "A major constituent of sentence or clause structure, traditionally associated with 'completing' the action specified by the verb. In its broadest sense, complement therefore is a very general notion, subsuming all obligatory features of the predicate other than the verb, e.g., objects (e.g., *She kicked the ball*) and adverbials (e.g., *She was in the* *garden*)." This notion of obligatory completion extends to prepositions, which obligatorily head noun phrase complements (e.g., *to the bank*).

complement clause. *See* clause.

composition [96]. Describes how larger linguistic structures are made up of smaller structures. In semantics, the compositionality principle attributes the meaning of a larger linguistic structure to the meanings contributed by the smaller units within it.

concessive [98]. "A word or construction which expresses the meaning of 'concession.' The point expressed in the main clause continues to be valid despite the point being made in the subordinate clause (the concessive clause). In English, the most widely used markers of concession are *although* and *though*."

conditional clause. *See* clause.

conjugation [100]. Verbs created from a base form that show the same range of inflections indicating such things as person, gender, number. For example, all verbs in the PFV conjugation use the same set of person-gender-number inflectional suffixes, and the IPFV conjugation uses a different set of inflectional affixes.

conjunction [101]. An "item or a process whose primary function is to connect words or other constructions."

constituent [104]. "A linguistic unit which is a functional component of a larger construction."

construct. *See* bound construction.

copula (verbal, nonverbal, null) [116]. A "linking verb, i.e., a verb which has little independent meaning, and whose main function is to relate other elements of clause structure, especially subject and complement." In Hebrew, the verbal copula is הי"ה; the existentials יֵשׁ and אַיִן can serve as noninflected, nonverbal copulas. Null copula refers to a copular clause in that the copula is phonologically null or covert; i.e., a "verbless" (or nominal) clause.

correspondence [118]. In semantics, correspondence theory of truth or meaning posits that there is a connection between a linguistic form and its referent that constitutes its truth value or meaning. *See* truth condition.

covert. *See* null.

deixis/deictic [133]. The process of (and as an adjective, the words used in) referring directly to the personal, temporal, or locational characteristics of the situation within which an utterance takes place, whose meaning is thus relative to that situation. Personal pronouns (especially first- and second-person) and demonstrative pronouns are deictic, as also are nonpronominal words such as הִנֵּה and עַתָּה. Deictic discourse mode refers to the anchoring of the interpretation of tense-aspect-mood/modality to the speaker's temporal or modal "now," sometimes referred to as the speaker's "deictic center" (see §4.3).

deontic. *See* tense-aspect-mood/modality.

directive. *See* tense-aspect-mood/modality: mood/modality.

discourse pragmatics [148, 379]. Discourse refers to a continuous stretch of text larger than the clause or sentence. Pragmatics is concerned with meaning in context, including extralinguistic contributors to meaning. Used in combination, these terms refer to the meaning of a linguistic expression within and influenced by its discourse context.

discourse representation theory [149]. "A semantic theory which seeks to extend model-theoretic semantics to accommodate sequences of sentences, and in particular to accommodate anaphoric dependencies across sentence boundaries."

dislocation (left and right) (= *casus pendens*) [273, s.v. "left dislocation"; 418, s.v. "right dislocation"]. A type of sentence in which one of the constituents appears in initial (left) or final (right) position and its canonical position is filled by a pronoun or a full lexical noun phrase with the same reference (e.g., *John, I like him/the old chap* or *I know that woman/her, Julie*).

dispositional middle. An intransitive expression that ascribes a disposition to the subject, as in *The glass is fragile* (i.e., is disposed to being broken).

distributed morphology [153]. "An approach to morphology . . . in which morphological processes are not localized within a single component but are 'distributed' throughout the grammar, involving syntactic as well as phonological operations."

ditransitive. *See* transitivity.

dynamic. *See* tense-aspect-mood/modality: situation aspect.

dynamic semantics [160]. An approach to semantics that characterizes the meaning of a clause in terms of its ability to change the information state of the discourse, as opposed to "static" approaches.

equative clause. *See* clause.

existential clause. *See* clause.

extension/intension [181, 248]. Extension refers to the entity or entities to which a word properly applies, also termed its *referent* or *denotation*. Intension refers to the defining properties of a word or its sense, what a word signifies (e.g., a computer is defined by having a screen, a keyboard, a processing chip, etc.). In the statement *Bill is looking for a computer*, the meaning of *computer* is opaque: Bill might be looking for a specific computer (extension) or for a computer of some sort (intension).

factitive [184]. A verb in which a cause produces a resultant state, such as *kill* (i.e., *make someone be dead*). *See* active-causative; resultative.

finite verb [189]. A verb that can occur on its own in an independent clause, as opposed to nonfinite verbs, which typically cannot.

focus (fronting) [192–93]. "A term used by some linguists in a two-part analysis of sentences which distinguishes between the information assumed by speakers, and that which is at the centre (or 'focus') of their communicative interest; 'focus' in this sense is opposed to presupposition. (The contrast between given and new information makes an analogous distinction.) For example, in the sentence *It was Mary who came to tea*, Mary is the focus (as the intonation contour helps to signal). Taking such factors into account is an important aspect of intersentence relationships: it would not be possible to have the above sentence as the answer to the question *What did Mary do?*, but only to *Who came to tea?*" In Hebrew, constituents are typically fronted (see fronting) to indicate focus.

formalist. Applied to linguistic theories that tend to focus on the internal structure of language, are concerned with rules of grammar, and often employ mathematical and logical notations in their analyses. Cf. functionalist.

formal semantics. An approach to meaning that employs mathematical and logical notations. Distinctives of the approach include the use of truth conditions and models to analyze meaning and the principle of compositionality. *See* composition.

fronting [201]. The transposition of "a constituent from the middle or end of a string to initial position. For example, the rule of '*Wh*-fronting' places a *Wh*-phrase (e.g., *Which books?*) in initial position, transposing it from the underlying noninitial position (cf. *John walked there* → *John walked where* → *where did John walk*)."

functionalist. Applied to linguistic theories that tend to focus on the communicative function of language, are concerned with the context of language usage, and tend to eschew mathematical and logical notations. *See* formalist; formal semantics.

generative grammar. A term introduced by Chomsky (1957) that refers to linguistic theories that conceive of grammar as a set of rules that "generate" only grammatical expressions.

generic/genericity. A noun phrase or clause that expresses a class, a general property, or a characteristic in contrast to "particular" noun phrases and clauses (e.g., *Lions are ferocious*). This category includes clauses traditionally termed gnomic, general, or, proverbial.

gram. Grammatical construction; here the term refers specifically to grammatical constructions in the tense-aspect-mood/modality (TAM) system. Broader than "conjugation" or "form," it includes any grammaticalized way of signaling TAM, including inflected verbal forms, periphrastic constructions, or irrealis-mood word-order inversion (see Dahl 2000: 23n2).

grammaticalization [218, s.v. "grammar"]. The process whereby a word with semantic content is used to express grammatical functions. "An example of grammaticalization (grammaticization) is the use of the English motion verb *go*, as in *She is going to London*, which has become a marker of tense in *It's going to rain*."

head [225]. "A term used in the grammatical description of some types of phrase to refer to the central element which is distributionally equivalent to the phrase as a whole." *See* noun phrase; verb phrase.

historical-comparative [91, 229]. Historical linguistics (also known as diachronic linguistics) studies the development of language. Comparative linguistics deals with the same historical data but focuses on relationships within language families. Combined, they refer to the study of historical development within a language family (e.g., historical-comparative Semitics). *See* typology.

homonymy [231]. Lexical items with the same form but different meaning, such as *bear* (an animal and a verb meaning "to carry").

hypotactic [233]. A subordinate clause that is marked by an overt subordinate word, in contrast to paratactic clauses, which are not marked overtly. Cf. the hypotactic relative clause *The man that I saw outside* with the paratactic relative clause *The man I saw outside*.

imperfective. *See* tense-aspect-mood/modality: viewpoint aspect.

implicit complement. A complement that is suggested by the meaning of the verb but is neither syntactically nor phonologically represented in the text. See §2.5.4.

contextual implicit complement. An implicit complement that can be reconstructed based on contextual elements.

deictic implicit complement. An implicit complement that is referred to by pragmatic deixis in the context, such as physically pointing to it.

generic implicit complement. An implicit complement that is interpreted stereotypically (i.e., absent of any contextual or deictic clues).

inchoative. The expression of the entrance into a state, as in *They became sick*. It is contrasted with a simple state, as in *They were sick*, and with inceptive, which refers to the initiation of a dynamic action, such as *They began working*.

intension. *See* extension/intension.

intransitive. *See* transitivity.

inversion [254]. A syntactic change "in which a specific sequence of constituents is seen as the reverse of another."

irrealis. *See* tense-aspect-mood/modality: mood/modality.

jussive. *See* tense-aspect-mood/modality: mood/modality.

light verb. A closed set of verbs that are identical with full verbs but contribute a non-compositional meaning to a monoclausal predication. For example, the Qal שׁו"ב as a full verb means "return," but as a light verb construction it adds the sense of "again" to another conjoined verb, forming a single predicate, "do *x* again."

linguistic typology [499, s.v. "typological linguistics"]. A branch of linguistics that studies the structural similarities between languages, regardless of their history or genetic relationship, in an attempt to establish a satisfactory classification, or typology, of languages. Typological comparison is thus distinguished from the historical comparison of languages—the province of comparative philology and historical linguistics—and its groupings may not coincide with those set up by the historical method. For example, in respect of the paucity of inflectional endings, English is closer to Chinese than it is to Latin.

minimalist program(me) [306]. "A development in generative linguistic thinking, which emphasizes the aim of making statements about language which are as simple and general as possible. The term 'programme' expresses the notion that this is an ongoing research initiative, not a fully articulated grammatical theory."

modality. *See* tense-aspect-mood/modality.

model-theoretical semantics [309]. A semantic approach in which truth conditions are posited for linguistic expressions relative to each model or "world" for which the described state of affairs is valid.

monovalent. *See* valency.

mood. *See* tense-aspect-mood/modality.

nominal clause. *See* null copula.

noun phrase (NP) [333]. A structural element consisting "minimally of the noun"; NPs may consist of a single noun (e.g., מֶלֶךְ, king) or may contain additional constituents that modify the noun (e.g., הָאֱלֹהִים אֲשֶׁר בָּרָא הָאָרֶץ, the God who created the earth).

null (**covert**) [335]. Generative grammar uses this mathematical term for "empty" or "zero" to refer to a "phonologically empty constituent" or "null element"—that is, a constituent that syntactically exists but is not phonologically overt (verbalized).

null copula. *See* copula.

null (**covert**) **complement**. A constituent that must exist, given the argument structure of a verb or noun phrase, but that is identifiable from a discourse antecedent rather than being phonologically overt.

null (**covert**) **subject**. A phrase used to refer to a subject that must exist, given the argument structure of a verb, but is not phonologically overt. Null subjects may or may not be reconstructible from context.

null (covert) verb. A verb that is not phonologically overt.

overt. *See* null (covert).

paratactic. *See* hypotactic.

perfect. *See* tense-aspect-mood/modality: aspect: viewpoint aspect.

perfective. *See* tense-aspect-mood/modality: aspect: viewpoint aspect.

periphrasis [358]. The use of separate words instead of inflections to express a linguistic meaning, as in *more wise* versus *wiser*.

phasal aspect. *See* tense-aspect-mood/modality: aspect.

pluractional/pluractionality. A term that refers to the expression of multiple events distributed over time (e.g., *He sang a song again and again*), locations (e.g., *She planted trees here and there*), or participants (e.g., *They all built houses*). The term features in discussions of interactions among verbal aspects. For example, a pluractional event consisting of multiple accomplishments or achievements may be viewed as an activity: *They are (each) building houses* is a pluractional activity with distribution across participants consisting of multiple accomplishments (i.e., *to build a house*).

pragmatics. *See* discourse pragmatics.

predicate [381]. A "major constituent of sentence structure . . . containing all obligatory constituents other than the subject" within a "two-part analysis" of clauses. *See* subject.

prepositional phrase (PP) [383]. The "set of items which typically precede noun phrases (often single nouns or pronouns), to form a single constituent of structure." Prepositions "can combine with not only an NP but also a PP (e.g., *since before breakfast*) [or] a clause (e.g., *since they finished their breakfast*)."

progressive. *See* tense-aspect-mood/modality: aspect: viewpoint aspect.

pronoun [391–92]. A term referring to the closed set of items that can be used to substitute syntactically for a noun phrase. Pronouns are often divided into classes, such as personal, demonstrative, interrogative, reflexive, indefinite, and relative.

protasis. *See* clause: conditional clause.

purpose clause. *See* clause.

realis. *See* tense-aspect-mood/modality: mood/modality.

reciprocal [404]. An intransitive verb that requires a plural subject and whose object is implied to be the same as the subject, as in *They kissed*. Most reciprocal verbs can also be nonreciprocal transitive in the singular or plural, as in *She/They kissed the Blarney Stone*.

reference/sense [407, 432]. *See* extension/intension.

reflex. A form or grammatical construction for which a pre- or proto-form may be reconstructed; reflexes that are related to the same pre-/proto-form are cognates.

reflexive [408]. An intransitive verb whose object is implied to be the same as the subject: *The child bathed.* Most reflexive verbs can also be transitive with either an overt reflexive pronoun, as in *The child bathed himself*, or a nonreflexive, as in *The child bathed her doll.*

relative clause. *See* clause.

relative tense. *See* tense-aspect-mood/modality: tense.

result clause. *See* clause.

resultative. A verb that indicates that a state exists as the result of a previous dynamic event. Similar and developmentally related to simple statives and perfect/anterior aspect. *See* factitive.

resumptive/resumption [415]. "An element or structure which repeats or in some way recapitulates the meaning of a prior element." In Hebrew, resumption occurs especially in relative clauses, where pronouns are the typical resumptive element, for example, הָאָרֶץ אֲשֶׁר עָבַרְנוּ בָהּ, "the land that they explored *it*" (Num. 13:32).

semantics [428]. A branch of linguistics that studies meaning in language.

sense. *See* extension/intension.

serial verb [434]. A construction in which verbs are linked in an underspecified way to express a single event, as in *I'll go see.*

situation aspect. *See* tense-aspect-mood/modality: aspect.

small clause. *See* clause.

specificational clause. *See* clause.

stages. Event structure based on a localist understanding (i.e., spatial location is fundamental). Situation types that have stages (activities and accomplishments) can be thought of spatially. For example, *Rob ate three burgers* suggests that at one stage Rob has eaten one burger, then two at a later stage, and so on. Similarly, *Jon was playing catch with his son* indicates that Jon was throwing the ball at one stage, catching it at another, and so on. By contrast, "states" (e.g., *Paul was sick*) and "achievements" (e.g., *Julie left town*) lack stages because they describe static situations (states) and transitions from one state to another (achievements; see §2.3).

state/stative. *See* tense-aspect-mood/modality: aspect: situation aspect.

subinterval property. A property of [–telic] events, in which if an event is true at a given interval, it is also true at any subinterval of that interval (see Cook 2012c: 60).

subject [461]. "A major constituent of sentence or clause structure, traditionally associated with the 'doer' of an action, as in *The cat bit the dog*. [Many] approaches make a twofold distinction in sentence analysis between subject and predicate." *See* predicate.

subordinate clause. *See* clause.

subordination [462]. "The process or result of linking linguistic units so that they have different syntactic status, one being dependent upon the other, and usually a constituent of the other."

substantive [463]. "Items which function as nouns, though lacking some of the formal characteristics of that class (cf. the 'substantival function' of adjectives, in *the poor, the rich*, etc.)."

syntagm [470]. A syntactic constituent.

telic [478]. A term used in aspect studies to describe an event with an inherent end/final point.

temporal clause. *See* clause.

tense. *See* tense-aspect-mood/modality.

tense-aspect-mood/modality (TAM). A bundle of features present in verbs, centered on the relationship of events in time and to reality.

aspect [38]. Refers "primarily to the way the grammar marks the duration or type of temporal activity denoted by the verb."

phasal aspect. A category distinguishing focus on or alteration of different phases of situation development, including focus on the beginning (e.g., *She began to read*), end (e.g., *He finished reading*), and alteration of the middle (e.g., *They continued to read/resumed reading/always read*). See §2.6.

situation aspect. A category distinguishing among event types in terms of their temporal structure. Four situation types commonly appear in the literature: **states** (situations that lack stages and lack a natural endpoint; e.g., *He is sick*), **activities** (situations that have stages but lack an inherent endpoint; e.g., *They play together well*), **accomplishments** (situations that have stages and a natural endpoint; e.g., *He built a house*), and **achievements** (situations that lack stages and consist of a transition from one state to a natural end state; e.g., *She won the race*). These are classified into **stative** (states) and **dynamic** (activities, accomplishments, and achievements) situation types. States are further divisible into **individual-level** (permanent) versus **stage-level** (temporary). See §2.3. Some also posit **semelfactive** as a situation aspect (see ex. 95c and the accompanying note).

viewpoint aspect. A category distinguishing among alternative perspectives on situation development. The two main viewpoints are the **perfective** (views the entire situation development; e.g, *She read the book*) and **imperfective** (views a portion of the situation development; e.g., *She is reading the book*). Others include **progressive** (very similar to imperfective), (**past, present, future**) **perfect/anterior** (views the ending of situation development and the resultant state of affairs; e.g., *She has read the book [so she is done with it]*), and **prospective** (the opposite of anterior, viewing the preliminary state of affairs to situation development; e.g, *He is going to pick her up tonight at 8 p.m.*). See §3.2.2.

mood/modality [312]. "Mood (modality, or mode) refers to a set of syntactic and semantic contrasts signaled by alternative paradigms of the verb, e.g., indicative (the unmarked form), subjunctive, imperative. Semantically, a wide range of meanings is involved, especially attitudes on the part of the speaker towards the factual content of the utterance, e.g., uncertainty, definiteness, vagueness, possibility." Mood and modality are often discussed in terms of alternative situations and the realis and irrealis contrast: whereas **realis** refers to the "actual" situation, **irrealis** refers to "alternative" situations that are related to the "actual" situation via a modal "accessibility" relationship. The two broad modalities belonging in the irrealis category are **epistemic** (statements of probability/possibility; e.g., *He must be there by now*) and **deontic** (statements of obligation/permission; e.g., *You should really be there*), alongside of which is **dynamic** (statements of ability; e.g., *He can jump the wall*). Deontic subcategories include the **directive** (imposition of will; e.g., *Be there tomorrow*), **volitive** (statements of will or desire, typically in first person; e.g., *I will be there tonight*), and **jussive** (statements of will or desire, typically in second or third person; e.g., *Let them go*). See §3.2.3.

tense [479]. A category for describing verbs that refers to how grammar indicates the time at which the action denoted by the verb occurs. **Absolute tense** describes the time of the event as a direct relationship to the time of speaking. **Relative tense** describes the time of the event as a relationship to some other time, typically associated with another event. See §3.2.1.

thetic. A clause containing all new information; i.e., the clause is entirely comment rather than topic-comment. *See* topic and §4.2.

topic (fronting) [48]. "The entity (person, thing, etc.) about which something is said, whereas the further statement made about this entity is the comment." In BH, constituents may be fronted (*see* fronting) or dislocated (*see* dislocation) to indicate topic.

transitivity (intransitive, transitive ditransitive) [494]. A classification of clauses based on the relationship of the verb to dependent constituents in the verb phrase. A transitive clause has a dependent direct object complement (*She baked bread*), whereas an intransitive one lacks one (*He ran*), and a ditransitive clause has both a dependent direct object complement and an indirect object one (*She gave him a present*).

trivalent. *See* valency.

truth condition [497]. Refers to the conditions under which a linguistic expression is true or meaningful.

typology. *See* linguistic typology.

unacccusative [500]. An intransitive verb whose subject originates as the patient object of the event (e.g., *The window broke*). Also referred to as ergative verbs.

unbounded(ness). *See* bounded(ness).

unergative. An intransitive verb whose subject is the agent of the event, as in *They talked.*

valency [507]. "The number and type of bonds which syntactic elements may form with each other." In this book, the term refers particularly to the number of arguments necessary to complete a verb phrase.

avalent. The valency of a verb licensing no arguments.

bivalent. The valency of a verb licensing two arguments (subject and VP complement).

monovalent. The valency of a verb licensing one argument (the subject).

trivalent. The valency of a verb licensing three arguments.

verbless clause. *See* copula.

verb phrase (VP). [510] A phrase consisting minimally of a head verb, but may also contain complement and adjunct modifiers of the verb—equivalent to predicate. *See* predicate.

verb switching. The phenomenon in which a verbal (inflectional) encoding of a predicate is taken over partially by a nonverbal (periphrastic) encoding strategy. E.g., the English simple present verbal inflection *The baby cries* has been partly displaced by the nonverbal (locative) encoding *The baby is crying*, specifically to describe events happening at the speech time (see Stassen 1997: 242).

viewpoint aspect. *See* tense-aspect-mood/modality: aspect.

volitive. *See* tense-aspect-mood/modality: mood.

WORKS CITED

Abbott, Barbara. 2010. *Reference*. Oxford: Oxford University Press.

———. 2011. "Reference: Foundational Issues." In *Semantics: An International Handbook of Natural Language Meaning*, edited by Claudia Maienborn, Klaus von Heusinger, and Paul Portner, 49–74. Berlin: De Gruyter.

Alexiadou, Artemis, and Edit Doron. 2012. "The Syntactic Construction of Two Non-active Voices: Passive and Middle." *Journal of Linguistics* 48 (1): 1–34.

Andersen, Francis I., and A. Dean Forbes. 2007. "The Participle in Biblical Hebrew and the Overlap of Grammar and Lexicon." In *Milk and Honey: Essays on Ancient Israel and the Bible in Appreciation of the Judaic Studies Program at the University of California, San Diego*, edited by Sarah Malena and David Miano, 185–212. Winona Lake, IN: Eisenbrauns.

Andersen, Francis I., and David Noel Freedman. 2000. *Micah: A New Translation with Introduction and Commentary*. Anchor Bible. New York: Doubleday.

Anttila, Raimo. 1989. *Historical and Comparative Linguistics*. Amsterdam: Benjamins.

Arad, Maya. 2005. *Roots and Patterns: Hebrew Morpho-Syntax*. Studies in Natural Language and Linguistic Theory 63. Dordrecht: Springer.

Austin, J. L. 1962. *How to Do Things with Words*. Oxford: Clarendon.

Baker, David W. 1973. "The Consecutive Nonperfective as Pluperfect in the Historical Books of the Hebrew Old Testament." PhD diss., Regent College.

Baker, Mark C., and Jim McCloskey. 2007. "On the Relationship of Typology to Theoretical Syntax." *Linguistic Typology* 11:285–96.

Bar-Asher, Elitzur. 2009. "A Theory of Argument Realization and Its Application to Features of the Semitic Languages." PhD diss., Harvard University.

Barr, James. 1961. *The Semantics of Biblical Language*. London: Oxford University Press.

Bauer, Hans. 1910. "Die Tempora im Semitischen." *Beiträge zur Assyriologie und semitischen Sprachwissenschaft* 81:1–53.

Bauer, Hans, and Pontus Leander. 1922. *Historische Grammatik der hebräischen Sprache*. Hildesheim: Olms.

Beckman, John Charles. 2015. "Toward the Meaning of the Biblical Hebrew Piel Stem." PhD diss., Harvard University.

Benton, Richard Charles, Jr. 2009. "Aspect and the Biblical Hebrew Niphal and Hitpael." PhD diss., University of Wisconsin.

Berlin, Adele. 1994. *Zephaniah: A New Translation with Introduction and Commentary*. Anchor Bible 25A. New York: Doubleday.

Bertinetto, Pier Marco. 2000. "The Progressive in Romance, as Compared with English." In *Tense and Aspect in the Languages of Europe*, edited by Östen Dahl, 559–604. Berlin: De Gruyter.

Bertinetto, Pier Marco, Karen H. Ebert, and Casper de Groot. 2000. "The Progressive in Europe." In *Tense and Aspect in the Languages of Europe*, edited by Östen Dahl, 517–58. Berlin: De Gruyter.

Bicknell, Belinda Jean. 1984. "Passives in Biblical Hebrew." PhD diss., University of Michigan.

Binnick, Robert I. 1991. *Time and the Verb: A Guide to Tense and Aspect*. Oxford: Oxford University Press.

Blau, Joshua. 2010. *Phonology and Morphology of Biblical Hebrew: An Introduction*. Linguistic Studies in Ancient West Semitic 2. Winona Lake: Eisenbrauns.

Bloch, Yigal. 2010. "The Prefixed Perfective in the Construction אָז יִקְטֹל and Its Later Replacement by the Long Prefixed Verbal Form: A Syntactic and Text-Critical Analysis." *Journal of Northwest Semitic Languages* 36 (2): 49–74.

Bloomfield, Leonard. 1926. "A Set of Postulates for the Science of Language." *Language* 2 (3): 153–64.

Boneh, Nora, and Edit Doron. 2008. "Habituality and Habitual Aspect." In *Theoretical and Crosslinguistic Approaches to the Semantics of Aspect*, edited by Susan Rothstein, 321–48. Linguistik Aktuell/Linguistics Today 110. Amsterdam: Benjamins.

———. 2010. "Modal and Temporal Aspects of Habituality." In *Syntax, Lexical Semantics, and Event Structure*, edited by Malka Rappaport Hovav, Edit Doron, and Ivy Sichel, 338–63. Oxford Studies in Theoretical Linguistics 27. Oxford: Oxford University Press.

Boulet, Jacques. 2019. "A Linguistic Reappraisal of the Biblical Hebrew Accusative." PhD diss., University of Toronto.

Boyd, Steven William. 1993. "A Synchronic Analysis of the Medio-Passive-Reflexive in Biblical Hebrew." PhD diss., Hebrew Union College.

———. 2017. "The Binyanim (Verbal Stems)." In *"Where Shall Wisdom Be Found?" A Grammatical Tribute to Professor Stephen A. Kaufman*, edited by Hélène Dallaire, Benjamin J. Noonan, and Jennifer E. Noonan, 85–125. Winona Lake, IN: Eisenbrauns.

Brown, Gillian, and George Yule. 1983. *Discourse Analysis*. Cambridge: Cambridge University Press.

Buth, Randall. 1994. "Methodological Collision between Source Criticism and Discourse Analysis: The Problem of 'Unmarked Temporal Overlay' and the Pluperfect/Nonsequential *Wayyiqtol*." In *Biblical Hebrew and Discourse Linguistics*, edited by Robert D. Bergen, 138–54. Winona Lake, IN: Eisenbrauns.

Bybee, Joan L., and Östen Dahl. 1989. "The Creation of Tense and Aspect Systems in the Languages of the World." *Studies in Language* 13:51–103.

Bybee, Joan, Revere Perkins, and William Pagliuca. 1994. *The Evolution of Grammar: Tense, Aspect, and Modality in the Languages of the World*. Chicago: University of Chicago Press.

Callaham, Scott N. 2008–11. “The Paranomastic Infinitive Construction as a Modality-Focusing Device: Evidence from Qatal Verbs.” *Zeitschrift für Althebraistik* 21–24:9–30.

———. 2010. *Modality and the Biblical Hebrew Infinitive Absolute*. Wiesbaden: Harrassowitz.

Carver, Daniel E. 2017. “A Reconsideration of the Prophetic Perfect in Biblical Hebrew.” PhD diss., Catholic University of America.

———. 2023. “Biblical Prophecy in Its Ancient Near Eastern Context: A New Interpretation of Jeremiah 30–33.” *Journal of Biblical Literature* 142 (2): 267–87.

Chomsky, Noam. 1957. *Syntactic Structures*. The Hague: Mouton.

———. 1986. *Knowledge of Language: Its Nature, Origin, and Use*. New York: Praeger.

———. 1995. *The Minimalist Program*. Cambridge, MA: MIT Press.

Cohen, Ariel. 2018. “The Square of Disposition.” *Glossa: A Journal of General Linguistics* 3 (1): article 90.

———. 2020. *Something Out of Nothing: The Semantics and Pragmatics of Implicit Quantification*. Current Research in the Semantics/Pragmatics Interface 38. Leiden: Brill.

Cohen, Ohad. 2013. *The Verbal Tense System in Late Biblical Hebrew Prose*. Harvard Semitic Studies 63. Winona Lake, IN: Eisenbrauns.

Comrie, Bernard. 1976. *Aspect*. Cambridge: Cambridge University Press.

Cook, John A. 2004. “The Semantics of Verbal Pragmatics: Clarifying the Roles of *Wayyiqtol* and *Weqatal* in Biblical Hebrew Prose.” *Journal of Semitic Studies* 49 (2): 247–73.

———. 2005. “Genericity, Tense, and Verbal Patterns in the Sentence Literature of Proverbs.” In *Seeking Out the Wisdom of the Ancients: Essays Offered to Honor Michael V. Fox on the Occasion of His Sixty-Fifth Birthday*, edited by Ronald L. Troxel, Kelvin G. Friebel, and Dennis R. Magary, 117–33. Winona Lake, IN: Eisenbrauns.

———. 2006. “The Finite Verbal Forms in Biblical Hebrew Do Express Aspect.” *Journal of the Ancient Near Eastern Society* 30:21–35.

———. 2008. “The Participle and Stative in Typological Perspective.” *Journal of Northwest Semitic Languages* 34 (1): 1–19.

———. 2012a. “Detecting Development in Biblical Hebrew Using Diachronic Typology.” In *Diachrony in Biblical Hebrew*, edited by Cynthia L. Miller-Naudé and Ziony Zevit, 83–95. Linguistic Studies in Ancient West Semitic 8. Winona Lake, IN: Eisenbrauns.

———. 2012b. “Hebrew Language.” In *Dictionary of the Old Testament: Prophets*, edited by J. G. McConville and Mark J. Boda, 307–18. Downers Grove, IL: IVP Academic.

———. 2012c. *Time and the Biblical Hebrew Verb: The Expression of Tense, Aspect, and Modality in Biblical Hebrew*. Linguistic Studies in Ancient West Semitic 7. Winona Lake, IN: Eisenbrauns.

———. 2013. “The Verb in Qoheleth.” In *The Words of the Wise Are Like Goads: Engaging Qoheleth in the 21st Century*, edited by Mark J. Boda, Tremper Longman III, and Cristian Rata, 309–42. Winona Lake, IN: Eisenbrauns.

———. 2014. "Current Issues in the Study of the Biblical Hebrew Verbal System." *Kleine Untersuchungen zur Sprache des Alten Testaments und seiner Umwelt* 17:79–108.

———. 2019. *Aramaic Ezra and Daniel: A Handbook on the Aramaic Text*. Waco: Baylor University Press.

———. 2020. "Finding Missing Objects in Biblical Hebrew (with an Appendix on Missing Subjects)." *Journal for Semitics* 29 (2): 1–21. https://orcid.org/0000-0002-3330-5180.

———. 2023. "How Systematic Is the Binyanim 'System' in Biblical Hebrew?" *Journal for Semitics* 32 (1): 1–14. https:doi.org/10.25159/2663-6573/13557.

———. Forthcoming. "The Biblical Hebrew Verbal System." In *The Cambridge Companion to the Bible and Linguistics*, edited by Stanley E. Porter. Cambridge: Cambridge University Press.

Cook, John A., and Robert D. Holmstedt. 2013. *Beginning Biblical Hebrew: A Grammar and Illustrated Reader*. Illustrated by Philip Williams. Grand Rapids: Baker Academic.

———. 2020. *Intermediate Biblical Hebrew: An Illustrated Grammar*. Illustrated by Philip Williams. Grand Rapids: Baker Academic.

———. Forthcoming. *Isaiah 40–55: A Handbook on the Hebrew Text*. Waco: Baylor University Press.

Craigie, Peter C. 1983. *Psalms 1–50*. Word Biblical Commentary 19. Waco: Word Books.

Creason, Stuart-Alan. 1995. "Semantic Classes of Hebrew Verbs: A Study of Aktionsart in the Hebrew Verbal System." PhD diss., University of Chicago.

Croft, William. 2003. *Typology and Universals*. 2nd ed. Cambridge Textbooks in Linguistics. Cambridge: Cambridge University Press.

Crystal, David. 2008. *A Dictionary of Linguistics and Phonetics*. 6th ed. Oxford: Blackwell.

Dahl, Östen., ed. 2000. *Tense and Aspect in the Languages of Europe*. Berlin: De Gruyter.

Dallaire, Hélène. 2014. *The Syntax of Volitives in Biblical Hebrew and Amarna Canaanite Prose*. Winona Lake, IN: Eisenbrauns.

Daniel, Michael. 2010. "Linguistic Typology and the Study of Language." In *The Oxford Handbook of Linguistic Typology*, edited by Jae Jung Song, 43–68. Oxford: Oxford University Press.

Davidson, A. B. 1901. *Introductory Hebrew Grammar: Hebrew Syntax*. Edinburgh: T&T Clark.

DeCaen, Vincent. 1995. "On the Placement and Interpretation of the Verb in Standard Biblical Hebrew Prose." PhD diss., University of Toronto.

DeClaissé-Walford, Nancy L., Rolf A. Jacobson, and Beth LaNeel Tanner. 2014. *The Book of Psalms*. New International Commentary on the Old Testament. Grand Rapids: Eerdmans.

Depraetere, Ilse. 1995. "On the Necessity of Distinguishing between (Un)boundedness and (A)telicity." *Linguistics and Philosophy* 18:1–19.

Detges, Ulrich. 2000. "Time and Truth: The Grammaticalization of Resultatives and Perfects within a Theory of Subjectification." *Studies in Language* 24 (2): 345–77. https://doi:10.1075/sl.24.2.05det.

Dobbs-Allsopp, F. W. 2004–7. (More) on Performatives in Semitic. *Zeitschrift für Althebräistik* 17–20:36–81.

Doron, Edit. 2003. "Agency and Voice: The Semantics of the Semitic Templates." *Natural Language Semantics* 11 (1): 1–67.

Driver, G. R. 1936. *Problems of the Hebrew Verbal System*. Edinburgh: T&T Clark.

Driver, S. R. 1913. *An Introduction to the Literature of the Old Testament*. New York: Scribner's Sons.

———. 1998. *A Treatise on the Use of the Tenses in Hebrew and Some Other Syntactical Questions*. Reprint, Grand Rapids: Eerdmans.

Dry, Helen Aristar. 1981. "Sentence Aspect and the Movement of Narrative Time." *Text* 1:233–40.

Ewald, Heinrich. 1879. *Syntax of the Hebrew Language of the Old Testament*. Translated by James Kennedy. Edinburgh: T&T Clark.

Fabb, Nigel. 2002. *Language and Literary Structure: The Linguistic Analysis of Form in Verse and Narrative*. Cambridge: Cambridge University Press.

Fassberg, Steven E. 1999. "The Lengthened Imperative קָטְלָה in Biblical Hebrew." *Hebrew Studies* 40:7–13.

———. 2001. "The Movement from *Qal* to *Piʿel* in Hebrew and the Disappearance of the *Qal* Internal Passive." *Hebrew Studies* 42:243–55.

Ferguson, H. 1882. "An Examination of the Use of Tenses in Conditional Sentences." *Journal of Biblical Literature* 2:40–94.

Filip, Hana. 2011. "Aspectual Class and Aktionsart." In *Semantics: An International Handbook of Natural Language Meaning*, edited by Claudia Maienborn, Klaus von Heusinger, and Paul Portner, 1186–217. Berlin: De Gruyter.

Folmer, Margaretha L. 1995. *The Aramaic Language of the Achaemenid Period: A Study in Linguistic Variation*. Orientalist Lovaniensia Analecta 68. Leuven: Peeters.

Fox, Joshua. 2003. *Semitic Noun Patterns*. Harvard Semitic Studies 59. Winona Lake, IN: Eisenbrauns.

Frege, Gottlob. 1892. "Über Sinn und Bedeutung." *Zeitschrift für Philosophie und philosophische Kritik* 100:25–50.

Frege, Gottlob, and Max Black. 1948. "A Translation of Frege's *Über Sinn und Bedeutung*." *The Philosophical Review* 57 (3): 207–30.

Gai, Amikam. 1982. "The Reduction of Tense (and Other Categories) of the Consequent Verb in North-West Semitic." *Orientalia* 51:254–56.

Garr, W. Randall. 2004. *Dialect Geography of Syria-Palestine, 1000–586 B.C.E.* Winona Lake, IN: Eisenbrauns.

———. 2021. "A Note on the Pluractional *Piel*." In *Ve-'ed Ya 'Aleh (Gen 2:6)*, vol. 1, *Essays in Biblical and Ancient Near Eastern Studies Presented to Edward L. Greenstein*, edited by Peter Machinist, Robert A. Harris, Joshua A. Berman, Nili Samit, and Noga Ayali-Darshan, 253–67. Atlanta: SBL Press.

Geiger, Gregor. 2013. "Participle: Rabbinic Hebrew." In *Encyclopedia of Hebrew Language and Literature*, edited by Geoffrey Khan, 3:36–39. Leiden: Brill.

Gelderen, Elly van. 2013. *Clause Structure*. Cambridge: Cambridge University Press.

Geniušienė, Emma. 1987. *The Typology of Reflexives*. Empirical Approaches to Language Typology 2. Berlin: De Gruyter.

Gentry, Peter J. 1998. "The System of the Finite Verb in Classical Biblical Hebrew." *Hebrew Studies* 39:7–39.

Goetze, Albrecht. 1942. "The So-Called Intensive of the Semitic Languages." *Journal of the American Oriental Society* 62:1–8.

Gordon, Amnon. 1982. "The Development of the Participle in Biblical, Mishnaic, and Modern Hebrew." *Afroasiatic Linguistics* 8 (3): 1–59.

Grasso, Kevin. "The Meaning of *Qatal*." *Journal for Semitics* 30:1–16. https://doi.org/10.25159/2663-6573/9299.

Grønn, Atle, and Arnim von Stechow. 2016. "Tense." In *The Cambridge Handbook of Formal Semantics*, edited by Maria Aloni and Paul Jacques Edgar Dekker, 313–41. Cambridge: Cambridge University Press.

Gropp, Douglas M. 1991. "The Function of the Finite Verb in Classical Biblical Hebrew." *Hebrew Annual Review* 13:45–62.

Gzella, Holger. 2009. "Voice in Classical Hebrew against Its Semitic Background." *Orientalia* 78 (3): 292–325.

Haggard, Bradley. 2022. "Metaphor and Atonement: A Conceptual Metaphor Study of the Sacrificial Prescriptions in Leviticus 1–16." PhD diss., Asbury Theological Seminary.

Hale, Mark. 2007. *Historical Linguistics: Theory and Method*. Oxford: Blackwell.

Hanson, Kristin. 2012. "Linguistics and Poetics." In *The Princeton Encyclopedia of Poetry and Poetics*, edited by Roland Greene, Stephen Cushman, Clare Cavanagh, Jahan Ramazani, and Paul Rouzer, 803–9. 4th ed. Princeton: Princeton University Press.

Haspelmath, Martin. 1998. "The Semantic Development of Old Presents: New Futures and Subjunctives without Grammaticalization." *Diachronica* 15 (1): 29–62.

———. 2004. "Does Linguistic Explanation Presuppose Linguistic Description?" *Studies in Language* 28 (3): 554–79.

Hatav, Galia. 1997. *The Semantics of Aspect and Modality: Evidence from English and Biblical Hebrew*. Studies in Language Companion Series 34. Amsterdam: Benjamins.

———. 2017. "The Infinitive Absolute and Topicalization of Events in Biblical Hebrew." In *Advances in Biblical Hebrew Linguistics: Data, Methods, and Analyses*, edited by A. Mosak Moshavi and Tania Notarius, 207–29. Linguistic Studies in Ancient West Semitic 12. Winona Lake, IN: Eisenbrauns.

———. 2021. "The Nature of the Infinitive Absolute." In *Linguistic Studies on Biblical Hebrew*, edited by Robert D. Holmstedt, 125–43. Studies in Semitic Languages and Linguistics 102. Leiden: Brill.

Heine, Bernd, Claudi Ulrike, and Friederike Hünnemeyer. 1991. *Grammaticalization: A Conceptual Framework*. Chicago: University of Chicago Press.

Held, Moshe. 1962. "The YQTL-QTL (QTL-YQTL) Sequence of Identical Verbs in Biblical Hebrew and in Ugaritic." In *Studies and Essays in Honor of Abraham A. Neuman*, edited by Meir Ben-Horin, Bernard D. Weinryb, and Solomon Zeitlin, 281–90. Leiden: Brill.

Hillers, Delbert R. 1969. Review of Ernst Jenni, "Das hebräische Piʿel: Syntaktisch-semasiologische Untersuchung einer Verbalform im Alten Testament." *Journal of Biblical Literature* 88 (2): 212–14.

Hogg, Richard M., N. F. Blake, Roger Lass, Suzanne Romaine, R. W. Burchfield, and John Algeo. 1992. *The Cambridge History of the English Language*. Cambridge: Cambridge University Press.

Holmstedt, Robert D. 2006. "Issues in the Linguistic Analysis of a Dead Language, with Particular Reference to Ancient Hebrew." *Journal of Hebrew Scriptures* 6: article 11.

———. 2009. "Word Order and Information Structure in Ruth and Jonah: A Generative-Typological Analysis." *Journal of Semitic Studies* 59 (1): 111–39.

———. 2011. "The Typological Classification of the Hebrew of Genesis: Subject-Verb or Verb-Subject?" *Journal of Hebrew Scriptures* 11: article 14.

———. 2013a. "Hypotaxis." In *Encyclopedia of Hebrew Language and Linguistics*, edited by Geoffrey Khan, 2:220–22. Leiden: Brill.

———. 2013b. "Investigating the Possible Verb-Subject to Subject-Verb Shift in Ancient Hebrew: Methodological First Steps." *Kleine Untersuchungen zur Sprache des Alten Testaments und seiner Umwelt*. "Schrift und Sprache": Papers Read at the 10th Mainz International Colloquium on Ancient Hebrew (MICAH), Mainz, 28–30 October 2011, 15:3–31.

———. 2014. "Critical at the Margins: Edge Constituents in Biblical Hebrew." *Kleine Untersuchungen zur Sprache des Alten Testaments und seiner Umwelt* 17:109–56.

———. 2016. *The Relative Clause in Biblical Hebrew*. Linguistic Studies in Ancient West Semitic 10. Winona Lake, IN: Eisenbrauns.

———. 2019. "Hebrew Poetry and the Appositive Style: Parallelism, *Requiescat in Pace*." *Vetus Testamentum* 69:617–48.

———. Forthcoming. *Biblical Hebrew Syntax: A Linguistic Introduction*. Grand Rapids: Baker Academic.

Holmstedt, Robert D., John A. Cook, and Phillip S. Marshall. 2017. *Qoheleth: A Handbook on the Hebrew Text*. Waco: Baylor University Press.

Holmstedt, Robert D., and Andrew R. Jones. 2014. "The Pronoun in Tripartite Verbless Clauses in Biblical Hebrew: Resumption for Left-Dislocation or Pronominal Copula?" *Journal of Semitic Studies* 59 (1): 53–89.

Hopper, Paul J., and Sandra A. Thompson. 1980. "Transitivity in Grammar and Discourse." *Language* 56:251–99.

Hopper, Paul J., and Elizabeth Closs Traugott. 2003. *Grammaticalization*. 2nd ed. Cambridge Textbooks in Linguistics. Cambridge: Cambridge University Press.

Huehnergard, John. 1988. "The Early Hebrew Prefix-Conjugations." *Hebrew Studies* 29:19–23.

Huehnergard, John, and Na'ama Pat-El. 2019. "Introduction to the Semitic Languages and Their History." In *The Semitic Languages*, 1–21. 2nd ed. Abingdon: Routledge.

Hurvitz, Avi. 1972. *Ben Lashon Le-Lashon: Le-Toldot Leshon Ha-Mikra Bi-Yeme Bayit Sheni*. Jerusalem: Mosad Byalik.

———. 1982. *A Linguistic Study of the Relationship between the Priestly Source and the Book of Ezekiel: A New Approach to an Old Problem*. Paris: J. Gabalda.

———. 2000. "Can Biblical Texts Be Dated Linguistically? Chronological Perspectives in the Historical Study of Biblical Hebrew." In *Congress Volume, Oslo 1998*, edited by A. Lemaire and M. Saebø, 143–60. Leiden: Brill.

Hurvitz, Avi, Leeor Gottlieb, Aaron D. Hornkohl, and Emmanuel Mastéy. 2014. *A Concise Lexicon of Late Biblical Hebrew: Linguistic Innovations in the Writings of the Second Temple Period*. Leiden: Brill.

Jenni, Ernst. 1968. *Das hebräische Piʿel: Syntaktisch-semasiologische Untersuchung einer Verbalform im Alten Testament*. Zürich: EVZ-Verlag.

———. 2000. "Aktionsarten und Stammformen im Althebräischen: Das Piʿel in verbesserter Sicht." *Zeitschrift für Althebräistik* 13:67–90.

———. 2005. *Studien zur Sprachwelt des Alten Testaments II*. Stuttgart: Kohlhammer.

———. 2012. "Nifal und Hitpael im biblische-Hebräischen." In *Studien zur Sprachwelt des Alten Testaments III*, edited by Ernst Jenni, 131–303. Stuttgart: Kohlhammer.

Jespersen, Otto. 1921. *Language: Its Nature, Development and Origin*. London: Allen & Unwin; New York: Holt.

Jones, Ethan C. 2020. "Middle and Passive Voice: Semantic Distinctions of the Niphal in Biblical Hebrew." *Zeitschrift für die alttestamentliche Wissenschaft* 132 (2): 427–48.

Joosten, Jan. 1998. "The Functions of the Semitic D Stem: Biblical Hebrew Materials for a Comparative-Historical Approach." *Orientalia* 67 (2): 202–30.

———. 2012. *The Verbal System of Biblical Hebrew: A New Synthesis Elaborated on the Basis of Classical Prose*. Jerusalem: Simor.

Joüon, Paul. 1923. *Grammaire de l'hébrew biblique*. Rome: Pontifical Biblical Institute.

———. 2006. *A Grammar of Biblical Hebrew*. Translated and revised by Takamitsu Muraoka. 2nd ed. Rome: Pontifical Biblical Institute.

Kahan, J. 1889. *Über die verbalnominale Doppelnatur der hebräischen Participien und Infinitive und ihre darauf beruhende verschiedene Konstruktion*. Leipzig: Vollrath.

Kamp, Hans, and Christian Rohrer. 1983. "Tense in Texts." In *Meaning, Use, and Interpretation of Language*, edited by Rainer Bäuerle, Christoph Schwarze, and Arnim von Stechow, 250–69. Berlin: De Gruyter.

Kamp, Hans, Josef van Genabith, and Uwe Reyle. 2011. "Discourse Representation Theory." In *Handbook of Philosophical Logic*, edited by Dov M. Gabby and Franz Guenthner, 125–394. Dordrecht: Springer.

Keenan, Edward L., and Bernard Comrie. 1977. "Noun Phrase Accessibility and Universal Grammar." *Linguistic Inquiry* 8 (1): 63–99.

Kim, Yoo-Ki. 2009. *The Function of the Tautological Infinitive in Classical Biblical Hebrew*. Winona Lake, IN: Eisenbrauns.

Kit, Olena. 2014. "On the Complex Eventive Structure of Dispositional Middle Constructions." MS thesis, McMaster University.

Klein, George L. 1992. "The Meaning of the Niphal in Biblical Hebrew." PhD diss., Annenberg Research Institute.

Kouwenberg, N. J. C. 1997. *Gemination in the Akkadian Verb*. Assen: Van Gorcum.

———. 2010. *The Akkadian Verb and Its Semitic Background*. University Park: Penn State University Press.

Krahmalkov, Charles R. 1986. "The *Qatal* with Future Tense Reference in Phoenician." *Journal of Semitic Studies* 31 (1): 5–10.

Krifka, Manfred, Francis Jeffry Pelletier, Gregory N. Carlson, Alice ter Meulen, Godehard Link, and Gennaro Chierchia. 1995. "Genericity: An Introduction." In *The Generic Book*, edited by Gregory N. Carlson and Francis Jeffry Pelletier, 1–124. Chicago: University of Chicago Press.

Kroeger, Paul R. 2005. *Analyzing Grammar: An Introduction*. Cambridge: Cambridge University Press.

———. 2019. *Analyzing Meaning: An Introduction to Semantics and Pragmatics*. Berlin: Language Science Press.

Kummerow, David. 2007. "How Can the Form יִקְטֹל be a Preterite, Jussive, and a Future/Imperfective?" *Kleine Untersuchungen zur Sprache des Alten Testaments und seiner Umwelt* 8 (9): 63–95.

———. 2013. *Object Predication in Tiberian Hebrew: A Typological Approach to the Nonverbal Copula*. Kleine Untersuchungen zur Sprache des Alten Testaments und seiner Umwelt 16. Kamen: Hartmut Spenner.

Kuryłowicz, Jerzy K. 1973. "Verbal Aspect in Semitic." *Orientalia* 42 (1–2): 114–20.

Lakoff, R. T. 1971. "If's, And's and But's about Conjunctions." In *Studies in Linguistic Semantics*, edited by C. J. Fillmore and D. T. Langendoen, 114–49. New York: Rinehart.

Lambrecht, Knud. 1994. *Information Structure and Sentence Form: Topic, Focus, and the Mental Representation of Discourse Referents*. Cambridge Studies in Linguistics 71. Cambridge: Cambridge University Press.

Lambrecht, Knud, and Maria Polinsky. 1997. "Typological Variation in Sentence-Focus Constructions." In *Proceedings of the Thirty-Third Annual Meeting of the Chicago Linguistic Society: Papers from the Panels*, edited by Kora Singer, Eggert Randall, and Gregory Anderson, 189–206. Chicago: Chicago Linguistic Society.

Lancelot, Claude, and Antoine Arnauld. 1975. *General and Rational Grammar: The Port-Royal Grammar*. The Hague: Mouton.

Langacker, Ronald W. 1997. "Generics and Habituals." In *On Conditionals Again*, edited by Angeliki Athanasiadou and René Dirven, 191–222. Amsterdam: Benjamins.

Levinsohn, Stephen H. 2000. "NP References to Active Participants and Story Development in Ancient Hebrew." *Working Papers of the Summer Institute of Linguistics, University of North Dakota Session* 44.

Lipiński, Edward. 2001. *Semitic Languages: Outline of a Comparative Grammar*. 2nd ed. Orientalist Lovaniensia Analecta 80. Leuven: Peeters.

Lyngfelt, Benjamin, and Torgrim Solstad, eds. 2006. *Demoting the Agent: Passive, Middle and Other Voice Phenomena*. Linguistik Aktuell/Linguistics Today 96. Amsterdam: Benjamins.

Lyons, John. 1977. *Semantics*. Cambridge: Cambridge University Press.

Macías, José Hugo García. 2016. "From the Unexpected to the Unbelievable: Thetics, Miratives and Exclamatives in Conceptual Space." PhD diss., University of New Mexico.

Mair, Christian. 2012. "Progressive and Continuous Aspect." In *The Oxford Handbook of Tense and Aspect*, edited by Robert I. Binnick, 803–27. Oxford: Oxford University Press.

Malchukov, Andrej L., and Viktor S. Xrakovskij. 2016. "The Linguistic Interaction of Mood with Modality and Other Categories." In *The Oxford Handbook of Modality and Mood*, edited by Jan Nuyts and Johan van der Auwera, 196–220. Oxford: Oxford University Press.

Mani, Inderjeet, J. Pustejovsky, and Robert Gaizauskas, eds. 2005. *The Language of Time: A Reader*. New York: Oxford University Press.

Matthews, Peter. 2001. *A Short History of Structural Linguistics*. Cambridge: Cambridge University Press.

McCarter, P. Kyle, Jr. 1984. *II Samuel: A New Translation with Introduction and Commentary*. Anchor Bible 9. New York: Doubleday.

McCawley, James D. 1993. *Everything That Linguists Have Always Wanted to Know about Logic*. Chicago: University of Chicago Press.

McFall, Leslie. 1982. *The Enigma of the Hebrew Verbal System*. Sheffield: Almond.

McNally, Louise. 2011. "Existential Sentences." In *Semantics: An International Handbook of Natural Language Meaning*, edited by Claudia Maienborn, Klaus von Heusinger, and Paul Portner, 1829–48. Berlin: De Gruyter.

Michel, Diethelm. 1960. *Tempora und Satzstellung in den Psalmen*. Bonn: Bouvier.

Milgrom, Jacob. 1991. *Leviticus 1–16: A New Translation with Introduction and Commentary*. Anchor Bible 3. New York: Doubleday.

Mikkelsen, Line. 2011. "Copular Clauses." In *Semantics: An International Handbook of Natural Language Meaning*, edited by Claudia Maienborn, Klaus von Heusinger, and Paul Portner, 1805–29. Berlin; New York: De Gruyter.

Miller, Cynthia L. 2003. *The Representation of Speech in Biblical Hebrew Narrative: A Linguistic Analysis*. Harvard Semitic Monographs 55. Atlanta: Scholars Press, 1996. Reprint, Winona Lake, IN: Eisenbrauns.

———. 2004. "Methodological Issues in Reconstructing Language Systems from Epigraphic Fragments." In *The Future of Biblical Archaeology: Reassessing Methodologies and Assumptions*, edited by J. K. Hoffmeier and A. R. Millard, 281–305. Grand Rapids: Eerdmans.

Montague, Richard. 1974. *Formal Philosophy: Selected Papers of Richard Montague*. New Haven: Yale University Press.

Moran, William L. 2003. *Amarna Studies: Collected Writings*. Winona Lake, IN: Eisenbrauns.

Moravcsik, Edith A. 2007. "What Is Universal about Typology?" *Linguistic Typology* 11:27–41.

Muraoka, Takamitsu. 1997. "The Alleged Final Function of the Biblical Syntagm <*Waw* + a Volitive Verb Form>." In *Narrative Syntax and the Hebrew Bible: Papers of the Tilburg Conference 1996*, edited by Ellen van Wolde, 229–41. Leiden: Brill.

Myler, Neil. 2018. "Complex Copula Systems as Suppletive Allomorphy." *Glossa: A Journal of General Linguistics* 3 (1). https://doi.org/10.5334/gjgl.214.

Naudé, Jacobus A. 2001. "The Distribution of Independent Personal Pronouns in Qumran Hebrew." *Journal of Northwest Semitic Languages* 27 (2): 91–112.

Naudé, Jacobus A., and Cynthia L. Miller-Naudé. 2016. "The Contribution of Qumran to Historical Hebrew Linguistics: Evidence from the Syntax of Participial Negation." *HTS Teologiese Studies / Theological Studies* 72 (4). http://dx.doi. org/10.4102/hts.v72i4.3150.

Naudé, Jacobus A., Cynthia L. Miller-Naudé, and Daniel J. Wilson. 2021. "The Negative Existential Cycle in Ancient Hebrew." In *The Negative Existential Cycle*, edited by Arja Hamari and Ljuba Veselinova, 101–20. Research on Comparative Grammar 1. Berlin: Language Science Press.

Niccacci, Alviero. 2006. "The Biblical Hebrew Verbal System in Poetry." In *Biblical Hebrew in Its Northwest Semitic Setting. Typological and Historical Perspectives*, edited by Steven E. Fassberg and Avi Hurvitz, 247–68. Jerusalem: Magnes; Winona Lake, IN: Eisenbrauns.

Notarius, Tania. 2013. *The Verb in Archaic Biblical Poetry: A Discursive, Typological, and Historical Investigation of the Tense System*. Studies in Semitic Languages and Linguistics 68. Leiden: Brill.

Pagin, Peter, and Dag Westerståhl. 2011. "Compositionality." In *Semantics: An International Handbook of Natural Language Meaning*, edited by Claudia Maienborn, Klaus von Heusinger, and Paul Portner, 96–123. Berlin: De Gruyter.

Palmer, Frank R. 1986. *Mood and Modality*. Cambridge Textbooks in Linguistics. Cambridge: Cambridge University Press.

———. 2001. *Mood and Modality*. 2nd ed. Cambridge: Cambridge University Press.

Pardee, Dennis. 2004. "Ugaritic." In *The Cambridge Encyclopedia of the World's Ancient Languages*, edited by Roger D. Woodard, 288–318. Cambridge: Cambridge University Press.

Partee, Barbara. 2016. "Formal Semantics." In *The Cambridge Handbook of Formal Semantics*, edited by Maria Aloni and Paul Jacques Edgar Dekker, 3–32. Cambridge: Cambridge University Press.

Peled, Yishai. 1992. *Conditional Structures in Classical Arabic*. Studies in Arabic Language and Literature 2. Wiesbaden: Harrassowitz.

Perlmutter, David M. 1978. "Impersonal Passives and the Unaccusative Hypothesis." *Annual Meeting of the Berkeley Linguistics Society* 4:157–90.

Polzin, Robert. 1976. *Late Biblical Hebrew: Toward an Historical Typology of Biblical Hebrew Prose*. Harvard Semitic Monographs 12. Missoula, MT: Scholars Press.

Porten, Bazalel, and Ada Yardeni. 1986. *Textbook of Aramaic Documents from Ancient Egypt*. Winona Lake, IN: Eisenbrauns.

Portner, Paul. 2009. *Modality*. Oxford Surveys in Semantics and Pragmatics. Oxford: Oxford University Press.

———. 2018. *Mood*. Oxford Surveys in Semantics and Pragmatics. Oxford: Oxford University Press.

Portner, Paul, and Barbara Hall Partee. 2002. *Formal Semantics: The Essential Readings*. Malden, MA: Blackwell.

Propp, William Henry. 1999. *Exodus 1–18: A New Translation with Introduction and Commentary*. Anchor Yale Bible 2. New Haven: Yale University Press.

Pustejovsky, James. 1991. "The Syntax of Event Structure." *Cognition* 41 (1): 47–81.

Pylkkänen, Liina. 2008. *Introducing Arguments*. Linguistic Inquiry Monograph 49. Cambridge, MA: MIT Press.

Qimron, Elisha. 1997. "A New Approach to the Use of Forms of the Imperfect without Personal Endings." In *Hebrew of the Dead Sea Scrolls and Ben Sira*, edited by Takamitsu Muraoka and J. F. Elwolde, 174–81. Leiden: Brill.

Rainey, Anson F. 1986. "The Ancient Hebrew Prefix Conjugation in the Light of Amarnah Canaanite." *Hebrew Studies* 27 (1): 4–19.

Reichenbach, Hans. 1947. *Elements of Symbolic Logic*. London: Collier-Macmillan.

Reinhart, Tanya. 1984. "Principles of Gestalt Perception in the Temporal Organization of Narrative Texts." *Linguistics* 22:779–809.

Rendsburg, Gary A. 1990a. *Diglossia in Ancient Hebrew*. American Oriental Series 72. New Haven: American Oriental Society.

———. 1990b. *Linguistic Evidence for the Northern Origin of Selected Psalms*. Society of Biblical Literature Monograph Series 43. Atlanta: Scholars Press.

Revell, E. J. 1984. "Stress and the *Waw* 'Consecutive' in Biblical Hebrew." *Journal of the American Oriental Society* 104 (3): 437–44.

———. 1989. "The System of the Verb in Standard Biblical Prose." *Hebrew Union College Annual* 60:1–37.

Reymond, Eric D. 2023. "Irregular Short-*Yiqṭol* Forms in Late Second Temple Hebrew." In *A Sage in New Haven: Essays on the Prophets, the Writings, and the Ancient World in Honor of Robert R. Wilson*, edited by Alison Acker Gruseke and Carolyn J. Sharp, 331–42. Münster: Zaphon.

Rissanen, Matti. 1999. "Syntax." In *The Cambridge History of the English Language*, vol. 3, *1476–1776*, edited by Roger Lass, 187–331. Cambridge: Cambridge University Press.

Rogland, Max. 2003. *Alleged Non-past Uses of Qatal in Classical Hebrew*. Assen: Van Gorcum.

Rothmayr, Antonia. 2009. *The Structure of Stative Verbs*. Linguistik Aktuell/Linguistics Today 143. Amsterdam: Benjamins.

Rothstein, Susan. 2004. *Structuring Events: A Study in the Semantics of Lexical Aspect*. Explorations in Semantics. Oxford: Blackwell.

Rubinstein, A. 1952. "A Finite Verb Continued by an Infinitive Absolute in Hebrew." *Vetus Testamentum* 1:362–67.

Ryder, Stuart A. 1974. *The D-Stem in Western Semitic*. Berlin: De Gruyter.

Sapir, Edward. 1921. *Language: An Introduction to the Study of Speech*. New York: Harcourt, Brace.

Sasse, H.-J. 1996. *Theticity*. Köln: Institut für Sprachwissenschaft der Universität zu Köln.

Saussure, Ferdinand de, Charles Bally, and Albert Sechehaye. 1959. *Course in General Linguistics*. Translated by Wade Baskin. New York: Philosophical Library.

Screnock, John, and Robert D. Holmstedt. 2015. *Esther: A Handbook on the Hebrew Text*. Waco: Baylor University Press.

Sellin, Ernst. 1889. *Die verbal-nominale Doppelnatur der hebräischen Participien und Infinitive und ihre darauf beruhende verschiedene Construktion*. Leipzig: Ackermann & Glaser.

Seow, C. L. 1995. *A Grammar for Biblical Hebrew*. Rev. ed. Nashville: Abingdon.

Shulman, Ahouva. 1996. "The Use of Modal Verb Forms in Biblical Hebrew Prose." PhD diss., University of Toronto.

———. 1999. "The Particle נָא in Biblical Hebrew Prose." *Hebrew Studies* 40:57–82.

———. 2000. "The Function of the 'Jussive' and 'Indicative' Imperfect Forms in Biblical Hebrew Prose." *Zeitschrift für Althebräistik* 13 (2): 168–80.

Siddiqi, Daniel. 2009. *Syntax within the Word: Economy, Allomorphy, and Argument Selection in Distributed Morphology*. Linguistik Aktuell/Linguistics Today 138. Amsterdam: Benjamins.

Siebesma, P. J. 1991. *The Function of the Niph'al in Biblical Hebrew*. Studia Semitica Neerlandica 29. Assen: Van Gorcum.

Smith, Carlota S. 1997. *The Parameter of Aspect*. Studies in Linguistics and Philosophy 43. Dordrecht: Kluwer Academic.

———. 1999. "Activities: States or Events?" *Linguistics and Philosophy* 22:479–508.

———. 2003. *Modes of Discourse: The Local Structure of Texts*. Cambridge Studies in Linguistics 103. Cambridge: Cambridge University Press.

———. 2006. "The Pragmatics and Semantics of Temporal Meaning." In *Proceedings of the 2004 Texas Linguistics Society Conference: Issues at the Semantics-Pragmatics Interface*, edited by Pascal Denis, Eric McCready, Alexis Palmer, and Brian Reese, 92–106. Somerville, MA: Cascadilla Proceedings Project.

———. 2008. "Time with and without Tense." In *Time and Modality*, edited by Jacqueline Guéron and Jacqueline Lecarme, 227–50. Studies in Natural Language and Linguistic Theory 75. Dordrecht: Springer.

Snider, Todd. 2021. "Light Verbs in Biblical Hebrew." In *Linguistic Studies on Biblical Hebrew*, edited by Robert D. Holmstedt, 169–90. Studies in Semitic Languages and Linguistics 102. Leiden: Brill.

Stassen, Leon. 1997. *Intransitive Predication*. Oxford Studies in Typology and Linguistic Theory. Oxford: Clarendon.

———. 2009. *Predicative Possession*. Oxford Studies in Typology and Linguistic Theory. Oxford: Oxford University Press.

Sweeney, Marvin A. 2003. *Zephaniah: A Commentary*. Hermeneia. Minneapolis: Fortress.

Talmon, Shemaryahu. 1978. "The Presentation of Synchroneity and Simultaneity in Biblical Narrative." *Scripta Hierosolymitana* 27:9–26.

Textor, Mark. 2011. "(Frege on) Sense and Reference." In *Semantics: An International Handbook of Natural Language Meaning*, edited by Claudia Maienborn, Klaus von Heusinger, and Paul Portner, 25–49. Berlin: De Gruyter.

Tropper, J. 1998. "Althebraisches und Semitisches Aspektsystem." *Zeitschrift für Althebräistik* 11 (2): 153–90.

Tsumura, David Toshio. 2007. *The First Book of Samuel*. New International Commentary on the Old Testament. Grand Rapids: Eerdmans.

Ullendorff, Edward. 1977. "Is Biblical Hebrew a Language?" In *Is Biblical Hebrew a Language? Studies in Semitic Languages and Civilizations*, edited by Edward Ullendorff, 3–17. Wiesbaden: Harrassowitz.

van der Merwe, Christo H. J. 1999. "The Elusive Biblical Hebrew Term ויהי: A Perspective in Terms of Its Syntax, Semantics, and Pragmatics in 1 Samuel." *Hebrew Studies* 40:83–114.

van Wolde, Ellen J. 2019. "The Niphal as Middle Voice and Its Consequence for Meaning." *Journal for the Study of the Old Testament* 43 (3): 453–78. https://doi.org/10.1177/0309089217743160.

———. 2021. "*Nifʿal* Verbs in the Book of Genesis and Their Contribution to Meaning." In *New Perspectives in Biblical and Rabbinic Hebrew*, edited by Aaron D. Hornkohl and Geoffrey Khan, 431–53. Cambridge Semitic Languages and Cultures 7. Cambridge: Open Book.

Vendler, Zeno. 1957. "Verbs and Times." *Philosophical Review* 66 (2): 143–60.

Verstraete, Jean-Christophe. 2007. *Re-thinking the Coordinate-Subordinate Dichotomy: Interpersonal Grammar and the Analysis of Adverbial Clauses in English*. Topics in English Linguistics 55. Berlin: De Gruyter.

Weingreen, J. 1959. *A Practical Grammar for Classical Hebrew*. Oxford: Oxford University Press.

Williamson, H. G. M. 1985. *Ezra, Nehemiah*. Word Biblical Commentary. Waco: Word.

Wilson, Daniel J. 2018. "Copular and Existential Sentences in Biblical Hebrew." PhD diss., University of the Free State.

———. 2019. "*Wayhî* and Theticity in Biblical Hebrew." *Journal of Northwest Semitic Languages* 45 (1): 89–118.

———. 2020. "The Thetic/Categorical Distinction as Difference in Common Ground Update." In *Thetics and Categoricals*, edited by Werner Abraham, Elizabeth Leiss, and Yasuhiro Fujinawa, 311–33. Amsterdam: Benjamins.

Wright, William. 1962. *A Grammar of the Arabic Language*. Cambridge: Cambridge University Press.

Young, Ian. 1993. *Diversity in Pre-exilic Hebrew*. Tübingen: Mohr Siebeck.

———. 1995. "The 'Northernisms' of the Israelite Narratives of Kings." *Zeitschrift für Althebräistik* 8:63–70.

———. 1997. "Evidence of Diversity in Pre-exilic Judahite Hebrew." *Hebrew Studies* 38:7–20.

——— 2005. "Biblical Texts Cannot Be Dated Linguistically." *Hebrew Studies* 46:341–51.

Young, Ian, Robert Rezetko, and Martin Ehrensvärd. 2008. *Linguistic Dating of Biblical Texts*. London: Equinox.

INDEX OF SUBJECTS

INDEX OF SCRIPTURE

Books of the Bible are listed in English canonical order, but the verse numbering is that of the Hebrew Bible.

Old Testament / Hebrew Bible

Genesis

Exodus

Leviticus

Numbers

Deuteronomy

Joshua

Judges

Ruth

1 Samuel

2 Samuel

1 Kings

2 Kings

1 Chronicles

2 Chronicles

Ezra

Nehemiah

Esther

Job

Psalms

Proverbs

Ecclesiastes

Song of Songs

Isaiah

Lamentations

Ezekiel

Daniel

Hosea

Joel

Amos

INDEX OF HEBREW EXAMPLES